D0932205

Radical Religion in America

Religion and Politics
Michael Barkun, *Series Editor*

Radical Religion in America

Millenarian Movements
from the Far Right
to the Children of Noah

Jeffrey Kaplan

Syracuse University Press

Copyright © 1997 by Syracuse University Press
Syracuse, New York 13244
All Rights Reserved

First Edition 1997
99 00 01 02   6 5 4 3

The paper used in this publication meets the minimum requirements of American National Standard for Information Sciences—Permanence of Paper for Printed Library Materials, ANSI Z39.48-1984. ♾™

Library of Congress Cataloging-in-Publication Data
Kaplan, Jeffrey.
Radical religion in America : millenarian movements from the far
right to the children of Noah / Jeffrey Kaplan. — 1st ed.
p.   cm.
Includes bibliographical references and index.
ISBN 0-8156-2687-8 (cloth : alk. paper). — 0-8156-0396-7
(pbk. : alk. paper)
1. Millenialism—United States.   2. Cults—United States.
3. United States—Religion.   I. Title.
BL503.2.K37   1996
291.2'3—dc20   96-25627

Manufactured in the United States of America

Contents

Jeffrey Kaplan is assistant professor of social sciences at Arctic Sivun-mun Ilisagvik College in Barrow, Alaska.

Foreword

MICHAEL BARKUN

Contemporary America is, by common agreement, in a period of unusual religious ferment. Indeed, the historian of religion William G. McLoughlin has spoken of it as the country's fifth "great awakening"—one of the nation's periodic spiritual upsurges. Writing in 1978, McLoughlin believed the current "awakening" would end by the early 1990s. Such, however, has not been the case, and there is every reason to believe that this time of religious upheaval will continue until at least the year 2000—that millennial time-marker that appears simultaneously as a sign of imminent fulfillment and of apocalyptic dread.

An important characteristic of this period has been the flowering of distinctly millenarian religion—belief systems that anticipate an imminent and radical overturning of the existing social order, with history reaching its penultimate conclusion. There have been such times before, notably in the 1830s and 1840s, when large numbers of Americans were drawn to millenarian religion, particularly in the Northeast. That was a time of mass movements, such as the Millerites, with their dramatic predictions of the Second Coming in 1843 and 1844; and also of utopian experiments, like the Oneida Community and the Shakers, building, as some have suggested, a "millennium in miniature." But even these vivid episodes pale before the millenarian religiosity of the present day.

Contemporary millennialism takes a bewildering variety of forms. There are the so-called "New Religious Movements," such as the Unification Church and the Montana-based Church Universal and Triumphant. There is the New Age in its many manifestations, including the "Earth Changes" literature with predictions of massive catastrophes. Within fundamentalist Protestantism, millennialism has reached unprecedented peaks of intensity, built upon the "dispensationalist" model of sacred history. Although official Catholic doctrine continues to eschew millenarian literalism, unofficial Catholic millennialism proliferates through an array of movements linked to Marian apparitions. Judaism, long hostile to messianic pretensions, has seen in the claims made for the Hasidic Lubavitcher Rebbe perhaps the most significant messianic movement since the seventeenth century.

All of these strands within the millenarian fabric are relatively visible. Some have developed within important religious traditions; others lead relatively independent lives but by virtue of size or aggressive outreach programs are well known and well studied. But they do not exhaust the contemporary millenarian scene. There are more exotic growths, little known to the general public and often ignored by scholars. It is these that Jeffrey Kaplan examines.

What Kaplan gives us here is remarkable for several reasons. First, he lays bare the beliefs of groups that few if any scholars have examined. Although a small literature exists about the Christian Identity movement, largely because of its links to the radical right, almost nothing systematic has appeared on Odinism and Ásatrú in America, or on B'nai Noah. The former group seeks to recover Norse-Germanic paganism, while the latter constructs a theology based on the covenant with Noah described in the Book of Genesis. Second, this book is ethnographic as much as it is an expedition into religious history. We see these groups as communities of believers, not merely as disembodied doctrines. Indeed, because the doctrines cut believers off so radically from the larger society, their coteries take on the appearance of groups of the besieged, simultaneously preoccupied with defense against a society perceived as hostile and riven with internecine ideological warfare.

Finally, Kaplan has broken free of one of the pervasive constraints in religious studies, the tendency to look at only one group at a time. Here, instead of the conventional single-movement case study, we find a genuinely comparative approach. As Kaplan demonstrates, the very estrangement that these groups feel from the larger society leads them into complex relationships with one another. This is the first exploration of America's millenarian religious underground that provides a sense of the interconnections pariah groups have with one another. A significant link for Kaplan is the anti-cult movement; the private organizations which act as self-appointed watchdogs of religious life, animated by the interests of mainstream faiths, the desire of families to pry converts loose, and the fear that cult groups may be built on bigotry and intergroup prejudice. This phenomenon, too, has been understudied and here receives one of its first analytical treatments.

The groups considered here are exceedingly small. Most reference works on American religion pay them little or no heed. Of what possible political significance could they be? Their political relevance exists at two levels. First, the millenarian community that Kaplan describes, together with the anti-cult movement, is itself a political system, where jockeying for power, factional disputes, and the ever-present fear of state regulation are common themes. Second, Christian Identity and some elements in Odinism have close links to the white supremacist radical right, and even though the numbers may be small, the capacity to become involved in major confrontations with authority is substantial. One need only point to the FBI's standoff with the Christian Identity Freemen in Garfield County, Montana, in 1996, where scarcely two dozen Identity believers became the focus of a major contest of wills.

In short, Kaplan has given us a path-breaking work that illuminates, as few others have, the dynamics of marginalized religion in contemporary America.

Preface

In a book so dependent upon the experiences and insights of others, it is no easy task to know where to begin to express the author's most heartfelt thanks to all who generously shared of their time and their ideas as the work gradually assumed its present shape. To begin at the beginning, then . . .

Thanks must go first of all to Prof. Karl J. Weintraub, Chairman of the Committee on the History of Culture at the University of Chicago, whose restrained exasperation assured that the dissertation that served as the genesis of the current work moved to an expeditious conclusion. Special thanks go to my dissertation director, Prof. Martin E. Marty, as well as to Profs. Jonathan Z. Smith and Bernard McGinn, the ever-patient readers of the sprawling work, whose support and advice were and are much appreciated.

It would be almost impossible to list all of the many scholars across the country—as well as in Europe and the Middle East—who gave so much of themselves to make this book possible. Prof. Michael Barkun of Syracuse University, Prof. David C. Rapoport of the University of California at Los Angeles, and Laird Wilcox, founder of the Wilcox Collection at the University of Kansas, were supportive of the work at every stage, for which I am most grateful. As the work began to take final shape, Prof. Heléne Lööw, Prof. Ehud Sprinzak, and Doug Milford provided many insights.

A deep debt of gratitude is owed to my institution, Arctic Sivunmun Ilisagvik College in Barrow, Alaska, for its unflagging generosity and support. Special thanks are due to our governing board, chaired by Richard Glenn, and to our dean of instruction, Jennifer Chang-Harty, and indeed to the entire community of the North Slope of Alaska, whom the college exists to serve.

Ultimately, however, thanks are due most of all to the many people who so generously shared their own deeply held religious and political beliefs. These, from a wide variety of religious traditions and shades of belief, are truly too numerous to list fully. They would, moreover, very likely be most surprised to find their names mentioned in the same breath. However, without their vital contributions, this volume would not have been possible. Therefore, to Pastor Dan Gayman, John Harrell, Thom Robb, the late Robert Miles, Eustace Mullins, Else Christensen, Steve McNallen, Ron Hand, Edred Thorsson, KveldúlfR Gundarsson and the redoubtable Stephan Grundy, William Bainbridge, James Chisholm, Gamlinginn, Garman Lord, Gert McQueen, Prudence Priest, Wilfred von Dauster, Robert Stine, R. N. Taylor, Valgard Murray, Aidan A. Kelly, J. David Davis, Rabbi Dov Ber Haskelevich, Rabbi Michael Katz, James Tabor, Laura Morgan, Shelley Shannon, Jack Roper, Gail Gans, Cynthia Kisser, Sondra Chesky, Elwood McQuad, Jan Keith, Lambert Dolphin, Joseph Grace, John Broekhoft, and to a good friend who introduced me to the world of Wing Chun, Phil Nearing, among many, many others, many thanks.

Thanks must be extended as well to the Harry Frank Guggenheim Foundation, whose generous support provided for a series of interviews with European activists, whose contributions were telling during the revision stage of this book. Of these, this work is particularly indebted to the former head of the Swedish Church of the Creator, Tommy Rydén, and his wife, Maude, for their hospitality and kindness.

Most of all, however, the greatest debt is owed to my wife, Eva Maria, for her years of patient support, which made this all possible.

Barrow, Alaska   JEFFREY KAPLAN
January 1996

Introduction

Apocalyptic millenarianism starts with a dream. It is a dream of a past that never was and of a future that may never be—a dream, in a word, of perfection. This dream, moreover, seeks to link a past golden age with a future promise of a world governed by a sinless elect under the benevolent rule of the Savior himself. The millennial dream has for two thousand years served as a beacon of hope to all, and as a call to action to a few. This book is about this tiny band of activists and their timeless dream. For these visionaries, the cataclysmic events of the apocalypse are the gateway from the troubles of this world to the promise of the millennial kingdom.

History records many instances of apocalyptic millenarianism. Most of these millenarians have been content to watch and wait and pray for the End; a few have taken up arms and attempted to "force the End." On occasion, they have even succeeded for a season in their seemingly quixotic endeavor. More often they have been disappointed, and those whose resort has been to arms have been crushed by the powers of this world. Apocalyptic millenarians today are few in number, geographically dispersed, and bitterly divided among themselves. Yet for all this, the dream has not lost its allure for a select few. This book is about this "righteous remnant."

When I began my research in 1989, the subject of contemporary apocalyptic millenarianism was of interest to few beyond a small coterie of academics. The choice of the radical right wing as a focus for this study narrowed the field still further. And so it would have remained had two key events not intervened.

On 19 April 1993, at Waco, Texas, the federal siege of the Branch Davidian compound reached its fiery denouement. In the American cultural heartland, there were expressions of sadness for the tragic fate of the children, which only slightly softened the consensus that the cult members had in some way "got what they deserved." Attorney General Janet Reno was lionized as the most popular personality of the floundering Clinton administration. In the more distant reaches on the map of American spirituality, however, the perception of Waco was considerably different. For many adherents of the New Religious Movements and for all of the believers in the myriad ideologies of the radical right wing, here was proof positive that our government had declared open season on each and every one of them.

Two years to the day later, a bomb destroyed the Federal Building in Oklahoma City, Oklahoma. The accused bomber's primary motivation was said to be his anger over the Waco tragedy. Suddenly, there was a frenzy of interest in the esoteric worlds of millenarian movements—particularly those movements that were connected with the radical right wing. By the mid-1990s, as militia groups continued to grow throughout the United States and (through the magic of computer technology) ideas emanating from the American radical right found receptive audiences in Europe and throughout the English-speaking world, the subject had taken on an import which could not have been foreseen at the inception of this research.

The majority of the millenarian appeals represented in these pages emanate from the most extreme sectors of the far right wing. Some, however, such as the philo-Semitic B'nai Noah or the diverse Ásatrú movement, defy political categorization. Their appeals are directed to vastly different segments of American society, just as their visions of impending apocalypse and chiliastic hope are strikingly at odds with each other. For all this, these movements form what can only be termed a "millennial community" by virtue of the characteristics that they do share as well as their complex interactions.

By strict definition, the term "millenarianism" refers to the biblical millennium, a 1,000-year post-historical period seen by Christians as a time of peace and plenty. Contemporary Christian eschatologies hold differing theories of the millennium. For some believers, Jesus will return to personally usher in and rule the chiliastic Kingdom (premillennialism); for others, the millennium will be purely the result of human effort, with Jesus' appearance reserved for the final phase of the drama (postmillennialism). The term "apocalyptic millenarianism" emphasizes the importance of a cataclysmic denouement of history as the necessary prelude to the birth of a new and better world. Apocalyptic millenarians within the Christian tradition are by definition premillenarians, but it is important to note that most American premillenarians are not apocalyptic. The point of differentiation centers on imminence—that is, the belief that the apocalypse is imminent and thus that some immediate action is incumbent on believers. Apocalyptic millenarians, therefore, see themselves as actors in the End Time drama. This engagement in the birth of a "new heaven and a new earth" separates the apocalyptic millenarian from those premillenarians who shelter in the promise of rapture, or escape from the worst ravages of the apocalypse. Finally, "Revolutionary millenarianism" refers to apocalyptic millenarians engaged in either a nonviolent quest to revolutionize an existing religious tradition or a movement that may involve a resort to violence in an effort to upset the sociopolitical status quo, and thus to "force the End."[1]

Increasingly, however, scholars have loosened these definitional requirements so as to include not only the Abrahamic traditions, each of which embodies a rich eschatological heritage, but non-Western religions as well.[2] In this view, the key consideration is whether or not the belief system emphasizes the reign of a sinless elect over a posthistorical chiliastic kingdom posited as perfect. By adopting this more malleable definition of millenarianism, it is possible to encompass professedly secular movements such as National Socialism and non-Christian religious movements such as Odinism.

With such an expanded lens, a huge variety of small, little-known religiopolitical groupings must be considered. Some order can be brought to this diversity through six analytical categories based on Michael Barkun's typology of white supremacists. That typology included Christian Identity groups, Ku Klux Klan groups, explicitly neo-Nazi groups, Reconstructed Traditions, Single Issue Constituencies/Lone Unguided Missiles, Idiosyncratic Sectarians, and an amorphous category, Hope Seeking a Means to Fulfillment.[3] Chapter 1 will offer examples of each of these categories, although particular emphasis will be placed on the key roles of Ásatrú/Odinism, the Church of the Creator, and the B'nai Noah in this typology.

In using an analytical framework such as this, however, a word of caution is in order. Adherents of these belief systems constitute a kind of pariah class in contemporary culture. As such, they have been banished to the farthest reaches of the cultural cosmos. In this isolation, adherents have been left to interact primarily with each other, and as a result an ideological synthesis has taken place over the last half century, culminating in a kind of apocalyptic orthodoxy. Thus, all of these groups share such primary characteristics as a Golden Age myth, the perception of a "theft of culture," scripturalism, a manichaean world view, a conspiratorial view of history, a vision of the group as a righteous remnant, an apocalyptic analysis of society, and a concomitant chiliastic dream.

This synthesis explains the tendency of many adherents toward membership in more than one group or belief system. Indeed, these seekers are embarked on an endless quest for the ultimate answer to society's ills. At the same time, it is important to make distinctions. For example, some groups are more susceptible than others to calls for violence. Moreover, the more distant a particular group tends to be from the values and beliefs of the mainstream society, the more difficult it becomes for an adherent to moderate or give up the belief system. For such as these, access to the American public square may be barred forever.

A remarkable feature of these highly diverse movements is the difficulty of differentiating ideological appeals that have many common beliefs yet at the same time are bitterly divisive and competitive for the allegiance of a limited pool of adherents. Equally striking is the fluidity with which seekers drift from one movement to another. Thus, the attempt to place believers in clear typological categories must be nuanced by the use of theoretical constructs of countercultural communities, such as that of the cultic milieu suggested by Colin Campbell, and the technique of religious mapping, championed by Martin Marty (among others).[4] Both systems posit deviance from the beliefs of mainstream society as the key analytical factor, with mapping theory seeking to locate a particular belief system in relation to the dominant culture and Campbell's cultic milieu documenting the close interactions of members within the oppositional subculture. Campbell's description of the cultic milieu is particularly relevant to a discussion of the constituent elements of the American millennial community:

> Cults must exist within a milieu which, if not conducive to the maintenance of individual cults, is clearly highly conducive to the spawning of cults in general. Such a generally supportive cultic milieu is continually giving birth to new cults, absorbing the debris of the dead ones and creating new generations of cult-prone individuals to maintain the high level of membership turnover. Thus, whereas cults are by definition a transitory phenomenon, the cultic milieu is, by contrast, a permanent feature of society.[5]

It is important to note, however, that the idea of the cults' quest for what Campbell refers to as "rejected knowledge" needs some modification when applied to the millenarians of the American radical right wing. The esoteric truths which these adherents seek have not been lost, as Campbell's cultists would have it. Rather, this knowledge is well known, albeit to a tiny conspiratorial elite whom these believers regard as the true powers of this world. The identities of these shadowy figures differ in the telling; for some they may be a cabal of Jewish manipulators along the lines of the Learned Elders of Zion, while for others they may be Trilateralists, Bilderbergers, or the blue-helmeted minions of the United Nations–dominated New World Order. The key linking factor, however, is that this knowledge has been suppressed rather than lost.[6]

The seeker after this suppressed knowledge carries on his or her search at great personal risk. From the seeker's perspective, the endeavor is nothing less than promethean. The costs are certainly great, the least of them being rejection. Friends and colleagues roll their eyes, family members exchange embarrassed glances, and the unenlightened populace (on whose behalf the lonely search has been undertaken) evince reactions from bored incredulity to knowing laughter. As the undaunted seeker delves further into the suppressed mysteries of the world, hitherto unknown vistas of knowledge and information open, and the vast reaches of the cultic milieu's many centers of esoteric lore become known.

Should the seeker persevere, however, he or she will begin to fear that there are ultimate costs which may yet be exacted. Here lies the very real paranoia of the movement, for the master conspirators from whom the seeker seeks to steal the fire of truth do not mean to let go of their treasure lightly. Thus the dire warnings of such theorists that their time may be short and that the enemy, utilizing the might of the American government (which they are believed to fully control), may soon grow fearful that the seeker has penetrated too closely to the heart of the long-suppressed truth and may strike back with the full ferocity at their command. Mark Koernke and Linda Thompson of the American militia movement are only the latest to express such fears publicly. They are hardly the first, and they most assuredly will not be the last.[7]

Given the obscurity of the religious communities that depend to a significant degree on this quest for suppressed knowledge, it may be helpful to consider briefly their approximate locations on a hypothetical religious map of America. For those sitting comfortably within the embrace of what Robert Bellah and others have dubbed the secularized, pluralistic civil religion of America, it is difficult to imagine why anyone would choose to reside beyond the comfortable mainstream of American society.[8] Here are found the Christian denominations, the mainline Protestant and Catholic churches, the conservative and reformed Jewish congregations, and increasingly, the Islamic *ummah* (community) and a host of imported Asian religious communities. Theirs is a comfortable world of "Sunday (or Saturday, or Friday) spirituality," of interfaith dialogue, and of an increasingly amorphous "Americanism" which serves as the glue binding together the communities of the American religious heartland. From the center of the map, it is not easy to accept that, to quote Martin Marty, "Out there, there be monsters."

Far beyond the heartland of the civil religion, however, lies a wilderness which most Americans prefer to believe is but a remnant of a darker time in our collective past, a time best forgotten. Just as in a bygone era the uncharted reaches of maritime maps were filled in with the monsters of the mariners' deepest fears, in the late twentieth century a particular region that lies beyond the safety of the American spiritual center has come to be peopled by that most feared and despised form of contemporary demonology, the belief systems that Michael Barkun has termed the "white supremacist synthesis."

At the heart of this constellation is Christian Identity. Neopagan Odinism, a belief system centered on the reconstruction of the pre-Christian Norse/Germanic pantheon, has in recent years taken on an increasingly important role in the wilderness of the radical right as well; the existence of a nonracialist counterpart, Ásatrú, provides an interesting contrast. Residing nearer to the borders of the American religious heartland is the B'nai Noah, the Children of Noah, whose powerfully philo-Semitic creed calls for the adoption by the non-Jewish world of a Noahide covenant separate from, and subordinated to, the Sinaitic covenant that binds the Jewish people to God. The complex interactions of the B'nai Noah with the denizens of the white supremacist world speak volumes to the efficacy of the cultic milieu theory. After an introduction to the history and themes of American millenarianism, these three case studies will concentrate on an examination of each group's theology/ideology, role in the milieu of the American millennial community, and orientation toward millenarian violence.

Interestingly, however, perhaps the most important component of the American millennial community is the so-called anti-cult movement. This term can be applied to a wide variety of "watchdog" groups, leading to a typology of watchdog movements and an examination of their interactions with the millenarian movements that they have undertaken to monitor. In the transition from quietist withdrawal to millenarian violence, the watchdog movements play a key role. Thus, a consideration of both the watchdog groups and the millenarian case studies can illumine the implications of the American millennial community for the dominant culture in the wake of events such as the 19 April 1995 bombing in Oklahoma City. Of primary importance, such a study will help us examine the fundamental questions of millenarian violence and of the existence of an oppositional cultic milieu.

Radical Religion in America

1

The American Millennial Community

Christian Identity

You know, one of the most difficult things in the Identity message is having the patience to wait until God's time before we start the war. And when he sends in his reinforcements is the only time we'll ever win. Because we will be fighting a holding action, backing up, backing up . . . base camp to base camp, up until the time He sends Michael, the Archangel.[1]

Christian Identity has evolved from an older, rather genteel doctrine known interchangeably as British Israelism or Anglo-Israelism.[2] British Israelism was perhaps based on the eccentric eighteenth-century theories of Richard Brothers, who claimed to have found, on the basis of a complex foray into biblical hermeneutics, proof that the Caucasian nations of Europe are in reality the ten lost tribes of Israel. At its nineteenth-century zenith, Anglo-Israelites on the whole tended to be substantial citizens, such as parliamentarians, businessmen, military officers, and bankers, who were often in sympathy with Jews and with the Zionist enterprise.[3]

British Israelism arrived in the United States and Canada by way of the writings of M. M. Eshelman, W. H. Poole, and J. H. Allen, all late-nineteenth- to early-twentieth-century figures. From Allen, the Church of God, Seventh Day took its doctrine, as did Herbert W. Armstrong's World Wide Church of God. The rather philo-Semitic teachings of these early British Israelites were transformed in the America of the 1920s and 1930s by the interaction of the tireless British Israel evangelist Howard Rand and the anti-Semitism of his associate, William J. Cameron. The Canadian-born Cameron would come to fame as the chief spokesman for Henry Ford and as editor of Ford's newspaper, the *Dearborn Independent*. It was the *Independent*'s 1920 series collectively titled "The International Jew" that would provide an entry for many Americans to the world of anti-Semitism. Cameron would leave British

1

Israelism in the 1930s, and Rand would distance himself from the movement in the same period, but the groundwork for the emergence of modern Christian Identity had been laid.

Identity came increasingly to identify the Jew as the literal offspring of Satan and as the human instrument for the diabolic theft of culture that Identity adherents strive to this day to rectify. By 1930, under the impact of the *Protocols of the Elders of Zion* and of the *Dearborn Independent*'s anti-Semitic series, a new Identity with a new passion for exposing and punishing the Jews for their theft of the birthright emerged.

Howard Rand, who died at the age of 102 in 1991, served as the venerable patriarch of the emergent Christian Identity movement despite his misgivings about its increasingly radical direction. Rand described his own realization of his Israelite heritage in terms of a kind of internal liberation, an almost Zen-like *satori* experience which stripped away the veils of ignorance to reveal a melding of the esoteric and the exoteric meanings of scripture:

> In the first place, to recognize who the Kingdom people are, to correctly identify the modern Israel of God in the world today, would provide the key to unlock the secrets of revelation, while the purport of the messages of the prophets would become correspondingly clear. Secondly, if Christendom would awaken to the realization that the Kingdom of God was established on earth at Mount Sinai, there would be an instant comprehension of the whole story the Bible tells.[4]

Doctrinally, the Christian Identity movement placed its primary stress on the so-called two seeds doctrine, whereby the Bible was held to be the exclusive history of the descendants of the race of Adam. The true Israelites are thus identified as the white race. The Jews represent a separate creation—the result of the seduction of Eve by Satan—with the issue of the union, Cain, as the carrier of the seed of Lucifer.

Put under a curse of eternal enmity, the two seed lines, that of white Adamic man and that of the children of Satan, the Jews, have been locked in struggle ever since. In this view, the Jews are not truly Israelites but are the synagogue of Satan (Rev. 2:9 and 3:9), who are believed to have dispossessed the true Israelites from knowledge of their actual identity. However, the Jews have failed to wrest from the Anglo-Saxons the covenant relationship with God. Other races are identified with the "Beasts of the field" (Gen. 1:25) who took human form as a result of illicit matings with wayward Adamites. Much of the racism in Identity circles follows from the view that, over the course of time, these nonwhite races have fallen under the control of the Jewish conspiracy for world domination.

The process by which Identity adopted this doctrine as orthodoxy is complex. William Cameron was a primary influence, but the key events involved extensive contacts between such anti-Semitic British Israel figures as C. F. Parker and Clem Davies in Vancouver and the West Coast American cadre of influential Identity figures associated with Gerald L. K. Smith. The most influential of these Californians were Wesley Swift, Bertrand Comperet, and William Potter Gale. The actual medium of exchange was a series of conferences, the first of which (in 1937) was attended by no lesser lights than Howard Rand and Reuben Sawyer, whose primary claim to fame lies in his being the first to combine Identity theology with Ku Klux Klan leadership. By the end of World War II, however, the development of Christian Identity doctrine shifted to the United States, with the coterie surrounding Gerald L. K. Smith as the key figures.

So important is Smith's influence in Identity doctrine—two generations of Identity teachers were directly associated with either his Christian Nationalist Crusade organization (Swift, Gale, and Comperet) or with his youth movement (Kenneth Goff and Dan Gayman)—that the question of his adherence to Identity beliefs must be addressed. The answer is far from clear: Smith's biographer, Glen Jeansonne, argues that he was an Identity believer, but Michael Barkun takes the opposite view.[5] Although it is true that Smith's long-lived periodical (1942–76), *The Cross and the Flag* did give some space to Identity figures—Swift and Comperet in particular—so long as they refrained from writing overtly Identity-based material, it is also true that Smith seems to have reserved *The Cross and the Flag* for political articles, with religion limited to vague affirmations of Christianity and Americanism, the better to hold together as broad a constituency as is possible in the fractious world of the far right. Smith did, however, explicitly state in his autobiography, *Besieged Patriot,* that Wesley Swift opened up the world of Identity hermeneutics to him, for which he was eternally grateful.

> One day, [Wesley Swift] said to me: "Mr. Smith, I would like to bring my Bible up to your hotel room and talk to you." He did, and he made one of the greatest contributions to my life that any man ever made. He opened the Bible and demonstrated to me with proper texts that Christ's worst enemies were not God's chosen people. He identified the "true Israel" which gave us the Messiah, and demonstrated to me that we were heirs to the covenant that God made with Abraham, and we were indeed Israelites. He later pointed out the text which reads, concerning those who had accepted Jesus Christ who might not be able to trace their lineage to Abraham: "Ye have been circumcised by faith."
>
> He demonstrated that the crucifiers of Christ were apostates, sons

basic C. I. ideology

of Satan, and the seed of Cain. He proved by scriptures that Jesus Christ was not a Jew as we now know Jews, and that God is going to give His kingdom to those who have accepted Jesus Christ, and not to those who caused His crucifixion and still justify it. The modern apostates may say that if they had it to do over again, they would not nail Him to a cross; but they, in fact "crucify our Lord anew" every day.[6]

In a separate tract, *Who Are The Chosen People? Certainly Not The Jews! (As We Now Know Jews)*, Smith reaffirmed this Identity affiliation.[7] It is therefore difficult to see how Smith in his later years could not be considered a Christian Identity adherent.

The newly energized doctrine of Christian Identity was soon to gain wide currency in the world of the American radical right. Adherents seem to have been drawn primarily from the ranks of conservative Protestant churches. Identity in the post–World War II era attracted a population of disaffected Protestant premillennialists whose hermeneutics of such passages as Rev. 2:9 and 3:9 could not be reconciled with their churches' enthusiasm for the Zionist enterprise. Jack Mohr and John Harrell are typical of this evolution.

This premillennial Protestant transition to Identity was facilitated by the apocalypticism characteristic of Christian Identity. Identity's eschatology is little different from that of Protestant fundamentalism, in all but one key element: the belief in rapture. Most fundamentalists await the eschatological "End of Days" secure in the knowledge that in the dreaded seven-year period of the Tribulation, when war, famine, and disease engulf the earth, they will be raptured into the air to await the inevitable conclusion of history at Jesus' side. Identity believers have no such hope of supernatural rescue. Rather, the Christian Identity believer is secure only in his ability to persevere—to survive by the grace of God but also by virtue of his own wits and through recourse to his own stores of food and weapons.

Why has Christian Identity appealed to these (and other) alienated seekers? The primary explanation lies in Identity's unique ability to meet the need of many members of the racialist right for spirituality, fellowship, and ritual in the context of a Christianity shorn of its Jewish roots. Moreover, Identity provides a hermeneutical key to unlocking the mysteries of past, present, and future while explaining to the faithful the reasons for their current perception of dispossession. Identity apprises these seekers of the golden past that was theirs until the machinations of the satanic Jews robbed them of the knowledge of their covenantal birthright, and it assures them of their promised future of happiness and terrestrial power.

Perhaps most importantly, Identity doctrine gives shape and substance to the conspiratorial suspicions of the faithful remnant. In this respect, the efficacy of the two seed theory centers on its ability to demonstrate to the faithful the truth of what (to the uninitiated) is the weakest link in the extravagant conspiracy scenarios which it is the passion of the Identity churches to unravel: how is it that the Jews have succeeded in keeping alive a centrally directed conspiracy against Christianity over the course of two millennia? Identity's explanation is as simple as it is elegant. The conspiracy is genetic. As the Bible says, "Ye are of your father the devil; and it is your will to practice the lusts and gratify the desires of your father. He was a murderer from the beginning, and does not stand in the truth, because there is no truth in him. When he speaks a falsehood, he speaks what is natural to him; for he is a liar and the father of lies and of all that is false" (John 8:44).

Christian Identity today is extraordinarily diverse. This is the inevitable fruit of a highly decentralized tradition in which individual (and highly individualistic) Identity pastors offer their flocks strikingly idiosyncratic messages based on Identity's distinctive approach to biblical hermeneutics. There is no center of orthodoxy, and in the post–Wesley Swift era, no preeminent figure to tie together the fractious world of independent Identity churches. The three leaders discussed below illustrate the diversity characteristic of modern Identity.

The Identity minister who has become almost synonymous with the construction of Christian Identity as the "theology of hate" is Richard Butler and his Aryan Nations compound at Hayden Lake, Idaho.[8] Butler, a disciple of Swift in California who moved to Idaho in 1973, possesses perhaps the strongest claim to be Swift's spiritual heir. In the late 1970s and early 1980s, Butler's star did indeed appear to be in the ascendant. His Aryan Nations compound became a mecca for the radical right, and his annual open house attracted adherents of a wide variety of far-right belief systems. A central attraction of this carnival was the weapons and survivalist training offered by Aryan Nation "experts," who in their snappy brown imitation Third Reich uniforms, veered as close to neo-Nazism as Christian Identity in North America has come. Further, the Aryan Nations' prison ministry appears to have been highly influential in the formation of the Aryan Brotherhood movement among white prisoners.[9]

Rev. Butler was one of the star defendants at the 1989 Fort Smith sedition trial. His legal position was at that point precarious. The revolutionary movement led by Robert Mathews and popularly known as the Order had emerged from the area around Hayden Lake, and several founding Order members were Aryan Nations residents. Worse, the printing press used in the Order's counterfeiting operation belonged to the Aryan Nations. Finally, when Robert West, another of the inhabitants of Butler's compound, was found to be unable to drink and keep quiet at the same time, he was murdered on orders from Mathews. His body has never been found.[10]

Butler, however, was acquitted of all charges at Fort Smith, and indeed he has been remarkably successful at skirting the law without actually crossing the line. At the same time, this innate caution does much to explain the precipitous decline in his fortunes in the 1990s. In essence, he preached a violent message while refusing to sanction—or even discuss—the possibility of violent actions. Thus, when Robert Mathews and the Order were at the zenith of their fortunes, donating large sums of cash to a number of far right wing movements, Richard Butler—whose Aryan Nations compound supplied the Order with much of its manpower—saw little if any of this largess. Mathews seems to have held Butler in some contempt.[11] As an aging Butler has begun to cast around for a successor, the Aryan Nations movement appears to be fragmenting. There are few realistic prospects for the movement to long survive Butler's demise.

Younger, more outspoken, and also peripherally connected to the Order is Pete Peters, an Identity minister based in northern Colorado. Peters, a well-known figure in the world of Christian Identity, first came to public notice during the investigation of the Order's connection to the murder of Denver radio talk show host Alan Berg, with the revelation that several members of the Order attended services at Peters' Laporte, Colorado, church. He has more recently been vilified for his authorship of a booklet that owes as much to Christian Reconstructionism as to Christian Identity. The tract, whose title—*Death Penalty for Homosexuals*—succinctly states its message, concludes that unless the ultimate penalty as mandated in Lev. 20:13 is carried out, "homosexuals will continue to spread their form of death and will continue to recruit the people's sons and daughters and threaten and carry out their threats against any who oppose them."[12]

Pastor Peters' efforts to step into the vacuum of Identity leadership brought on by the decline of Butler's influence and by the further splintering of the movement in the wake of the Fort Smith fiasco have brought him little more than increased difficulties with state authorities. An opportunity to assert his claim to influence presented itself following the events which took place in Ruby Ridge, Idaho, on 21–22 August 1992. There, in an event that would eerily resemble a small-scale version of the federal action at the Branch Davidian compound in Waco, an eighteen-month stakeout of the cabin of Identity adherent Randy Weaver culminated in the deaths of a federal marshal, Weaver's fourteen-year old son, and his wife—shot in the head while holding her infant daughter in her arms. The battle electrified the world of Christian

Identity. By chance, this drama was played out during the week-long Scriptures for America Bible Camp conducted in Colorado by Peters. Following the camp, Peters attempted with limited success to channel the outrage felt throughout the far right wing into an organized movement that would seek to prevent such an event from happening again. The means to achieve this felicitous outcome would be either legitimate political action or, if no other recourse were possible, by fighting back rather than allowing the federal government to eliminate the faithful one by one.[13]

So fractious is the world of Christian Identity that it almost goes without saying that Pete Peters has had little success in his quest to unite the small, far-flung kingdoms that are the Identity ministries in North America. Thus, Identity appears to have played little role in the formation of the militia movement that in fact has coalesced in reaction to the events in Waco and Ruby Ridge. Worse, the authoritarian personality noted by academic theorists in regard to those susceptible to right-wing ideologics, while overstated, does seem to have come home to roost in the case of Peters. A stubborn man, convinced of his own basic rightness, Peters held fast to his principles for over two years of complicated legal wrangling with the state of Colorado over a minor election law violation which carried a small fine. By refusing all efforts at compromise, Peters had amassed fines plus interest of over $10,000. On 26 February 1993, the state of Colorado seized his church and froze his bank accounts in an effort to make good on the debt.[14] Undaunted, Peters continued to find innovative ways to proselytize. He has pioneered the use of the internet computer network as a repository for Identity literature, and his ministry recently has followed the example of another Idaho Identity minister, Dave Barley, by taking his case to the public via satellite television.

Pastor Dan Gayman, head of the Church of Israel (COI) in Schell City, Missouri, is arguably the premier theologian in the modern Christian Identity movement. Where a Richard Butler could gather a group of the disaffected and dream of revolution, and a Pete Peters could urge the Identity community to unite for self-defense against a government seen as bent on the destruction of the righteous remnant, Dan Gayman would urge the faithful to withdraw to the greatest possible degree from the surrounding society and to prepare as best they can for the imminent End of Days. This is not to say that Pastor Gayman is a pacifist. A student of Kenneth Goff (himself an acolyte of Gerald L. K. Smith), Gayman in his younger years was closely identified with the most radical wing of Identity believers.

Gayman's biography is somewhat difficult to reconstruct.[15] In his own words,

I had the good fortune to be born into a home where God and scripture were considered important. Some of my earliest childhood memories include church services in Denver, Colorado, where I was born . . . I became interested in scripture at a very early age, studied the Bible along with other textbooks at a rural one room country school, and made it a point to try to read the Bible through once a year when I was in high school. . . . At the age of 21, I began preaching and doing evangelistic work among rural Churches of Christ in southwest Missouri . . . I was preaching Kingdom/Israel truth at all of these small Churches of Christ at that time.

As early as 1960, I began placing total focus on the Gospel of the Kingdom. At that time . . . I was preaching just up from our present Church of Israel sanctuary. We were holding spring, summer, and fall conferences throughout the 1960s, and these conferences became formal festival celebrations in 1970. Throughout the 1960s, we published a church magazine called *Zions Restorer*. This publication became *Zions Watchman* in 1973 and was later shortened to *The Watchman*. The Gospel of the Kingdom has been a focal point of the Church since about 1960. I should hasten to add that various portions of the Kingdom were preached in the church in the 1940s and 1950s by my maternal grandfather, Jesse F. Cruz.

Gayman discovered Kingdom theology "with a keen sense of interest" in the early 1950s through Herbert W. Armstrong's *Plain Truth Magazine* and Howard Rand's Destiny publications. He later sent for British Israel World Federation (BIWF) material. Gayman soon veered away from the mild doctrines of Anglo-Israelism as propounded by Herbert W. Armstrong and the BIWF, opting instead for the racialist and anti-Semitic wing of the movement. In this, he was much influenced by the *Dearborn Independent* series. (He also had read the *Protocols of the Elders of Zion,* but these were never a strong influence.) His youthful interest in British Israelism is of particular note, given his family's connection to the Church of Christ (Temple Lot), a dissident Mormon sect with centers in Denver and three other cities;[16] a significant number of Mormons have been drawn to the various belief systems of the far right, if not specifically to Christian Identity.[17] However, Gayman's reluctance to discuss his upbringing as a member of a minority Mormon community makes it impossible to do more than speculate on possible connections. What is certain is that Gayman's adoption as a young man of racialist Christian Identity would serve as an important line of demarcation between his faction and that of his brother Duane in their battle for control of their church in the early 1970s. By 1972, the impact of Dan Gayman's racialist Identity theology and his crusading zeal had split the Church of Israel, leading to a divisive law suit pitting brother against brother. The resulting court case cost Dan Gayman all but 20 acres of the church's property.[18]

Dan Gayman received his primary training in Kingdom theology under Denver-based Identity minister Kenneth Goff, a teacher to many current figures in the movement, at Goff's Soldiers of the Cross Training Institute in Denver in 1964–1965.[19] Immediately prior to this education, however, Gayman took his first substantive step into racialist activism, unsuccessfully attempting to turn the church youth camp into something of a Christian Identity adult seminary that would provide, besides theological education, weapons and survivalist training. Armed with Goff's teachings and a much strengthened sense of mission, Gayman returned to Schell City to win election as Church of Israel pastor and as editor of the church's newspaper, *Zions Restorer,* which henceforth would become a stridently racialist organ.

Why this sudden turn to activism took place is an important question. The ferment of the 1960s was one obvious catalyst, but on a deeper level, that unsettled time clearly stimulated an underlying apocalyptic millenarianism, which defines the Church of Israel to this day. This world view is evident in the 5 March 1972 resolution through which Gayman sought to effect the takeover of the Church. This resolution vowed to:

1. prepare a people for the return of Jesus Christ to earth;
2. establish [the Church] as a place of retreat for God's people;
3. establish a storehouse of the Lord as the economic order of God in these latter days; and
4. bring . . . Adam's race under the influence of the Gospel of the Kingdom of Jesus Christ . . . under the administration of . . . the Gospel as contained in the Articles of Faith and Practice.[20]

By the mid-1990s, the Church of Israel has become an international ecclesiastical organization, which conceptually has been divided into twelve dioceses, each named for one of the tribes of Israel. Pastor Gayman heads the Diocese of Manasseh, named for the son of Joseph and covering the United States. How many of these dioceses are operational is unclear, although there is evidence of substantial COI activity in Great Britain and in South Africa.[21] The congregation of the COI is about 100 individuals residing in the vicinity of Schell City, with an international mailing list of subscribers to the *Watchman* and to the large cassette tape ministry which the church opened in 1977.[22] The COI in the late 1970s operated a Christian Day School, but recent movement literature has stressed home schooling (as well as home birthing) and the operation of home churches presided over by the family patriarch where an Israelite congregation is unavailable.[23]

Gayman's acceptance of money from the Order (see chapter 2) led to his appearance as a prosecution witness in the Fort Smith sedition trial. Since then, he has maintained a low profile in Identity circles. His Church of Israel publications continue to stress adherence to non-violence as well as to warn the faithful of the impending cataclysm and thus the need to retreat from the cities to the relative safety of the rural redoubts of America.

Save for the tiny band of National Socialist faithful, no movement has been as thoroughly demonized as has Christian Identity—nor has any movement offered so thoroughgoing and devastating a critique of the America of the 1990s. Isolated from the dominant culture by its emphasis on anti-Semitism and racism, relentlessly pursued by the watchdog organizations whose self-appointed mission it is to raise the *alarum* over such overt expressions of "hate" as the those embraced by the Identity churches, Christian Identity is the most spiritually—and often the most physically—distant outpost on the map of contemporary American religiosity.

Ku Klux Klan Groups

> Throughout the millenniums of warfare between the Aryan and the Jew, neither we nor they have ever "won." The victories each has in turn known, when spread over the centuries, equal stalemate. However, Aryan technology has shrunk the whole earth to the size of one battlefield. The eternal war, which can most properly be called a Conflict Of The Ages, has taken a final turn. The age-long conflict approaches the last battle—Ragnarök, Armageddon—is about to be fought, and there will be only one survivor of this struggle.[24]

In the contemporary demonology of American culture, few organizations elicit a more negative reaction than does the Ku Klux Klan. Fear of the Klan—and perhaps for whites a shared collective shame for the power which the movement accrued both in the Reconstruction-era American South and in a number of Northern states in the 1920s—is deeply rooted in the collective American consciousness. It is a fear which at once attracts and bedevils Klan recruits, who often find that their initial attraction to the Klan's mystique of secrecy and popular fear wanes with the realization that virtually any public activity undertaken by the Klan is certain to be met by a far greater crowd of counter-demonstrators. Worse, covert Klan operations appear to be undertaken at the sufferance if not at the outright invitation of government authorities, given the success of federal agencies at infiltrating Klan ranks and inducing Klan leaders to cooperate in federal investigations.

Thus, for a Klan group to undertake or even seriously contemplate violent action is tantamount to organizational suicide. As individuals, klansmen face lengthy incarceration for their criminal acts through newly adopted hate crime sentence enhancement provisions available in many states. On the organizational level, the successful use of civil litigation initiated by such watchdog organizations as the Klanwatch Project of the Southern Poverty Law Center on behalf of victims of Klan violence has successfully shut down those Klan organizations whose members do perpetrate acts of violence.

The model for this strategy is a successful civil case brought by Morris Dees on behalf of Beulah May Donald, whose son Michael was murdered in 1981 by three members of the United Klans of America (UKA). The killers were caught and convicted of criminal charges. The Klanwatch civil action, however, was taken against the UKA and the organization's Imperial Wizard, Robert Shelton. The jury found that, although Shelton knew nothing of the killing in advance, the UKA was responsible for the acts of its members. Thus, in 1987, Mrs. Donald was awarded control of the group's Tuscaloosa headquarters, including its printing equipment. This effectively put the United Klans of America out of business.[25]

Given these powerful disincentives to violence, it is not surprising that the already fragmented Klans in North America would enter into a bitter battle of polemics over the tactics of nonviolence vs. the Klan's tradition of violent activism. Emerging from this internecine debate are two very different approaches: the call to revolutionary violence, championed by such firebrands as Louis Beam of Texas and Dennis Mahon of Oklahoma, as opposed to Arkansas-based Thom Robb's attempts to market the Klan as a civil rights group for white people, modeled on the example of Martin Luther King![26]

Louis Beam, the author of the manichaean and apocalyptic analysis of contemporary history which opened this section, is a rarity among Klansmen. Undeniably intelligent, articulate, and widely read—and the driving force behind the dreaded right-wing computer bulletin boards of the late 1980s—Louis Beam has lived a life that many Klansmen and would-be Klansmen can only fantasize. A Vietnam veteran, Beam preaches the dream of revolutionary violence and has himself not been loath to take up the dangerous existence of the underground fugitive. The most celebrated of Beam's exploits may well be the shoot-out in which Mexican federal officers attempted to take Beam and his wife into custody. In the ensuing confrontation, Beam's wife managed to pin down the arresting officers, allowing her husband to make good his escape. Beam's charmed life did not end with his return to the United

to hurt or not to hurt people?

States, where he and his fellow defendants were acquitted of all charges in the ill-starred 1989 sedition trial held at Fort Smith, Arkansas. He remained free through the mid-1990s.

kkk
goal

Beam's successes should not, however, obscure the essential futility of his primary quest: to modernize the Ku Klux Klan by unifying its many disparate factions and forging the organization into an effective vanguard revolutionary force. This ideal, developed with the help of the late Robert Miles and others, is referred to as the "Fifth Era Klan," a Klan capable of a clear-eyed analysis of the incompetence and treason that have been the history of the Klan since the original movement was disbanded in 1869, as well as of an honest appraisal of the remarkably poor quality of recruits the present day Klan organizations have managed to attract. Only when these difficulties are addressed and rectified will Beam's ecumenical call to take up arms, overthrow the current sociopolitical order, and ruthlessly take vengeance on "lying politicians, criminal bureaucrats, racial traitors, communists, assorted degenerates, culture distorters, and those who resist the implementation of lawful constitutional government"[27] be more than a distant dream. In the meantime, Beam's ecumenism is aptly demonstrated in his extra-Klan contacts, ranging from his close association with Richard Butler's Christian Identity Aryan Nations compound in Idaho to the sort of generic Odinism suggested by his equation of the Christian Apocalypse with the Norse end-time scenario of Ragnarök, in the quotation above.

Dennis Mahon is no Louis Beam, but he too has come to represent a revolutionary voice in Klan circles—so much so that, having come to much the same analysis of the Klan's current status as Beam, he amicably left the Klan in 1992 for Tom Metzger's White Aryan Resistance (WAR). Prior to his defection to WAR, Mahon was best known for his association with Terry Boyce's Confederate Knights of America Klan chapter and for his calls to arms in the Knight's journal, *White Beret*. His occasional forays to Europe and Canada on behalf of the Klan have garnered some press attention as well. Mahon's drift from the KKK to WAR illustrates well the applicability of Campbell's theory of the cultic milieu to the radical right, but of greater interest is his frank analysis of the Klan. Interspersed between intemperate attacks on Thom Robb ("the Grand Lizard") for his attempts to remake the image of the Klan from a revolutionary force to a civil rights group is a telling appraisal of the current state of the Klan:

> after 12 years of proudly wearing the robe of the Invisible Order, I feel that Tom Metzger's leadership and personal strategies fit my personality and mind set better at this time of my life. Also, I just got tired of

seeing so many mistakes in tactics and ideology of the leaders of the other 25 or so Klan groups in Zoglandia. So many of these mini-fuhrers of these other Klans have embarrassed me with these displays of weakness and idiotic statements of "Niggers are the cause of all our problems—we got to kill the niggers—nigger this, nigger that." It's like a broken record.

The Jewsmedia always link the Klan with "lynching niggers." The average "Joe Six-pack" out there, whenever he thinks of a Klansman, pictures an uneducated hick half drunk, in bib overalls, with tobacco juice dripping down his chin, burning a cross on some poor Blacks [sic] lawn, and the Klansman stating how he "put the nigger in his place." Unfortunately, many Klansmen knowingly fit the media stereotype.[28]

Mahon continues his analysis throughout the premier issue of his post-Klan vehicle, *The Oklahoma Excalibur.* The effortless penetration of Klan leadership ranks by government agents as well as by informants reporting to private watchdog groups is decried, as are the tactics of nonviolence and staged events in which Klan groups are seen as demonstrating peacefully until they are attacked by anti-Klan demonstrators (the forte of Thom Robb). For Mahon, the contradictions of the modern Klan became intolerable, and thus the switch to WAR.

During an interview in Chicago in 1991, Identity minister and Klan leader Thom Robb made the surprising declaration that, virtually alone among members of the radical right in America, he was pleased with media coverage of his Knights of the Ku Klux Klan. Indeed, to the extent that it is possible for the Ku Klux Klan to get positive media coverage, Robb's message of love for the white race while eschewing any (public) negative comments on other races has dovetailed nicely with a certain trend in American society toward the reinforcement of ethnic as opposed to national identity.[29] However, Robb's kinder, gentler Klan is unlikely to do much to erase the intensely negative associations which the organization engenders in Americans, and as Dennis Mahon's writing amply demonstrates, it has done much to further divide an already disintegrating movement.

How low the Ku Klux Klan's fortunes have ebbed in recent years is clearly documented by the watchdog community. According to Anti-Defamation League (ADL) figures, total Klan membership in 1988 was between 4,500 and 5,000 members, representing the lowest Klan membership total in fifteen years. Klanwatch's Klan census concurs with the ADL's 5,000 figure, and both agree that the Klan shows little hope of upward growth.[30] So dire are the Klan's current fortunes that in its 1991 report on the KKK, the ADL was moved to write:

Although the Klan's decade-long decline has stopped, and it may begin to grow again—especially if the current recession becomes lengthy and severe—there is little prospect of the hooded order once again becoming a significant force in the land . . . considered from the standpoint of the nation as a whole, the KKK has only limited present and potential significance.[31]

The primary importance of the declining Ku Klux Klan groups in the cultic milieu of the radical right lies in their limited ability to provide for the Klan's few promising recruits a port of entry to the broader world of the radical right. In addition, the Klan's vague affirmations of Christianity and its near-deification of the white race mix well with other white supremacist ideologies (such as Christian Identity). However, given the Klan's marginal stature and the widely held perception within the radical right that Dennis Mahon's critical view of Klan adherents is accurate, little further attention will be given to the movement in these pages.

Ásatrú/Odinism

Brothers will fight
and kill each other,
siblings
do incest;
men will know misery,
adulteries be multiplied,
an axe-age, a sword-age,
shields will be cloven,
a wind-age, a wolf-age[32]

Odinism, a reconstruction of the Viking-era Norse pantheon, plays a vital role in the world of the radical right and in the wider universe of the cultic milieu.[33] In terms of mapping theory, Odinism is located at the spiritual crossroads linking the racialist appeals of the radical right to the occult/magical community of Wicca and neopaganism. This linkage occurs primarily through Odinism's nonracialist counterpart, Ásatrú, though Ásatrú is becoming increasingly distinct from Odinism. Devotees of the same Norse/Germanic pantheon, Ásatrúers tend to eschew overtly racist constructions of their tradition, concentrating instead on the ritual and magical elements central to all Wiccan/neopagan religions.[34]

The diverse occult community, consisting of such belief systems as neopaganism, Wiccan witchcraft in its myriad forms, Satanism real and imagined, and the New Age movement, has since the 1960s moved ever closer to the American mainstream—a drift that was symbolized by the high profile given the magical religions at the World Parliament of Religions gathering in Chicago in 1993. As denizens of the cultic milieu, Odinists practice an imaginative blend of ritual magic, ceremonial forms of fraternal fellowship, and an ideological flexibility which allows for a remarkable degree of syncretism with other white supremacist appeals—National Socialism in particular. Odinists ironically tend to subscribe to a number of beliefs which are explicitly Christian. Anti-Semitism, for example, would have puzzled the pagan-era Norse, as would have the various conspiratorial fantasies which are ubiquitous in the radical right.

Odinism as it is presently understood appeared before Ásatrú. Although Odinism's precise origins are far from clear, its surge of popularity may have centered in the profound social and political crises that engulfed Germany in the chaotic period of the Weimar Republic. In this time of intermingled chaos and decadence, wandering groups of displaced or simply disillusioned German youth, known collectively as the German Youth Movement, began—perhaps as a lark, perhaps with more serious intent—to make sacrifices to Wotan. Many of these young people would in the Nazi era give up their wanderings for the chiliastic excitement of helping to build the Third Reich.[35] Indeed, the old gods were hardly alien to the architects of the Third Reich. A fascinating if eccentric literature has grown up around the mystical endeavors of leading figures in the Nazi party, of which the revival of Germanic paganism was but one manifestation.[36]

As Hitler was rising to power in Germany, the occult implications of National Socialism were gaining the attention of mystics outside of Germany. One such, an eccentric Australian named Alexander Rud Mills, was an unabashed Nazi sympathizer and a believer in a form of racial mysticism which posited pre-Christian Anglo-Saxon society as the Golden Age of the British people. In the 1930s, Mills began to turn his dreams toward the reconstruction of that perfect time in this degenerate age. Following a path that also would be trod by such modern groups as Ben Klassen's Church of the Creator and the most extreme sectors of the Russian group Pamyat, Mills' diagnosis held that the contemporary malady of civilization was due to the malign influence of the Jews, and as Christianity was built on the foundation of that "vile Middle Eastern Abrahamic cult," it had to be severed from the soul of the descendants of the Anglo-Saxon race as surely as one would excise a cancer. Out of this process of reasoning came Mills' most influential book, *The Odinist Religion: Overcoming Jewish Christianity.*[37] *The Odinist Religion* was only the first of a number of writings—mostly in tract form—which Mills would churn out, but it is the most revealing of the gradual process through which he attempted to disengage his thought from the deeply ingrained paradigms of the dominant Christian culture. *The Odinist Religion* is in reality a manichaean treatise, deeply wedded to a world view and an imagined history in which Europe is the true birthplace of civilization, whence white men descended from a common ancestor (named either George or Sigge). This progenitor is posited as the culture bearer to the world, whose offspring built the Egyptian pyramids and founded empires. From this imagined history and theft of culture motif, Mills adds conspiracy theories, dire warnings against usury and miscegenation, and finally the claim that Christ did not die on the cross!

Mills would win few converts to his Anglecyn (later Anglican) Church of Odin, but his writings would be kept alive in the world of the right-wing publishing houses. He was rediscovered by Else Christensen and her husband Alex in the early 1960s, during the course of reading such right-wing staples as Francis Parker Yockey's epic treatise on Western culture and the malign role of the Jews, *Imperium,* and Oswald Spengler's *Decline of the West.* In the midst of such influences, it was Mills who inspired the widowed Else Christensen to form the Odinist Fellowship in the early 1970s. The publication in 1971 of the first issue of the Fellowship's journal, *The Odinist,* coincided with the discovery of the Norse pantheon by other seekers—most notably Stephen McNallen, who at virtually the same time founded the Viking Brotherhood (an Ásatrú group). Mrs. Christensen recalls:

> When confronted with Rud Mills' ideas and the political atmosphere of the time, I suppose that I finally realized that the problems were more of a spiritual nature than political. We chose the Scandinavian mythology as, at the time, the animosity between Anglo Saxons and Teutons (aftermath of World War II) was still lingering; Scandinavian was neutral; a rational choice, not because I'm Danish.[38]

Through the mid-1990s, Christensen is said to have remained so enamored with Mills' work that she obtained a complete collection of A. Rud Mills' writings and effects, and it seems clear that a primary area of differentiation between Odinists and Ásatrúers is a knowledge of Mills.[39] In addition to the impact of Mills, other primary differentiating factors include the facts that Odinists (1) have far more contact with the other sectors of the white supremacist constellation than most Ásatrú adherents would find palatable; (2) are wedded to a conspiratorial view of history; (3) evince a pronounced warrior ethic that emphasizes the desire to some day strike back in some form at the dominant culture for its perceived injustices; (4) have a strongly racialist strain of thought, which verges easily and often into racial mysticism; and (5) emphasize a reductionist concentration on reviving an idealized form of Viking tribal values. By contrast, the Ásatrúer takes on the ambitious and complex task of reconstructing their religious, communal and magical practices in the context of the modern world.

The heady combination of National Socialism, the occult, the Viking mystique, and the quest for community has proved irresistible to other long-standing elements of the white supremacist constellation as well. Of these, perhaps the most revealing of the processes by which racialist adherents seek to exploit the Norse/Germanic revival are the activities of George Dietz. Dietz, a German immigrant and long-time figure in American neo-Nazi circles whose primary income appears to be derived from the sale of anti-Semitic and racist literature through his Liberty Bell Publications, took note of the revival of Odinist groups in the United States. Through one of his younger associates, Ron Hand, Dietz created the Odinist Study Group (OSG) as a front operation for his own National Socialist movement. Hand, operating under his own name in Odinist affairs and the name Reinhold Dunkel in NS circles, enjoyed complete autonomy as leader of the group, although in the Byzantine world of American National Socialism, independence is a relative term. This period saw intensive conflicts between Hand and the creative Ben Klassen and National Socialist White People's Party leader Matt Koehl.[40]

By the late 1970s or early 1980s, Dietz had come to believe that Germany was probably dead to a possible National Socialist revival and that the last hope for a Nazi resurgence was the United States. Odinism, he reasoned, might be the engine for a future National Socialist America. The extent of Dietz's knowledge of the Odinist revival is uncertain. He clearly knew of Else Christensen, but whether he knew much more is questionable. The original plan appears to have been to gather a list of local Odinist groups and to infiltrate them, turning them gradually towards National Socialism. However, this plan could not be carried out because Dietz had decided to sell his mailing list (of which the Odinist Study Group was a part) to other groups. Ironically, this had the effect of bringing the OSG to life, in the form of a mail order kindred (local group); the inclusion of the OSG's address in certain right-wing lists—especially those of Joseph Dilys in Chicago—and word-of-mouth publicity brought in a number of seekers from across the country, many of them in the prisons. Soon, however, Hand lost interest in Odinism, and began directing letters to the OSG to Mike Murray of the Ásatrú Alliance.

The organizational history of the Ásatrú movement is relatively straightforward, but it is as difficult to define the movement itself as it is to trace the complex paths which led the members of the community to embrace Ásatrú. The term *Ásatrú* is an Icelandic word which means "belief in the Æsir" (gods), a fitting misnomer for a community that embraces belief in the Vanir (elemental gods) and also in a host of lesser wights (beings). While the contemporary adherents of Odinism and Ásatrú would appear to be traveling in opposite directions—from early brotherhood to battle—it is the *wyrd* (fate) of both to reside together in the borderland linking the worlds of the occult with the white supremacist constellation.

It is clear that the ranks of Ásatrúers existed long before the appearance of an organized Ásatrú community. The testimonies are many, but taken together, they tend fall into several categories. Most common are what could be called the awakening of childhood memories. In the 1950s and 1960s, storybook adaptations of Norse mythology, often beautifully illustrated, were popular gifts for young boys. Several present day Ásatrúers report gaining an interest in the Northern Way from this source. A second port of entry into Ásatrú flows from the influence of pop culture or the desire to become involved with the occult or magical community as a teenager or young adult. Of particular influence, recalls Stephen McNallen—the founder of the organized Ásatrú movement in the United States—was the historical novel *The Viking* by Edison Marshall (and the subsequent film starring Kirk Douglas), which contrasted the values of Ásatrú with those of Christianity.[41]

With so many awakening to the rebirth of Ásatrú, it was only a matter of time before organizations would be formed to link these scattered believers into some form of community. Remarkably, no less than three independent groups sprang up in three countries at roughly the same time. Although this study centers solely on the American groups, it is important to note that Ásatrúarmenn in Iceland was formed by the late Svienbjörn Beinteinsson in 1973, and in the same year, the Committee for the Restoration of the Odinic Rite was founded by John Yeowell in England.[42] The first American Ásatrú organization, the Viking Brotherhood, was formed in Texas by Stephen McNallen. It is the Viking Brotherhood, later renamed the Ásatrú Free Assembly (AFA), to which the organized Ásatrú community in America traces its roots.

Although Else Christensen's Odinism and Stephen McNallen's Ásatrú were at their inception difficult to distinguish, by the late 1970s the two movements had come to differ considerably. The primacy of racialism in Odinism was at the heart of this division, and flowing from this division comes the primary emphasis that McNallen placed on ritual and spirituality as opposed to Mrs. Christensen's emphasis on politics. At that time, the inherent tensions within the Ásatrú Free Assembly (race being but one of many sources of conflict) would shatter any hopes of a unified movement. How difficult the issue of race—and that

[handwritten margin note: Odinism > Ásatrú were too diff. to unify]

of National Socialism—was for the fledgling Odinist/Ásatrú movement was illustrated in 1978, when the tiny National Socialist White Workers Party (led by American Nazi Party veteran Allen Vincent) obtained a meeting room in San Francisco by claiming to be "The Odinist Society."[43] McNallen's reaction marked a decisive break with the racialist roots of the modern Odinist revival:

> [This] Nazi-Odinist identification has persisted down to this day, but most of us either learned to live with it or simply hoped it would go away if we ignored it.
> The Ásatrú Free Assembly announces the end of that tolerance.
> We . . . sympathize with the legitimate frustrations of white men who are concerned for their kind and for their culture. These concerns are fully justified. It is a tragedy that these men are driven to radical groups such as the NSWWP because there is no well-known, responsible organization working for white ethnic awareness and identity.[44]

It is somewhat ironic, but nonetheless not atypical of small, fledgling religious communities, that relatively marginal issues can often become divisive far out of proportion to their centrality to the religion itself. So it is with race and Ásatrú. Although self-identified Odinists are often drawn to the belief system by preexisting racialist beliefs, Ásatrúers are a considerably more diverse community for whom racial pride, while important, is in most instances secondary to the greater considerations of spirituality and the "remagicalization" of the world.[45] At the same time, however, the presence of racialist and National Socialist adherents at Ásatrú Free Assembly gatherings was a problem which by the late 1970s could no longer be ignored. The struggle for the soul of the movement—which would continue for at least two decades—was being waged in earnest, and the pressures on McNallen were formidable. It was this accumulation of pressures, personal and organizational, which in 1987 brought about the demise of the AFA.

The AFA had simply become too great a strain, personally and financially, on Steve McNallen and Robert Stine who, with their wives Maddy and Kelly respectively, were trying to hold the faltering organization together. All were putting in approximately sixty hours per week on the organization and trying to exist on "get by" jobs (McNallen himself working for a time as a jail guard). The AFA could not support a permanent staff financially, and with the constant pressure of the race question which saw a minority of the movement pushing the leadership to adopt an overtly racialist stance, the combined pressures simply became too much to bear. When the realization set in that the AFA was simply not going anywhere, McNallen called it a day and folded the organization.[46]

Two successor organizations would fill the post-AFA void: the Ásatrú Alliance, headed by Mike Murray of the Arizona Kindred, and the
Ring of Troth, founded by Edred Thorsson. The latter group would
eschew race and concentrate instead on revitalizing the magical traditions of the pagan Norse-Germanic peoples, while at the same time as-
piring to create an Ásatrú priesthood modeled closely on that of the
early Christian church.

The Alliance, however, is a more complex case. One of the guiding
spirits behind the Alliance is Mike Murray. As a teenager in Phoenix,
Murray was involved in the local National Socialist scene through
Rockwell's American Nazi Party. With the commander's 1967 assassination, Murray remained briefly with the renamed party under Matt
Koehl and was a member of the odd National Socialist White People's
Party's Nazi Motorcycle Club commanded by Mike Brown. In those
days he jauntily signed his letters with a hearty "Heil Hitler!" However,
like many activists who were connected to the ANP, the fragmentation
of the Koehl era and the common perception within the movement that
Rockwell's successor was more interested in fundraising than revolution, Murray left the world of National Socialism and in the early
1970s found Else Christensen's Odinist Fellowship where he eventually
served as vice president. Murray first met McNallen in 1972, but it was
not until 1980 that, deeply moved by the spirituality of the rituals led
by McNallen, Murray would officially join the Ásatrú Free Assembly.
With the 1987 breakup of the AFA, Murray and a select group of
others were left with the corpse of the organization, which he revi-
talized as the Ásatrú Alliance.[47] With the mantle of leadership on his
own shoulders, Murray faced his first challenge from National Socialist
ranks. In dealing with the problem, he reacted in precisely the way
McNallen had in 1978.

The occasion for this event was a 1988 issue of *Speaking Out,* an
eccentric National Socialist publication of the New Dawn, an organization whose leader (and only known member) was Michael Merritt of
Burbank, California. New Dawn promoted the idea that National Socialism and Hitler cultists in general were perceived in such negative
terms by the American public that the ideals of National Socialism
would never be implemented unless their name and rhetoric were radically revised. Merritt's mission was thus to put "old wine in new bottles" by marketing National Socialism as the New Philosophy and as
American Socialism. Following long-standing practice in racialist right-
wing circles, Merritt obtained an issue of the Ásatrú Alliance journal,
Vor Trú, which listed the names and addresses of all AA member kindreds and promptly published this information, implying that these kindreds were in agreement with National Socialist ideals. This publicity

clearly displeased some of the affected kindreds, and Murray was left with the task of contacting Merritt and insisting that Murray's letter of protest be published in the next issue of *Speaking Out,* and that Merritt cease to publish this directory in the future. The key section of Murray's letter read, "The Alliance does not advocate any type of political or racial extremist views or affiliations. We do not support the *New Dawn* nor share its views."[48]

The other national Ásatru organization, Ring of Troth, was very much the brainchild of Edred Thorsson. It emerged contemporaneously with the Ásatrú Alliance on 20 December 1987, from the wreckage of the Ásatrú Free Assembly. The organizational blueprint for the Troth was set out in Thorsson's *A Book of Troth,* which "is the official, basic document of the organization known simply as 'The Ring of Troth.'"[49] The group has survived a series of disasters which would have doomed a less determined organization. By the mid-1990s, led by William Bainbridge and boasting a High Rede (board of directors) which features such promising young scholars as KveldúlfR Gundarsson, the Troth has emerged to become in a very real sense the most accessible face of the Odinist/Ásatrú community. While Odinism has found a comfortable niche in the white supremacist constellation (and thus, off the map of contemporary cultural discourse), individual Odinists interact with the Ásatrú community primarily in the pages of Ásatrú Alliance's publication *Vor Trú* and at the Ásatrú Alliance Althings (annual gatherings). By contrast, the Ring of Troth sits squarely within the Wiccan/neopagan community, and is so diverse that its core and peripheral members are identified with such unlikely bedfellows as several strains of Satanism *and* with that scourge of Satanists (real or imagined), the cult awareness movement! The Ring of Troth reflects an astonishing diversity, including members with inter-racial marriages and kindreds who boast Jewish, black, homosexual, and even transsexual members.

Thus, while the Alliance inhabits a border area linking the magical/neopagan community with the millenarian theorists of the white supremacist world, they are intertwined as well with the decidedly non-racialist Ring of Troth. No better example of the Alliance-Troth connection could be given than the case of William Bainbridge. Bainbridge is a member both of the Arizona Kindred in the Ásatrú Alliance and is the steersman of the Ring of Troth. Cross-membership in the Ásatrú Alliance and in the Ring of Troth may be common due to the Troth's practice of enrolling all subscribers to their official journal, *Idunna,* unless the subscriber specifically declines membership on the subscription form.

Bainbridge makes a key point in his analysis of the Ring of Troth when he contends that the Troth has existed in its current form only since March 1992. Until then, the organization was in chaos, buffeted on all sides with controversies of its own making. Specifically, three unrelated revelations swept through the Ásatrú community in the first year of the organization's existence: Edred Thorsson's (and later, James Chisholm's) connection to Michael Aquino's Satanist group, the Temple of Set; the same cast of characters' involvement in sadomasochistic activity; and the case of Rob Meek, the group's rising star, who exposed in particularly lurid terms Thorsson's Satanist activities. As the controversy over the Temple of Set was reaching its peak, Meek was arrested in Dallas and accused (and later convicted) of the murder of his wife. Given this triple shock, it is a testament to the viability of the Ring of Troth (or to the protection of the gods) that the organization survived at all.

The revelation of Thorsson's connection to the Temple of Set (and in particular its Order of the Trapezoid) engendered an intensely negative reaction in the Ásatrú community. Thorsson argues, with considerable justification, that his connections with Satanism and with both the Church of Satan and the Temple of Set were known to many within the Ásatrú community. However, there is considerably less documentation for Thorsson's belief that McNallen (or any other Ásatrú figure) fully understood the "left hand path" that he had chosen, much less approved of it.[50] In any case, and again illustrative of the theory of the cultic milieu, Thorsson was hardly the only Ásatrúer to hold membership not only in the Temple of Set but in a number of occult/magical belief systems. This tendency toward serial membership is mirrored in the Odinist world, where Odinists have long been associated with National Socialist groups as well as with other appeals throughout the racialist right wing. For many in the world of Ásatrú, however, Satanism was simply incompatible with the neopagan Northern Way.

Many participants in the controversy are unanimous in their recollection that Rob Meek in particular went to considerable lengths to publicize the "Satanist infiltration" of Ásatrú. According to Chisholm, Meek was motivated by "repeated viewings of Geraldo's Satanism specials."[51] Meek apparently learned about Thorsson's Temple of Set affiliation after a young female Setian boasted at a Dallas occult bookstore of knowing Thorsson. The local occult community being as small and interconnected as it was, it took little time for this news to get to Meek. According to Thorsson's recollection, Meek had held a grudge for some time because Thorsson had not deigned to communicate with Meek as the latter's star was rising with the Ring of Troth. Add to this the fact that in the course of the Temple of Set controversy, when four or five letters were exchanged between the two, Thorsson apparently refused to rise to Meek's support of the Vanir (elemental deities) against the Æsir, and the break was irreparable.[52]

Perhaps the most dispassionate and thus enlightening "insider" view of this period is provided by KveldúlfR Gundarsson:

> The whistle was blown on Edred Thorsson by Rob Meek late in 1988; Meek campaigned ceaselessly throughout Ásatrú to make sure everyone knew about the Temple of Set. Edred's mention of Aquino in *Runelore* and *A Book of Troth* proved it beyond a doubt. In late spring of 1989, James Chisholm also admitted his membership in the TOS. By this time, the issue had seriously inflamed what I believe (though not having been active in the early years, do not know) to have been a long standing degree of dislike between Thorsson and some members of the AA. Edred and Jim then wrote very stupid letters to the 1989 Althing—Edred identifying Wotan/Odhinn with the "Prince of Darkness"[53] . . . which sealed their status as outcasts in Ásatrú as a whole and established a perception of the Ring of Troth as merely a sort of outer court of the Temple of Set. This badly damaged the group's growth potential for a couple of years; however it [the Troth] was not very large when the event took place. Edred's ambiguous position was also something of a difficulty from the beginning: he had no desire to take a place, but kept writing and trying to structure the ideology of the group. He went through several titles, including "Drighten," before settling on "Warden of the Lore."
>
> Ultimately, Edred and Jim realized that, while they were involved in the Troth, it would never gain any sort of acceptance.[54]

The reaction against Thorsson was indeed strong, and began with the reception of his and Chisholm's letters at the AA's 1889 gathering, Althing 9, at which a statement was adopted declaring that there could be no connection between Ásatrú and Satanism. In particular, the Alliance went on record as opposing

> any connection between Ásatrú and the "prince of darkness" or any other alien deities . . . [in particular with] outlandish . . . Mediterranean archetypes, deities, philosophies and ideas into our pure faith . . . We shall have no part in any attempted rehabilitation of Nazi occultism[55] [because] the Nazis did more damage to our Folk and to Germanic spirituality in two decades than any group since our forced conversion to Christianity, and we shall never be fooled . . . into forgetting the unspeakable consequences for our Folk of the "Thousand Year Reich." Regarding Edred Thorsson, we recognize his unique and irreplaceable contribution to our rediscovery of our spiritual and magical heritage . . . because of the great respect we all felt for Thorsson and his work, we have been all the more hurt and dismayed to learn of

his recent and extensive connection with Satanism . . . In secretly asso-
ciating himself with satanic organizations, and insinuating satanic
teachings into his work, particularly in the Rune Gild, Edred has let us
down, and if, as rumored, he has regarded us as sheep to be manipulated and led about without explaining the origin of his teachings or
the direction of his leadership, then he has unforgivably insulted us as
well. However, the Alliance has no intention of leading inquisitions or
pronouncing anathemas. The All Father [Odin] has always been a stir-
rer of strife, and, as his children, we do not fear the free competition of
ideas.[56]

Meanwhile, the Ring of Troth in Texas were hardly passive ob-
servers to all this. Fending off attacks from Meek on one front and from
the Alliance and other Ásatrú sources on the other, Dianne Ross, the
ever-loyal editor of the Troth's journal *Idunna,* opened a line of defense
in the form of a most unusual two-page letter sent individually to
Idunna subscribers/Ring of Troth members. The letter appears to have
been intended to complement a year-long campaign of defense and
counterattack conducted by the Thorsson/Chisholm axis. (Thorsson's
contributions came in the form of open letters, none significantly different in content than the "Open Letter to the Arizona Kindred" which
was read at Althing 9.) Ross stated:

> While I am writing to you, it seems perhaps timely to touch briefly
> on the allegations made regarding possible "Satanic" influences on the
> Troth. I have been a member of the Ring of Troth for eight months
> and have attended meetings of the Irminsul Hearth in Austin [Thors-
> son's kindred] on a weekly basis. I have seen absolutely no "Satanic"
> influences within the Troth and certainly in no way is the Troth seen as
> a recruitment ground for the Temple of Set. (And I am not an unobser-
> vant sort.) I am not a member of the Temple.
>
> Edred Thorsson and James Chisholm have been unbelievably kind
> and helpful in my quest to find my way back to the ancient Gods and
> Goddesses. They both spend between twenty and thirty hours a week
> in their dedication to this religion, in addition to their full time jobs.
> This, of course, is an understatement. Really, they have given all their
> adult lives. I have never seen them do anything to harm another living
> soul and they have always gone out of their way to teach and encour-
> age. Certainly that has been my experience with other members of our
> hearth as well. I would not have even known of any of this business if
> it had not been for Rob Meek in Arlington [Texas] and it seems to me
> that everything has been blown completely out of proportion. In the
> eyes of the Christians we are all Satanic . . .
>
> I say all of this in hopes you will use your intelligence and influ-
> ence to put an end to all this malfeasance. Please consider that just
> possibly the fires of discontent have been fueled by the tendencies of

those who find it easier to criticize and damn than to spend the energy required for constructive long-term work on behalf of the folk. If Rob Meek would spend his time writing on the Vanic Gods and Goddesses and their mysteries we would all be the better for it. He despises Od-hinn and is so frustrated that the good books written in recent times have all been by written by Odians. Rather than find out if he can produce a major writing of quality from a Vanic perspective it seems he finds a perverse satisfaction in causing strife and dissension. Each one of us in this religion is precious and we must try to understand and respect our differences.[57]

This letter is rich in allusions to several of the central religious mo-tifs attendant to the current reconstruction of Ásatrú in the modern world; indeed, Rob Meek's rebellion (or betrayal) is posited here as arising from this ethos. Most striking perhaps, is the assertion—correct in the case of fundamentalists—that Christians consider neopagans Sa-tanic by definition. Ásatrú, like Odinism, is explicitly anti-Christian. This may be expressed with varying degrees of intensity, ranging from the contemptuous "White-Krist" of Thorsson to Gundarsson's simple refusal to capitalize "christian." However it is expressed, it is based on the belief that Christianity displaced the old religion and its native values, replacing it with an alien, Mediterranean cult, which had the effect of devastating the culture of the Norse/Germanic peoples. The undoing of that historical disaster is one of the central goals of Ásatrú today; this goal is implied in Ross's cryptic words of caution, "What will happen when the time comes to confront our real opponents when they come to understand our aim?" This confrontation is seen by most Ásatrúers as inevitable, given the pronounced intolerance which they perceive to be inherent in Christianity. Many believe that Meek was induced to take this action by televised warnings of the machinations of Satan on this earth—hardly a prevalent view among neopagans but an article of faith in fundamentalist Christianity (of which Arlington, Texas, is a heartland).

However, even if Christian intolerance was the context for Meek's actions, the proximate causes might well have been drawn from the Eddas and the sagas themselves. None of the images in the last para-graph of Ross's letter are new to Norse mythology: Odin as strife-stir-rer, the war between the Vanes and the Æsir, jealousy and revenge. Here, however, the themes are brought together and applied to a real life situation in the world of contemporary Ásatrú.

At about the same time that Ross and others were defending Thors-son from charges of Satanism, their task was made more difficult by the controversy surrounding Thorsson's connections to sadomasochistic practices. Thorsson for his part made no secret of this, but as with all of his activities, there was a religious dimension to the newest scandal which few Ásatrúers were ready to accept or understand. For Thorsson, it is through extremes—the polarity of pain and pleasure, for example—that one achieves transcendence, and transcendence is the very essence of the Odinnic archetype. Moreover, Odin in one of his aspects is known as the god of fetters. The idea for the actualization of this form of sexuality in a ritual context appears to have been drawn from the novel, *Story of O,* although Thorsson also points out that two traditional cultures (northern Europe and Japan) utilize these practices in a religious context.[58] It is unclear how such activities first became public, but the Ásatrú community was soon apprised of the accouterments of Thorsson's shamanic journeys into the dark side of Odin. Unkind jokes about the "Roissy Kindred" aside, Thorsson had never tried to hide his interest in various forms of shamanic sex magic, and even in his popular-market books had given broad hints about the magical use of sadomasochistic practices. For example, borrowing loosely from Eliade, he offers this description of the use of seith (shamanic trance) magic:

> To work seith . . . you must first achieve an altered state of consciousness. Traditionally, this was done with a variety or combination of techniques, including drugs, sleep deprivation, fasting, sensory overload, and even physical tortures, which might be combined with chanting, dancing, and perhaps the playing of some rhythmic instrument.[59]

It would be atypical for Edred Thorsson to actuate any practice without making an organization and/or a religion out of it, and so was born the Order of the Triskelion. The Triskelion refers to the three-pronged signet ring worn by the habitués of Roissy, the domicile in which O is introduced to the polarities of pain and pleasure. There are two Triskelion suborders, the Roissy Society for male dominants and female submissives and the Onyx Circle for female dominants and male submissives. Advancement in the group, as in the Temple of Set and the Rune Gild, is by initiation, and membership is by invitation.[60]

The dust from the revelations of Satanism and of sadomasochism had hardly settled on the Ásatrú community when news of murder began to filter out of Texas, all the more shocking when it was learned that the accused killer was Rob Meek. Meek's history is typical of the seeker within the cultic milieu. He came to Ásatrú in 1985 in the course of a spiritual quest that he undertook at the urging of his mother, then dying of lymphatic cancer in his native San Antonio. Born in 1963 into a religious Episcopalian family and educated in the local Christian school system from 1976 to 1979, Meek investigated Islam, Eastern religions, and a number of other religious ports of call before finding his way to the then headquarters of the Ásatrú Free Alliance, the Northern European Heritage Center in Breckenridge, Texas, manned by Stephen McNallen and Robert Stine.[61] Meek adopted the AFA philosophy and returned to Arlington, where he founded a small kindred that disbanded with the dissolution of the AFA.

In 1987 he married Anne Harrington, who was to become a force in Ásatrú as the founding editor of the journal *Northways*. Coming into contact with Mike Murray and the Ásatrú Alliance, Meek, now more commonly known by his magical name of Ingvar Solve Ingvisson, reestablished a kindred in Arlington in 1988. Learning of the Ring of Troth, he quickly joined, working his way within a year to membership on the initial High Rede, while returning to the University of Texas at Arlington to pursue a B.A. in General Studies.[62]

Soon, however, a literal dark shadow cast a pall over the career of Ingvisson/Meek. He was diagnosed with a brain tumor, which in time would grow and, according to some who knew him, take on a kind of personality for Meek, who gave it a name, referred to it at times as a friend, and on occasion conversed with it. He was, in fact, becoming increasingly unstable, and his dramatic denunciation of Thorsson for Satanic activities should in retrospect be seen in this light. Indeed, Ásatrú was but another spiritual way station which he put behind him even as the Troth was reeling from the Satanism controversy.

The story would not end there. On the evening of 18 February 1991, Meek murdered his wife, reportedly in her sleep, and buried her body at a landfill near the Dallas airport. Following his arrest, he was ritually cursed throughout the Ásatrú community.[63] For the Ring of Troth, however, the event—with which they had nothing to do, save by association—was a second disaster. Meek was simply too deeply involved in the conflict with Thorsson and the Troth over Satanism for disclaimers pointing out that he was no longer a member of the Ring of Troth or even an adherent of Ásatrú at the time of the crime to make much difference.[64] In the minds of many, Satanism and murder were of a piece, and the Ring of Troth was twice cursed.

Clearly, Edred Thorsson—and James Chisholm as well—were simply too controversial to remain associated with the Ring of Troth if that organization was to survive. Thus, by 1991, the search was on for a new Steersman who would be free of damaging associations with the Troth's turbulent past. The search was focused outside of the Texas epicenter of the organization, and was undertaken with some urgency. With the group in disarray, there was talk throughout Ásatrú circles of forming a new, nonracialist grouping separate from the Ásatrú Alliance but free as well from the taint of the Troth's current difficulties.[65] Eventually, the choice fell on the disgruntled former Thing-speaker of the

Ásatrú Alliance, Phil Nearing of the Old Northwest Kindred, centered in Chicago.

Phil Nearing had by this time severed his relationship with the Alliance. In a letter dated 6 January 1991, he tendered the resignation of the Old Northwest Kindred, stating that it was in the "intellectual, political and spiritual interests" of the kindred to leave the organization; while they would be interested in continuing contacts with individual kindreds, they nonetheless wished to be on the record in opposition to "any fascist and racist interpretations of Ásatrú and [were] not interested in interacting with groups or individuals who follow these lines of thought."[66]

Shortly after this, Nearing, by now increasingly disgusted with the racialism of the Alliance wrote a letter to the Troth stating that he was not an enemy of the latter organization but in fact something of an ally, and this opened a considerable correspondence. At this time, however, Nearing first got wind of the murder of Rob Meek's wife; the murder was confirmed by Chisholm over the phone, although the latter expressed some surprise that Nearing had heard about it so soon. With these scandals, Nearing was convinced privately that he would have nothing to do with leading the organization.[67] Still, when he was invited in July 1991 to meet with Thorsson and Chisholm in an Austin, Texas, restaurant to discuss Nearing's accepting the Steersmanship, the chance to meet Thorsson and assess the situation firsthand was simply too inviting to pass up. From the perspective of the Austin group, primarily composed at this point of Thorsson, Chisholm, and the new *Idunna* editor, Þórfinn Einarsson, the very fact that Nearing and company would take the trouble to fly down to Texas was evidence that "something was going to happen," even if no assurances or commitments had been made in advance. In the event, however, they "acted like a bunch of tourists," according to Thorsson.[68]

In fact, this is precisely what the putative candidates were. Tales of the macabre doings in Austin were sufficiently lurid as to make the invitation irresistible. Still, Nearing deemed it advisable to bring trusted friends with him, and thus he asked William Bainbridge and one other well-known independent Ásatrúer (whose name is withheld upon request) to attend. Both agreed, and their separate accounts of the meeting are consistent in every important detail.

The most complete account of this meeting, and of the subsequent transfer of power to Prudence Priest and the "de-Thorssonization" of the Ring of Troth, is offered by the anonymous participant. His extended account is worth noting:

> In July 1991 . . . Nearing . . . asked me to join him and William Bainbridge . . . to meet Edred Thorsson face to face. Nearing told me on the telephone beforehand that Thorsson had asked him to accept

the post of Steersman of the Ring of Troth because Chisholm was ready to resign . . . I agreed . . . partly out of curiosity because it would enable me to meet the notorious Edred Thorsson . . . During dinner, we talked about a wide range of topics, many not related to Ásatrú at all. (No one ever mentioned "The Temple of Set" throughout the entire weekend.) I found Thorsson to be a quiet, reserved man, about 40—obviously intelligent and well versed in all the subjects we discussed. There seemed to be nothing unusual or "weird" about him. We arranged to meet again the next morning . . . The next morning (Saturday) the three of us arrived at Thorsson's house. There we were met in the living room by Edred Thorsson, James Chisholm, Dianne Ross, and Þórfinn Einarsson. After the introductions had been made, we all went into another room. There was a large table with three chairs on each of its long sides. Thorsson sat down in the middle chair on one side, with Chisholm on his right and Ross on his left . . . Chisholm was wearing a large Mjölnir (Thor's Hammer) around his neck outside of his shirt. After a few preliminary remarks, Thorsson offered the Steersmanship to Nearing and, as he did so, Chisholm took the Mjölnir off his neck and prepared to hand it to Nearing . . . At this point, Nearing said he felt that he could not accept the Steersmanship because he did not have enough people in Chicago to properly run the Ring of Troth. Thorsson was obviously completely surprised by this. Chisholm sat there holding the Mjölnir in his hands unsure of what to do next. Thorsson then turned to Bainbridge, and asked him if he would consider being the Steersman. Bainbridge said no, citing the same reasons Nearing had given. Then, to my utter amazement, Thorsson offered the Steersmanship to me. Like the others, I too refused to accept it, giving once more the reasons Nearing had given. After a few awkward moments, Chisholm replaced the Mjölnir around his own neck and we all went back into the living room . . . the subject of the Steersmanship never came up again . . .

It took some time to find a new leader for the Ring of Troth, but Prudence Priest accepted the office of Steerswoman/Steersman from James Chisholm at a ceremony held just north of San Francisco in March 1992.[69]

With the transfer of the Steersmanship to Priest, the first phase of the Ring of Troth—the era of Edred Thorsson—came to a close. The Ring of Troth's second phase, however, would do little to stabilize the organization. Thus, in 1995, in the wake of accusations that Priest intended to bring Thorsson back into the fold and of her failed attempt to ease KveldúlfR Gundarsson out of his increasingly prominent role, Priest was herself ousted and William Bainbridge took over as interim Steersman.

Bainbridge is correct in his assertion, offered as a plea for patience, that the current Troth is in fact a new creation. The Ásatrú Alliance, currently in a period of expansion, is structured much as it was before.

What, then, can be said about the future of these Ásatrú organizations, and indeed about the Ásatrú community as a whole?

In Weberian terms, as these have been adapted to the academic study of New Religious Movements, it is the Ring of Troth—with all of its turbulent history—rather than the Alliance that would seem to best fit the profile of a movement destined to succeed. Its original charismatic founder, Edred Thorsson, a true visionary but a hopeless administrator, routinized his own (and thus the organization's) charisma by investing it in the High Rede and left much of the decision making to that body. By contrast, in the Ásatrú Alliance, no such routinization has occurred. In theoretical terms, this should not bode well for the post-Mike Murray future of the Alliance.[70]

This theory, however, is an academic construct, very much in keeping with the ROT's scholarly orientation. Unsurprisingly, the view from the Alliance's vantage point is quite different. In the words of the Wulfing Kindred's Robert Taylor:

> I think it would be accurate to describe [the ROT] as academic rather than intellectual. . . . The majority of those in the Alliance are coming from the soul—a gut feeling towards Asatru. . . . Troth people are coming basically from the head. For those in the academic world what someone thinks or says is of paramount importance. In an academic environment nothing much ever really happens or is done. It's a world where ideas are of the first order of importance.
>
> For myself as well as for most of the Alliance members it's less important what you think or say as what you do. It's more a world of concrete actions and deeds . . . [the ROT's] focus seems to be everywhere except their own culture. They are cosmopolitans and cultural pluralists. Academic nomads lost in the by-ways and hi-ways of the Global village. They can write books about runes and play-act at being Vikings, but in the end they are empty soulless vessels with little relevance to reality. . . . Few of them have had to survive in combat, prison or inner city streets.[71]

By 1996, Robert Taylor's words seem to have been prophetic. The Troth, wracked by internal dissension and plagued by splits based more on personality than on substance, has begun to unravel. The always contentious email lists by which Troth members communicate has for years been a forum for the most divisive personal invective imaginable. The Troth's journal, *Idunna,* has seen editors brought in and then dismissed for instituting too critical an editorial policy.[72] The Ring of Troth simply shows few signs of stabilizing, despite the able leadership of William Bainbridge.

The Alliance on the other hand shows every sign of slow but steady growth. Indeed, Steve McNallen whose reemergence on the Ásatrú scene was heralded by the creation of a new national organization, the Ásatrú Folk Assembly, has recently applied to have his own kindred admitted to the Ásatrú Alliance.[73] Why then has the Alliance prospered while the Troth, Weberian constructs aside, continued to founder?

It would seem that, at root, the institution of the High Rede, which Thorsson sought to invest with the leadership of the Troth, was both unready to accept the burden of running a national organization and unable to bring order to the administrative chaos left behind by the mercurial Thorsson. In this sense, it mattered little whether Nearing, Bainbridge, or Priest took over the organization. Each of these figures would have had to deal with the High Rede, which itself is composed of strong personalities who have proved resistant to submitting to any leader, regardless of that leader's qualifications. Moreover, the scattered membership of the Troth has proven equally reluctant to follow the initiatives of the High Rede. When Bainbridge did take over the organization in the wake of Priest's ouster, one of the first orders of business was the attempt to "democratize" the Troth, and in 1996 an election is underway for Steersman while an attempt is being made to open the Rede itself to elections.

The Ásatrú Alliance, beset by its own severe problems inherited from the waning days of the Ásatrú Free Assembly, went through its own period of severe turmoil. These conflicts (discussed in chapter 3) came to a head at several of the early Alliance Althings. However, from the beginning there was a conscious design among the Alliance leadership to avoid the pitfalls of a centralized leadership or a single, charismatic figure. The Alliance's "charisma," therefore, was invested in the institution itself, and the functions of running the organization were split up among several key adherents. The Alliance, in stark contrast to the Troth, never attempted to exercise control over local kindreds. While the Troth's Elder Training Program undertook the ambitious task of creating an Ásatrú "priesthood," the Alliance left the spiritual direction of its member kindreds to the local leadership. This practice had the effect of minimizing internal friction. Moreover, although the Alliance Althings, which met to set policies and directions for the organization, were often fractious in the immediate post-AFA period, the insistence of the AA leadership to officially eschew questions of politics and race has in recent years minimized these cleavages considerably.[74]

Steve McNallen's newest national organization, the Ásatrú Folk Assembly, in 1996 is roughly the size of the old Ásatrú Free Assembly, which is to say, small. Its structure is similar to the original Ásatrú Free Assembly, as are its rituals. Indeed, the new AFA can even boast of the reincarnation of the seminal Ásatrú publication, the *Runestone,* as its primary publication (bolstered by the mailing list of imprisoned Else Christensen's Odinist Fellowship).

Given the application of McNallen's kindred to join the Ásatrú Alliance, the creation of a new AFA would seem somewhat superfluous. McNallen was moved to organize the Ásatrú Folk Assembly by reports—much exaggerated as it turned out—that the "universalist" (i.e., nonracialist) adherents of the Ring of Troth had made inroads into the Alliance with their message that anyone could be an Ásatrúer. For McNallen, as for Murray and most members of the Alliance, Ásatrú is the religion of the descendants of the northern European peoples. McNallen, however, had maintained little direct contact with Murray for several years and so took these rumors seriously. The new AFA was therefore created to maintain what McNallen sees as the integral link between ancestry and religion, between biology and spirituality. Ultimately, McNallen hopes that the new AFA will one day be in a position to be a voice for the interests of the Norse/Germanic peoples, even if those peoples do not accept Ásatrú as their religion.[75]

In the great racial divide, the new AFA seems to be attempting to hold to the old AFA's middle ground position, although McNallen notes that he considers involving himself in politics on an almost daily basis. The new organization, like the original AFA, continues to draw to its ranks National Socialists and other strongly racialist adherents, but McNallen continues to try to steer these discussions into more constructive areas that would try to broach solutions to problems rather than simply to wallow in despair over the current state of the nation.[76]

The AFA's future is at this point uncertain. It serves the same constituency as does the Ásatrú Alliance, and despite the new AFA's boast of a number of functioning guilds (i.e., Warriors, Brewers, etc., along the model of the old Ásatrú Free Assembly), there is little evidence that these ambitious plans have gone beyond the discussion stage.[77]

Nationalist Socialist Groups

Right now this movement is plagued with little self-appointed SS groups who spend huge bucks in assembling SS paraphernalia and putting it on for secret photographic sessions that almost smack of queers coming out of the closet—indeed, in some cases, that is what it is. The fact is (and we had better start admitting some of these unpleasant facts) that this movement has a distinct tendency to attract faggots because of the leather-macho image that the System Jew media imparts to the SS uniform.

in the past year we have had here in North Carolina as "house guests" . . . a 32-year-old 300 pound psychotic who tried to play junior Martin

Bormann, spent his time here insulting, threatening, and spreading rumors about other Party members, and would throw screaming tantrums like those of a four-year-old child when opposed. One person described these fits as "a bearded Gerber baby on a rampage" . . .

And this is in Carolina, admittedly the best and most selective unit in the Party! The other units are even worse . . . drug addicts, tattooed women, total bums and losers, police informers, the dregs of urban life.[78]

More a study in political pathology than a viable political movement, the highly disparate world of explicitly neo-Nazi groups in North America is notable both for its high profile activism—they are a visible feature of the landscape of every right-wing march—and for its minuscule size. In spatial terms, no movement is more distant from the American cultural mainstream. This is not to say that National Socialist (NS) groups are without influence—quite the opposite is true—but if the radical right wing is fractious, National Socialism is fratricidal. The movement has been preoccupied with internecine rivalries since 1967, when Commander George Lincoln Rockwell was assassinated in Arlington, Virginia.[79] Matthias Koehl inherited Rockwell's American Nazi Party (ANP), changing its name to the National Socialist White People's Party (NSWPP) and beginning what would be an ongoing feature of the movement since then, a seemingly unending round of purges and angry resignations. Such high profile Christian Identity figures as James Warner and Ralph Forbes began their careers in the radical right in the ANP, only to be harried into other quarters of the cultic milieu through this process of Koehl-era fragmentation. Dr. William Pierce and Harold Covington, whose widely shared observations of the quality of adherents that neo-Nazi movements in North America manage to attract opened this section, were purge victims as well.[80]

In the 1990s, National Socialism is a highly idiosyncratic collection of "leaders" scattered around the country whose unenviable task it is to lead a tiny and unsavory band of followers towards the institution of a New Order. The Euro-American Alliance (Maj. D. V. Clerkin, "fuehrer"), the American National Socialist Party (Hale McGee, "fuehrer"), and the American Nazi Party (Jim Burford, "fuehrer") are but a few examples. Moreover, the movement is bitterly divided between the conservative majority of party activists, who favor the theory of mass action that calls for carefully building a broad revolutionary coalition, and those few who favor immediate revolutionary violence on the model of 1960s-era left-wing guerrilla movements. The National Socialist group most involved in this form of revolutionary violence is, unsurprisingly, moribund. The National Socialist Liberation Front (NSLF) was founded in the early 1970s by Joseph Tomassi, who was purged from the NSWPP by Koehl on the grounds that he allowed young women and marijuana parties in party headquarters. Tomassi responded by forming the NSLF on the model of left-wing terrorist groups of the day. Tomassi was assassinated by an NSWPP adherent in 1975, leaving behind a cadre which included David Rust, Karl Hand, and James Mason. Both Rust and Hand are currently incarcerated.[81]

Whether the strategy of mass action or that of revolutionary violence is favored, the ultimate dream is frankly millennial. It is a dream which is, to the faithful, very much worth fighting for. According to Koehl, "Like a true disciple, [Rockwell] would be propagating the Millennial Idea as the rallying banner of an embattled race." Rick Cooper of the National Socialist Vanguard is even more explicit: "We know 'Armageddon,' which many (we included) believe is the biblical word for race war, will climax a tribulation period at which time the bankers will close their doors. What we have been attempting to determine now is a possible trigger incident that will cause the bankers to close their doors."[82]

It is no easy task to single out a preeminent leader in contemporary National Socialist ranks. Many have passed through the movement, but almost all have gravitated to other racialist appeals less stigmatized by the negative public image of Nazism and less prone to attract the sort of adherents decried by Covington. What remains are a small group of true believers—Hitler cultists in every sense of the term—along with a relative few for whom veneration of the Third Reich does not stand in the way of an objective analysis of the current condition of the movement nor of the flexibility to adapt National Socialist doctrine to the exigencies of the contemporary United States. Several of the more influential of the modernist "little fuehrers" serve to illustrate how a movement with so few adherents—and those held in contempt by their own leaders no less than by the far right wing generally—could enjoy as much influence as it does.

There is little question that the single most influential neo-Nazi in the American radical right today is National Alliance leader William Pierce. It was Pierce, writing under the pseudonym of Andrew Macdonald, who authored *The Turner Diaries,* which strongly influenced the founder of the Order, Robert Mathews. Indeed, Mathews was once a member of the National Alliance before his discovery of Christian Identity and Odinism—as was Tom Martinez, the man whose betrayal would cost Mathews his life. Pierce's career considerably predated *The Turner Diaries,* however. A Ph.D. physicist who resigned a professorship at Oregon State University to become a core member of Rockwell's American Nazi Party, Pierce edited the ANP's quarterly journal, *National Socialist World.* He remained with the ANP for three years after Rockwell's assassination, until that organization's internal upheavals forced him into the arms of veteran anti-Semite Willis Carto and his National Youth Alliance. As with every one of Carto's associations, this affiliation was short-lived, and the National Alliance was born. After 1978, the National Alliance was joined by a new Pierce creation, the Cosmotheist Church, whose primary tenet of faith appears to be "Thou shalt not deny Dr. Pierce tax exempt status," as had the Internal Revenue Service in that year.[83]

Pierce's pre–*Turner Diaries* influence in the world of the radical right was based less on his Rockwellian pedigree than on his own ecumenical approach to National Socialism. No mere Hitler cultist, Pierce has consistently eschewed the swastika or other overt displays of Third Reich nostalgia. Instead, his journals (*Attack!* and its successor *National Vanguard,* and the internal *Action* and its successor *National Alliance Bulletin*) have consistently been not only literate but also intellectually challenging—no mean feat, in this milieu! Moreover, Pierce has managed to remain on good terms with a considerable number of radical right figures; for example, he was perhaps the last man that Church of the Creator creator Ben Klassen could call a friend before Klassen's 1993 suicide. This too was no mean feat, and Pierce's reward was the opportunity to buy Klassen's North Carolina property at the bargain price of $100,000.[84]

It is, however, *The Turner Diaries,* and perhaps also its successor, *Hunter,* for which Pierce will best be remembered. *The Turner Diaries* is the most accurate encapsulation available of the seductiveness of the chiliastic dream that led a certain segment of the radical right to ignore the glaring disparity between the forces of the state and those of the "revolution" and to enlist in Robert Mathews' quixotic Order. After 1984 with the Order crushed and the dream of the "revolutionary majority" in tatters, Pierce launched the novel *Hunter* into the void to suggest to the dispirited movement that all was not lost. Rather, a change in tactics was in order, with the lone-wolf assassin providing for the moment the only realistic outlet for revolutionary violence.[85]

By contrast, Rick Cooper and Gerhard (Gary) Lauck do not approach the status of William Pierce in the world of the radical right. At the same time, both do enjoy a certain degree of influence in National Socialist circles, Cooper in North America and Lauck abroad, most notably in Germany. Their approaches to NS doctrine are polar opposites: while Cooper seeks to adapt NS principles to the creation of a small, separatist utopian communalism, Lauck unabashedly dreams of world revolution and pledges explicit fealty to the ghost of Adolph Hitler.

Lauck's name is perhaps better known. Through translations of its newspaper *New Order,* Lauck's National Socialist Party/Overseas Organization (NSDAP/AO) reaches an audience throughout Europe, the

Americas, and South Africa. In America, *New Order* is published and distributed from a post office box in Lincoln, Nebraska. Lauck's current loner status in the world of American National Socialism may have been the result of an ill-starred alliance with Frank Collin, the head of the National Socialist Party of America (NSPA) in Chicago in the late 1970s. Collin's reign ended ingloriously, although hardly atypically. First, it was revealed that Collin was half-Jewish—his father had been a prisoner in the Nazi concentration camp at Dachau. As if this wasn't enough, Harold Covington, his rival for NSPA "power," made the fortuitous discovery (while rifling through Collin's desk) that the half-Jewish fuehrer also had a weakness for pedophilia and did not hesitate to photograph his dalliances with a number of young boys. As a result, Collin was sent to prison, Covington inherited the NSPA and moved its operations to North Carolina, and the luckless Lauck found a new calling: translating American neo-Nazi propaganda and smuggling it into Germany. The NSDAP/AO was founded in 1974 following his expulsion from West Germany for giving a speech on American National Socialism. Undaunted, Lauck tried again in 1976, at which time he was arrested, briefly incarcerated, and banned from entering the country for life.[86] Finally, in 1995 Lauck's luck ran out again and he was arrested in Denmark and extradited to Germany.

Rick Cooper's National Socialist biography is less colorful than that of Gary Lauck. A former member of Koehl's NSWPP, Cooper and cofounders Don Stewart and Fred Surber (also NSWPP veterans) made a virtue out of necessity by stating at the inception of their National Socialist Vanguard (NSV) that the organization would not accept followers. Rather, the NSV would work to create a separatist enclave which they called Wolf Stadt, ultimately intended to provide a refuge for the "righteous remnant" of the racialist right. Wolf Stadt would be built from the proceeds of a group of private businesses established by the trio in Salinas, California.

The NSV migrated from Salinas to Oregon and then to Washington, with the service companies reportedly doing worse at each location. Nonetheless, the NSV could hardly be accused of obfuscation. Among its ventures were Nordic Carpet and Upholstery Cleaning, Hessian Janitorial Service, Quartermaster Laundry, and the memorable Galactic Storm Troop Amusement Center![87]

Cooper's influence in National Socialist circles stems from his affability—he has never met a racialist ideology in which he couldn't find at least some positive points—and from the role of his *NSV Report,* which provides something of a friendly tabloid documenting the recent doings of the radical right and reviewing the latest books, television programs, and films that might be of interest to what the NSV calls the

White Nationalist community. Still, it would be atypical of the American National Socialist milieu for a leader, however self-effacing, to remain forever above the fray. Thus it should have come as no surprise when, in 1995, Cooper was moved to write a history of the movement that frankly laments the post-Rockwell fate of the American Nazi Party and singles out for particular criticism Matt Koehl, in prose only slightly less purple than that of Harold Covington. Like Covington, however, he ends on a note of hope:

> As we all see before us our unstoppable Movement, arising as a Phoenix bird, blossoming flower or some other symbol of rebirth, we must not become demoralized or think it odd that our Movement had its beginning with a small group in New York City, infiltrated by a group of homosexuals and financed by Jewish money for such is not a weird phenomenon but a natural metamorphosis; after all, isn't that the way it has been with all great religious and political movements?[88]

The willingness of both Cooper and Pierce to forge alliances across ideological chasms is the key to the riddle of how a movement as small as National Socialism could exercise the considerable influence that it does on the radical right wing. The minuscule group of literate, intelligent propagandists that North American National Socialism has managed to produce in the wake of Rockwell's assassination has proven to be a valuable resource for a broad spectrum of radical right-wing appeals. Moreover, beyond the influence of written texts lies once again the marked tendency within the cultic milieu of seekers to drift continuously from one appeal to another. This cross-membership pattern is decried by a number of participants, among them Dan Gayman. Gayman himself, however, had his own early flirtation with National Socialist fashion: in his younger years, he and Buddy Tucker occupied the Gayman family church at the height of a feud with his brother clad in homespun imitations of storm trooper uniforms![89]

zionist

206: occupational gov't.

Church of the Creator

The "creators," as the adherents of the Church of the Creator like to be called, are highly idiosyncratic individuals who profess fealty to no one. This might seem odd given their affiliation with a movement that styles itself a "church" and that was headed by a charismatic and highly authoritarian leader. However, despite these organizational trappings, the Church of the Creator (COTC) remains a mail order ministry in every sense of the word. Beyond an ever-changing core of would-be successors to the "Pontifex Maximus" Ben Klassen, the COTC membership is diffuse and no more substantial than a name on an application form and sufficient funds to pay dues and buy literature. An avocation for distributing the COTC newspaper *Racial Loyalty* to anyone willing to buy or accept a copy is also highly desirable.

This diffuse organizational structure, combined with a histrionic racialist appeal, brought the COTC a scattered group of worldwide adherents that at its height probably numbered no more than three thousand, of whom about one hundred were "ordained ministers."[90] Throughout the COTC's more than twenty years of tumultuous existence, creators have been implicated in a number of invariably random acts of racially motivated street violence. This violence is at once encouraged by the tone of COTC literature and overtly discouraged by the cautious Klassen's practice of framing the most violently racialist prose with disavowals of any intent to foment violent behavior among his church's "ministers."

The COTC centers on the belief that Christian Identity's quest to wrest back the divine covenant from the Jews is misguided. Rather, the COTC accepts the nearly universal perception that Christianity is built upon the foundation of Judaism and that Jesus himself was a Jew. Thus, Christianity itself is Jewish and therefore anathema—as is any society that would embrace such a Jewish religion (styled JOG or Jewish Occupation Government). Following this line of reasoning, the Pontifex Maximus deduced that as Christianity is built on a lie, so then all religions must be false; as the Jews are the font of all of the lies of this world, all religions are Jewish creations consciously constructed to enslave the world.[91]

Having rejected the existence of God or any other supernatural being, the COTC has erected in His place a religion which is an odd blend of rewritten Christianity, health faddism, and scabrous racism. Theologically, the COTC's program is primarily negative: literally thousands of pages are devoted to debunking religious belief, especially those religions seen as appealing to potential COTC recruits. Thus, COTC publications attack every belief system from Mormonism to Odinism, but it is Christianity that comes in for particular vilification:

> Where did the idea of Christianity come from? . . . [from] the Jews, who were scattered throughout the Roman Empire, [who] have been *Master Mind-manipulators* of other peoples from the earliest beginnings of their history. They have *always been at war* with the host peoples they have infested like a parasite . . . They had tried military opposition and failed miserably, being no match for the superlative Romans. They looked for an *alternative—mind-manipulation through religion*—and they found the right creed in a relatively unimportant *religious sect called the Essenes.*
>
> So let us proceed further . . . exposing the ridiculous Jewish story

known as Christianity, which I prefer to call the "spooks in the sky" swindle, the greatest swindle in history.[92]

With so much time devoted to attacking other religious faiths, it is little wonder that Creativity provides little in the way of a creed of its own. What passes for a COTC creedal statement is contained in the Sixteen Commandments of Creativity, along with a number of "credos" which do little more than recycle the aphorisms which abound in Klassen's writings. So important are the Commandments that the COTC asks little more of ministers than an adherence to these basic doctrines.

The Sixteen Commandments

1. It is the avowed duty and the holy responsibility of each generation to assure and secure for all time the existence of the White Race upon the face of this planet.

2. Be fruitful and multiply. Do your part in helping to populate the world with your own kind. It is our sacred goal to populate the lands of this earth with White people exclusively.

3. Remember that the inferior colored races are our deadly enemies, and the most dangerous of all is the Jewish race. It is our immediate objective to relentlessly expand the White race, and keep shrinking our enemies.

4. The guiding principle of all your actions shall be: What is best for the White Race?

5. You shall keep your race pure. Pollution of the White Race is a heinous crime against Nature and against your own race.

6. Your first loyalty belongs to the White Race.

7. Show your preferential treatment in business dealings to members of your own race. Phase out all dealings with Jews as soon as possible. Do not employ niggers or other coloreds. Have social contact only with members of your own racial family.

8. Destroy and banish all Jewish thought and influence from society. Work hard to bring about a White world as soon as possible.

9. Work and creativity are our genius. We regard work as a noble pursuit and our willingness to work a blessing to our race.

10. Decide in early youth that during your lifetime you will make at least one major lasting contribution to the White Race.

11. Uphold the honor of your race at all times.

12. It is our duty and privilege to further Nature's plan by striving towards the advancement and improvement of our future generations.

13. You shall honor, protect and venerate the sanctity of the family unit, and hold it sacred. It is the present link in the long golden chain of our White Race.

14. Throughout your life you shall faithfully uphold our pivotal

creed of Blood, Soil and Honor. Practice it diligently, for it is the heart of our faith.

15. Be a proud member of the White Race, think and act positively. Be courageous, confident and aggressive. Utilize constructively your creative ability.

16. We, the Racial Comrades of the White Race, are determined to regain complete and unconditional control of our own destiny.[93]

The Sixteen Commandments are quintessential Ben Klassen. Calls to racial pride and group solidarity are interspersed with Klassen's fascination for eugenics and National Socialist imagery. More intriguing, however, are the ambiguous suggestions of violence contained in commandments 2, 3, 8 and 10. The earth is posited as the exclusive domain of the white race, but no suggestion is offered as to how this felicitous denouement is to take place. In commandment 3, Klassen calls for *lebensraum* by "expand[ing] the White race, and . . . shrinking our enemies." Commandment 8 mandates the purging of "Jewish thought and influence" in an effort to cleanse the earth of all but the white race, while commandment 10 urges the faithful to undertake at least one act that will make a lasting difference to the status of the white race. Are these calls for a "final solution," or merely a chiliastic dream? Klassen's writings could easily support either interpretation.

Klassen's suicide in 1993 capped a chaotic period in the existence of the Church of the Creator, and the fate of Creativity in the post-Klassen era is uncertain. Formed in 1973 either as the fruition of a burst of religious illumination or as a tax dodge, the Church of the Creator came to appeal to an audience increasingly composed of skinheads and prisoners. By the late 1980s, the COTC had enjoyed considerable growth while in the process gathering more than its share of enemies in the competing camps of the right-wing synthesis. By 1992, however, the COTC began to falter. Klassen's advanced age and failing health—and perhaps the death of his wife of many years—necessitated a search for a new Pontifex Maximus. In rapid succession, Rudy Stanko, Charles Altvatar, Mark Wilson, and Dr. Rick McCarty were named as Klassen's successor. Attacks on Klassen mounted, usually—in the stereotypical form of far right invective—with accusations that Klassen was a homosexual and a Jew. Finally, on 6 August 1994, Klassen took a number of boxes of documents to a local recycling center, returned to his home, and ingested the contents of four bottles of sleeping pills. He reportedly left behind a suicide note that referred to a passage in his *White Man's Bible* asserting suicide to be an honorable way to end a life that was no longer worth living.[94]

Creators were officially notified of Klassen's demise through a letter dated 12 August 1993 from the COTC's successor of the moment, Dr. Rick McCarty. That letter said in brief:

> In the early hours of Sunday, August the 8th our beloved founder and friend Mr. Ben Klassen passed away. I learned of this from Klassen's daughter Monday morning. She told me his last thoughts were about you. How important and significant each one of you are in the survival of our race and religion. The faith he has in each of you to continue with the courage you have always shown. To make a stand and not to back down. To take up the banner of the COTC and to carry it to victory . . .
>
> In his last book: Trials, Tribulations and Triumphs, Mr. Klassen writes "At 75, this is undoubtedly the last book I will write. I have dedicated the last twenty years of my life and all my worldly resources to try and awaken the White Race to its impending peril, and I have done all I can. Now the younger generation must pick up the torch and fight the battle."[95]

Even in death, Klassen continued to be a lightening rod for the internecine feuds of the radical right. What has emerged is a rather sordid story which, whatever its truth, has come to be widely accepted throughout the movement. Best articulated by Harold Covington writing under the pseudonym "Winston Smith," the final years of Klassen's life were lived in the shadow of persistent rumors regarding his own past and of internal conflict that engulfed the COTC. Smith's mocking obituary best imparts the flavor both of the particular rancor that Klassen aroused and of the vicious infighting so typical of the competing appeals of the radical right wing:

> Benny Klassen is dead, and it's a Whiter and Brighter world without him. The founder of the "Church of the Creator" sodomy cult, the man whose deviate sexual lifestyle was so notorious that American Skinheads nicknamed him "Old Benny Buttfuck," the self-proclaimed greatest Aryan genius who ever lived—most probably a rabbi's son from Vilna—came crawling back to his cult's ashram in Otto, North Carolina in the early weeks of July. Over a year ago he had fled into hiding, in fear of prosecution for a cult-related killing in Florida.
>
> In the early morning hours of August 7th, Klassen swallowed the contents of four bottles of sleeping pills. The Macon County sheriff reports that the quondam Maximum Pontoon left a rambling and incoherent suicide note on a yellow legal pad by his bedside. Considering Klassen's wonted verbosity, the sheriff was lucky he didn't decide to turn it into another lengthy, excruciatingly boring book . . .
>
> For twenty years, Benny Klassen performed one gigantic act of psychological and political sodomy on us all. He never had any real

religious or political message. It was all a gull, warmed-over classical anti-clericalism framed in the manner of Talmudic responsa, mixed with crude race baiting and pseudo-scholarship, garnished with soft core pornography and served up on a bed of crap . . .

Yet the turgid gibberish in his interminable books was reverenced as inspired wisdom; the most arrant nonsense in his so-called theology was seriously debated; and flaming bird-brained idiots that we are, all but a few of us accepted the liver-lipped old baboon at his own estimation of himself. The reason is simple and shameful: money. Klassen was a millionaire, and with pitifully few exceptions Movement people and Movement leaders in particular genuflect in the presence of wealth. Our public spokesmen and most prominent personalities are largely self-seeking, venal frauds who are incapable of distinguishing between the cool riffle of a roll of hundred dollar bills and the Voice of God. I'd give anything if it weren't so. But it's true.

And so we tolerated among us a Moloch who devoured our children. The roster of Klassen's victims is a long one . . . [here follows a lengthy list of COTC related deaths]

Given the general depravity of our so-called leaders, I can understand why many of them kept their lips firmly pressed against Klassen's withered buttocks in hope of catching some of the dribble from his overflowing bank accounts. But you'd think they might at least have managed a mumble or two of protest when the vile monster started killing kids.

Enough. The already depleted remnants of his cult are collapsing like a house of cards even as I write. Let it perish along with he who gave it life . . .

We sank low during the Klassen years. Now let us see how high we can rise.[96]

The B'nai Noah

It has been said by millenarians throughout the ages that the search for signs and portents heralding the imminence of the End is never undertaken in vain. That such certain and incontestable wonders will pass unnoticed by the great mass of society is hardly surprising; indeed, this seeming blindness may itself be interpreted as further proof that the End is nigh. Thus, it went largely unremarked when, on 20 March 1991, President George Bush signed Public Law 102-14, a bill passed by Congress as "A Joint Resolution to Designate March 26, 1991 as Education Day, USA." Intended as a gesture to the influential Lubavitcher movement headquartered in Crown Heights, New York, this apparently inconsequential act would have a powerful if unintended impact on several sectors of American millenarian thought. It was seized upon by two sets of adherents—the militantly philo-Semitic B'nai Noah, or Chil-

dren of Noah, and the bitterly anti-Semitic Christian Identity groups—
as clear and incontestable proof of the imminence of the End.

At first glance, the juxtaposition of these two apparently incongruous belief systems may seem fanciful, but upon closer examination, they are inextricably linked. Both groups base their appeals on the concept of covenant, and in particular, on the covenant relationship binding the Jewish people to God. For the B'nai Noah, the aim is to share in the covenantal relationship through what the movement has come to call "covenant plurality," or the acceptance of the "gentile covenant" that they believe has been in effect since the time of the deluge and that operates side by side with the Mosaic covenant of the Jewish people. Conversely, Identity Christians see themselves as the victims of the most monstrous theft of culture in recorded history, that perpetrated by the Jews, who by demonic guile have dispossessed the Anglo-Saxons of the knowledge of their own covenantal heritage. It is in the struggle to revive dormant memories of these lost covenant relationships and to institute a chiliastic Kingdom on earth that the B'nai Noah and the adherents of Christian Identity come into contact in America's cultic milieu.[97] This interaction powerfully reinforces both the ideology and the eschatology of the groups involved.

The B'nai Noah are a small but growing movement whose scope is international (and indeed, in the internal view of many in the core of the movement, metahistorical) and who have received levels of press coverage in the United States and in Israel that would suggest far greater numbers than the several thousand adherents who in fact comprise the movement.[98] The central dogma of the B'nai Noah centers on adherence to the seven Noahide commandments (the establishment of courts of justice and the prohibitions against blasphemy, idolatry, sexual sins, murder, theft, and eating the limb of a living creature) found in Tract Sanhedrin 56a of the Babylonian Talmud.[99] The movement emerged in the mid-1970s from a series of discussions between Vendyl Jones of Texas and J. David Davis of Athens, Tennessee, both former Protestant fundamentalist ministers.

David Davis's path to the B'nai Noah began in the winter of 1973–1974, in a quest for the historical Jesus. This quest brought him to the Second Temple period. He found a *Mishna* and began to read it, realizing that he needed to learn about Judaism. In 1979–1980, he first ran across books on the Noahide movement while engaged in a study of all 28 chapters of the Book of Acts. The most important of these texts were Rabbi Harvey Falk's *Jesus the Pharisee,* which contained a letter by Rabbi Jacob Emden on the Noahide Code,[100] and the *Seven Laws of Noah* by Aaron Lichtenstein. The more he read, the further he (and his associates Vendyl Jones and Jack Saunders) drifted from Christianity. It became clear that an organized movement was called for, and a number of names for the new movement were proposed, with such appellations as God-fearers and Fearers of Heaven being considered and rejected. With the B'nai Noah name came the determination to concentrate the new "ministry" on the importance to gentiles of the Seven Laws of Noah, under the tutelage of Jewish rabbinical teachers. Neither goal has proved easy to accomplish, and the difficulties encountered by the B'nai Noah reflect the powerful strain of messianic excitement that has propelled the movement from its inception. This excitement was reflected in the first B'nai Noah publication, in 1991:

> Frankly, what is happening in our day is somewhat new. We are in a new situation; one which we hope, through the grace of haShem will lead to messianic times . . . This is in the spirit of Isaiah 2 and 11, which tells of the nations coming to Jerusalem to learn the "Way of haShem," leading to messianic times when the earth is filled with the knowledge of haShem as the waters cover the sea (Zechariah 14:9) . . . all nations can be taught of God and learn the way of God for this planet. The Noahide concept is the beginning of that great goal.[101]

The key event in the consolidation of the B'nai Noah movement from a loose coalition of geographically dispersed and often spiritually isolated individuals into a viable religious movement took place at the First Annual International Conference of B'nai Noah, which was held in Fort Worth, Texas, during 28–30 April 1990. The event was the culmination of a frenetic burst of activity by the B'nai Noah leadership. Their aims can be divided into two distinct areas: alliance building and proselytizing activities. It is a measure of the uniqueness of the B'nai Noah among New Religious Movements that the effort to build alliances with outside (Jewish) entities and individuals took precedence over the need to recruit a significant number of committed adherents. Indeed, it is possible that the energy required to build and maintain alliance relationships with elements of the fractious Jewish world may be in part responsible for the relatively small number of individuals who have chosen to become Noahides.

The Lubavitcher (Chabad) movement appears to have been the first to be approached by the B'nai Noah, and it is the Chabad community that has perhaps given the most intensive thought to the messianic implications—as well as to the potential risks—of Noahidism. The late Rebbe Menachem Schneerson had for a number of years led the movement into a period which one scholar refers to as one of "acute messianism." Even in such a period of messianic tension, however, the Lubavitcher community was shocked when, in 1982, the Rebbe first spoke of the need to spread the news of the Noahide commandments to the gentile community. After 1982, the Rebbe said on many occasions that the Noahide Code must be instituted.[102] The Lubavitcher Rebbe may have seen the Noahide Code more in terms of an ideal construct than as a sectarian movement. This would explain why, although there is some Chabad involvement with the B'nai Noah as teachers, the Lubavitchers remain distinctly wary of any close identification with the B'nai Noah. Indeed, the Rebbe has never publicly mentioned the existence of an organized B'nai Noah movement. Thus, at the First International Conference of B'nai Noah, despite promises of participation, Chabad sent no official delegation.

The success of the 1990 Texas conference paved the way for the alliance that may prove to have the most far-ranging import of the numerous connections being forged between the B'nai Noah and the Jewish world. It was at this conference that the local Noahide groups coalesced to form an international movement, the Agudat Karem B'nai No'ach (Union of the Vineyard of the Children of Noah), which asked for and received the blessing—and official sanction—of the Chief Sephardi Rabbi of Israel, Mordechai Eliahu.[103]

The rabbinical alliance which is the most illustrative of the metahistoric aspirations of Noahidism involves Rabbi Chaim Richman, director of public affairs for the Temple Institute in Jerusalem. The Temple Institute is one of a welter of often competing Jewish movements that seek in various ways to reconstitute the Third Temple and thus to usher in the era of messianic redemption. So close has this relationship become that B'nai Noah adherents Jack Saunders, James Tabor, and David Davis have been named the Institute's official representatives to the non-Jewish world. For its part, the Institute endeavors to distribute B'nai Noah materials to gentile visitors to the group's Jerusalem museum of Temple implements.[104]

The Noahide laws and the B'nai Noah movement came to the attention of Christian Identity for the first time when President Bush signed Public Law 102-14 on 20 March 1991 and a *Wall Street Journal* article which publicized the Noahide movement appeared by chance on the same day.[105] To the millenarian adherents of the white supremacist constellation, this act constituted both a prime sign of the imminence of the End and proof positive that ZOG had at last consolidated its hold on America. The resolution itself, composed of 10 paragraphs of lofty platitudes, contains two operant passages: "the ethical values and principles [which] have been the bedrock of society from the dawn of civilization . . . [were then] known as the Seven Noahide Laws"; and a two-paragraph tribute to Rabbi Schneerson on the occasion of his eighty-ninth birthday, which fell on 26 March of that year.[106]

Ironically, none of the seven Noahide laws would find much disagreement throughout the American right wing today. Taken together, however, and related to the Babylonian Talmud (held by right wingers to be diabolic),[107] the Noahide laws were interpreted through the manichaean framework with which these millenarian believers view the development of the putative post–cold war New World Order. The impact of the Education Day resolution was further magnified by the revelation in the publicity surrounding the resolution's signing that there was already a Noahide sectarian movement gaining converts among Christians.

For the adherents of so manichaean a belief system as Christian Identity, the blame can be laid at the door of the Talmudic Jew and an age-old conspiracy against the people of God.[108] For the B'nai Noah, the fault can be traced to another group of malign outsiders: Hellenized and pagan gentiles whose influence attributed a divinity to Christ which Jesus never claimed. For both, the only possible answer to the finding of Christian iniquity is to separate from the mainstream of Christian culture.

The apocalyptic interpretations of the B'nai Noah movement prevalent throughout the white supremacist constellation appear to reinforce the movement's internal sense of metahistoric importance. Here again, in the self view of the believers, they are a righteous remnant intent on holding fast to the truth as they know it in these, the Last Days.

2

Christian Identity

All things will change or transform [handwritten annotation]

Millenarian Theology

[Identity] is probably the final gasp of Christian theology, which says in effect we are Jews, and those who call themselves Jews are impostors. This brings us full circle . . . with this feat of mental gymnastics; the serpent is biting its own tail so to speak. . . . A member of the inner core of the Minutemen had a fixation on this Identity stuff. He had a number of reel-to-reel tape recordings of Wesley Swift preaching these ideas. It was really entertaining. We literally fell off our chairs clutching our sides with laughter—tears streaming down our cheeks, it was so ludicrously funny. Things like "all blacks had originated on Mars" and so forth.[1]

Any consideration of the theology of Identity Christianity must begin with the proviso that Identity has no center of orthodoxy, few universally accepted dogmas, and with the possible exception of Dan Gayman, no theologian worthy of the name. It is little wonder, then, that Identity theology is in a state of constant flux. Be this as it may, Identity does generally hold to a set of beliefs which do translate to a rough sort of orthodoxy, albeit an orthodoxy which is subjected to a constant process of review and refinement. These beliefs are drawn primarily from an idiosyncratic approach to biblical hermeneutics, with the creation story of Genesis of primary importance. This theological flexibility is well illustrated by the central problem of the origin of the Jews.

The theological process by which Identity determined the Jews to be, in Jack Mohr's redolent phrase, "Satan's Kids" involved the addition of a racialist gloss to the seventeenth-century pre-Adamism of Isaac de la Peyrère.[2] Identity doctrine generally holds Adam to have been a relative latecomer to the earth. Predating him were a host of other, lesser races identified in Genesis as "the beasts of the field" (Gen. 1:25). These pre-Adamic races took on added importance after the serpent (most often identified as Satan) literally seduced Eve, who thereby gave birth

47

to two "seed lines," one (Abel) of good Aryan stock through Adam, and the other (Cain) the demonic son of Satan. Cain, in Identity theology, was the progenitor of the Jews, as his subsequent matings with non-Adamites created a race genetically predisposed to carry on a timeless conspiracy against the Adamic line, a race that today has achieved almost complete control of the earth. (This observation explains the efficacy of the epithet ZOG or Zionist Occupation Government for the American body politic.) From this doctrine springs the self-image of the Identity believer as the righteous remnant doomed to suffer the persecution of the demonic Jew until the soon-coming return of the Lord at the head of an avenging host. To this manichaean scenario Wesley Swift and William Gale added ever more fantastic overlayers of preterrestrial history, space battles and UFOs, and many another products of the cultic milieu of 1950s America.

For all its eclecticism and eccentricity, Identity theology's concentration on the eschatological import of the Jews is of considerable interest. It is this obsessive search for the truth behind the perceived power of the Jews that links the Identity world not only to the wider constellation of white supremacist appeals but to a two-millennia old tradition of Christian anti-Semitism as well. Identity has evolved several versions of the two seeds doctrine in its approach to the centrality of the Jews. While all Identity adherents would accept the dogma that those who are known as Jews are literally satanic, their origins are interchangeably posited as springing either from the unholy union of Satan with Eve or from the conversion of the barbaric Khazar tribe to Judaism or to both for that matter.[3]

The "two seeds" doctrine, which was considered in chapter 1, has become ubiquitous in Identity circles and flows from a particular hermeneutical approach to inerrant text:

> I know your afflictions and your poverty—yet you are rich! I know the slander of those who say they are Jews and are not, but are a synagogue of Satan. (Rev. 2:9)

> I will make those who are of the synagogue of Satan, who claim to be Jews though they are not, but are liars—I will make them come and fall down at your feet and acknowledge that I have loved you. (Revelations 3:9)

These two passages linked with John 8:44 quoted earlier form the cornerstone of Identity theology. In this view, the target of divine wrath is unambiguously held to be the Jews, who by demonic cunning have conspired to dispossess the true Israelite heirs from their covenantal birthright. Further proof texts are found in both Old and New Testament sources—with recourse made to intertestamental literature as well—but in each case the passages cited are selected carefully to reflect maximum opprobrium on the Jews. Indeed, in this effort to construct fragment by fragment a clear indictment of the Jews as usurpers, the literature of Identity Christianity refers to such Jewish texts as the Babylonian Talmud as well as to such modern secular works as those of Arthur Koestler or Francis Parker Yockey, in a manner that raises these almost to the level of Holy Writ.[4] These texts are in turn subjected to a process of hermeneutics and disseminated to the faithful. Jack Mohr's formulation is typical:

> Jesus did not practice the "religion of the Jews." He abhorred it. The religious beliefs taught in the synagogues of Judea during Christ's lifetime . . . Jesus condemned these as being "children of Satan."
>
> Are you naive enough to believe that a religious book which encourages incest, such as the Sanhedrin volume of the Talmud does; or unnatural intercourse; or rape of non-Jews; or bestiality, as found in this filthy volume; do you believe that this could be the basis of Jesus' teaching? If you do, you are guilty of the vilest form of blasphemy.[5]

This selective retrieval of text, however, is not intended entirely as an expression of contempt for the Jews. The Identity believer also accrues significant benefits from the sincere profession of Identity faith, as was demonstrated by Howard Rand in chapter 1.

Moreover, to realize "the whole story the Bible tells" is to have in hand the very meaning of life. God's plan for the divinely ordered life on earth will be revealed to the believer, as will the history of the covenantal relationship between God and the Anglo-Saxon and kindred peoples. Of more pressing import, however, are the outlines of the imminent apocalyptic denouement of history and of the chiliastic life to come. The eschatological speculations of Identity Christians are varied, but they are invariably dramatic, imbuing the believer with an aura of almost constant tension. Great forces are seen to be at work in the world, and the tiny righteous remnant are at the center of this apocalyptic struggle.

Despite the strikingly different eschatological visions current in the Identity world, a clear pattern is discernible. First, the world is plunged into chaos, triggering events similar to those described in the Book of Revelations. The foci of this conflict are the epicenter of the battle, Jerusalem, and the last redoubts of the faithful, invariably seen as the rural areas of the United States. At the point when this struggle culminates in the biblical horrors of the apocalypse, the Identity believer, despairing of the rapture's promise of supernatural safety, knows that he must survive these events by virtue of his foresight in correctly reading the signs of the End and acting accordingly. From these beliefs flow the marked tendency of the Identity community to eschew the cities whenever possible and also the frequency with which Identity adherents adopt survivalism as a way of life. Finally, each Identity theorist treasures a chiliastic vision of a posthistorical world in which the faithful will be rewarded and the enemies of God punished.[6] Remarkably, these visions tend toward the gentle imagery of the world as it was before original sin:

> Every race was created by Yahweh and was pronounced very good (Gen. 1:31). Every race bears the original design of God in skin color and all other unique qualities established by the act of creation. The Christian view must be that every race has its particular life purpose in the plan of God. Moreover, it must be true that what God created perfect in the beginning will be a part of His Kingdom design in the end. We believe that every race as created in its pristine original design will be resident within the Kingdom when Jesus Christ rules this earth. Every race will occupy that portion of the earth assigned to them by their God. There can be no hatred for the various races that Yahweh has created and placed upon His earth.[7]

Christian Identity eschatology is clearly no "pie in the sky" set of speculations. Rather, it is closely matched to the everyday lives of its adherents, who in turn live each day as if it were their last. How could it be otherwise when proofs of the End are so abundant? In a hermeneutical act similar that undertaken by earlier millenarians,[8] Identity Christians glean the signs of the times from events in the physical world as seen through the prism of sacred text. For a flavor of this earlier approach to millenarian speculation, consider such timeless texts as the following.

> But mark this: There will be terrible times in the last days. People will be lovers of themselves, lovers of money, boastful, proud, abusive, disobedient to their parents, ungrateful, unholy, without love, unforgiving, slanderous, without self-control, brutal, not lovers of the good, treacherous, rash, conceited, lovers of pleasure rather than lovers of God—having a form of godliness but denying its power. Have nothing to do with them. (2 Timothy 3:1–5)

> Dearly beloved brothers, believe the Holy Spirit who speaks in us. We have already told you that the End of the world is near, the consummation remains. Has not faith withered away from mankind? How many foolish things are seen among youths, how many crimes among prelates, how many lies among priests, how many perjuries among dea-

cons! There are evil deeds among the ministers, adulteries in the aged, wantonness in the youths—in mature women false faces, in the virgins dangerous traces! (Pseudo Ephraem, 6th–7th century)[9]

There is little to distinguish these despairing observations from the millennial speculations of the present day. There is the same discouragement with the behavior of the young, with the failings of the clergy and the Church, and with a world from which the virtues of the society of the writer's youth seem to have forever disappeared. This commingling of text and current events—the Bible and CNN in current parlance—is typical of the eschatological longings of millenarians through the ages. In this respect, Dan Gayman's writings are again instructive. In the late 1970s, his *Zions Watchman* carried a column that presented the reader with the seven leading signs of the day, modeled on the Seven Trumpets of Revelation motif. Based on a careful analysis of the news, these included in two typical months in 1977:

July, 1977
1) The U.N. Genocide Convention; 2) the construction of concentration camps throughout the U.S. to hold "Patriots"; 3) The invitation to Russian officials to observe American army maneuvers; 4) possible war in the Middle East; 5) Trilateral [Commission] restrictions on U.S. military exports; 6) a headline quoting a Jewish spokesman as fearing a new holocaust, because ". . . the Bible points out that Jews are the children of the devil . . ."; and 7) American civil defense plans.

November, 1977
1) U.N. treaties on economic, social and cultural rights and on civil and political rights; 2) a water shortage in the western U.S.; 3) the Soviet acquisition of a laser range finder; 4) an estimate that whites will soon be a minority in the U.S. due to immigration and high non-white birth rates; 5) a survivalist call to store food; 6) forced busing and white urban flight; and 7) the Panama Canal Treaty.[10]

Another *Watchman* updated these signs for the 1990s. By that time, relevant events included race mixing, AIDS, drugs, sexual sins, abortion, the EEC Common Market, the Mexican Free Trade Zone proposal, and general economic upheaval. Other Identity journals carry much the same fare, offering apocalyptic signs ranging from AIDS to the birth of the Noahide movement.[11]

Despite the remarkable volume of apocalyptic signs and portents offered in the pages of Identity journals, there is virtually no attention paid to such natural phenomenon as floods and earthquakes, which were in earlier days the primary currency of millenarian speculation. (Indeed, even for the various New Age and neopagan groups who do posit the End in terms of ecological disaster, these cataclysms are invariably held to be the result of purely human action.) For Identity Christians, the ravages of nature pale in significance beside the specter of atomic annihilation. For example, Identity journals gave little apocalyptic credence to the floods which devastated the American midwest in 1993; by contrast, whole Identity ministries (such as that of John Harrell in Illinois) have been built on the fear of nuclear war.

Harrell's ministry, the Christian Patriots Defense League (CDPL)—and such spinoff organizations as the Conservative Christian Churches of America, Citizens Emergency Defense System, Save America Gun Club, Women's Survival Corps, Paul Revere Club, and last but hardly least, the Civilian Air Force—are based primarily on the premise that nuclear war is inevitable. Thus, elaborate if fanciful survivalist plans are offered for a brief bout of postapocalyptic irregular warfare, after which the tiny righteous remnant will inherit the earth. Interestingly, none of Harrell's many "Paul Revere Club" newsletters mention among their "signs of the times" any natural disaster, although they mine the news obsessively for any manmade event that could be interpreted within an apocalyptic framework.[12]

Perhaps no better example of the process by which a specific doctrine is offered to the Identity community by a particular leader, considered throughout the diverse world of the Identity faithful, and then either rejected and forgotten or accepted as dogma can be given than the strange case of George Washington's prophetic vision for America. Washington's vision came to be widely accepted, an unquestioned tenet of belief among Identity adherents, only after a complex process of selection, hermeneutics, and dissemination. The actual origin of the story is impossible to reconstruct. According to the tale itself, the vision was related by one Anthony Sherman to Wesley Bradshaw on 4 July 1859. Mr. Sherman was at the time 99 years old—the precise age of Abraham when God bestowed upon him the Covenant in Gen. 17—and in 1777 was with George Washington at Valley Forge. The vision itself took the form of a dream, which Washington described to Sherman. In highly allusive language, Washington recounted that "a singularly beautiful female" came to him in his sleep, and addressing him as "Son of the Republic," guided him through a series of apocalyptic visions whose central motif involved the American republic engulfed in the tribulations of war and famine. The cause of these fearful scenes was suggested by "a shadowy angel," who placed "a trumpet to his mouth and blew three distinct blasts; and taking water from the ocean, he sprinkled it upon Europe, Asia and Africa." From these continents arose a black and terrible cloud, which settled to earth and resolved into armed men "who moving with the cloud, marched by land and sailed by sea to

America, which . . . was enveloped by the volume of the cloud." America is fated to survive this tribulation, according to the vision, only so long as the Republic keeps faith in God, the land, and the union.[13]

A common source for the many retellings of this vision was reprinted in a September 1958 issue of Howard Rand's *Destiny* magazine. An anonymous editorial introduction[14] does much to illustrate the communal process of the examination and selection of Identity beliefs:

> Editors Note: The Vision of George Washington related to Anthony Sherman at Valley Forge has been published a number of times in former issues of Destiny Magazine over the past 27 years. However, in every case the edition of Destiny in which it was published quickly sold out. In Destiny for December 1957 reference was made to this vision in commenting on the racial issue the Supreme Court of the United States dropped into our midst. It was pointed out editorially that the feeling engendered as a result could become a major contributing factor that would involve the colored race, for the father of our country, George Washington, saw Africa as one of the continents to be joined with Europe and Asia in the final troubles which would afflict us. Due to the demand, we are again publishing this vision and, in doing so, we are following the style of handling as it appeared in Destiny for July 1950 when we quoted a dispatch from Rome as evidence that the vision is coming true.[15]

So thoroughly accepted in Identity circles is the belief in Washington's vision that it is invoked as a call to action as well as a hermeneutical device. In the process, Washington himself has been elevated to the level of a prophet. For example, John Harrell and Jack Mohr use the vision as a survivalist appeal.[16] C. A. "Eddie" Seckinger, president (and presumably sole member) of the Christian Anti-communist Party and of the fanciful "Adamite Army," uses it as a call to arms: "The Adamite Army is being build outside the United States of America to come to the AID of the American People when they are on their knees, as it is written in the last part of Washington's vision . . . We only want to do our part when the whole world comes up against that great Nation."[17]

While Washington's vision has achieved the status of unquestioned dogma in Christian Identity theology, other appeals—such as the alleged anti-Semitic warnings of Benjamin Franklin, or the "vision" of General McClellan—have failed to achieve such widespread acceptance.[18] The McClellan vision is in fact an extension of the Washington vision. In it, Gen. Washington (in his "Son of the Republic" guise) appears to Gen. McClellan in a dream, confirming that the Civil War was predicted in his original vision and warning that the worst, a global onslaught against America, was yet to come. The original source of the vision is claimed to be the 8 March 1862 edition of *The Evening Courier* of Portland, Maine. The vision in its current form is credited to an undated article by one Pastor Curtis Clair Ewing and is distributed in the form of a double-sided mimeographed sheet by Pastor Grant H. "Wings" Barker of the Gospel of the Kingdom Mission in El Cajon, California.

For all of its variety, Identity hermeneutics is marked both by a pronounced democratic spirit and by an intense competition between Identity pastors for the allegiance (and financial support) of a tiny and far from affluent community of believers. The democratic spirit of Identity theology is typified by Dan Gayman's invitation to his live congregation (as well as to listeners in his tape ministry) to offer rebuttal to any and all of his interpretations. Thus, even such basic tenets of racialist Kingdom doctrine as the belief that the Jews are the Satanic offspring of Eve and the devil or the reliability of *The Protocols of the Elders of Zion* have recently come into question.[19] This spirit of open debate is common to Identity and can be heard on cassette sermons of Identity pastors as diverse as Gayman, the fiery Pete Peters, and the relatively moderate Dave Barley.

However, the democratic spirit of Identity hermeneutics does nothing to ameliorate the starkly contra-acculturative nature of the Identity message. For example, the enthusiasm of the fundamentalist and evangelical churches for the Jewish enterprise in Israel is anathema to Identity adherents. So too is the pluralism of the American public square. American religious pluralism is decried as "Judeo-Christianity," in Identity terms a vile syncretism aimed at perverting true Christianity and, not incidentally, serving to keep the secret of the Jewish usurpation of the covenant hidden. Thus, for the adherents of Christian Identity, Judeo-Christianity is a contemptuous term for the perceived Jewish subversion and conquest of mainstream Christianity.

Christian Identity: A Theology of Violence?

For all its democratic spirit, the world of Identity hermeneutics remains intensely competitive. Beyond the personalities of the pastors (which is in reality of primary importance), the central focus of this competition is played out over the question of violence. Identity Christianity has long been labeled "a theology of violence," and on rare occasions, this has been true.[20] More often, Identity has been a quietist community, noting the signs of the End but seldom acting upon this knowledge. There is in the white supremacist millennial community an inherent dynamism: in normal times, the quietist majority of millenarian adherents primarily seek to withdraw to the greatest possible degree from a society seen as inherently contaminating; on occasion, however, and under circumstances which are still far from clear, these groups may emerge as violent centers of revolutionary activism.[21] If not destroyed in a hopeless confrontation with government authorities or (more commonly) rent asunder by internal divisions, these groups may then return to the withdrawal mode to prayerfully await the End of Days.

This activist/quietist split marks the deepest cleavage in the Identity community, and it is around this issue that the competition between Identity theorists for followers is most keenly felt. To examine this divisive internal debate, we must consider three forms of violence: rhetorical, defensive, and revolutionary millenarian.

Rhetorical violence is ubiquitous in the milieu of Christian Identity. Richard Butler has appeared in these pages as the *exemplar par excellence* of Identity as the "theology of hate," and for his pioneering prison ministry. The premier issue of Butler's prison outreach newsletter, *The Way*, appeared in June 1987 and proudly featured a long letter from imprisoned Order veteran David Tate.[22]

Typical of the Aryan Nation's penchant for violent rhetoric is a grandiose flier distributed by the group in the 1980s:

RACE TRAITORS
Those guilty of fraternizing socially or sexually with blacks now stand warned that their identities are being catalogued.
The country is in a Second Revolution which will restore complete authority into the hands of those people of European ancestry.

Those persons of alien race will be deported to Asia or Africa.

White persons consorting with blacks will be dealt with according to
the Miscegenation Section of the Revolutionary Ethic:
1. Miscegenation is Race Treason;
2. Race Treason is a Capital Offense;
3. It will be punished by death, automatic, by Public Hanging

Negroes involved in Miscegenation will be Shot as they are apprehended.
The
Revolutionary Government
of the
Aryan Nation[23]

Rev. Butler's conspicuous lack of action to back up these angry words may be hastening the fragmentation of the Aryan Nations movement. Security chief Floyd Cochrane left the movement and publicly renounced his racist views, and heir apparent Carl Franklin also departed, forming the New Church of Jesus Christ Christian of Montana.[24] Ku Klux Klan figure Louis Beam tried to shore up the group, but seems to have had little interest in replacing Butler. Indeed, so low have Butler's fortunes sunk that at the 1993 Aryan Nations Congress, less than one hundred people made the trek to Hayden Lake.[25] Moreover, there appear to be few realistic prospects for the movement to long survive Butler's demise.

Pastor Dan Gayman has taken a very different approach to the issue of violence in the wake of the Fort Smith trial, at which he was forced to appear as a reluctant witness for the prosecution. Moreover, Gayman apparently received at least $10,000 from the Order, although at FBI insistence during the Fort Smith trial, this money was returned.[26] Following his testimony, and in the context of the increasing violence of the federal government in combating Identity's rural redoubts, Gayman publicly rejected the violence of Identity rhetoric.

These new-found principles of nonviolence were announced in a 15 January 1982 resolution adopted by the congregation of Pastor Gayman's Church of Israel:

> be it hereby known that the CHURCH . . . and the Board of Trustees, the Pastor, and the congregation of the same in America and throughout the world do not offer this Church as a sanctuary, cover, or "safe house" for any person or persons, organizations or groups, that teach civil disobedience, violence, militant armed might, gun-running, paramilitary training, hatred of blacks, reprisals against the Jews, Posse Comitatus, dualist, odinist [sic], Ku Klux Klan, Neo-Nazi, national socialism [sic], Hitler cult, stealing, welfare fraud, murder, war against the government of the United States, polygamy, driving unlicensed vehicles, hunting game without proper licenses, etc.[27]

This declaration was followed by a series of scriptural teachings (based on Romans 13) mandating submission to all but the most unjust of secular authorities and culminated with a stern denunciation of the fictional commandos from time immemorial, the Phineas Priesthood.[28]

This disavowal of violence placed Gayman squarely within the Christian Identity mainstream. Most other Identity leaders also preach a message of nonviolence and of submission to civil authorities. The primary center of opposition to these voices is the prison constituency so eagerly courted by such leaders as Richard Butler. How successful Butler has been in this prison ministry may be seen in the experience of pastor Raymond Bray of the Lord's Work Identity ministry in Austin, Kentucky:

> I am very much aware of the hatred that prevails in most of the so-called "Identity" groups; much of it has been directed at me at one

time or another. I usually get three letters from . . . [prisoners]. The
first one requests our paper and calls me "white Nationalist Brother."
The second disagrees with just about everything they found in the
American Ephraimite [The Lord's Work's outreach publication] and
any other literature that they have received from us, and the third denounces me as a mentally retarded heretic and traitor to my race and
demands that I stop mailing to them.

[In November 1991] I began getting requests for inclusion on our mailing list from prisoners all over the Northeast. Then one prisoner rec-
ommended that I state in the paper that I was part of Butler's bunch,
so that I could become more popular among the prison population. I
told him flatly that Butler was misleading people and how he was doing it. My popularity disappeared overnight after that; I almost never
hear from a prisoner now. There seems to be a Nazi network within
the prison system that puts [the] Bell System to shame.[29]

Beneath the occasional displays of rhetorical violence, the primary
form that violence takes in Identity is defensive. Defensive violence may
be defined as violence undertaken as a last resort to defend an enclave
into which a single adherent or a group of believers have withdrawn to
sever to the greatest degree possible contact with the dominant culture.[30]
Rural Identity encampments (which seek primarily to disengage from
the dominant society) too often find themselves embroiled with state
authorities over relatively minor issues ranging from building codes to
firearms possession. These disputes, on occasion, evolve into armed
confrontations. A classic example was the April 1985 siege of the Covenant, Sword and the Arm of the Lord's compound in rural Missouri.
    The Covenant, Sword and the Arm of the Lord (CSA) was perhaps
the most idiosyncratic Identity ministry to emerge in the 1980s. James
Ellison, the leader of the CSA, was a polygamist who came to be contemptuously referred to as "King James of the Ozarks," a title that
brought much derision from Robert Miles after Ellison's appearance as
the government's star witness at the Fort Smith sedition trial.[31] Before
his self-serving conversion to government informant, however, Ellison's
CSA compound poured out a steady stream of violent rhetoric as it
strove to become the armorer of the radical right. An article in a 1982
edition of the *C. S. A. Journal* states the group's purpose succinctly:

    Warfare is coming to our nation and to our people! Warfare as
    this world has never seen before! Warfare that will surely end all war-
    fare. The battle of the ages will be between two forces, climaxing in a
    period of contest between the manifested, glorious sons of the almighty
    God of all creation and the completely manifested sons of the devil
    himself, for all creation to watch and behold!

> This warfare is in the genes of every true son of God, as it is in the genes of our enemies. This enemy has been known by many names throughout the ages. Today he is known as the JEW, sworn to destroy the white race and its religious heritage, Christianity. The warfare was declared by God in Genesis 3:15.[32]

In its heyday, the CSA compound was the elite training ground of choice for would-be paramilitary enthusiasts throughout the disparate appeals of the radical right wing. The group's *Survival Manual* remains one of the better guides to guerrilla operations and it is unparalleled in the world of Christian Identity.[33] Given the intensity of CSA rhetoric on arms and revolutionary violence, it is surprising that the compound surrendered to federal officers without a shot being fired. This precedent may well have been a source of the tragically mistaken decisions in the siege of the Branch Davidian compound in Waco and in the Randy Weaver drama, where it was expected that the groups would peacefully surrender after an initial show of bravado.

Ellison remains an elusive figure within the milieu of the radical right. Almost universally despised for his role at Fort Smith, condemned for his regal pretensions no less than for his practice of polygamy and for the empty bravado of CSA rhetoric when federal agents surrounded his compound, little is known of Ellison the man. In a remarkable series of letters to the Swedish race activist Tommy Rydén written from his federal prison cell, Ellison speaks of his beliefs and of his sense of abandonment by the movement in which he once had such influence:

> Thank you for writing to me. You do not know how much your letter means to me at just this time. I am sure the Holy Spirit was directing you to write. Your letter came at a time when I had begun to wonder if there were any faithful believers out there who are praying for me . . .
>
> I would offer a word of encouragement to you if you will receive it. Be ever so careful of political attachments, they tend to lead us into bondage rather than to the spreading of freedom and the truth . . .
>
> In my case, I was led into the movement by Yahuah by my love for the people of Israel and by my desire to see unity. It was Yahuah's doing to place me in a place where He could use me to expose the evil and adulterous mixture that was in the movement. Any time an adulterous mixture exists, it is a stench in the nostrils of our holy God (El) . . . My love for Yahuah will help me to expose the evil that is among the "Identity" movement.[34]

Ellison accompanies this missive with copious biblical proof texts, but of interest here is both his sense of estrangement from the Identity movement and his curious choice of metaphors, given his own history of polygamy. Significantly, Ellison promises to pass on Rydén's letter to his wife (singular), who is of Swedish descent.

Later, as the correspondence matures, Ellison becomes more at ease, and the discussion centers increasingly on the recurrent themes of Ellison's life, weapons and polygamy:

> In regard to the natural things, I have fired and handled most of the light infantry weapons of the western military. I am familiar with the Chinese AK 47 and the Chinese and Warsaw Pact versions although I have not fired them all . . . I have seen the new AK 74's and some of the new plastic mines and hand grenades that are being used in Afghanistan by the Russians. One thing that they have that is far superior to the west is their RPG 7 and RPG family of shoulder fired missiles.

Ellison goes on for some time in this technical vein, before turning to the question of polygamy:

> You mention the point of multiple marriage, or a man having more than one wife or mate, rightly called "Polygyny", (which is different than "Polygamy"), look it up. I am not a Mormon. In regard to my wives, yes I have more than one. As you know, so did many of the great men of our people all through history. Abraham had Sarah, Hagar, and Keturah . . . [other biblical precedents are offered as well] All through the scriptures it is recorded that OUR people practiced this principle. It is the enemy who fears that we will thus multiply and subdue the earth as we have been commanded by our Father. One thing to note is that this is not for every man of our people. Also a man needs to learn to be faithful to ONE wife and provide for her and her children before he thinks of any others. Even then it should be by agreement of the elders of the local body of believers or by counsel or at least very carefully. I say again it is not for all. Our enemy does not want any more of our kin [kind] in the earth so there is great resistance and misunderstanding about it. I only entered into it by direct command to me from Yahuah that I was to do this.[35]

Although Ellison surrendered his CSA compound and turned state's witness, other individuals associated with the group have opted for violence. Richard Snell, for example, was executed on 19 April 1995—the day of the Oklahoma City bombing—in Texarkana, Texas, for the murder of a black Arkansas state trooper during a routine traffic stop. Before this murder, Snell was involved in a series of terrorist acts, culminating in the murder of a pawnshop owner during a robbery in Texarkana, Arkansas. The victim, William Stumpp, was believed by Snell to be Jewish, and thus he "needed to die."[36] Snell apparently acted out of a sense of frustration with the reluctance of the Covenant, Sword, and the

Arm of the Lord to turn its violent rhetoric into revolutionary action. He may have been emulating the revolutionary violence of the Order as well.

Snell's crimes were those of an individual, not as a member of the CSA. An important question arises at this point: what can be said of the individual psychology of the adherent in the more violent reaches of the movement? Psychological explanations for extremism of any sort are a risky venture, and one best left to the province of experts.[37] On rare occasions, however, a source emerges through which the mind of the extremist may be held up to view, both through the external perspective of the psychiatrist and through the self view of the adherent. Such a source may be found in Snell's prison newsletter, *The Seekers*.

During his appeal process, Snell published—with some considerable embarrassment—a transcript in which his psychological state is discussed in most unflattering terms by a forensic psychiatrist appointed by the court. The testimony of the expert, Dr. Brad Fisher, was printed by Snell because:

> Whether it's expedient or not, fairness demands we let you read what the enemy thinks of us, after all it was your tax dollars that paid the expert to dig out all this info. After reading, you will not only have what we wrote, what our friends have to say, or what dear old mother may have said, but a balance of opinion assisting you to arrive at your own conclusions. We believe we owe this to you who have stood by us in this ordeal and to all who may read our opinions in the future. Is this fair?[38]

Dr. Fisher's conclusions were straightforward enough. He found that from at least 1983, Snell was suffering from a "paranoid delusional disorder," with a second axis diagnosis of a "paranoid personality disorder." The symptoms of this delusion were primarily a conspiratorial view of history, the view that the U. S. government has fallen to a shadowy group of conspirators known as ZOG (which Fisher mistakenly calls the Zionist Occupation Group), that the minions of this cabal have participated in the persecution of Snell personally, and that said persecution commenced years before his attraction to Identity theology and drove him out of his photography business in the 1960s. Worse yet, "He believes that Armageddon and race wars will happen within the next two years." So advanced was this paranoia that the suicide of his son, Ken (connected to despair over drug use) was posited by Snell as the fault of ZOG—the entity ultimately responsible for the proliferation of drugs in America.

And what did the prisoner have to say to all this? On the death of his son, Snell wrote:

Ken's suicide: abruptly my thoughts were plucked as by an eagle snatching his prey and lifted back in time to an event shrouded in the cloak of attempted forgetfulness. A chilling rain was falling on that cold December morning in '78, the weeping family, a circle of friends who could find no comfort, the preacher intoning "Ashes to ashes, dust to dust . . ." as an unopened casket was lowered into a dark hole in the sandy loam of South Arkansas. Unopenable because a twelve-gauge shotgun under the chin does a trick to one's head.

And was Snell insane?

Deluded? God, let it be so! A prison cage will become a palace if suddenly evidence is presented that this nightmare was only paranoia, merely a bad dream without reality. Time will tell. I must—and can rest in this.

For true revolutionary violence one need look no further than the Order.

A tribute to the men of Nordland, a tribute to Robert J. [Mathews], and a tribute to brotherhood. You are now seated around the table of Valhalla, victims of a corrupt and evil world. To some you are a memory, but in our hearts you live on.[39]

The revolutionary violence of the Order was quite distinct from the lone-wolf depredations of Richard Snell. The *Bruders Schweigen* or Silent Brotherhood, more popularly known as the Order, was an unprecedented event in the annals of the American radical right wing. The Order was an active terrorist movement built on tactics borrowed in equal parts from the left-wing terrorist groups of the 1960s and the inspiration provided by William Pierce's novel *The Turner Diaries*. The Order was an example of a millenarian revolutionary movement par excellence, which could with impunity challenge the vastly superior forces at the disposal of ZOG, confident in the power of God to assure ultimate victory.

The Order was founded in 1983 by Robert Mathews, a veteran of the tax protest movement who had gravitated to Pierce's neo-Nazi National Alliance. Mathews, a charismatic and visionary leader, was the virtual embodiment of the applicability of Campbell's theory of the cultic milieu to the radical right wing. From his roots in tax protest and National Socialism, he was by the time of the Order's birth closely identified with Christian Identity, and he was eventually reported to have become an Odinist as well. In a letter published after his death, Mathews talked at some length about his background in the movement and about his dreams for the future. Although the authenticity of the document is subject to question, the letter has been widely republished throughout the spectrum of the American radical right; moreover, it has been translated and republished throughout Europe, where in the milieu of the racist right, Robert Mathews has come to be virtually beatified. In both the United States and Europe, the letter is commonly believed to be genuine.

TO THE EDITOR:

For the past decade I have been a resident of Northern Pend Oreille County [Washington]. When I first arrived in Metaline Falls, I had only twenty-five dollars to my name, a desire to work hard and be left alone, and the dream of someday acquiring my own small farm.

During my three years at the mine and seven years at the cement plant, I can safely say that I was known as a hard worker. I stayed out of the bars and pretty much kept to myself. Anyone who is familiar with Boundary Dam Road knows how my late father and I carved a beautiful place out of the woods. [But] . . . I was not left alone.

Within months of my arrival the FBI went to the mine office and tried to have me fired from my job . . . fortunately, [my foreman] had a deep and lasting dislike for the Feds . . .

This campaign of harassment and intimidation began because of my involvement in the Tax Rebellion Movement from the time I was fifteen to twenty years old. The Government was on me so much in Arizona that during one incident when I was eighteen, IRS agents shot at me for nothing more than a misdemeanor tax violation.

I left Arizona and the Tax Rebellion when I was twenty. I left not out of fear of the IRS or because of submission to their tyranny, but because I was thoroughly disgusted with the American people. I maintained then as I do now, that our people have devolved into some of the most cowardly, sheepish degenerates that have ever littered the face of this planet.

I had hoped to start a new life in the state of Washington, but the ruling powers had other plans for me. When I learned of their highly illegal attempt to have me fired, I wrote a letter to their Seattle office and told them "I would take no more, to leave me alone, or I would respond in such a way that could be very painful to certain agents."

After the letter they gradually started to let me be.

I soon settled down to marriage, clearing my land, and reading. Reading became an obsession with me. I consumed volume upon volume on subjects dealing with history, politics and economics. I was especially taken with Spengler's "Decline of the West" and "Which Way Western Man?" I also subscribed to numerous periodicals on current American problems, especially those concerned with the ever increasing decline of White America.

My knowledge of ancient European history started to awaken a wrongfully suppressed emotion buried deep within my soul, that of racial pride and consciousness.

The stronger my love for my people grew, the deeper became my hatred for those who would destroy my race, my heritage, and darken the future of my children.

By the time my son had arrived, I realized that White America, indeed my entire race, was headed for oblivion unless White men rose and turned the tide. The more I came to love my son the more I realized that unless things changed radically, by the time he was my age, he would be a stranger in his own land, a blonde-haired, blue-eyed Aryan in a country populated mainly by Mexicans, Mulattos, Blacks and Asians. His future was growing darker by the day.

I came to learn that this was not by accident, that there is a small, cohesive alien group within this nation working day and night to make this happen. I learned that these culture distorters have an iron grip on both major political parties, on Congress, on the media, on the publishing houses, and on most of the major Christian denominations in this nation, even though these aliens subscribe to a religion which is diametrically opposed to Christianity.

These are the same people who Ex-Senator William J. Fulbright and the late General Brown tried to warn us about. Henry Ford and Charles Lindberg tried vainly to warn us also. Had we been more vigilant, my son's future would not be so dark and dismal.

Thus I have no choice. I must stand up like a White man and do battle.

A secret war has been developing for the last year between the regime in Washington and an ever growing number of White people who are determined to regain what our forefathers discovered, explored, conquered, settled, built and died for.

The FBI has been able to keep this war secret only because up until now we have been doing nothing more than growing and preparing. The government, however, seems determined to force the issue, so we have no choice left but to stand and fight back. Hail Victory!

. . . I am not going into hiding, rather I will press the FBI and let them know what it is like to become the hunted. Doing so it is only logical to assume that my days on this planet are rapidly drawing to a close. Even so, I have no fear. For the reality of my life is death, and the worst the enemy can do to me is shorten my tour of duty in this world. I will leave knowing that I have made the ultimate sacrifice to ensure the future of my children.

As always, for blood, soil, honor, for faith and for race.
Robert Jay Mathews[40]

In fact, Mathews did not teach the FBI what it was to become the hunted. Instead, on 9 December 1984, he died in a hail of FBI gunfire on Whidby Island off the coast of Washington state. The long-cherished dream of many of the denizens of the American radical right—that the nation might awaken to the truth of its "subjugation" at the hands of an alien conspiracy and might purify itself through the cleansing violence of a popularly-based revolution—died with him.

The Order's brief revolutionary career was, by the standards of the American radical right, dazzling. The murder of Denver radio personality Alan Berg was perhaps the best known of the Order's actions. Of greater import to the various ideological outposts of the radical right, however, were a series of thefts, including two armored car robberies in Seattle and in Ukiah, California, the proceeds of which financed a number of groups throughout the movement.[41]

The Order announced its presence and its intent ostentatiously enough, with a declaration of war against ZOG. The government, however, accorded the announcement a reception not unlike that depicted in the Peter Sellers film *The Mouse That Roared,* in which a similar document made no impression whatever; in fact, the announcement only came to light after the Order had demonstrated that it was in earnest. For its part, the broader movement's initial reaction to the Order is instructive. Typical was the warning of Rick Cooper's National Socialist vehicle, the *NSV Report:*

> We have received word that the federal government is planning a major "sting" operation against "Klan and Nazi terrorists" in collaboration with the Anti-Defamation League of the B'nai B'rith. Going under the name(s) of the "Secret Army Organization" and/or the "Silent Brotherhood" or some similar label, this counterfeit operation is under the auspices of the Bureau of Alcohol, Tobacco and Firearms (BATF) and/or the FBI, and is designed to entrap naive and unsuspecting racial activists. The procedure is for government agents to approach a prospect with the offer of several hundred dollars in deposit money, whereupon he is told to await further instructions—presumably of a highly illegal nature, involving bombing and assassination. Once the person accepts the money, he is "hooked" (i.e., he is guilty of an indictable offense as part of an illegal conspiracy), the preferred method of the government for putting racial activists out of business.[42]

Neither the government's skepticism nor the conspiratorial suspicions of the movement should come as a surprise. From the government's perspective (in those distant pre–Oklahoma City days), the declaration of hostilities on the part of a tiny and highly idiosyncratic band of revolutionaries would have been perceived as ludicrous. In the lifetime of federal agents, serious American terrorist bands were exclusively left-wing groups such as the Weathermen or the Symbionese Liberation Army. The government could well be excused for agreeing with

George Lincoln Rockwell's view that the radical right wing consists primarily of "cowards, dopes, nuts, one-track minds, blabbermouths, boobs, incurable tight-wads and . . . hobbyists."[43] The Order was in living memory unprecedented.

For the denizens of the radical right, the manichaeism of the movement colored the early perception of the Order. In this conception, the tiny righteous remnant are engaged in a hopeless battle with the forces of this world. The earth in these latter days is the province of Satan, and as in the Book of Job, God has given the adversary leave for a season to do as he will. Thus, the elect can not but persevere against the "powers and principalities" armed with little more than their faith. In movement literature, the human face of the Enemy loom's grotesquely large: the Jew becomes superhuman, capable of plotting dark deeds millennia in advance and today standing astride this world like a colossus, in ultimate control of the American government, of the press, and indeed of the world. The dark skinned races—the so-called Mud People—have fallen under the sway of the Jews and thus have come unknowingly to serve their nefarious ends.

Little wonder that with such vast forces arrayed against them, the adherents of radical right-wing ideologies would doubt the reality of the Order. How much better it is to put hope of temporal salvation in such risk-free fantasies as the Phineas Priesthood! The Phineas Priests, a literary invention of Identity figure Richard Kelly Hoskins, are a timeless order of avengers who are the mirror image of the conspiratorial Jew, a movement selflessly dedicated to tracking down the worst of God's enemies and slaying them without mercy. The Phineas Priesthood is an attractive dream in that it is safe: the believer can yearn for the appearance of a Phineas priest with all the ardor that other residents of the American cultic milieu yearn to be rescued by UFOs.[44]

The Order, however, was decidedly not safe. Adopting the life of the full-time revolutionary is extremely rare in the world of the radical right. Radical right violence is primarily an impulsive act, carried out by part-time revolutionaries against convenient targets of opportunity or symbols of some change in the status quo.[45] In this milieu, Robert Mathews' call to take up arms against the federal government could not have met with any reaction other than disbelief. This reception was anticipated in the apocalyptic tenor of the Order's declaration of war.

It is now a dark and dismal time in the history of our race. All about us lie the green graves of our sires, yet, in a land once ours, we have become a people dispossessed . . .

While we allow Mexicans by the legions to invade our soil, we murder our babies in equal numbers. Were the men of the Alamo only a myth? Whether by force of arms or by the force of the groin, the result of this invasion is the same. Yet we do not resist.

Our heroes and our culture have been insulted and degraded. The mongrel hordes clamor to sever us from our inheritance. Yet our people do not care.

Throughout this land our children are being coerced into accepting non-Whites for their idols, their companions, and worst of all, their mates. A course which is taking us straight to oblivion. Yet our people do not see . . .

All about us the land is dying. Our cities swarm with dusky hordes.

The water is rancid and the air is rank. Our farms are being seized by usurious leeches and our people are being forced off the land. The Capitalists and the Communists gleefully pick at our bones while the vile hook-nosed masters of usury orchestrate our destruction. What is to become of our children in a land such as this? Yet still our people sleep . . .

To these three kinsmen [John Singer, Gordon Kahl, and Arthur Kirk] we say: "Rise, rise from your graves, white brothers. Rise and join us! We go to avenge your deaths. The Aryan yeoman is awakening . . . War is upon the land. The tyrant's blood will flow."[46]

Needless to say, the right wing did not rise up. After this stirring call to arms, it was not long before Mathews would damn white America as "sheeple" [i.e., sheep people]. Mathews himself would die in a gunfight with the FBI, the building where he made his last stand burning down around him as he fought. The remaining Order adherents (save for Tom Martinez) are now in the maximum security prisons of America; Martinez spends his days in the federal witness protection program, under sentence of death by decapitation for his betrayal of the movement.

The Order's story is not over, however. Robert Mathews has found in death the army of followers he never had in life. He is lionized as a movement martyr—and indeed as its greatest hero—in Europe and in North America. Gary Lee Yarbrough, from his prison cell, holds forth on movement matters in the United States, while in Sweden he is listed as editor of the White Aryan Resistance (VAM) prison newsletter.[47] David Lane is today the Order's Odinist eminence grise.

What went wrong? From the Identity perspective, ironically, the problem was one of pluralism. The presence of non-Christians (i.e., Odinists or simply agnostics) was enough to deprive the movement of God's favor, without which no millenarian revolutionary appeal could hope to prevail. This criticism was made by Richard Kelly Hoskins, whose Phineas Priests by contrast are said to have survived for millennia because of their absolute fealty to the Christian faith.[48]

Perhaps the most fitting epitaph for the Order is offered by Gary Yarbrough. Writing in 1993, Yarbrough frankly admits the failure of Mathews' strategy of creating a vanguard movement that would pave the way for a mass uprising:

> The conventional resistance techniques hitherto employed by our causes [sic] diverse factions have proven to be a failure to our cause and only aid and abet the enemies . . . Therefore we must abandon the old strategies and opt for a more judicious approach to victory . . . Our enemies, via illegal and subversive tactics . . . have infiltrated and polluted our above ground institution. Conventional tactics such as: recruiting members and associates from the populace, mass gatherings and meetings, rallies, protests, etcetera, are no longer profitable, viable, or judicious to employ. Therefore, we must switch from the conventional approach to irregular tactics and implement strategies that are less of a security risk to ourselves and will augment our success. The only way to battle and triumph over such an eminent adversary is via covert, clandestine, irregular and guerrilla tactics. We must utilize the very techniques that the enemy employs against us! . . . The only way to fight terror is with a greater terror![49]

Before the battle can be joined however, the feuding kingdoms of radical right-wing belief must overcome their differences and unify around the primary issue of race:

> Whether you are National Socialist, Klan, Odinist, Christian Identity, Skinhead, Creator, or any other cult, creed, faith or persuasion of our cause does not matter. For the essence of our cause, regardless of our diversity is RACE!, our common genetic heritage . . . OUR FAITH IS OUR RACE, AND OUR RACE IS OUR FAITH!!!

Once this unity is achieved, the movement will be ready to take the offensive, utilizing the small cell or lone-wolf tactics urged by such movement stalwarts as Louis Beam (in his "Leaderless Resistance" essay) and William Pierce (in his follow-up to *The Turner Diaries, Hunter*). As Yarbrough stated it,

> Our overt publishing agencies should be the only component of our cause that is revealed to the scrutiny of our enemies, [revealing nothing] except what "WE CHOOSE" to reveal to them. All other components should be concealed and clandestine. The bulk of our resistance forces should be comprised of individuals, or small nuclear units of teams no larger than five or six members. These individuals or nuclear units will conduct their resistance efforts in whatever capacity they feel capable of instituting. At this time in our conflict, our number one priority is to enlighten, educate and convert new prospects to our

cause. This is where our publishing agencies play a vital role . . . I do not exclude or rule out illegal activity or physical confrontation with the adversaries of our racial cause. We may not be prepared for this type of warfare, but its time has come nonetheless . . . The enemy must learn that they cannot murder and imprison us with impunity.

Unity would be no easy achievement in this milieu, however. While adherents drift from movement to movement, ideology to ideology (as the cultic milieu theory predicts), the movements are nevertheless strongly competitive. Far more the norm is the view of Richard Kelly Hoskins, whose postmortem on the Order was that it was too inclusive, and that the only hope of victory lies in the purity of the Identity faithful's love of the Lord.

3

Odinism and Ásatrú

Theology and Millenarianism

Hail to the gods that are dead! They are the future rule of lords![1]

> Is Ragnarök an ongoing process, such as some Odinists believe, or
> is it going to be one giant upheaval as stated in the Völuspá? I
> have noticed that there are a few similarities between Ragnarök and
> Armageddon.
>
> I also notice that Jesus was hung upon a tree and marked with a
> spear just as ODIN was. Also, in olden times THOR, FREY and ODIN
> were worshipped as a trinity just as the FATHER, SON and HOLY GHOST
> are now; THOR being the GOD of the common man, was given prior-
> ity—just as JESUS is today.[2]

The choice of Ásatrú/Odinism as one example of the numerous pre-
Christian traditions which have been (and are being) reconstructed
at the end of the twentieth century is based on three factors: compatibility, location, and viability. Compatibility is implied by location, but
the concept goes much further. Odinism, in its most extreme racialist
form, is quite compatible with many sectors of the right-wing constellation, as its attractiveness to the late Robert Mathews and to other members of the revolutionary Order as well as to certain skinhead groups
demonstrates. The strongly millenarian and chiliastic overtones of the
apocalyptic "twilight of the gods," Ragnarök, and its aftermath provide
a bridge to the potential racialist adherent, connecting those from fundamentalist and evangelical Christian backgrounds to Odinism.

At the other end of the racialist spectrum, that of the Ásatrúer, compatibility indicates strong linkages binding the adherent with the occult
community on the one hand, and with the dominant culture (of which
the Ásatrúer is a productive member) on the other. Location is important in that, as in the cases of oppositional monotheistic, millenarian,
and messianic communities, Ásatrú and Odinism inhabit the most dis-

69

tant reaches of the Wiccan/neopagan world,[3] forming a defined border region through which ideas and individuals may pass from the millenarian community into the magical/occult world and back again. In this context, viability is defined in terms of the opportunity which these adherents have before them to reestablish their religion as a living tradition, which may then enjoy the natural growth and development that can only come to a New Religious Movement through the passing of the belief system from a community of first generation converts to their children.[4] The key to this viability is found in the unusual concentration of genuine scholarship with which Ásatrú has been blessed. This scholarly approach to the reconstruction of Odinism/Ásatrú contrasts sharply with the purely intuitive methods by which most other neopagan traditions have been reinvented.

The selection of ritual texts available to the Ásatrú community is impressive by any measure. Of these, the earliest and in some respects most interesting are the Ásatrú Free Assembly rituals, available in a three volume set from World Tree Books. This material predates the scholarly contributions of Edred Thorsson and of KveldúlfR Gundarsson and owes much to the experiential approach to ritual characteristic of Wicca. The first true scholarly contribution to Ásatrú ritual was Thorsson's *A Book of Troth* (1992), which remained the standard until the publication of Gundarsson's impressive corpus of material. With the work of Thorsson and Gundarsson, Ásatrú/Odinism made a decisive break with Wicca and much of the rest of the occult/magical community, as the ritual content of the religion became increasingly tied to a historical tradition rather than to the florid imaginations of its adherents, as is invariably the case in the Wiccan world.[5]

As our understanding of the Norse/Germanic tradition is based primarily on written Christian era records, the pagan context of the religion is surrounded by controversy. Modern Ásatrúers are thus heavily dependent on the work of scholars for the raw material on which their own elaborate reconstructions of Ásatrú's ritual content are based. Of these scholarly sources, none is more controversial than Georges Dumézil. In his influential book *Gods of the Ancient Northmen* (1973), Dumézil posits a tripartite division of the Norse-Germanic pantheon, a division which serves to validate his primary theories of a common Indo-European ideology—in effect, an Ur-religion from which modern Western religious systems descend.[6] The central tripartite division differentiates fundamental cosmic principles: the maintenance of cosmic and juridical order; the exercise of physical prowess; and the promotion of physical well-being. Applied to the Norse/Germanic pantheon, these functions distinguish the roles of such priestly, governing, and justice-dispensing deities as Odin and Tyr from the warrior/guardian role of

Thor, and both of these roles from those of the agricultural and herding deities Freyr or Freya. Dumézil applies this theory with great ingenuity at successively more narrowly defined levels of the tradition, although the results of the exercise are not as satisfying as in the case of the application of the same tripartite theory to Vedic religions. The overlap between the various functions of the Norse/Germanic pantheon is simply too great for so precise a classification. It is, however, a remarkable aspect of the Ásatrú revival that so esoteric a debate has been conducted with such passion among a decidedly nonacademic community of adherents.[7]

Although the Dumézilian debate may seem esoteric at first glance, it does not take place in isolation. Rather, it is one strand of a deeper debate within the Ásatrú/Odinist community, a debate that reaches to the heart of the current reconstruction of the tradition. The central question posed by Ásatrúers and Odinists alike is, simply, how best can the long dormant Northern Way be brought to life in this time and in this place? This question is the proximate genesis for the formulation of two conflicting theories: the modernist and the genetic theories of transmission. A comparison of these two theories provides a key to understanding the shape of contemporary Ásatrú/Odinism.

Two important preliminary points must be made regarding this analysis. First, it is difficult for an overwhelmingly monotheistic society to take seriously the suggestion that the pagan community invests its pantheon of gods with the same aura of sanctity—or a comparable degree of faith—as do adherents of the Abrahamic religions in relation to their God.[8] This widespread public skepticism finds considerable support in the literature emanating from the Wiccan/neopagan community itself, which affords evidence that many of these reconstructed spiritual traditions are as much deifications of contemporary socio-political grievances (i.e., Wicca and feminism, various manifestations of earth spirituality and ecology, and the like) as they are manifestations of polytheistic belief. The issue becomes even more confused with the strong impact of psychological and psychoanalytical concepts on the emerging theodicies of many of the reconstructed traditions. These difficulties not withstanding, to attempt an analysis of Odinism and Ásatrú from a psychological, sociological, or historical perspective (as an interesting specimen of contemporary phenomenology) while discounting the concrete impact of the gods and goddesses on the lives of the adherents of the Northern Way is to miss the vital heart of the reconstruction of the tradition. To many of the adherents, the gods and goddesses are real.

This is not to say that—to take a grossly simplified example—Odin exists and Yahweh does not, or more to the point, that Odin is Yahweh by another name. The Ásatrú pantheon is dealt with in a considerably different manner than a Jew, a Christian, or a Muslim would entreat his God. The relationship is less one of creator to creation or of distant, all-knowing, and all-powerful spirit to weak, mortal flesh than it is one of father to child or of tribal elder to youthful warrior. Ásatrúers do not bend the knee even to Odin, and the deities as well as the lesser spirits are a very real part of the everyday lives of many of the adherents.

At the same time, the Ásatrú/Odinist communities are primarily a band of first generation converts whose faith and practice must be considered in the context of their having been born into monotheistic (or sometimes agnostic) families and their having come of age in a monotheistic (albeit increasingly secularized) American culture. For the gods to become a natural part of the lives of the community, for their worship to become less a conscious act of differentiation from the dominant culture and more of the sort of subconscious belief which is at the heart of the faith of religious monotheists, it will be necessary to hand down the faith to a generation born into the belief system.

For most adherents of the Northern Way, this transformation from a monotheistic to a polytheistic worldview is as yet partial. Perfecting this faith through ritual practice, through textual study, and through trial and error is a day to day affair. In this sense, it is praxis rather than theological speculation which is the true test of the success of the reconstructive effort. Yet theology is important, and for the adherent, the gods are real, if yet imperfectly perceived.

The second preliminary point is more succinctly made. The Ásatrú and Odinist communities are very young, and the borders dividing them remain fluid. Just as it is no easy task to demonstrate a definite point of demarcation between the adherents of Odinism and the Ásatrú community, so too is it daunting to attempt to delineate hard and fast divisions between adherents of the two reconstructive strategies analyzed below. However, although some overlap is unavoidable, there are clear differences in approach, and these cleavages are important. Moreover, if history is any guide, these diverse approaches to the reconstruction of the faith may well harden as the community matures. If this occurs and remedial steps are not taken, these differences may prove more divisive than the issue of race. Indeed, it has over time been theological questions such as these which have often become the bases for the kind of sectarian divisions that so often turn a religious community into warring camps. If Ásatrú/Odinism in particular is to survive in the face of the powerful opposition coalesced against it, these sectarian tendencies must be avoided.

With this background, the first reconstructive strategy to be considered will be that of modernism.

The Modernist Theory

Although it is impossible to document with precision, it is clear that the overwhelming body of Ásatrúers fit comfortably into this category. The modernist approach to the reconstruction of the tradition corresponds to the generally accepted meaning of the term "neopagan," in that the primary task of the religious community is to bring to life the soul of the pre-Christian tradition—its religious practices and beliefs, its texts, its forms of magic (especially, in Ásatrú, the runes), and indeed as much of its cosmology and theodicy as possible—*within the constraints of the modern world*. Modernity, or postmodernity, is the key concept. Among Ásatrúers of the modernist camp, the goal is not a return to the life of the eleventh century, when the conversion of Iceland took place.[9] Rather, to this group reconstruction means that the recovered heathen spirituality must be fully cognizant of the exigencies of living as a minority religious community in contemporary America.

In this conception, the religion should not have to be hidden for fear of adverse reactions from employers, family, or friends. Neither should the Northern Way be perceived as a threat to the American status quo, to the state, or to any of its citizens. Rather, as the rituals, mythos, cosmology, and theodicy are reconstructed, the primary effort should be centered on integrating the spiritual essence of the ancient materials into lives that, beyond the sphere of alternative spirituality, appear to differ little from other Americans of the same racial, educational, and economic backgrounds. Thus, the ultimate goal may be the creation of an entirely new *weltanschauung* that is neither fully pre-Christian nor fully modern (or postmodern) but rather a powerful synthesis of the two. This, it is hoped, will present an attractive religious model which may, if the gods are willing, one day supplant Christianity and restore to the world a natural order that the conversion to Christianity interrupted but did not entirely extinguish.

The two primary systems by which this tradition is being recovered are seith and galdor magic. *Seith* is essentially a form of shamanic magic. *Galdor,* a magical form with a number of practical applications, involves the use of language in all cases and (in one specific working) centers on the use of rune staves. Galdor is practiced today for purposes including divination, warding (talismanic magic), and sympathetic and hex magic, to name but a few.[10] It is in the adaptation of these systems for practical use in the contemporary world, along with the hermeneutics attending the Eddic and saga literatures, that the conception of the modernist reconstruction of the tradition is best illustrated.

Of the materials at the heart of the reconstruction of the Northern

Way, none are more important than the efforts being invested in rune lore. The runes are central to the Northern Way, serving to differentiate the Norse/Germanic tradition from other neopagan communities. They are an initial port of entry for a number of contemporary Ásatrúers who report being drawn to the tradition by an interest in the runes. There are currently no less than four major runic alphabets, known as *Futharks* by virtue of an anagram of the first six letters. In the world of modern Ásatrú, there exists no consensus over which of these are most efficacious for contemporary use. Purists, among them KveldúlfR Gundarsson, argue for the twenty-four-stave Elder Futhark as the most viable for magical uses.[11] Edred Thorsson, however, who (along with Freyja Aswynn of Great Britain) is the primary force behind the reconstruction of the runic traditions, maintains that the Elder Futhark should be reserved for solely magical purposes and the younger Anglo-Saxon Futhark be used for other communications, due to its closer correspondence to the English alphabet.[12]

The precise origin of the Elder Futhark is lost to history, and even the uses for which the few surviving inscriptions (which date from between the first and eighth centuries C.E.) were intended are subjects of scholarly dispute. There is no controversy, however, as to the mythic origins of the runes, and it is this mythos which forms a primary tenet of contemporary Ásatrú belief. On this view, the runes originated with the "passion of Odin," the nine days and nights during which, pierced by a spear, he hung from Yggdrasil, the World Tree.

> I know that I hung
> on the windswept tree
> for nine full nights,
> wounded with a spear
> and given to Odinn,
> myself to myself;
> on that tree
> of which none know
> from what roots it rises.
>
> They did not comfort me with bread,
> and not with the drinking horn;
> I peered downward,
> I grasped the 'runes,'
> screeching I grasped them;
> I fell back from there. (*Hávamál* 138145)[13]

While Thorsson and other Ásatrúers have explored in considerable depth the shamanistic implications of this myth, it is the use to which the hard-won runes were put by Odin and the Norse/Germanic pantheon (and their contemporary cult) which concerns us here. Thorsson points out that the word *rún* (rune) means "mystery" in Icelandic; he contends that the greatest of these mysteries—and the primary symbol of the potency of runic magic—is illustrated by a secret tradition that reveals in part the riddle of what Odin whispered into the ear of his slain son, Baldur, the most beautiful and beloved of the gods.[14] Thorsson believes that word, either *rún* or a phrase containing the term, imparted the secrets of life and death, of past and future, and allowed Baldur (following the apocalypse of Ragnarök) to return to the earth (Midgärd) and to invest it once again with light, with beauty, and with life. To Thorsson, and to other contemporary rune magicians, the ultimate prize of the quest to recover runic knowledge through magical means is nothing less than this: the recovery of the ancient knowledge, the hidden mysteries of the gods in which past and future are revealed to the present, leading to the union of the nine worlds of gods, wights, and men.

When reference is made to a rune in this magical context, three interdependent aspects are involved: the sound, the stave or shape, and the hidden lore of the rune. Each rune in the Futhark thus has an independent "personality"—its own use, its own history, and its own mysteries.[15]

Perhaps the best way to illustrate the concept of the modernist approach to the reconstruction of the tradition is through a series of brief anecdotal examples of the applicability of the lore to the everyday lives of the Ásatrú community. Let us first juxtapose two recent articles which illustrate the sacred and the mundane uses of the runes in contemporary Ásatrú. One of the better examples of sacred praxis is offered by Gundarsson in an article illustrating the creation of a drinking horn. Following a series of historical examples of drinking horns and their runic inscriptions taken from the saga literature, Gundarsson selects as his text a passage from the Second Lay of Gudhrún in which the heroine drinks from an enchanted horn covered with rune staves. The meaning of the passage is explained in terms of the interaction of the herbs and the runes, which work together to produce their intended effect: "Runic formulae on a horn can either be geared towards a specific end, or generally chosen to enhance whatever is done to the draught in the horn."[16] In the second article, mundane application of the runes is offered by Gamlinginn, who proudly presents a thirty-one-stave standardized alphabet with accompanying phonetic values which he calls the Standard International Futhark (SIF). The SIF is currently available in computer fonts for IBM compatible and Macintosh PCs.[17]

Gamlinginn in fact appears to have inspired Ymir Thunarsson, a former member of the High Rede of the Ring of Troth and the leader of Eagles' Reaches (one of the more idiosyncratic kindreds in modern Ásatrú), to step forth and boldly proclaim the obvious: if, as Gamlinginn predicts, Ásatrú is poised to become a major global force after the fall of Christianity, it is important for every true man and woman to practice worship, ritual, and magical workings on a daily basis. This assertion, and its accompanying suggestions for useful rituals, makes explicit a widely felt perception regarding the Ring of Troth:

> All too often the leadership of the movement known as Ásatrú takes to the high road of scholastic achievement and as a byproduct their writing has taken on the form of a university lecture or a grand thesis beyond the scope of common folk . . . for our movement to truly succeed we must reach and inflame both the hearts and minds of the everyday person male and female alike . . . [after Christianity's fall] "How do I transform myself into one worthy to be named true and good?" . . . The answer is really so simple that I feel that many of my more scholarly friends may have missed it. IT IS THROUGH THE POWER AND RITUAL OF DAILY WORKINGS![18]

A primary goal of ritual, of course, is to remagicalize the world. James Chisholm offers an unexcelled example of this in his utilization of the Lay of Alvis as source text for a series of blessings (worship rituals) and workings (magical acts) centered on the dwarves, whose aid can be secured in various tasks and whose happiness and good will one would want to assure in any case.[19] Elsewhere, Chisholm argues for the reconstruction of the sacred dramas that accompanied the Ostara holiday. These were, according to Chisholm, Vanic rites (and thus primarily sexual in nature), which are recorded in the lays of Skirner, Svipdag, and Sigrdrifa. As these texts were redacted in Christian times, and the rites shorn of their sexual content, Chisholm suggests various methods by which the rituals could be revived—albeit with the sexuality attendant on the pre-Christian original modified considerably to suit contemporary American sensibilities.[20]

Another series of articles from the now defunct Ásatrú journal *Mountain Thunder* offer practical applications of the textual tradition. Charles Armour, an adherent from the mountains of Colorado, presented a long running series on herbal lore.[21] A series by Tony Wolf on the warrior tradition, emphasizing often somewhat fanciful forms of "Norse martial arts," were also based (rather loosely) on textual sources.[22]

The incessant debate over race within Ásatrú may be the most important example of praxis in the modernist reconstruction of the tradition. In this discourse, the more racialist adherents tend to take on faith the proposition that, because Norse/Germanic societies were demonstrably of one racial stock, this "felicitous" condition must reflect the exclusivist racial consciousness of the Golden Age forefathers.[23] The most outspoken voices for racial inclusion in Ásatrú, however, tend to utilize materials drawn from the tradition that are adapted to the context of contemporary America.

KveldúlfR Gundarsson is perhaps the prime example of the "PC Pagan" available in contemporary Ásatrú.[24] He rarely misses an opportunity in his writings to uncover—often through complex hermeneutics—an important role for women in the history of the tradition. On this precedent, women are invited to take an honored place in the reconstructed tradition, as fully equal partners with male Ásatrúers. In a scholarly rebuke to those who would take up Odinism (or Ásatrú) as a means to give vent to racialist feelings, as well as to the more scholarly adherents of metagenetics (considered below), Gundarsson points to the historical record, which shows no hesitation among the Norse or among the German tribes to freely intermarry with any outsiders who were in proximity. He points out (with some irony, given the constituency of contemporary Ásatrú) that "the Norse who settled Iceland brought along Irish thralls . . . with whom they interbred so freely that blood type groupings show the average Icelander to be 25% to 75% Irish."[25] Moreover, the gods themselves interbred frequently: the Æsir with the Vanes, both with giants, gods with humans (and Loki with a horse, on one memorable occasion). Indeed, adoption of outsiders into the tribe (or Troth) is proven to have been a common institution for gods and men in the texts, just as the sagas prove that true birth and ancestry do not guarantee that one is true of soul. Finally, in an indirect rebuke to metageneticists, Gundarsson argues that the sagas prove conclusively that no current adherent of Ásatrú can claim pure descent from the pagan Golden Age. By accepting Christian baptism (as all eventually did), they were cut off from the soul line of the ancestors, with attendant loss of "the gods and goddesses . . . the ancestral kin-fetch and the personal fetch as well."[26]

Gamlinginn, despite unconvincing protestations of naïveté, is certainly the most astute member of the Ásatrú community in the ways and wiles of the world—particularly in the reaction of state authorities to small, nonconformist religious or political groupings whose beliefs are deemed to be inconvenient. An independent Ásatrúer, he has been extremely outspoken in his demand for an Ásatrú community open to anyone, regardless of their race or previous religious affiliation. Gamlinginn seems motivated to undertake this crusade at least in part by a clearly political impulse that belies his claims to puzzlement at the ways of the world. In his speech to Althing 12 in May 1992, he urges the racialist and nonracialist factions to cease what had by then become a virtual civil war, for "Ásatrú today is a tiny band surrounded on all sides by huge numbers of hostile forces. The only thing that has so far kept the encircling forces from launching a devastating attack is that Ásatrú is so small that most of its potential enemies are unaware of its existence. And we all know that could change at any moment."[27] This plea however, is not posited merely in terms of political expediency: again, the textual heritage is presented, coupled with a challenge to follow the true path and to become part not of the past but of the future— a post-Christian future. In this context, Gamlinginn cites perhaps the most quoted text in contemporary Ásatrú, verse 76 of the *Hávamál:*

> Cattle die, kinsmen die,
> oneself dies the same;
> but words of praise never die
> for those of great renown.

> Each of you has been given a chance to be remembered thousands of years from now. In fact, each of you has been given a chance for something far more important than just being remembered. Each of you has been given a chance to change the course of history.[28]

Gamlinginn returns to this subject in 1993 in the pages of *Mountain Thunder,* adopting a tone more closely approximating Gundarsson's textuality than the emotional approach of Althing 12's address to the Ásatrú Alliance. He begins by quoting a passage attributed to Odin in the Prose Edda, apparently chosen to support the universal embrace of the gods for the people of Midgard (earth):[29]

> Then said High One: "It will take a vast amount of knowledge to cover them all, but it is swiftest to say, that most of these names have been given (to him) because, the many different nations speaking different tongues in the world, all wanted to change his name into their own tongue in order to address and pray (to him) for themselves."[30]

With this as a proof text, Gamlinginn asserts that there must be no place for racism in Ásatrú, concluding:

> In the Modern Age, racists will become more and more isolated from mainstream society (and reality), living lonely, bitter and paranoid lives.

> Those of us who have spent our lives fighting both alongside and against many of the world's diverse ethnic groups learn to appreciate the essential similarities of all humans, and to ignore the superficial

differences. Every life is filled with combat situations; physical, mental, and spiritual. When facing combat, it is always better to pick allies who share with you the Viking values of Ásatrú than those who share only your skin color.[31]

Not every example of modernist praxis need be so serious, however. Once again, the highly unusual Texas kindred Eagles' Reaches provides an example of the lighter side of the Ásatrú movement. Egil's Saga makes mention of an object known as a *niðing* pole, which, adorned with suitable runic inscriptions, is erected to hex enemies, particularly incoming ships. The niðing pole was apparently rarely used, either because it was regarded as a deterrent that was never meant to be utilized (as in the more recent Mutually Assured Destruction nuclear doctrine) or simply because it was felt to be unmanly to use magic against a foe whose attack was on a mundane plane and should be met on equal terms. In any case, when Ymir Thunarsson apparently became embroiled in a dispute with a Native American shaman resident in the Houston area, Eagles' Reaches erected with all due ceremony a niðing pole with the intent to ease the offending holy man on a permanent journey to another plane of existence.[32]

A final example of the modernist reconstruction of the Norse/Germanic tradition illustrates again the juxtaposition of the sacred and the mundane in contemporary Ásatrú. In recognition of the dearth of available female marriage partners in the Ásatrú community, one young Ásatrúer writes:

> I am in the process of seriously courting a beautiful heathen maiden . . . [thus] in addition to making toasts and wishes at Yule on the subject of how much I wanted to find a compatible woman (still quite rare in Ásatrú), I also promised Frija that I would write a story focusing on her as a votive offering if she would help with this. I am now in the process of writing that story—quite a difficult task as it requires a viewpoint completely different from my own. When I am done, I will take one copy, bless it, and ritually sink it . . . I am planning to have this done at or before Ostara.[33]

The Geneticist Theory

For the adherents of Odinism and for the more racialist adherents of Ásatrú, there is little doubt that the transmission of the tradition and the sole criterion for membership is through genetic inheritance (i.e., race). The question of the transmission of tradition was just as pertinent to Stephen McNallen in the earliest days of the Viking Brotherhood or to later Ásuatrú leaders such as Edred Thorsson and Mike Murray as it is to these racialist adherents. While some Ásatrúers assert that the genesis of the reawakening of the tradition was a direct revelation from the gods,[34] for other Ásatrúers the question of origin is not so straightforward. It is for this reason all the more pressing. The primary theory which has evolved from the movement to explain these imponderables is metagenetics.

The idea of metagenetics appears to have begun with Stephen McNallen and first appeared in a brief, five-page exposition in the original *Runestone* magazine.[35] Since then, the theory has been fleshed out considerably by Edred Thorsson. What is perhaps most remarkable about metagenetic theory is that, despite the high status of its proponents and despite the considerable intellectual effort that has been lavished on its formulation (particularly at the hands of Thorsson), it has remarkably few adherents in either Ásatrú or Odinism. Indeed, even those closest to McNallen and Thorsson, Robert Stine and James Chisholm respectively, evinced no interest in the idea.[36] Despite this isolation, the theory is of considerable interest and may one day find its way out of the periphery of the Ásatrú and Odinist world.

What makes metagenetics so difficult for many to accept is its base assumption: the tradition (i.e., culture) is a matter of genetic inheritance, and it is for this reason that the compulsion to reawaken the Northern Way has come upon some but not others. Put another way, the reason that the gods choose to act through individuals of a particular national and racial stock is that the religious heritage that the gods personify never died, but rather has been handed down from generation to generation—albeit in a dormant state—until a time that the gods deem propitious for the rebirth of the Norse/Germanic tradition.

The fact that the gods have apparently chosen this time and this place as the setting for their reemergence is the key to the analysis of Ásatrú/Odinism as a millenarian belief system. With the defeat of the gods at the apocalyptic battle of Ragnarök, there began a dark period of the earth's history known as the Wolf Age. For the adherent of Ásatrú/Odinism, the reappearance of the gods heralds the end of this bleak period and the onset of a longed-for chiliastic period of a world reborn. Although this belief does not precisely equate with the permanent and totalistic transformation foreseen by Christian apocalyptic millenarianism, there is sufficient similarity to allow for a common discourse between Christian and neopagan apocalypticists. As the mixed Christian Identity and Odinist composition of the Order demonstrates, this theological affinity has considerable impact in the world of action.

Before examining the specifics of metagenetic theory, however, we may consider briefly why so few have been drawn to it. As explicated by McNallen in *The Runestone* and as developed in a number of later forums by Thorsson, metagenetics falls into the same middle-ground chasm that has bedeviled the old Ásatrú Free Assembly, the Ásatrú Alliance, and to a lesser extent the Ring of Troth. On the one hand, the notion of culture as hereditary violates much of the fundamental liberal dogma of our age, and (in less sure hands than those of Thorsson or McNallen) raises the specter of racism and the dreaded "Nazi occultism" epithet which has rather unfairly become synonymous in Ásatrú circles with Thorsson's adventures in the Temple of Set's Order of the Trapezoid. Thus, the theory is simply anathema to the antiracialists of the Ring of Troth and to much of independent Ásatrú. On the other hand, there has been no rush among Odinists or Ásatrú Alliance members to embrace the theory either. The explanation for this seems obvious as well. Metagenetics is no simple racist dogma; rather, it depends heavily on psychological theories of cultural transmission (most notably, Jungian archetypes), central Norse beliefs such as reincarnation within family lines, a grab bag of esoteric doctrines drawn from a variety of traditional cultures, and a selective but varied corpus of references from the contemporary social sciences. Put bluntly, these are rather deep intellectual waters. Thus, metagenetics sinks like a stone between the warring Ásatrú and Odinist camps.

Stripped to its essentials, metagenetics—"the science for the next century"—is Jung writ large.[37] Jung's metaphor for the applicability of archetypes to the Weimar-era reemergence of the worship of Wotan sums up the basis of metagenetic theory perfectly:

> Archetypes are like riverbeds which dry up when the water deserts them, but which it can find again at any time. An archetype is like an old water-course along which the water has flowed for centuries, digging a deep channel for itself. The longer it has flowed in this channel, the more likely it is that sooner or later the water will return to its old bed.[38]

When placed in the context that Jung provides in his essay "Wotan," the idea that the genetic descendants of the Norse/Germanic peoples should be the exclusive heirs of the religious tradition contains no hint of the racialist and exclusivist reputation with which Ásatrú has come to be associated in recent years. As McNallen writes in his introduction to "Metagenetics,"

> One of the most controversial tenets of Ásatrú is our insistence that ancestry matters—that there are spiritual and metaphysical implications to heredity, and that we are thus not a religion for all of humanity, but rather one that calls only its own. This belief of ours has led to much misunderstanding, and as a result some have attempted to

label us as "racist", or have accused us of fronting for totalitarian political forms.

In this article we will discuss, fully and at length, a science for the next century which we have named "metagenetics." For while that science deals with genetics, it also transcends the present boundaries of that discipline and touches on religion, metaphysics, and (among other things) the hereditary nature of Jungian archetypes. The foundations of metagenetics lie not in totalitarian dogma of the 19th and 20th centuries, but rather in intuitive insights as old as our people. It is only in the last decades that experimental evidence has begun to verify these age-old beliefs.[39]

The evidence "verifying" these beliefs is certainly eclectic. Quoted among other scientific and religious notables are such diverse luminaries as the Danish brain specialist Dr. N. Jule-Nielson, ESP researcher Dr. J. B. Rhine of Duke University, Dr. Timothy Leary of LSD exploration fame, Dr. Ian Stevenson of the University of Virginia Medical School (who authored a highly controversial volume on reincarnation), and Dr. Daniel G. Freedman of the University of Chicago (who has written on ethnic differences among newborns). It is Jung, however, with his theories of the collective unconscious and its resident archetypes, who forms the centerpiece of the presentation:

> Most modern students of Jung miss a key fact. Jung stated explicitly that the archetypes were not culturally transmitted but were in fact inherited—that is to say, genetic . . .
>
> But Jung was not satisfied to make this connection. He went on to say that because of this biological factor there were differences in the collective unconscious of mankind. Boldly, he asserted that, "Thus it is a quite unpardonable mistake to accept the conclusions of a Jewish psychology as generally valid. (This statement must be taken in context. It is not some irrelevant anti-Jewish remark, but instead stems from the growing rift between Jung and his Jewish teacher, Freud.) Nobody would dream of taking a Chinese or Indian psychology as binding on ourselves . . . with the beginning of racial differentiation, essential differences are developed in the collective psyche as well. For this reason, we cannot transmit the spirit of a foreign religion 'In globo' into our own mentality without sensible injury to the latter."[40]

Although scholars of religion would find historical reason to demure from this statement, given the long history of the diffusion of religious creeds across racial and cultural boundaries without noticeable "sensible injury" to the religious belief system, the theory does have an undeniable efficacy in trying to unravel (in terms accessible both to religion and to twentieth-century science) the emergence of Ásatrú in the modern world. Further, according to this theory, "if we, as a people, cease to exist, then Ásatrú also dies forever. We are intimately tied up with the fate of our whole people, for Ásatrú is an expression of the soul of our race."[41] At the same time, it is also true that "this does not mean that we are to behave negatively toward other people who have not harmed us. On the contrary, only by understanding who we are, only by coming from our racial 'center,' can we interact justly and with wisdom with other people on this planet."[42] Clearly, this attempt to define a "middle way" in racial terms has rendered metagenetic theory uniquely uninteresting to adherents on either side of the racialist divide in contemporary Ásatrú/Odinism.

Edred Thorsson would flesh out metagenetic theory considerably, most notably in an article in *Idunna,* in a chapter of *A Book of Troth,* and (less directly) in a talk given to the Pagan Student Alliance at the University of Texas at Austin.[43] By the early 1990s, Thorsson came to believe that part of the problem with having the concept accepted more widely in the Ásatrú world lies in the word itself, as the term "genetics" has accrued rather negative connotations "in the pop-intellectual world."[44]

In his talk at the University of Texas, Thorsson anticipates the obvious intellectual criticism that the original "Metagenetics" article would attract, namely, that at root it assumes that in the roughly eight hundred years since the triumph of Christianity, the genetic pool remained essentially pure, while in fact (to use the Jungian metaphor) the "old river bed" has been fed by too many fresh tributaries to ever hope to resume its old course. In response to this criticism, he posits four distinct components of culture which "blended together give us a true picture of any historical society, ancient or modern . . . 1) ethnic culture, 2) ethical culture, 3) material culture, and 4) linguistic culture."[45] Therefore, metagenetic or purely racial aspects of inherited culture account for only one-fourth of a particular culture. Language and material/ethical culture are more than enough to account for an adherent's attraction to Ásatrú, even if he or she is not a direct descendent of the Norse/Germanic blood line. Indeed, in Thorsson's exposition, linguistic affinity holds as much importance in the reawakening of the tradition as does racial heritage.

In his *Idunna* article, Thorsson expounds at greater length on the possibilities and the shortcomings of metagenetic theory.[46] He points out yet again that race is a nineteenth-century European construct that would have been incomprehensible to the ancestors, as would the dualistic *weltanschauung* which underpins the simplistic division of the world into good and bad, light and dark, etc. Further, he adds to the linguistic and cultural aspects of communal cohesion a graduated series of historically resonant patterns of association, which (from macro to micro level) are nation, tribe, kindred, family, and individual. These break down to three traditional organizational structures which are involved in the current rebirth of the tradition. The familial tie is genetic, and thus metagenetic writ small. The tribal level is certainly genetic, but given the institutions of alliance, adoption, and intermarriage, is also a voluntary form of association. Finally, there is the associative level, which is nongenetic and thus purely voluntary. Properly speaking, the first two levels may be said to be Ásatrú itself, while primary Ásatrú organizations such as the Rune Gild or the Ring of Troth belong to the associative level of organization. Does this observation, then, invalidate associative groupings as true Ásatrú organizations? If not, does this openness invalidate metagenetic theory? According to Thorsson,

> The genetic or metagenetic argument is powerful . . . but it has its definite weaknesses in a revivalist scheme. Principle among these is that carried to its logical conclusion it ends in an equation of "racial purity" and "divine contact." For if we say that someone is in contact with the Germanic gods because they are mainly of Germanic descent, then we could end that because someone else (anyone else) has more Germanic blood then he is automatically more in contact with these archetypes. The ultimate conclusion of such a simplistic and static reasoning would quite obviously be absurd, and what is more, not very convincing. To this important metagenetic, biological line we must add other factors, 1) language, and 2) culture, in order to come up with a complete rationale for German revivalism. Language is a paradigmatic mind-set which encodes the psyche of all who speak it with certain conceptual modes and possibilities. People who have a Germanic language as their Mother Tongue (i.e., English, German, Dutch, or any of the Scandinavian dialects) and who have grown up in cultures formulated by Germanic traditions and thought may also be impressed with the spirit of Ásatrú/Odinism. Culture is a complex sociological mixture of all that goes into the life of a people, and encompasses both the concepts of ancient cultural continuity and environmental influence.[47]

With this impressively Dumézilian formulation of metagenetics as but one of a three-pronged complex of factors (genetics, language and culture), Thorsson is able to reach the reasonable conclusion that "since race was never a real category of allegiance for the ancients, why should it be one now?" With this formulation, reached as a consequence of having given thought to the skeletal suggestions of McNallen's original article, it is possible to posit the importance of the theory, despite its present dearth of adherents.

The Odinist Path

Wotan's power has long been broken. I live now only in the hearts and memory of those of you who feel the life-force you once rejoiced to live. You shared my life-force, and in death I honored you as heroes to be with me in Valhalla. Now there is little left to honor. The Ravens fly out daily to bring me word of your deeds, only to return to Valhalla to tell me that which I loath to hear. You are dying, my Aryan kinder, of a sickness of your racial soul. The god-like graces I gave to you, which every other race but yours recognized, you have thrown down into the dust.[48]

The Odinist path takes up where the Ásatrúers' geneticist path ends—with race. In this sense, Odinism is a religion of race and of blood. The return of the gods is posited as the culmination of an apocalyptic End Time drama that liberally blends elements of Christian eschatology with the Norse Ragnarök tradition. The return of the Golden Age pantheon is a much-longed-for event in these dark days, for the return of the gods will mean a return to the days of racial purity, of harmony, and of universal happiness. As the above quotation graphically demonstrates, the present Wolf Age is one of uninterrupted darkness and despair for the faithful.

The gods, however, are ever present and available to the descendants of the Norse and Germanic peoples. In this understanding, metagenetics as derived from Jungian theory again plays a role. In the words of imprisoned Order member David Lane,

Having studied the works of Carl Jung, I believe the old Gods are a potential colossus within our collective subconscious. The old Gods and the old religion were exclusively ours, and thus, relate to our race-soul. Through the myths and legends we find a link to our past, and a rudder for our floundering racial vessel.[49]

Odinists, like Ásatrúers, posit the tribal ethos of Germany and Scandinavia before the coming of Christianity as a Golden Age. Unlike the Ásatrú community, however, the Odinist seeks to reconstitute that golden time virtually unchanged in the postapocalyptic modern world. The Odinist dream is of battle, of Valhalla, and of a world restored to the ancient virtues of folk and of tribe. That this dream is reminiscent of National Socialism is no accident. The borderline separating racialist Odinism and National Socialism is exceedingly thin, and much of the material produced by racialist Odinism contains explicit odes to Hitler and to the Third Reich.[50]

Odinists differ from Ásatrúers in another way as well: their powerful sense of conspiratorialism. For Odinists, there is no doubt as to the
identity of the enemy: in accord with the established orthodoxy of the
racialist right wing, it is the Jew who stands behind the evils of this
world. Not the least of these evils (in the Odinists' view) is the lamenta-
ble condition of the white race. Surrounded by hostile "aliens," brought
low by the superhuman machinations of the Jewish rulers of this world,
the Odinist—like the Identity Christian and the minister of the Church
of the Creator—sees the white race as nearing extinction. It is with this
self-view of the faithful as part of a dying righteous remnant that the
Odinist must choose between the same grim alternatives as all other
oppositional belief systems: to fight back against impossible odds, or to
withdraw and seek to persevere until such time as the gods deem it
propitious to join the new battle of Ragnarök.

The Question of Violence: the Ásatrú Community

It is a remarkable irony that, aside from the actions of the Order,
the most serious instance of violence associated with the Ásatrú/Odinist
community is associated with the decidedly nonracialist Ring of Troth.
Moreover, an incident involving the Ásatrú Alliance had the potential
for a similar disaster; fortunately, cooler heads prevailed on that occasion. These acts of violence—a domestic dispute that ended in murder
and an angry confrontation over a banner at an Ásatrú Alliance gathering—are clearly atypical of the Ásatrú community and are offered as a
contrast to the revolutionary violence of the Order and the (so far) random violence of the racialist Odinist community.

The first of these incidents, Rob Meek's murder of his wife, was
considered at some length in chapter 1. The incident involving the Ásatrú Alliance did not end in a similar tragedy, but is considerably more
typical of the forms of violence associated with the Odinist community.
As with the Ring of Troth, the events involving the Alliance must be
placed in context, especially that of the emotional debates over race and
over who may and who may not be an adherent of the Northern Way.
Robert Stine recalls the waning days of the old Ásatrú Free Alliance:

> We, Stephen McNallen, his wife Maddy Hutter, Kelly LaZatte, my
> wife, and yours truly, made the AFA too large of a monster for us to
> control, it thus broke free and devoured us . . . I went to the first Texas
> Althing and had a great time, the second Texas Althing I attended I
> stayed there . . . We moved the AFA headquarters from Steve's house
> into an office/store front in downtown, in Brekenridge [sic], Texas. All
> was going well, I guess the sign I painted for the storefront is still
> there. Then the Texas economy went bust, I lost my job, in short order

Steve lost his job, Kelly and I lived on what she could make doing laundry in an old folks home, Steve and Maddy lived on savings, we held on trying to make it, the AFA could not make enough to support us, so I was determined to get out.[51]

It is clear in retrospect that even had these problems of organization and leadership been solved, the breakup of the AFA was probably inevitable. While still a relatively minor factor, race played a role in the group's demise that was far out of proportion to its importance in the reconstruction of the tradition. The AFA, despite its highly decentralized organizational character, was no mere mail order church; rather, the emotional heart of Ásatrú is community, and the numerous local and regional gatherings for seasonal religious ceremonies (*blots*), for *sumbels* (religious ceremonies characterized by ritual drinking behavior), and for folk moots (general gatherings for primarily social purposes) are in fact celebrations of this communal spirit. At the apex of these gatherings is the Althing, a national assembly of kindreds gathered for religious ceremony, competitive games, and (unlike other Ásatrú gatherings) the discussion of political as well as of social topics. Althings determine the organizational policies to be pursued during the coming year; they are free gatherings of equals, and the parameters of debate are virtually unlimited. Thus, race could be politely ignored by the leadership, but debate on the issue (like criticism of the leadership itself) could not be stifled. It was the Althings that brought the inherent tensions and contradictions of the AFA to a head. It must be emphasized that the primary purpose of the Althing for most of those who attend is a weekend of fun, mead (honey wine), athletic contests, and most of all, a celebration of community. When talk turns to more substantive matters, however, cleavages soon become apparent; tempers become frayed, and the rhetoric turns hot. Bob Stine and others describe a number of incidents at these early post-AFA althings, which in aggregate, appear to represent tensions inherited from the demise of the AFA.[52]

These incidents were harbingers of things to come at Althing 9, held in Arizona in 1989. There exist in Alliance circles a number of versions of the events at Althing 9, but what is most striking is the remarkable consistency of accounts regarding the event. More remarkable still—and largely unknown to the Ásatrú community—there exists a two-hour tape recording of the central confrontation at the Althing 9 Council. Thus, a rather full story can be pieced together from interviews with participants from both camps, supplemented with the recorded material. The story provides a valuable insight into the powerful emotive ties which bind individual Ásatrúers, as well as into the centrifugal forces which so often rend small, tightly bound religious communities. Interestingly, although the underlying issue was racialism in the Alliance, at no time does the subject appear to have been addressed directly. Rather, the battle was waged over the interpretation of the Alliance by-laws, and more centrally, over the meaning of a flag, over the ties of troth and blood brotherhood, and in the minds of some, over the soul of the movement. When the subject of racialism was raised by the Old Northwest Kindred, the Council was engrossed in the issue of the damage to the movement which Edred Thorsson's involvement in the Temple of Set had brought about. The sudden change of subject caught the Council completely by surprise.[53] It is the suddenness of the confrontation that most stands out in the recollections of those involved. Indeed, it is inconceivable to some that the Old Northwest Kindred had not arrived at the Althing site with a preconceived agenda, and many afterward felt that they and the Alliance had been manipulated by the Old Northwest Kindred.[54]

The Old Northwest Kindred—at the time centered in Chicago, with about a dozen members—arrived at the Althing site early and were guests in the home of Mike Murray in Payson, Arizona. Four members had made the trip: Phil Nearing, who was to be elected to replace Murray as Speaker of the Alliance; Robert Stine; a long time Ásatrúer and head of the Brewers' Gild;[55] and Scott Enslin, a.k.a. Bagelwolf. All drove to Arizona in the same car, and although there was apparently some tension within the group, nothing was planned or said about provoking a confrontation at the Althing.

Probably, however, the issue was not far from the minds of the members of the Old Northwest Kindred, for some aspects of Althing 8 had left a bad aftertaste among them. A cadre of National Socialists were present at the earlier event, and although they tended to be relegated to the periphery, one incident did occur. One kindred from the Washington state area included the Wiccan/Jewish wife of one of the members. This became known, and some objections were raised to her presence, apparently by California adherent Dan West (a.k.a. Redbeard, King of the Thor's Hammer Kindred).[56] Most participants, however, followed the lead of the women from the Arizona Kindred and went out of their way to make her feel welcome. The racialism present at Althing 8 had a particularly negative effect on the head of the Brewers Gild (who pointed out that if the racists in AA were left unchallenged, they would simply bring in their friends and subvert the movement) and on Scott Enslin (whose mother was Jewish, leaving him with an obvious distaste for expressions of anti-Semitism).[57]

The determination to make a stand on the race issue at Althing 9 may have crystallized during the Old Northwest Kindred's stay in Murray's house. In conversation, Murray made an anti-Semitic remark to which Enslin took exception. Although the latter said nothing at the time, that ended his relationship with Murray.[58] However, while Althing 8 provides the context for Northwest's actions, the precipitating cause was the presence of the eccentric leader of the New York/New Jersey–based Ocean Kindred, Paal-Erik Filssennu. Filssennu's primary claim to fame is his quixotic quest to reclaim Greenland as an ethnic homeland, his invention of a language for this putative mini-state (contemptuously referred to by some as mock-Icelandic), and his leadership of the National Socialist–oriented Amerist Folk Bund.[59] At Althing 9, Filssennu set up a literature table next to Old Northwest's campsite. Enslin took an immediate interest; he pulled up a lawn chair, took each of the many pieces of literature one at a time, read it thoroughly, and quietly tossed the item back on the table before taking up the next item for inspection. It was in the course of this meditation on Folk Bundism that Enslin noticed that the flag of the future Amerist Folk Republic was in fact flying over the central "sacred space" of the campground—the very area where blots and sumbels were held and where oaths were sworn and the gods propitiated. Clearly, in his view, the banner was being used as a political symbol, and as such was in clear violation of the by-laws forbidding political stands by the organization. It had to come down immediately, and Enslin had little difficulty in winning the Old Northwest Kindred to this position.[60]

Complicating the matter was Mike Murray's insistence that the flag was his personal Tyr banner and that under it a member of Old Northwest had once sworn a warrior's oath of eternal troth to Murray when both were members of the Warrior's Gild.[61] Thus, the Old Northwest demand that the flag be lowered was not only a shock but in Murray's eyes an act of ultimate betrayal. All participants interviewed report that violence appeared to be the likely outcome of the confrontation. Although no Ásatrú gathering has ever resulted in violence, the combination of emotional argument, large amounts of alcohol, and the presence of guns at these events always offers the possibility of, at minimum, an unfortunate accident. With this in mind, the Old Northwest Kindred formulated a plan by which, if a battle ensued, they would be ready. Armed with a single 9mm pistol and an assortment of edged weapons, each member was assigned a designated target (with Murray being the first to go); having neutralized the primary targets, the "Brewer" and Phil Nearing were to retreat to the car, with Stine and Enslin providing cover. The point appears to have been to assure that when the authorities were apprised of the battle, at least the Old Northwest version of events would be available to counter that of what they believed would be a united front put up by the Arizona Kindred and its supporters.[62] Nearing, however, a martial arts teacher of the *Wing Chun* school, wouldn't hear of leaving. The Brewer's respiratory problems made him an obvious choice to go, but the loss of the kindred's best fighter made little sense. Thus, Enslin was chosen to replace Nearing in the car, leaving Stine and Nearing to fight a rear-guard action to allow for their escape.[63]

In the end, following hours of emotional but nonviolent debate, Murray's position that the banner was his personal (and thus apolitical) symbol did not prevail.[64] Murray, enraged and wishing to avoid violence, turned the speakership over to William Bainbridge, left the argument with his mead horns, and sat under his banner. The Old Northwest carried the day, Phil Nearing was elected Thingspeaker, and Althing 10 was planned for the Ohio home of Robert Stine. The cost was high, however. Old Northwest determined that, after Althing 10, they would leave the Alliance, and later evinced some disgust that they had not done so earlier. Both the Brewer and Scott Enslin have left active participation in organized Ásatrú, the former to return to academia, the latter becoming a merchant seaman.[65] The Alliance soon returned to what it always was, a group with a majority of racialist kindreds but with an increased determination to keep the Alliance on a nonpolitical footing.[66]

Althing 10 was held without incident in Ohio, and it returned to the pattern of previous events: religious ceremonies, contests, and ritual drinking and boasting, with the Council Meeting most notable for inconsequential discussions. A good part of the credit for diffusing the lingering tensions from Althing 9 may be credited to Stine, who as host elected to move the event grounds from the usual easily accessible public park to a beautiful lake shore in a distant, hidden valley, whose primary attraction (beyond the scenery) was the utter impossibility of getting in or out without a local guide. It is perhaps unremarkable that being thrust into an area that, in Bob Stine's words, was like returning to the tenth century served to focus the collective mind on cooperative and nonconfrontational pursuits! For his part, Murray and other Alliance members recall going to Althing 10 primarily to fulfill their obligation to Old Northwest, but continue to believe that the confrontation at Althing 9 was manipulated by Old Northwest in a manner consciously designed to harm the Alliance.[67]

By 1995, the stabilization of the Alliance was reflected in its organizational rules. While explicitly endorsing the metagenetic position of membership as open to the genetic descendants of the Norse-Germanic people, the Ásatrú Alliance rigorously moved to separate politics from the national organization while at the same time guaranteeing the rights of member of kindreds to function on the local level without interference. So important are these regulations in avoiding the potentially violent conflicts that beset earlier Althings that the 1995 laws of the Ásatrú Alliance are here set out in full:

BY LAWS OF THE ASATRÚ ALLIANCE
PROPOSED AT ALTHING—JUNE ɪɪ, 2243 RUNIC ERA

1. ASATRÚ IS THE ETHNIC RELIGION OF THE INDIGENOUS NORTH-ERN EUROPEAN PEOPLE.
2. THE ASATRÚ ALLIANCE IS A FREE ASSOCIATION OF INDEPENDENT KINDREDS SEEKING TO PRESERVE AND PROTECT THE ANCIENT FAITH OF OUR ANCESTORS.
3. THE ALLIANCE IS ORGANIZED ALONG TRIBAL/DEMOCRATIC LINES, PERMITTING THE FULL EXPRESSION OF OUR RELIGIOUS OPIN-IONS. STRIVING FOR THE PRESERVATION AND SANCTITY OF OUR ASATRÚ FAITH.
4. THE ALLIANCE IS APOLITICAL; IT IS NOT A FORUM FOR, NOR WILL IT PROMOTE ANY POLITICAL VIEWS OF, THE "LEFT"OR "RIGHT." OUR SACRED TEMPLES, GROVES, THINGS AND MOOTS WILL REMAIN FREE OF ANY POLITICAL MANIFESTATIONS.
5. THE ALLIANCE DOES NOT ESPOUSE A PRIEST CLASS. EACH KIN-DRED IS FREE TO DETERMINE ITS OWN SPIRITUAL AND TRIBAL NEEDS.
6. THE ALLIANCE WILL PROMOTE THE GROWTH OF ASATRÚ THROUGH THE SPONSORING OF NATIONAL AND REGIONAL THINGS AND MOOTS. WE WILL ALSO PUBLISH BOOKS, MAGAZINES AND NEWSLETTERS, AS NEEDED TO ACHIEVE OUR GOALS.
7. A THINGSPEAKER WILL BE CHOSEN FOR ALTHING BY THE HOST KINDRED. THE THINGSPEAKER MAY CONVENE THE THING AS NEEDED. ALTHING DELEGATES OF RECORD WILL SERVE AS A STANDING LEGISLA-TIVE BODY WITH FULL AUTHORITY OF THE THING, UNTIL THE COMMENCEMENT OF THE NEXT ALTHING. THE THINGSPEAKER OR ANY DELEGATE OF RECORD CAN CALL FOR A CAUCUS OF DELEGATES FOR A SUITABLE CAUSE.
8. THE THING HAS ABSOLUTE AUTHORITY IN DEALING WITH BY LAWS AND OTHER ISSUES OF THE ASATRÚ ALLIANCE.[68]

The document goes on to note rules governing the structure of member kindreds, mandating that each kindred have at least three members, but that the Alliance will not interfere in local affairs unless specifically petitioned to do so by the local group. In a brief section on individual members, it is noted that while any member of an Alliance kindred is a member of the Alliance, and that any local kindred of three or more members may petition to join the Alliance, no individual member will be accepted unless he or she is first accepted by a member kindred.

The Question of Violence: Odinism

> Robert Jay Mathews was an Odinist, and the finest man I've known. In Valhalla he waits for those who fight for the life of the Folk. I don't think he cares if you are a Creator, a Christian, or an Odinist, but only that you are White and Proud.
>
> But for my part, his Gods are the Folk's Gods, and they are my Gods.[69]

Given that Odinism is a religion of battle, that Odin and Thor in their warrior aspects are seen as models for emulation, and that much of the literature of youthful Odinists is given to the glorification of the berserker ideal, it is remarkable how little actual violence is associated with American Odinists. Else Christensen, the founder of the first organized racialist Odinist organization in the United States, saw her mission as one of defusing this potential violence, particularly among her prison constituency.[70]

Violence emanating from the Odinist community has thus been largely rhetorical. The calls for violence—invariably presented either as vengeance for the machinations of the predatory Jew or as berserker rage—are ubiquitous in the Odinist world. Threats emanating from racialist Odinists have on occasion been directed at Ásatrúers as well. In 1989, a classic example of the latter involved Mike Murray of the Ásatrú Alliance several years ago; ironically enough, his transgression in this case was his overly "liberal" position on the subject of race. Murray, like McNallen before him, was in the unenviable position of trying to hold to a middle ground in which all views could be accommodated within the Alliance but the organization itself would not violate its by-laws by taking an official position. This pressure was played out in the pages of the Alliance journal *Vor Trú*, and more devastatingly, at Althing 9. Most revealing of the irrevocability of the split between Odinists and Ásatrúers, however—and of Murray's own task—is a series of letters published in the open forum of *Vor Trú*.

A key front in the contest between Odinism and Ásatrú is found in the prisons. Throughout the 1980s, Odinist centers have conducted—invariably at the request of the inmates themselves—an important outreach ministry in the prisons of America, competing with Christian Identity for the allegiance of white racialist prisoners. Ásatrú, however, is rarely mentioned in the prison context, and most Ásatrúers would have it no other way. It was therefore something of a surprise when Murray published in the pages of *Vor Trú* a letter from Kevin Hunt, a prisoner from Nebraska. The letter itself was remarkable in that it eschewed any but the most elliptical reference to race. It concentrated instead on an emotional paean to the gods, including the declaration that life in prison is "a constant battle, filled with pain and anger, sorrow and bitterness, but from the bonding of each brother of our kindred and the help from Ásatrú folk in the free world, we can find sanctuary from all this."[71] In his reply, Murray attempted to counter the strongly negative feelings aroused by prisoners among most Ásatrúers—an aversion that appears to center largely on radical expressions of racism and on the threat that these prisoners may present to the Ásatrú community upon release.

> These fellows are not a bunch of racist punks. They are sincerely trying to practice their ancestral faith within the walls of the prison. They hold regular gatherings where their families join them from the outside and hope to join the mainstream of the Ásatrú community after they have paid their debt to society. I believe they are worthy of our support and encouragement.[72]

If Kevin Hunt is no racist punk, the same could not be said for Dane, the self-styled spokesman for the Ram's Horn Kindred, the Tyr's Song Kindred, the Kindred Motorcycle Club, and the New York State Odinist Prisoners Alliance. Responding to an essay from Australian Kim Peart that stated that Viking society was in no sense racist and thus the Ásatrú community as well should be open to any race or previous faith,[73] Dane presented a succinct encapsulation of the Odinism of the Order's David Lane and of the most strongly racialist members of white Odinist prison groups. Of more immediate import, his letter illustrated in graphic terms how little middle ground there was between the more strongly racialist Odinists and even the most right wing strains of Ásatrú. The very fact that Peart's letter was published in *Vor Trú*, a journal seen with some justice as being heavily tied to the Arizona Kindred, is posited by Dane as evidence that the Alliance in general and the Arizona Kindred in particular are race traitors and should be subjected to a war of reprisal.

> our community has determined that our people have once again been misled and that the Arizona Kindred is promoting the corruption of our folk through bastardization, mongrelization and assimilation which is not only suicide but genocide; and that our communities must not only distance ourselves from the Alliance, but demand a Holy War, so to speak, so that the Alliance will remove the corrupters or discontinue referring to itself as Odinist.
>
> Our offense at his [Peart's] statements are such that were he a representative of a nation, we would declare war against such an insult . . . Perhaps he should more closely study the "Havamal" and the Eddas . . .

> We've been educating and gathering those who hear the call. You
> people get tired of fantasy island and pretending and heed the words of
> the High One—life is struggle, not fun and games. Awaken or perish.
> We serve Asgard.[74]

The letter—with its dire warnings of "corrupters" and "holy war,"
its reference to the primacy of sacred text, and its clear chiliastic aspirations—reads as something very much akin to texts emanating from the
radical wing of Christian Identity.[75] In his reply, Murray draws a distinc-
tion between Odinist values and those of Ásatrú. Beginning with a lec-
ture on the value of free speech and the role of *Vor Trú* in promoting
discourse within the community, Murray concludes:

> If Ásatrú is indeed the embodiment of freedom for our Folk, we
> should remain diligent and defend freedom of thought and expression
> in the pages of *Vor Trú*. Many of the most controversial letters and
> articles represent the thoughts of a very small minority of our readers,
> but yet the majority should be aware of what others who claim to be
> Ásatrú hold to be true.
> For the record, *Vor Trú* is a journal of Ásatrú. Never once in our
> pages have we stated that we are Odinist.[76]

Within the Odinist community itself, the justification for the resort
to force in defense of the race is encapsulated in David Lane's ubiquitous "14 words": "We must secure the existence of our people and a
future for white children."[77] With this formulation, the recourse to violence is both justified and encouraged. With the sole exception of the
Order, however, such violence has to date been episodic—the province
of Odinist skinheads indulging in street violence with little or no planning and less justification. Typical of this sort of random violence is one
incarcerated California skinhead who writes:

> You asked what I'm in for. Well I tried to force a baseball bat
> down a Jews [*sic*] face. I got 3 years for it. Then when I was in Folsom
> I stabbed a Rat so I've got to do the whole 3. I've got 10 months left
> . . . I've got to finish my time here in the hole too . . .
> Have you met any Skins before? . . .
> I am right now . . . the inventor of a little plan to try and bring the
> Skins who are into that Jew worshipping Christian crap out of it . . . I
> feel a person who calls himself a Christian & then claims White Power
> is a very confused person . . . Christianity has already put our race . . .
> in a gutter.[78]

This sort of random violence represents only a minority of the
movement, however. Other Odinist skinhead leaders call instead for ac-

tion and perseverance, noting the futility of impulsive street violence to effect real change and also that the government would like nothing better than to warehouse racialist fighters in the prisons of America. George Eric Hawthorne, the founder of the white power record label Resistance Records and publisher of the journal *Resistance,* voices just such an appeal in the Spring 1995 issue:

> These sort of attacks accomplish absolutely NOTHING, and have cost us hundreds of our best men who are currently rotting away in ZOG's dungeons because they lacked the foresight and direction necessary to act as revolutionaries instead of reactionaries. Beating some worthless mud to death is not an act of revolution, it is an act of poor judgment. The *Protocols of the Learned Elders of Zion,* which is the doctrine outlining ZOG's plan for global domination, says that our enemy can *count on the White man to sacrifice long term victory for short term satisfaction.* We must stop acting in accordance with their plans and start acting in accordance with our own LONG RANGE PLAN FOR WHITE REVOLUTION. This means staying out of jail whenever it is avoidable. Remember, this is a war and you are living behind enemy lines. Act accordingly.[79]

The incarcerated Order activist David Lane has similar dreams of a revolution imbued with the violence needed to cleanse the earth of the corruption he sees as inherent in modern multiracial society. Despite his connections with adherents of Christian Identity, Lane's Odinist writings provide the most clearly articulated Odinist theology of violence available. Moreover, based on his Order pedigree, Lane's writings are becoming ubiquitous throughout the milieu of the radical right, giving his pronouncements an authority that extends far beyond the narrow confines of the Odinist community. In Lane's strategic view,

> Resistance to tyranny within an occupied country necessarily forms into certain structures. Most basic is the division between the political or legal arm, and the armed party which I prefer to call Wotan as it is an excellent anagram for the will of the Aryan nation. The political arm is distinctly and rigidly separated from Wotan. The political arm will always be subjected to surveillance, scrutiny, harassment, and attempted infiltration by the system. Therefore the political arm must remain scrupulously legal within the parameters allowed by the occupying power. The function of the political arm is above all else to disseminate propaganda. The nature of effective propaganda is magnificently detailed in *Mein Kampf,* and condensed in [Lane's] *88 Precepts.* The political arm is a network and loose confederation of like minded individuals sharing a common goal.
>
> Wotan draws recruits from those educated by the political arm.

When a Wotan "goes active" he severs all apparent or provable ties with the political arm. If he has been so foolish as to obtain "membership" in such an organization, all records of such association must be destroyed or resignation submitted.

The goal of Wotan is clear. He must hasten the demise of the system before it totally destroys our gene pool. Some of his weapons are fire, bombs, guns, terror, disruption, and destruction. Weak points in the infrastructure of an industrialized society are primary targets. Individuals who perform valuable service for the system are primary targets. Special attention and merciless terror is visited upon those white men who commit race treason. Wotan has a totally revolutionary mentality. He has no loyalty to anyone or anything except his cause. Those who do not share his cause are expendable and those who oppose his cause are targets. Wotan is mature, capable, ruthless, self-motivated, silent, deadly, and able to blend into the masses. Wotan receives no recognition for his labors for if the folk knows his identity then soon the enemy will also. Wotan are small autonomous cells, one man cells if possible. No one, not wife, brother, parent or friend, knows the identity or actions of Wotan.[80]

Lane employs the imagery of Wotan as warrior and the revolutionary as Wotan—a god on earth. Such discourse is of a piece with metagenetic theory, which holds that the essence of the gods is inherent in the genes of the white race. It also fits well with the "leaderless resistance" concept of Louis Beam and with William Pierce's second novel *Hunter.* In the wake of the failure of the Order, there has been a general malaise in the revolutionary dreams of the racialist right that the images of the lone-wolf assassin, the solitary berserker, or the fictional heroes of the Phineas Priesthood have sought to fill. Gone even for Order veteran Lane is the certainty of a mass, popular revolutionary uprising along the lines of *The Turner Diaries.* Moreover, the dream of a white separatist homeland—which fired Robert Mathews and many others in the white supremacist world in the 1970s and 1980s—has faded as well. What is left is the life of the underground revolutionary, the man with no ties to society, no family or friends, only a grim purpose and an undying love for his dying race. Few men fit this description, but the dream is sufficiently alluring to attract a few would-be revolutionaries—and most of these, as George Eric Hawthorne points out, are locked up and forgotten in ZOG's prison system.

Lane's *88 Precepts,* like his "14 words," have become the common currency of the revolutionary right and are thus deserving of some attention. The precepts themselves recycle many of the same themes as Ben Klassen's Sixteen Commandments of Creativity. Indeed, Lane's focus on what he calls "Laws of Nature" so closely resembles the

Church of the Creator's ideology that he is compelled at times to explicitly separate himself from any connection to Creativity.[81]

Lane begins his list of precepts with the observation that Nature has immutable laws and that harmony and human happiness are best achieved by obedience to these laws. At the apex of nature's laws is the imperative to preserve the race (15). History, in his view, is a mere construct, as are deistic religions, whose promises of an afterlife were concocted purposely to minimize resistance to the evils of this world: "History, both secular and religious, is a fable conceived in self-serving deceit and promulgated by those who perceive benefits (6)."[82] The search for the deeply hidden truth, therefore, is the highest calling of the human race. Borrowing the Christian connotations of the term, Lane offers discernment as the greatest weapon that the seeker after truth may possess: "Discernment is a sign of a healthy people. In a sick or dying nation, civilization, culture, or race, substance is abandoned in favor of appearance" (16).

Although Lane advises against hatred for other races when members of those races have done nothing to harm the white race, he then offers a version of history that suggests that all other races in fact have in some way harmed the white race:

> The White Race has suffered invasions and brutality from Africa and Asia for thousands of years, for example, Attila and the Asiatic Huns who invaded Europe in the 5th century raping, plundering, and killing from the Alps to the Baltic and Caspian Seas. This scenario was repeated by the Mongols of Genghis Kahn 800 years later. (Note here that the American Indians are not "Native Americans," but are racial Asians.) In the 8th century, hundreds of years before the Crusades and 8 centuries before Blacks were brought to America, the North African Moors of mixed-racial background invaded and conquered Portugal, Spain, and part of France. So, the attempted guilt trip placed on the White Race by civilization's executioners is invalid under both historical circumstances and the Natural Law which denies inter-specie compassion. The fact is all races have benefited immeasurably from the creative genius of the Aryan people. (20)

How this historical scenario comports with the earlier assertion that all history is false is unexplained, but it serves at once to deny the postcolonial accusation that European civilization owes a debt to anyone and to assert that all races have profited from the "creative genius of the Aryan people." Here as elsewhere in the *88 Precepts,* however, race supersedes all other considerations. History, natural science, politics—all of these are subordinated to the concept of race.

Sexuality and the social organization of the white race is of considerable concern to Lane's *88 Precepts*.

34. The instinct for sexual union is part of Nature's perfect mechanism for specie preservation. It must not be repressed; and its purpose namely reproduction, must not be thwarted either. Understand, that for thousands of years, our females bore children at an early age. Now, in an attempt to conform to, and compete in, an alien culture, they deny their Nature-ordained instincts and duties. Teach responsibility, but, also have understanding. The life of a race springs from the wombs of its women. He who would judge must first understand the difference between what is good and what is right.

35. Homosexuality is a crime against Nature. All Nature declares the purpose of the instinct for sexual union is reproduction and, thus, preservation of the specie. Homosexuality does not reproduce or preserve the specie. It is unnatural and, therefore, a suicidal perversion.

36. Sexual pornography degrades the Nature of all who are involved. The woman is reduced to an object and sex to animal coupling.

37. That race whose males will not fight to the death to keep and mate with its females will perish. Any White man with healthy instincts feels disgust and revulsion when he sees a woman of his race with a man of another race. Those who today control the media and affairs of the Western World, teach that this is wrong and shameful. They label it "racism." As any "ism;" for instance the word "nationalism," means you promote your nation, racism merely means you promote and protect the life of your race. It is, perhaps, the proudest word in existence. Any man who disobeys these instincts is anti-Nature.

Lane then turns to the political system, analyzing democracy as transitory and all leaders as tyrants, before turning to a discussion of the nature and utility of propaganda. It is here that Lane's own bitter experience comes through most clearly: "The patriot, being led to the inquisition's dungeons or the executioner's axe, will be condemned the loudest by his former friends and allies; for thus they seek to escape the same fate" (60). Lane concludes his discussion with a call for vigilance:

88. These are sure signs of a sick or dying Nation. If you seek any of them, your guardians are committing treason: 1) mixing and destruction of the founding race; 2) destruction of the family units; 3) oppressive taxation; 4) corruption of the Law; 5) terror and suppression against those who warn of the Nation's error; 6) immorality: drugs, drunkenness, etc.; 7) infanticide (now called abortion); 8) destruction of the currency (inflation or usury); 9) aliens in the land; 10) materialism; 11) foreign wars; 12) guardians (leaders) who pursue

wealth or glory; 13) homosexuality; 14) alien culture; 15) religion not based on Natural Law.

Of course, none of these signs is hard to find in this—or in any—age. Having discerned these signs of social decay, what choice does the race warrior have but to strike back? Given the strategic situation, he must at present do so as a lone wolf. Any association or larger group will be too risky, given the omnipresence of ZOG. To those who have decided to take the lonely course of the Wotan, Lane's advice is succinct.

Death to Traitors

In particular, if you are a white male who commits race treason, the day is coming when you will be visited by Wotan. Your demise will be unpleasant.

Judges, lawyers, bankers, real estate agents, judeo-christian preachers, federal agents, and other assorted treasonous swine take note, Wotan is coming. Your wealth, your homes, your women, and your lives are at risk when you commit treason. Pray that you die quickly. One day Wotan will feed your repulsive carcasses to the vultures and bury your bones under outhouses that our folk may forever pay fitting tribute to your memory. That day is called "Ragnarok."[83]

4

The B'nai Noah

Thus says the Lord of Hosts: In those days ten men, out of all languages of the nations, shall take a hold of the robe of him who is a Jew, saying, Let us go with you, for we have heard that God is with you.

—Zechariah 8:23

The inclusion of the philo-Semitic B'nai Noah or Children of Noah may at first glance seem incongruous in a book devoted largely to racialist and anti-Semitic belief systems. This problem was briefly addressed in chapter 1, with the introduction of the B'nai Noah community and the discussion of the mirror-image ideological resemblances between the B'nai Noah and Identity Christianity. Moreover, the interactions between the B'nai Noah and the other members of the American millennial community once again suggest the existence of a cultic milieu beneath these millennialist groups, taking Colin Campbell's formulation beyond its original application to deviant religious groups. To illustrate this point, we may consider briefly some further affinities between the B'nai Noah and the Christian Identity movement.

The B'nai Noah community is in reality no less radically contra-acculturative within their own families and communities than are the most outspoken of racialist millenarians. With respect to the latter, an outside observer might expect that Christian Identity believers would not be surprised to find themselves excluded to a great degree from the surrounding culture. Such rejection, however, always seems to catch Identity adherents unprepared.[1] Similarly, it seems to come as an even greater shock to the B'nai Noah that they too have been excluded from the communities in which they were once influential pillars. This is especially true of those adherents—J. David Davis, Jack Saunders, and Vendyl Jones most notably—who as fundamentalist Protestant ministers were once considered community leaders in small, closely knit southern towns.[2] Even some of those B'nai Noah who have not taken high profile positions, however, have found themselves isolated and excluded, and have discovered that even their children have lost friends.[3]

At the same time, like the racialist adherents of Christian Identity, the behavior of some B'nai Noah has often been intentionally scandalous. Intentionally scandalous behavior is not only typical of sectarian movements but is a defining feature of fundamentalism as a global religious phenomenon as well. Indeed, the sociologist Rodney Stark has suggested that for a new religious movement to survive, it must maintain a delicate balance between behavior that is sufficiently scandalous to differentiate itself from the mainstream religious community (and thus to attract members) but not so scandalous or esoteric that it becomes notorious and thus is unable to either expand or to retain its following.[4] For the B'nai Noah, such behavior commenced with the removal from church buildings of such symbols of communal normality as steeples, crosses, and the like, and deepened with the penetration of a doctrine—the de-divinization of Jesus—seen as heretical at best or satanic at worst by the community. All of this was capped by a flow of strangers, including Jewish rabbis and Hassidic teachers, into towns that never before had actually seen a Jew in person.[5] Forays by journalists bringing unwanted publicity into the lives of people who have historically prided themselves on their ability to solve problems within the family and the community added further tension to the situation. Little wonder, then, that missives such as the following have appeared with some regularity in the movement's literature:

> We have been told that we have been deceived by the devil and are probably demon possessed ourselves. People are warned not to talk to us, for if they do they will go away believing the way we do. We somehow are able to cast some mysterious spell and alter the way people believe. I realize that we live in the twentieth century, but from some of the things people have been reported to have said I think we have slipped back into the dark ages, or at least to the times of the Salem Witch hunts in which numerous innocent people were tortured or killed.[6]

> Dear David [Davis] and Fellow Noahides, Greetings from the Noahide community in Amarillo, Texas. We would like to take the opportunity to thank your group in Athens for including our group . . . in your weekly studies from the Torah, via speaker phone hook-up. Turning from pagan Christianity to the one and only God of Israel has left us isolated, alone, without much fellowship (as you can well understand) from being active in any spiritual way with our former "Christian" brethren.[7]

It is fortunate that the B'nai Noah have thus far not been the targets of violence in their communities or from outsiders. Their contra-accul-turative stance has in fact caused some splits in the families of ad-herents,[8] at the same time as their outspoken embrace of the Jews, publicized through an active media outreach,[9] has attracted the atten-tion not only of adherents of Christian Identity but of other elements of the American racist right. The lightening rod for the movement, J. David Davis, has indeed been called names,[10] received a good deal of racist and anti-Semitic literature, and reportedly even received some death threats on his answering machine. Davis, however, underplays the volume or importance of these.[11]

Apparently, several B'nai Noah have received hate literature through the mail. The material sent to Davis was clearly not a product of Chris-tian Identity; rather, it seems to have originated with Joe Dilys of Chi-cago. Dilys, a long-time racist loosely associated with neo-Nazism, is eclectic in his racist affiliations. He is memorable for his most famous quote: "The synagogue is an embassy of Hell. Every Rabbi is an ambas-sador of Lucifer." The material received by Davis included the anti-Semitic newspaper *The Truth At Last;* literature from the Institute for Historical Review, a Holocaust revisionist group; and various neo-Nazi publications, including an issue of William Pierce's National Alliance organ, the *National Vanguard,* emphasizing Jewish control of the Amer-ican media and including sheets of racist cartoons from the SS Action Group in Dearborn, Michigan and racist jokes from the National White People's Party of Tifton, Georgia. Perhaps the most unusual additions to this collection of arcania are two documents published by the Remain Intact "ORGAN"ization (emphasis in original)—a group in Larch-wood, Iowa, headed by Russell Zangger, which is dedicated to ending the practice of infant circumcision. Remain Intact provides graphic drawings and emotional prose to drive home its point.

More important than these postal bouquets are the reactions of friends and families to the adoption of Noahide beliefs. This isolation from the mainstream of the Christian community on the part of both the B'nai Noah and Christian Identity has led both groups to respond with a virtually identical rejection of mainstream Christianity. For both, the belief that modern Christianity not only derives from Judaic roots but in essence has become an unnecessary and illegitimate belief system stems again from a similar hermeneutic approach to scripture and an almost identical interpretation of history. For example, James Tabor, a trained specialist in early Christianity at the University of North Caro-lina, became interested in the Noahide movement through his academic field. He had developed the theory (based partly on Acts 15) that Paul was trying to form a messianic Noahide movement led by James, brother of Jesus.[12] Tabor writes:

> Classic Christianity, as it developed from the late 1st century CE onward, is far, far removed from the true Biblical Faith. *To put it simply, Christianity is not the ancient path. It is a new, almost wholly pagan, Hellenistic, quasi-Gnostic, amalgamation . . .*
> *The Christians lost touch with the Hebrew language and modes of thought, and with the long and fruitful history of rabbinic exegesis and understanding of Scripture . . . The Hebraic roots of the movement were totally severed.*
> To those with eyes to see, Christianity became "mystery Babylon the Great," incorporating into one great unified system Western Paganism and Greek rationalism.[13]

Further,

> Early gentile "Christianity," might be more accurately classified as a B'nai Noah movement, *despite the later heretical developments within Christianity which made Jesus a second deity.* B'nai Noah . . . instructs gentiles to turn directly to the One God as He is revealed in the pages of Scriptures. This is clearly reflected in Acts 15 and Paul's instructions to his gentile converts in letters like *1 Corinthians* (see chapters 5–10) and *1 Thessalonians 1:9* states ". . . how ye turned to God from idols to serve the living and true God." He instructs the gentiles on the seven Noahide Laws. These were made binding on the gentiles by none other than Jacob (James), brother of Jesus, and leader of the Nazarine Sect. They were among the "God-fearers."[14]

Similarly, for the adherents of Christian Identity, Judeo-Christianity is a contemptuous term for the current perceived Jewish subversion and conquest of mainstream Christianity. According to Dan Gayman:

> In order for you to understand why America is being captured from within and is making no resistance to the barbarian hordes attacking us from without, you must walk inside the modern church, and you must examine what is being taught from the pulpits . . . Only when you have examined these Fables from the ancient darkness of the *Jewish Babylonian Talmud* can you begin to understand why a nation of more than two hundred million people will allow their country to be taken from them, their Christian heritage trampled underfoot, their children destroyed . . . The blame lies with those preaching Jewish Fables in the modern churches of America and the western world, and we must go inside these churches and expose lie upon lie, fable upon fable, and let the TRUTH of Jesus Christ and the Word of God expose

the Jewish Fables for what they really are . . . *the preachment of Satan and his children the Jews.*[15]

It is a short step from a feeling that Christianity as it is practiced in the modern world has somehow gone wrong to a finding that the problem lies not as much with the contemporary church as it does with events in the formative stages of Christianity; thus the Identity demonization of the Jew and the B'nai Noah rejection of "Hellenized" Christianity.[16]

Finally, it is in the effort to enlist allies and to combat enemies that the dimensions of the millennial/messianic community can best be seen. Both sets of adherents, despite their dreams of future growth, are well aware of their minority status and are acutely conscious of their isolation and unpopularity within their respective religious and geographical communities. Thus, a great deal of effort must be put into cementing alliances and defending against attacks. Christian Identity has something of an advantage over the B'nai Noah in this regard because they function within a wider constellation of white supremacist groups. Within this fluid constellation of belief systems, patterns of alliance can be detected on both the leadership and ideological levels. In terms of leadership, serial and concurrent allegiances are common among Identity leaders. For example, Tom Metzger has drifted from Christian Identity to the Ku Klux Klan to neo-Nazi beliefs, before at last settling on his own group, the White Aryan Resistance (WAR). Going in the opposite direction, Ralph Forbes, a would-be candidate for office in Arkansas at the head of the New America First Party, began his career in George Lincoln Rockwell's American Nazi Party and, following a drift through various radical right groupings, now sees himself as a Christian Identity pastor. However, Christian Identity has had little success in building alliances with the wider culture. In fact, despite some efforts at taking the concerns of Christian Identity adherents to elected officials[17] and to the general public, Identity Christianity remains largely unknown to most Americans.

The B'nai Noah find themselves in a considerably more isolated position than does Christian Identity. Unlike Identity, whose racial ideology serves to build alliances among groups and individuals who have little interest in Kingdom theology, the B'nai Noah have no natural outside constituency for their message. Therefore, they must rely on support from the Jewish community just as they depend on the rabbinate for education and for guidance. This effort, however, is proving to be somewhat more problematic than would appear on first glance. The Jewish community is itself fragmented along ideological lines, and the B'nai Noah have become somewhat enmeshed in these conflicts.

It is important to note that the relationship between the B'nai Noah and the Jewish community has developed at the initiative of the B'nai Noah themselves. A prominent exception to this rule was the case of Rabbi Israel Chait. Rabbi Chait traces his involvement to the day in March 1991 when he read a *Wall Street Journal* article publicizing David Davis and the B'nai Noah. Seeing a gentile who truly understood that the wisdom of Torah is for all people and who further recognized that Christianity is a form of paganism and thus idolatry, Rabbi Chait felt the need to contact him, as did three of Rabbi Chait's students.[18] This instance of contact being initiated by Jews remains exceptional, however. Usually, the B'nai Noah's courtship of the Jewish community has been no easy task, and the effort has taken a variety of forms. Once a relationship is formed, however, the B'nai Noah largely subordinate themselves to the direction of the Jewish rabbinical authorities. At the same time, there are clearly limits to this control; rabbinical leadership is influential but in the last analysis purely advisory.[19]

The effort to enlist Jewish support began in earnest in the mid-1980s and involved two major outreach efforts: towards the Lubavitcher movement on the one hand, and on the other, towards local Orthodox rabbis. These efforts had by 1989 achieved sufficient success to suggest greater possibilities to the B'nai Noah and to their rabbinic teachers. In that year, Vendyl Jones took the lead in organizing the First Annual International Conference of B'nai Noah, which was duly held in Fort Worth, Texas, during 28–30 April 1990. It was at this conference that the local Noahide groups coalesced to form an international movement, the Agudat Karem B'nai No'ach (Union of the Vineyard of the Children of Noah), which asked for and received the blessing—and official sanction—of the Chief Sephardi Rabbi of Israel, Mordechai Eliahu.[20]

The initiative towards the Chief Rabbinate seems to have occasioned some internal controversy in B'nai Noah circles. In opposition, Rabbi Michael Katz was a strong advocate of trying to connect the B'nai Noah with elements of the Heredi community (ultra-Orthodox Jews)—particularly with Agudat Israel and perhaps with Mizrachi as well.[21] Rabbi Katz's calculation was shrewdly political; in his view, the institution of the Chief Rabbinate had become so scarred by a long history of compromise and scandal that a B'nai Noah alliance with the Chief Rabbis would preclude a far more intellectually and spiritually rewarding alliance with the Heredim. David Davis chose to disregard this advice, apparently impressed with the institutional weight of the Chief Rabbinate and perhaps calculating that the Heredi parties would sooner reconcile themselves to the B'nai Noah connection with the Chief Rabbis than would the Chief Rabbinate to an exclusive B'nai Noah/Heredim alliance.

The alliance forged by the B'nai Noah with Rabbi Chaim Richman, director of public affairs for the Temple Institute in Jerusalem, was considered in Chapter 1. The Institute believes that, by fashioning the implements of priestly Temple service according to exact halachic specifications and by finding the ashes of the perfectly created red heifer for sacrifice as demanded in Jewish law for the reconsecration of the Temple, they are in fact rebuilding the Temple. God will then complete the job, in a manner which the Institute does not care to specify.[22] Tabor asserts that the Temple Institute is happy with the B'nai Noah because the latter's existence allows the Institute to deal with gentiles without compromising their ideals; for their part, the B'nai Noah have warned the Institute members to beware of fundamentalists because "they want the Temple rebuilt so they can have another holocaust."[23]

At the same time, not all B'nai Noah adherents nor all of their rabbinical advisors are entirely pleased with the association of the group with the Temple movement. Off the record, some express reservations ranging from the potential of this alliance to alienate other (particularly Heredi) sectors of Jewish opinion to the distasteful nature of the animal sacrifices required in a revived Temple cult—a process which one noted contemporary scholar, Jacob Neusner, has described as "a holy barbecue . . . [which] many Jews today would see [as] repulsive."[24]

It is with this internal view of the adherents of the Noahide movement—that they are at once a sign and an agent of the Last Days—that the major divergence of the millenarian/messianic aspects of the B'nai Noah with those of Christian Identity occurs. Most Christian Identity adherents view themselves merely as potential survivors of the Tribulation, whose mission is to hold true to their identification with biblical Israel and to persevere through the imminent horrors of the End Times so as to be able to see with their own eyes the glory of the parousia. No formulation of Identity doctrine posits Kingdom believers as in themselves constituting a sign that the End of Days is upon us. This, however, is precisely the self-view of the B'nai Noah, a deeper understanding of which requires that the B'nai Noah's theology be addressed.

Theology and Messianism

The creedal statement of the contemporary B'nai Noah centers entirely upon the movement's adherence to the seven Noahide commandments: the establishment of courts of justice and the prohibitions against blasphemy, idolatry, sexual sins, murder, theft, and eating the limb of a living creature. Evolving from that deceptively simple framework, however, is an emerging theology which is remarkably complex.

This philosophical depth may be attributed to the contributions of such scholarly adherents as James Tabor as well as of the core of rabbinical authorities who have become associated with the movement. To fully appreciate the religious message of the B'nai Noah, it is necessary to consider the movement's perception both of its earliest roots in the New Testament period and of its reemergence in modern times.

The historical development of the Noahide laws are a matter of some controversy. It is commonly agreed that the term itself refers to a set of seven commandments said to have been revealed by God to Noah, based on a juxtaposition of the covenant entered into by God with Noah in Genesis 9 and the earlier Adamic covenant of Genesis 2:16–17. Clearly, possible esoteric interpretations aside, the convergence of the Adamic and Noahide covenants yield only two definite commandments: a ban on murder and certain dietary restrictions. Nevertheless, the two covenants were merged in the Talmudic literature (Sanhedrin 56–60 and Yoma 67b) into a set of seven commandments which came to be known as the Noahide laws.[25] So well accepted did this formulation become that by the Middle Ages, Maimonides could confidently assert:

> Six precepts were given to Adam: prohibition of idolatry, of blasphemy, of murder, of adultery, of robbery, and the command to establish courts of justice. Although there is a tradition to this effect—a tradition dating back to Moses, our teacher, and human reason approves of those precepts—*it is evident from the general tenor of Scriptures* [emphasis mine] that he (Adam) was bidden to observe these commandments. An additional commandment was given to Noah: prohibition of (eating) a limb from a living animal.[26]

Unremarkable in themselves, these commandments may have been a source of polemical contention between the Jews and the gentiles as early as the debates held under the auspices of the Emperor Julian (361–363 C.E.).[27] The basis of this heated contention appears to be less the commandments themselves than the universal application of the law envisioned by the rabbis of the day. This polemic, from the Jewish perspective, held that although the Torah and the 613 halachic laws were incumbent only upon the Jewish people, the seven Noahide laws constitute a minimal compact, obedience to which is binding upon the "children of Noah," the gentiles, as well as upon the Jews.

The first literary source of which we are aware, and the basis for later Mishnaic and Talmudic consideration of the Noahide laws, is found in the Tosefta (supplement), a collection of pharisaic and Mishnaic-era traditions that were not included in the Mishnah:[28]

> Seven commandments were the sons of Noah commanded: (1) concerning adjudication (*dinim*), (2) and concerning idolatry (*abodah zarah*), (3) and concerning blasphemy (*gilelat Ha-Shem*), (4) and concerning sexual immorality (*giluy arayot*), (5) and concerning bloodshed (*shefikhut damim*), (6) and concerning robbery (*ha-gezel*), (7) and concerning a limb torn from a living animal (*eber min ha-hy*).[29]

Tract Sanhedrin of the Babylonian Talmud[30] points to the difficulty of taking in isolation any particular doctrinal tenet from this convoluted body of rabbinical opinion. While the commentators in Tract Sanhedrin agree in general on a seven-fold law as binding upon the children of Noah, they are in some disagreement as to what the pertinent seven commandments should be:

> The rabbis taught: Seven commandments were given to the children of Noah, and they are: Concerning judges, blasphemy, idolatry, adultery, bloodshed, robbery, and that they must not eat of the member of the body while the animal is still alive. Rabbi Hananiah b. Gamaliel said: Also the blood of the same. Rabbi Hidka said: Also castration is forbidden to them. Rabbi Simeon said: Also witchcraft. And Rabbi Jose said: All that is forbidden to them in the portion on witchcraft [Deut. 18:10–12] shall be forbidden to a descendant of Noah.[31]

In addition, these sources are in considerable disagreement as to the proper order of the Noahide laws.[32]

Whatever the precise list of seven commandments, the key questions from the Christian perspective concerned the application of the death penalty to the gentiles and the composition of the courts mandated for the enforcement of the Noahide code. Again, the Babylonian Talmud is anything but clear. On the question of whose courts will be competent to try a son of Noah, the sources are contradictory. Rabbi Ahu b. Jacob holds that "just as the Israelites were ordered to set up law courts in every district and town, so were the sons of Noah likewise enjoined to set up law courts in every district and town."[33] A consensus does emerge, however, holding with Rabbi Johanan that "it makes no difference in which court he should be tried."[34]

The contemporary observer of this legal argument will be excused for the perception of an air of unreality surrounding the entire debate. One respected contemporary halachic authority argues that "in the Jewish Commonwealth, separate judiciaries were established: one exercised jurisdiction over the Jewish populace and administered Jewish law while the other sat in judgment upon non-Jewish nationals and rendered justice in accordance with the provisions of the Noahide Code."[35] The problem with this formulation, however, is that the Noahide code appears to postdate the Commonwealth considerably. The same argument must be made in response to theories suggesting that the brief reign of the Hasmonians (c. 140–63 C.E.) may have occasioned the imposition of Noahide law.[36] If indeed the Noahide code was never enacted on a practical level, what are we to make of the detailed rabbinical debate as to the establishment of courts, rules of evidence, and problems of jurisdiction and competence? It is impossible to answer to this question with any certainty, but it would appear that there were two major practical effects of the Noahide debate. In the short term, the Noahide controversy served to regulate the internal communal aspects of Jewish interaction with non-Jews.[37] Second, it is possible that the commentators engaged in the debate not as a matter of sterile academic disputation but as a source of legal precedent for a future in which the Noahide Covenant could be implemented—i.e., for the messianic era to come.

Such an interpretation could explain the merely sporadic attention given to the particulars of the Noahide code over the centuries, especially when contrasted to the considerable attention given the question of imposing a court system on the children of Noah by Maimonides and other medieval sources.[38] Moreover, it would be difficult to posit a hypothesis holding for a practical application of the Noahide laws that would account for the impossible rules of evidence or for the complete impotence of the Jews to establish a court system that would be binding even on the Jewish community itself, much less on a gentile population.[39] Maimonides held that the Jewish courts were indeed enjoined to appoint judges over the population of resident aliens under their authority, while Noahides not under Jewish control are nonetheless obligated to appoint judges over themselves to enforce the remaining six Noahide commandments.[40] Maimonides, however, was well aware that in the premessianic era, Jews could do nothing either to establish courts or to enforce in any way the Noahide code on a recalcitrant population.[41] Even the rulings enjoining the appointment of judges were offered in the context of a commentary on the dire retribution taken by the sons of Jacob in response to the rape (or seduction) of Dinah (Gen. 34).[42]

The death penalty for transgression of the Noahide laws is another point that is central to the Noahide controversy. It is clear that the consensus of the rabbinical authorities does indeed hold that death must be meted out to anyone violating at least some of the Noahide commandments (although again, the sources disagree on precisely which of the laws should be at all times and in all places capital crimes):[43]

Rabbi Ya'akov bar Aha found in Sefer Aggadeta deVei Rav: "A descendant of Noah may be put to death on [the ruling of] one witness, without formal preliminary warning [that his crime is a capital offense]. The witness must be a male but may be a relative." In the name of Rabbi Ishmael, it is said "[a] descendant of Noah may be put to death for feticide as well."[44]

The sources also disagree on the method of execution, with some holding for strangulation and others for decapitation.[45]

For Maimonides, the theoretical punishment for transgression of any of the six prohibitions of the Noahide code is—with some exceptions made for exculpatory circumstances—death.[46] Moreover, the primary justification for the behavior of the sons of Jacob in reprisal for the unfortunate experience of Dinah was the failure of the men of Shechem (Hivites) to establish a court to try Shechem for his transgression.[47] Additionally, Maimonides makes clear that the application of the death penalty is different for Jews and for Noahides, with Noahide crimes held to be capital offenses in far more instances than those of the Jews, even when the offenses are similar.[48] Maimonidin praxis is once again fraught with exceptions:

> A Noahide who inadvertently violates any of the commandments is exempt from all punishment . . .[49]
> A Noahide who is coerced by a man of violence to transgress any of the commandments mandatory upon him, may transgress it. Even if he is forced to worship idolatry, he may do it, because Noahides are not commanded to sanctify the Name (of God).[50]

Thus, the sources leave us with a detailed collection of rulings mandating death for a range of transgressions and insisting on the power of Jewish courts (or of gentile courts under Jewish control) to enforce these rulings. However, practical safeguards render the entire corpus of statutes effectively moot.

Although the coming of the Jewish Enlightenment in the eighteenth century and the steady inroads of secularization and assimilation into the surrounding gentile society caused the Noahide code to become less important for the emergent *maskilim* (enlighteners), the code demonstrably remained a serious topic for scholarly discussion—and not only in the yeshivas of the Orthodox. One recent commentator traces the Noahide debate from its Talmudic origins through the medieval commentators to such influential contemporary figures as Rabbi Abraham Isaac Kook, the first Chief Rabbi of mandatory Palestine, and the late Lubavitcher Rebbe Manachem Schneerson.[51] The spiritual father of the modern B'nai Noah movement, however, is Rabbi Elijah Benamozegh of Leghorn, Italy (1823–1900). Although his theology in some ways resembles that of Rabbi Kook, for Rabbi Benamozegh the Noahide laws formed a primary basis of his teaching, and it was around him that the first group of Christian Noahides formed. So close was this embrace that the first edition of his massive manuscript "Israel and Humanity" was edited in 1914 by Aimé Pallière, the Noahide whose own book *The Unknown Sanctuary: A Pilgrimage From Rome to Israel* would influence the contemporary B'nai Noah.

Rabbi Benamozegh's legacy is built on the twin foundations of his immersion in the mysticism of Kabbala and of his reading of halacha (Jewish law)—at least insofar as halacha concerns the interrelationship of the Mosaic and Noahide codes. What emerged from this marriage of the transcendent and the legalistic was a vision of Judaism as a universal religion whose appointed role in these premessianic times is to serve as a kind of priesthood for the nations:

> For Judaism, the world is like a great family, where the father lives in immediate contact with his children who are the different peoples of the earth. Among these children there is a firstborn, who in conformity with ancient institutions, was the priest of the family . . . Such is the Jewish conception of the world. In heaven a single God, father of all men alike; on earth a family of peoples, among whom Israel is the "firstborn," charged with teaching and administering the true religion of mankind, of which he is priest. The "true religion" is the Law of Noah. It is the one which the human race will embrace in the days of the Messiah, and which Israel's mission is to preserve and propagate meanwhile.[52]

According to Benamozegh, the Jewish people have performed this role for all of their long history. Thus, the historicity of the God-fearers is unquestioned,[53] and the creation of a loosely formed Noahide community under Aimé Pallière is seen as but the latest manifestation of this age-old phenomenon. Yet Benamozegh's learning went far beyond the confines of Jewish scholarship; he read widely in the European intellectual currents of his day, and he was thus quite aware of the anti-Semitic thought which was very much in vogue in some circles. It is probably with this in mind that he wrestles with some of the less sanguine implications of the priestly role of the Jews. Holding that the Jews were a "servant people" for whom the domination of other peoples would be alien, Benamozegh states:

> To be sure, at certain periods Jews have indeed nourished chimerical hopes of universal domination, but Judaism is not responsible for these patriotic dreams. Rather, it is the dreams which imply the existence of more reasonable doctrine, one so elevated that it was bound to degenerate, among the less refined spirits, into something more flattering to the national pride.[54]

With this apologia, Rabbi Benamozegh begins his discussion of the Noahide code itself. Although he is willing to accept seven as the number of commandments, he holds (with the majority of commentators) that within this basic corpus there is a vast range of related obligations. In addition, the Noahide could voluntarily choose to obey any of the remaining 613 Mosaic laws incumbent on the children of Israel. Moreover, until the destruction of the Temple and the Diaspora, courts of law did exist under Jewish control to enforce the law on the Noahides. Associationalism—the association of other divine beings with God—would be permitted the Noahide. He or she is therefore free to venerate Jesus or the saints, so long as this worship does not compromise the Noahide's commitment to monotheism. With respect to the prohibition of murder, Benamozegh holds that although ignorance of the law is an acceptable defense for the Jew, the Noahide is obligated to learn of the code and of the penalty of death for the transgression of this and other of the laws of Noah. (Murder is in this conception so broadly defined that it include abortion and euthanasia.) Conversely, the laws relating to sexual sins are more liberal for the Noahide than for the Jew, with marriage forbidden only with the natural sister, mother-in-law, and mother, and with homosexuality prohibited in all cases.[55]

Rabbi Benamozegh is unlikely to have influenced the contemporary B'nai Noah movement directly, as his work appeared in English only in 1995. Before that, he was known only through Aaron Lichtenstein's *The Seven Laws of Noah* (which includes one of Benamozegh's letters to Pallière) and through the *Encyclopedia Judaica*. Indeed, Rabbi Benamozegh is largely a forgotten figure in the world of nineteenth-century Jewish scholarship. In a manner rather reminiscent of Rabbi Abraham Isaac Kook, the reasons for this may involve his powerful universalist theology which, deeply informed by Kabbalistic mysticism, falls between Judaism's deeply held ethnic particularism and the indifference of the non-Jewish world. In the question of the respective rabbis' intellectual legacy, however, the similarity ends. For Rabbi Benamozegh, the reverence for his thought deeply held by such contemporaneous Noahides as Pallière and the circle around him, and the opportunity for a new generation of B'nai Noah to come to know his thought through the new Paulist Press edition, may assure the survival of his spirit of universalism. Rabbi Kook may not be so fortunate. After a period of eclipse, his legacy fell on his son, Rabbi Tzvi Yehuda Kook, and was transformed into a fundamentalist theology centered primarily on the sacrality of the full Land of Israel. Thus was born the Israeli settlement movement, Gush Emunim, from the circle of the younger Kook's followers at his yeshiva, Mercaz Herav.[56]

Since the days of Maimonides, then, the Noahide Laws have not fared well in the consciousness of the majority of Jews. The process by which a central strand of religious belief is lost by all but the most austere guardians of the tradition is common enough, although any explanation for the survival of some elements of a tradition and the loss of other, once-vital tenets must be speculative at best. Perhaps the most adequate hypothesis, at least for the Abrahamic traditions, centers on the availability to the adherent of inerrant text supported by authoritative exegetical material. For the Noahide debate, this seems to be the key factor. The Old Testament mentions the Noahide covenant only in Genesis 9, where God specifically commands mankind to obey only two prohibitions, that forbidding murder and a dietary restriction on the eating of an animal still containing blood. This is reprised in the New Testament (Acts 15:20, 29) by three prohibitions (idolatry, sexual impurity, and dietary restrictions), which brought the Noahides into subsequent Christian discourse.[57] The rest of Noahide law—including the dread penalty for disobedience—enjoys no such foundation in inerrant text. With the modern day diminution of the authority of these religious virtuosi, the Noahide code gradually came to be lost to all but the most devoted cadre of followers of rabbinical teachings.

A contemporary rabbi deemed by many to be the greatest Talmudist of the modern age, Rabbi Joseph Dov Soloveitchik, illustrates the controversy from the perspective of modern Yeshiva orthodoxy:

> Rabbinic interpretation of the Covenant made with Noah (Gen. 9) deduces the seven Noahide Laws whose observance is obligatory for all gentiles, while the Jew is enjoined to fulfill a more stringent and demanding discipline. Gentiles governed by those seven laws are judged worthy of eternal life.[58]

On the Christian side of the debate, there does not appear to have been great concern with the Noahide question. The Pseudepigrapha, for example, retains only two mentions of the Noahide covenant,[59] both faithful to the Genesis 9 formulations. The concept of the Noahide covenant itself does not seem to have figured prominently in the thinking of the early fathers of the Church. Nor did it have the same resonance among the medieval authorities as it enjoyed in the thought of Maimonides; rather, the attention of Christian authorities was given to apocalyptic speculations in which the biblical deluge marked an important epoch. For the great Calabrian abbot Joachim of Fiore (d. 1202), for example,

> Saint Augustine, when he discussed the ages in *The City of God,* said that there was one age from Adam to Noah, another age from Noah to Abraham. When he said this, he added: "Not because the second age

has the same number of years as the first, but because it has the same number of generations," These *tempora,* therefore, ought not to be reckoned according to their number of years but according to their generations.[60]

In Jewish terms, Joachim used the Noahide Covenant to "count the end."

In the post-Enlightenment period, the Noahide covenant would arouse renewed interest among those Protestant theologians concerned with using the Bible to divide history into a series of dispensations, leading up to the parousia. The earliest formulation of dispensationalist theory, mostly concerned with the Adamic covenant, was a minority trend in seventeenth-century Dutch Pietism championed by a Leyden professor of theology named Johannes Coccieus (d. 1669). Coccieus, remembered (if at all) as the father of Federal Theology, argued for the then-novel position that the system of grace pervades the Old as well as the New Testament, and gave dispensationalist theory much of its modern form.[61]

Modern dispensationalism is credited to the founder of the Plymouth Brethren, the British cleric John Nelson Darby (d. 1882). Darby divided history into a series of seven consecutive dispensations, a framework accepted in turn by Dwight L. Moody, William E. Blackstone, and C. I. Scofield. These dispensations are: 1) Age of Innocence (Eden to the Fall); 2) Age of Conscience (Fall to the Flood); 3) Age of Human Governance (Noahide Covenant); 4) Age of Promise (Abrahamic Covenant); 5) Age of Law (Mosaic Covenant); 6) Age of Grace (Covenant established through Christ); and 7) The Millennium.[62] Each successive covenant is seen by dispensationalists as having been abrogated through man's disobedience; the final act of disobedience is posited as ending the Age of Grace and ushering in the horrors of the apocalypse. The *Scofield Reference Bible,* first published in 1909 and later updated in 1967, was the most important event in the dissemination of dispensationalist beliefs.[63] Left unsolved in dispensational theology is the problem that, even though the Noahide covenant is known as human government, few specifics are offered as to the precise nature of the law which is to govern the Third Dispensation.

The scant attention given by modern Christian sources to the Noahide code makes the story of the most immediate Christian precursor of the current B'nai Noah all the more remarkable. This was the French Catholic convert to Noahidism, Aimé Pallière (1875–1949). Pallière's spiritual evolution began with an intense Catholicism, progressed to a strong attraction to Judaism, and detoured to the Salvation Army, before being introduced to the concept of Noahidism by Rabbi Benamozegh.[64] The "movement" begun by Pallière—in fact more an ecumenical discussion group than a movement—bears some resemblance to the current efforts of the B'nai Noah. Like the latter movement, the early publications of Pallière's group and their well-advertised public discussions attracted the welcome attentions of the popular press, and letters began to pour in from around the world.[65] There was also the same highly intellectual approach to the subject, prominently featuring Hebrew language study, along with great doctrinal flexibility, allowing each adherent to take from Judaism—beyond the seven laws—whatever he or she may wish. Finally, both groups come to the identical historical conclusion: Christianity is merely a form of messianic Judaism that, purged of Hellenistic thought, would return to the pure Hebraism which Pallière conceived to be the essence of modern Judaism.

At the same time, one difference is worth noting. Pallière and his circle came from Catholic backgrounds—indeed, at least one adherent, Pére Hyacinth, was a Catholic priest. By contrast, most of the current American B'nai Noah come from fundamentalist Protestant backgrounds, bringing with them a far more literal attachment to text and to inerrancy and a somewhat more manichaean view of the world than would have occurred to Pallière.

Pallière's activities were halted by the Nazi occupation of France. The condition of European Jewry in those years was hardly conducive to the sort of close cooperation mandated by Noahide beliefs. Pallière survived the war, however, emerging to complete an Italian version of his book, *Il Santuario Sconosciuto*, which was published three years after his death in 1949.[66] Aimé Pallière's life, and the book which recorded his spiritual journey, have come to serve as models for the contemporary B'nai Noah.

On the Question of Idolatry

Where previous chapters conclude with a discussion of the potential of a movement for a resort to violence, the B'nai Noah are hardly likely to take up arms to "force the End." If the B'nai Noah movement is to be involved in any form of violence, it will most likely be as a result of the intense conspiratorial suspicions of the anti-Semitic groups who were among the first to discover the existence of an organized B'nai Noah movement. For this reason, this chapter will conclude with a discussion of the most radical element of B'nai Noah doctrine, the belief that Christianity is in reality a form of idolatry. It is this belief, coupled with the Talmud's mandate of death for idolaters, that forms the heart of the radical right wing's indictment of the B'nai Noah. Thus, we must also consider the intensely negative anti–B'nai Noah polemic that has been a feature of the literature of Christian Identity and other radical right appeals since the early 1990s.

Of the seven Noahide laws, the most important in the view both of the B'nai Noah and of Identity Christians is the prohibition against idolatry. On this subject, there appears to be a remarkable convergence of views, with adherents of both groups concluding that from the perspective of the Noahide movement, Christianity is in fact a form of idolatry and is thus prohibited to anyone seeking "a share in the life to come."[67] So important is the concept of idolatry that Maimonides restates an ancient tradition when he holds that "the commandment against idolatry is (the equivalent of) all (other) commandments . . . and anyone who rejects idolatry thereby accepts the entire Torah."[68] For one contemporary source, the commandment to abjure idolatrous behavior constitutes the only strictly religious duty incumbent on Noahides.[69] A brief examination of the historical development of the idolatry doctrine in the Jewish sources, however, demonstrates that the question is not so simple.

The clear prohibition against idolatry directed at the Jewish people—"You shall have no other gods before me"—may reliably be traced to the Decalogue (Ex. 20:3 and Deut. 5:7).[70] It is considerably less clear at what point this prohibition was extended to non-Jews. In all likelihood, the basic assumption that gentiles were irredeemably idolatrous by nature was not transformed into a more positive determination to turn non-Jews away from idolatry until the formulation of Noahide law.[71] When the question of gentile idolatry was addressed in the biblical period, it was posed in terms of regulations incumbent on the resident alien (ger toshab) and (significantly, in terms of the current B'nai Noah/Christian Identity polemic) was at all times linked to the concept of Jewish suzerainty.[72] The early rabbinical literature considered the question of turning gentiles toward monotheism, but this consideration was theoretical at best and tended toward the view that this blessed eventuality would take place in the context of a general conversion at the dawn of the messianic era.[73]

The first serious discussion of combating gentile idolatry appears to stem from the Talmudic literature, and in particular the Babylonian Talmud.[74] As we have seen, the concept of the Noahide code of law was first fully explicated in the Babylonian Talmud, as was the theoretical sanction of death for transgressors. Although the Noahide code and the penalty of death never left the realm of the theoretical, the acceptance of the Talmudic literature as normative within Diaspora Judaism had the practical effect of gradually changing the rabbinic view from one of ceding to gentiles a virtual license to engage in idolatry until the onset of the messianic era to one which saw gentile society as not necessarily inherently idolatrous.[75] This opened greater possibilities for Jewish inter-action with their gentile hosts, at the same time as it stimulated a dis-cussion of the death penalty for transgression of the Noahide covenant that took on an increasing liveliness over time.[76]

Increased interaction with host communities brought Jews into greater dialogue both with pagan society and with Christians. The view of the early rabbinical authorities in this context is (relatively) unam-biguous; according to Rabbi Tarfon (first century C.E.), pagan idolaters were better than Christians (or perhaps Gnostics, the reference is un-clear) in that pagans disavow God through ignorance while Christian idolaters "know him and yet deny him."[77] In later sources, however, the discussion tends to be more nuanced. The most important relevant doc-trinal issues are Christological, in particular the Trinity, the incarnation, the broader association of Jesus with the Godhead, and to a lesser ex-tent, the veneration of saints. Where early rabbinical sources tended to view Christianity as idolatrous by definition,[78] this view came by the Middle Ages to be modified considerably. In this period, a consensus seems to have arisen that Christianity occupied a middle ground be-tween pure idolatry and the perfect monotheism of the Jews.[79] Indeed, medieval thinkers from Maimonides to Judah HaLevy argued that both Islam and Christianity had vital roles to play in providential metahis-tory, holding that God had brought both belief systems into being so as to prepare the ground for the imposition of pure monotheism on the world during the messianic era.[80] It should be noted, however, that both of these figures lived in Islamic lands, and they argued that although Christianity has elements of idolatrous worship, Islam was a pure monotheism.

The doctrinal elements of Christianity which from a Jewish perspec-tive would suggest the possibility of idolatry were handled in different ways. Most European rabbinical authorities argued that if only Chris-tians would follow the ethical mandates of the Noahide code, even the Trinity and the cult of saints are allowed to them.[81] This eminently prac-tical view avoids the logical inconsistency of simultaneously rejecting both the divinity of Jesus and the efficacy of saints and insisting that those who engage in such worship are not by definition idolaters. Be this as it may, the consensus of rabbinical authorities from the medieval period to the present—knowing full well that they lacked the power to influence their Christian neighbors and that Jewish survival, already tenuous, depended on a modicum of sufferance on the part of the gen-tile nations—prudently ruled that for non-Jews, Christianity did not constitute a form of idolatry. To further confuse matters, Jewish con-verts to Christianity were deemed guilty of idolatry.[82]

This rabbinic exercise in diplomacy, however, did not obviate the very real doctrinal difficulties presented by Christianity. Here too, distinctions were drawn. For example, the veneration of saints was viewed as a lesser problem than the central doctrines of the Trinity, associationalism, and the incarnation.[83] Naturally, this problem was addressed more comfortably from the safety of Moslem lands, most notably by Maimonides. For him, idolatry consisted most dangerously of what may be termed associationalism (Heb. *shittuf*), that is, the association of anyone or anything with God. It is the association of Jesus with God which is at the root of the development of the Trinity—and the incarnation itself—into central Christian doctrines.[84] We are thus left with a dichotomous view: in Christian lands, the Jew is not to regard Christianity as idolatrous, but at a safe remove, he is to think of at least some aspects of Christian doctrine as idolatry. This view is illustrated by the circumspection of Elijah Benamozegh, who at no time states—either in writing nor apparently in conversation—that Christianity is in any way idolatrous. Rather, "you can remain within this Christianity, on condition, of course, that it be reviewed and corrected by the Jewish priesthood."[85]

In particular, Rabbi Benamozegh suggests that the problem with Christianity that is most in need of correction centers on Christology:

> As to the person of Jesus . . . that on condition that divinity be not attributed to him, there would be no reason whatever not to make him a prophet, to consider him a man charged by God with an august religious mission, without because of this altering any part of the ancient word of God, and without abolishing for the Jews the Mosaic Law, as his disciples pretended to do, misrepresenting his explicit teachings. see Matthew V, 17–19.[86]

In other words, the central thrust of Noahidism is to de-divinize the person of Jesus. Failing this, what is left—as was stated implicitly in the nineteenth century and more explicitly in the twentieth—is a perception of Christianity as in essence a form of idolatry. The view has come to be stressed more forcefully than in the past in some rabbinical quarters in the context of a renewed polemical debate with Christianity. Thus, the late Steven Schwarzschild, a rabbinical figure who has written about the Noahides since the early 1960s and who is a major influence on the contemporary B'nai Noah movement, states:

> My own view is, however, that, since we are no longer living in the Christian Middle-Ages, and neither even atheism nor the candid condemnation of idolatry is at all likely to bring life endangering consequences upon us,[87] [the line of decisions holding Christianity to not be idolatrous] should be treated as what it was—*a hora'ah lesha'ata,* "a

temporary, prudential measure," which has long since lost its power. This is so especially, I wish to argue in view of the fact that the single most important Jewish and human truth is at stake—the uniqueness, the incomparability of God and the morality necessarily entailed by that truth.[88]

Clearly, Christian Identity theorists are not wrong in their supposition that in Jewish eyes, and in particular in the view of those involved in the Noahide movement, Christianity is seen as idolatry. Moreover, at least in theory, death is the penalty to be paid by idolaters, and the putative courts empowered to exact this punishment will be either Jewish or under Jewish control. To Identity Christians, imbued with a manichaean view of the world and convinced that history is a conspiratorial process in which the master conspirator is the shadowy figure of the elite Talmudic Jew, the notion that the death penalty was never more than theoretical is meaningless. A sure proof that the apocalypse is imminent is the perception that the world is getting worse and that the timeless conspiracy of the Jews against the people of God, the remnant of true Israel, is only now coming to fruition. The Noahide movement is interpreted by Identity theorists as just such a sign of the End.

Christian Identity Discovers the Noahides

As we have seen, the *Wall Street Journal* article first alerted the Identity world to the existence of the B'nai Noah. Consternation followed with the revelation that the Noahide Code was based on the Babylonian Talmud, a text much feared and despised by the Identity faithful. To understand this strongly negative reaction of the Christian Identity believers, one need only examine the anti-Semitic literature that serves as a primary source of Identity's apocalyptic millenarianism. In one such influential text, Rev. I. B. Pranaitis's 1892 *The Talmud Unmasked*,[89] a number of talmudic passages are given special prominence, some of which deal specifically with aspects of the seven Noahide laws:

VII. THOSE WHO KILL CHRISTIANS SHALL HAVE A HIGH PLACE IN HEAVEN
In Zohar[90] (I, 38b, and 39a) it says:
"In the palaces of the fourth heaven are those who lammented over Sion and Jerusalem, and all those who destroyed idolatrous nations . . . and those who killed off people who worship idols are clothed in purple garments so that they may be recognized and honored."[91]

VIII. JEWS MUST NEVER CEASE TO EXTERMINATE THE *GOIM*; they must never leave them in peace and never submit to them

In Hilkoth Akum (X, 1) it says:
"Do not eat with idolaters, nor permit them to worship their idols; for
it is written: *Make no covenant with them, nor show mercy unto them*
(Deut. ch. 7),
2) Either turn them away from their idols or kill them."[92]

Apparently to insure that the reader does not fail to understand that
the idolaters referred to above are in fact Christians, and to imply that
the cross is thus seen in the Talmud as constituting an idol, *The Talmud
Unmasked* closes with several specifically anti-Christian quotations:

In Zohar (I, 25a) it says:
"The people of the earth are idolaters, and it has been written about
them: Let them be wiped off the face of the earth. Destroy the memory
of the Amalekites. They are still with us in the Fourth Captivity,
namely, the Princes [of Rome] . . . who are really Amalekites."[93]

While *The Talmud Unmasked* may be credited with helping to create the atmosphere in which the Noahide laws could be interpreted as a
prime sign of the End, it could not have done so in isolation. Rather,
there is a large body of anti-Semitic literature that would seem to validate elements of the Christian Identity hermeneutical approach to the
Noahides.[94] Of these, none has been more influential than *The Protocols of the Elders of Zion*. From this text, it is necessary to abstract but
a single element: the question of judges, and specifically, the inherent
right claimed by the "Elders" to judge the gentile nations.

Under our influence, the execution of the laws of the *goyim* has been
reduced to a minimum. The prestige of the law has been exploded by
the liberal interpretations introduced into this sphere. In the most important and fundamental affairs and questions judges decide as we dic-
tate to them, see matters in the light wherewith we enfold them for the
administration of the *goyim,* of course, through persons who are our
tools though we do not appear to have anything in common with
them.[95]

The core texts constituting the basis of the millenarian right's understanding of the Noahide controversy, from Genesis through Jubilees
to the *Protocols,* all suggest to the adherent a powerful strain of manichaeism, a starkly dualist struggle of the forces of good against the
forces of darkness. In this view, all events form a chain of causation that
will bring to fruition the most dire predictions of imminent apocalypse.
It was not long before such interpretations emerged throughout the
white supremacist constellation. Although it is impossible to state with
certainty precisely who was the first to sound the alarm, a remarkably

similar group of themes quickly made their way through the underground maze of newsletters, bulletins, cassette sermons, and Kingdom meetings, forming a sort of apocalyptic orthodoxy that illustrates the linkages binding diverse ideological elements into a coherent subculture.

Two senior Identity figures seem to have dominated the interpretation of the Noahide controversy, Earl Jones in New Mexico and Gordon Ginn in California. In a 1991 article, Jones, a prestigious Identity pastor and conspiracy theorist, admits the possibility that the signing of the "Noahide Bill" has no eschatological implications—but immediately goes on to demolish this notion. Jones reminds his readers of the radical secularization that has taken prayer and the Ten Commandments out of America's schools, and contrasts the replacement of "now illegal" Christmas crèche scenes with public displays of the Chanukah menorah (which have occasioned no legal repercussions). He then examines each of the noble-sounding Noahide commandments in the light of their possible implications for Christians, an examination replete with villains and knaves, from J. David Davis to the "*sayanims* (those volunteers for Zionism working in the congressional offices of Washington)" who "received their orders from the Nazis (Zionist Princes) and Congress bit hook, line and sinker."[96] How clever the proponents of these innocuous-sounding laws were can be seen from the implications of each, according to Jones's analysis. For example, the prohibition of blasphemy against God could hardly be rejected by any Christian—at least until one recalls that Jesus was put to death by the Pharisees on exactly this charge. Remember, he warns, just who will be sitting in judgment of whom under such laws. Given the conspiratorial nature of the Jew, what better Trojan horse than the Noahide laws could be found to subordinate Christian Americans to their Jewish overlords?[97]

Pastor Jones gives credit to another newsletter, *Smyrna*, for bringing Public Law 102-14 to his attention.[98] *Smyrna*, a modest Identity newsletter published in Fortuna, California, is the vehicle for Gordon Ginn, the current religion editor of the National Religious Foundation. Ginn has since had his name taken off the journal, and the reasons for this reveal much about the psychology of the movement: "*Smyrna* no longer places the name of its editor on the masthead. Until recently Gordon L. Ginn, Ph.D. was printed there, and he remains as Founder and Editor. However, it was decided that too many people either believe or disbelieve information based upon who the writer/editor is, and what academic degree is behind his name. We disagree with that kind of thinking."[99] No less than Pastor Jones, *Smyrna* sees the Education Day resolution in starkly millenarian terms: "History is grinding to an end. The signs are everywhere. Possibly one of the most prominent signs of the times that tells us the 'last days' are upon us is the passage of House

Joint Resolution 104 on March 20, 1991, which became Public Law 102-14."[100]

Smyrna in turn credits the *Wall Street Journal* for its information on the general content of the Noahides. At the same time, and alone among Identity theorists, *Smyrna* has taken the trouble to obtain material directly from the Noahide movement itself: articles from *The Gap,* the organ of the movement published by J. David Davis in Athens, Tennessee, and the newspaper articles taken from a variety of often obscure Jewish sources that are gathered together in *The Root and Branch Noahide Guide.* Thus, for the precise threat which the Noahides present to Christian civilization—and for the death penalty hanging over the head of every Christian—full credit is given to an article in *The Gap* written by Rabbi Michael Katz. Rabbi Katz is quoted:

> All would agree however, that only the seven [which] are derived from the Torah (either in the commandments to Adam or those to Noah) are capital sins, the transgression of which is punishable by execution. Jews are bound to enforce the Noahide Code to the extent that it is possible given their own circumstances of exile.[101]

So seriously does *Smyrna* take the threat of the Noahide laws that the entire issue for September/October 1991 is devoted to a consideration of the problem. Putting the Noahide controversy in the context of the recent Gulf War and of predictions by none other than the Lubavitcher Rebbe Menachem Schneerson of imminent messianic redemption,[102] *Smyrna* reiterates its warning that the End is near, adding a number of supporting source documents. The diverse listing of sources include various unnamed journals from the mainstream churches (dubbed contemptuously "Jewish Christian" periodicals), sources from the *Noahide Guide* (uncredited), the *Encyclopedia Judaica,* and the *Jewish Encyclopedia.*[103]

Between the *Smyrna* alarm and Pastor Jones's hermeneutics crystallized the interpretation of the Noahide controversy that would hold sway throughout the white supremacist constellation. Indeed, Jack Mohr, a major Identity figure from Bay St. Louis, Mississippi, appropriated not only the issue but the distinctive wording of Jones's formulation:

> You can be assured, that the Jewish "*sayanims*" (volunteers for Zionism) who infest the halls of Congress, did the job . . . These "*sayanims*" received their orders from the real NAZIS (Zionist Princes) and our Congress, as usual with their heads in the sand, swallowed the Zionist bait, "Hook, line and sinker."[104]

It remained for the various sectors of the white supremacist constellation to pick up on the issue and to consider what, if anything, should be done in response. For its part, *Smyrna* submits that history teaches that change can come via one of only two methods, the ballot or violence, and opts for the former, offering readers a form letter to send to their representative or senator.[105] Pastor Jones suggests no course of action, seeing the adoption of the Noahide laws as but another piece in the vast conspiratorial jigsaw puzzle that he has dedicated his life to unraveling.[106] In Sacramento, California, the National Justice Foundation (NJF), featuring the same Gordon Ginn, Ph.D. as its religion editor, published an article that adds further analysis, apparently without suggesting any definite course of action.[107] Most notable among the NJF hermeneutics is the suggestion that the first Noahide commandment (that proscribing idolatry) could easily be interpreted as outlawing the "possession of artifacts such as a cross, a semblance of the baby Jesus, a statue of the Virgin Mary, Buddha and others for this would violate the prohibition of idol worship."[108]

Pastor Fred Butler of *The Shepherd's Voice* in Elizabethtown, Kentucky, is unique among Identity pastors for having made a visit to Israel and for his praise for the kibbutzniks he met there. Responding to reader requests, Butler reprints the Education Day resolution, crediting a newspaper published by Don Bell in Florida for the text of Public Law 102-14, the extreme racialist newsletter of James Warner's Christian Defense League in Louisiana for background information on the Lubavitcher movement, and of course *Smyrna* for "primary source" documentation including relevant quotes from the *Wall Street Journal* and from *The Gap*.[109] Pastor Butler's interpretation of all this is apocalyptic: "America, tribulation is promised, and tribulation we will get unless there is a national repentance! Our country is more evil than Sodom and Gomorrah. Can we expect to sleep with the devil and not pay the price?"[110] If Butler hears the hoofbeats of the Four Horsemen in the echoes of the Noahide movement, his response is conventional enough: he reprints a one-paragraph form letter provided by a "corresponding Pastor" and suggests that it be sent to the reader's representative or senator.[111]

Pastor John Harrell of the Christian Patriots Defense League (CPDL) of Flora, Illinois, believes that the greatest danger of the Noahide laws is that they originate in the Talmud, not the Bible. Moreover, in his view the laws could result in the killing of Christians. Although he doesn't know whether Congress and ultimately the President were simply ignorant or darker forces were at work, he fully subscribes to the notion that the U.S. government is a Zionist entity, rendering the accidental passage of the Noahides most unlikely. However, while the Noahide controversy indicates that we are living in "dangerous times," he is not convinced that the event is a clear sign of the End.[112]

Dr. H. Graber of the Church of Christ in Israel in Mariposa, California, in his *Kingdom Courier* newsletter reproduces the Noahide laws and offers a brief analysis of each that does not differ significantly from any of the views considered above. Pastor Graber, following some stridently apocalyptic rhetoric, ends by meekly suggesting that a strong letter to the reader's local congressman might be in order.[113]

The White Angel Isaac Sons of Lincoln, North Carolina, are a group located at the most radical fringes of the Identity movement. They take up the Noahide debate by republishing an article by Paul Hall of the Identity Christian *Jubilee* newspaper from Midpines, California. The Hall article is a carefully footnoted recitation of the case against the adoption of the Noahide laws, which obliquely breaks with the quietist majority of the movement over the question of the appropriate response:

> Others having reported on the Noahide Law/Education Day nightmare have suggested writing to your congressman and complaining. While this is certainly a time honored method of attack with varying levels of success, it is not what THE JUBILEE can honestly suggest. The devils are not going to cast themselves out.
>
> Don't take it personally! Remember, the evil that has befallen our land is simply Yahweh's punishment for our national sins . . . Fortify your families, fellow remnant, and watch as the Babylonian ship of state sinks.[114]

Hall may have been something of a latecomer to the Noahide debate, but he took the lead in warning of the dimensions of the threat posed by the adoption of the Education Day resolution. Opening a subsequent series on the Noahide laws, Hall notes that a second Education Day resolution had been offered in Congress to honor the ninetieth birthday of Rabbi Schneerson.[115] Not one to be caught off guard twice, in the interim he had obtained the book *The Path of the Righteous Gentile* by Chaim Clorfene and Yakov Rogalski, and in addition had conducted a telephone interview with a spokesman for Habad House in Crown Heights, New York. Pastor Hall's presentation closely follows *The Path of the Righteous Gentile,* emphasizing the death penalty for transgression of the Noahide code, demonstrating again the Talmud's alleged anti-Christian and pornographic nature, and concluding with an examination of the Christianity-as-idolatry issue.[116]

The *Omega Times,* a derivative Identity newsletter published by the Solid Rock Bible Church of Smithville, Oklahoma, credits several of its readers for an article on the Noahide movement which appeared in the

Tampa Tribune.[117] Under the mistaken impression that J. David Davis and his congregation in Tennessee had converted to Judaism, the *Omega Times* decries a Davis statement that Christianity is paganism, his rejection of the virgin birth and the resurrection, and his denial of the divinity of Jesus. According to the newsletter, such a teaching as this "new Phariseeism" could only come, "directly from Satan via his seed (literally . . . Gen. 3:15, John 8:44, etc.)." Vendyl Jones is then introduced as a "proselyte" of the Davis group, with the twofold conclusion being that the evil of the Talmud is at the root of the offending doctrines and that Jones's research institute (the Institute of Judaic-Christian Research) proves once again how nefarious is the concept of Judeo-Christianity.[118] A more recent issue of the *Omega Times* gloats:

> THE TALMUDIC "NOAHIDE LAWS" passed into US "law" as a memorial to a Jewish rabbi, as reported in the Omega Times last year, caused quite a disturbance among real "CHRISTIAN PATRIOTS" (Americans). As verification and sanctification of this blasphemous and traitorous act, YOUR President Bush "CELEBRATED HANUKKAH AT THE WHITE HOUSE" last December (America today/Atlanta Journal/Sileven).!!!!!!!!!!!!!!!!!!!!!!!!!![119]

Finally, the Noahide controversy has been brought before the more affluent sectors of far right wing thought through a long treatment that appeared in *Criminal Politics.*[120] *Criminal Politics* appears to have the ambition of becoming the *Time Magazine* of the far right: a weekly replete with glossy cover, an all-star staff of contributing editors (including such notables as the influential conspiracy theorist Eustace Mullins and the South African journalist Ivor Benson), and featuring prominently an investment and portfolio service for its readers. All for the price of $187.50 per year![121] The January 1992 issue prints the basic facts of the controversy, throws in helpful photographs of the Lubavitcher Rebbe and of a Torah scroll, artfully suggests a massive conspiracy that has deluded many Christians (not the least of whom was J. David Davis), and holds the World Zionist Organization (WZO) as at the root of this latest manifestation of the timeless conspiracy. It proposes no course of action, however.[122]

The early discovery of the Noahide movement by the racialist constituents of the radical right demonstrates again the applicability of the cultic milieu concept to a broad spectrum of oppositional religiopolitical movements that exist as a kind of American millennial community. Despite their widely disparate theological and ideological tenets, these groups do interact with each other—often to a considerably greater degree than they do with the dominant culture. Thus it is with the Children of Noah and the Christian Identity movement. While most Americans are unaware of the existence of either community, Identity Christians are intensely aware of the activities of the B'nai Noah, while the B'nai Noah for their part have been made quite aware of this attention from Identity Christians.

5

The Anti-Cult Movement/ Watchdog Groups

On your walls, Jerusalem, I have posted watchmen; they will never be silent, day or night.

—Isaiah 62:6

The rise of the militant anti-cult movement in America marks a new chapter in the history of human bigotry. The new bigotry turns both the ideology and the new scientific perspectives of the Enlightenment into the effective tools of modern scapegoating. The use of modern science and technology in the scapegoating solution was pioneered with great energy and effectiveness by the Nazis.[1]

—J. Gordon Melton and Robert L. Moore

Can't we all just get along?

—Rodney King, 1992

Virtually without exception, every religious movement examined in these pages has drawn upon itself the attention of a highly motivated cadre of opponents dedicated to the task of "exposing" the alleged dangers of the movement. The jury associated with this court of public opinion may be a religious denomination, but it may as easily be the general public or the agencies of local, state, or federal government. Often, not content with merely publicizing the iniquities of the movement, these watchdog groups may organize to harass, intimidate, or even outlaw the target group. Whatever form the opposition takes, it seems to be an immutable law of nature—or perhaps a confirmation of the axiomatic truth of the Hegelian dialectic—that for every millennial or messianic group that takes wing and seeks to spread its "good news"

127

there arises an equally strongly motivated group of enemies who seek to counter by any available means the millenarian or messianic message.

Each of the movements considered above has had this rather unhappy experience, and it is in the complex interactions of the two groups of adherents—the thesis and the antithesis, to borrow again from Hegel—that the final dynamic of the "community of seekers" becomes most clear, a process that may culminate in a degree of symbiosis that locks the seemingly irreconcilable groups into an incongruous embrace. Thus, Christian Identity has its Anti-Defamation League (ADL), its Klanwatch, and most recently, its Simon Wiesenthal Center just as surely as its forerunner British Israelism had the Anglican Church and its American denominational opponents. The B'nai Noah, although too new to have drawn the level of organized opposition that other movements have aroused, lost no time in attracting the interest of a watchdog group dedicated to monitoring and exposing each and every one of its alleged conspiratorial machinations: Christian Identity! The Ásatrú community draws attention from the same elements of the religious anti-cult movement that take an interest in the neopagan and Wiccan community generally, but there are signs that with the increasing identification of Odinism with the revolutionary right, the same largely Jewish opponents of the right wing (most notably the ADL) are taking an interest in the movement as well. Indeed, one prominent Ásatrúer has sought to preempt this interest by taking it upon himself to report on the movement's doings to Klanwatch!

Paradoxically, the role of the anti-cult movement (ACM) is to bring the message of the target group to the attention of the dominant cultural community—albeit in often grotesquely distorted forms. Ironically, the upstart millenarian or messianic movement often first gains access to the mass media as a by-product of the effort to demonize it. This media exposure in turn makes the movement known to other concerned sectors of society, most notably to the churches and the agencies of the state. However, the mass media is open to anyone wishing to partake of its product, and quite often the group's message is conveyed to a more receptive audience of the alienated or simply the curious, and the ranks of the target movement tend to swell in this way. Further, millenarian or messianic groups often become aware of the existence of other oppositional religious movements through this process of anti-cult alarums broadcast through the popular media. Thus, the formation of alliance or vendetta relationships often results from a careful perusal of the morning newspaper; such indeed was the case with the Christian Identity–B'nai Noah embrace.

Regardless of the unanticipated effects of publicizing the message of the enemy, however, the anti-cult movement accrues for itself some important benefits. First, it finds itself in something of the position of the high priest of an esoteric god. By monitoring, interpreting, and disseminating the ideology and the objectives of the target group, the ACM becomes in itself a key player in the drama; the object of the ACM's attentions thus appears more significant than its meager membership would indicate. As the ACM holds a monopoly on the distant rumblings emanating from the as-yet-invisible god, it becomes sought after by those interested in the oracular wisdom that the self-appointed priesthood is alone in a position to dispense. With the public recognition of this monopoly comes the perception that the ACM priesthood fulfills a vital social role, a role that must for the common good be performed as efficiently as possible. Thus, funds roll in and the high priests undertake a round of public appearances to enact the timeless role of the "warner" (Ezek. 3:19). In recognition of the demands of modernity, materials must be produced that are suited to a variety of media and to a diverse target audience so as to further spread the message of fear.

Finally, in perhaps the greatest irony, subtle but unmistakable changes occur in the nature of both the evil god and its high priesthood. Just as a generation of American gangsters of the Lucky Luciano and Meir Lansky era of the 1930s were said to have been so affected by James Cagney's Hollywood portrayal of their world that they almost unconsciously came to imitate the actor's cadences, dress, and on-screen attitudes, so too in many ways have the "cult" and "countercult" come to fulfill the most dire stereotypes each has constructed of the other.

As the complex interactions of cult and countercult unfold, the vital role played by the various watchdogs in the American millennial community must be addressed. Save for a relatively small number of religiously based ACMs emanating from the Protestant fundamentalist and evangelical communities, the ACMs could hardly be described as millenarian. At the same time, the impact of a seemingly implacable enemy on an oppositional millennial community—predisposed as it is to a strongly manichaean worldview and a powerful sense of hidden conspiratorial machinations behind almost any political event—should not be underestimated. Thus, in the discourse of the target community, the ACM is often blown up to superhuman proportions—its overarching power taken as a matter of faith. This is the key to the effortless adaptation by right wing millenarians of, say, the ADL's activities into ever-widening conspiratorial scenarios involving the U.S. government, the putative New World Order, and ultimately the age old battle with Satan himself. This process would also explain the immediate post-Waco suspicions that the Cult Awareness Network, through the activities of one of its operatives, was somehow responsible for the tragedy. Thus, the activities of the ACMs are offered as proof positive of the prophesied End Time persecution of the righteous remnant and thus serve to confirm the millennial excitement of the constituents of the millennial community.

Definition of the Anti-Cult Movement

The term "anti-cult movement" did not come into vogue until the 1970s, and by strict definition, the movements considered in these pages do not constitute cults. Nor for that matter do the myriad groups covered under the rubric of ACM constitute anything coherent or organized enough to be called a movement. Indeed, the precise definition of a cult is the subject of considerable scholarly rancor. Most scholars who are concerned with New Religious Movements tend to follow J. Gordon Melton and others in discounting the utility of the term altogether, given its strongly negative connotations. This is particularly the case in the aftermath of the People's Temple mass suicide in 1978. In concurrence with this scholarly consensus, no space will be expended in pursuing an unproductive quest for a definition of the term "cult."[2] Just as the definition of millenarianism has been expanded over the years by scholars interested in bringing under their analytical lens non-Western movements and religious traditions that lack any conception of a posthistorical millennial epoch, so too can we understand the anti-cult movement as encompassing an array of groups who have constituted themselves as watchdogs over a broad range of religious organizations.

ACMs—whose primary purpose is to act as watchdogs (or high priests) over their chosen targets—come in many forms, derive from a variety of backgrounds, and possess different capabilities and goals. In general, however, an ACM may be defined as any organized group which, motivated primarily either by religion or by secular political considerations, coalesces in opposition to one or more newly emergent religious or political movements. An ACM is understood to be a small core group of highly motivated individuals who may in time obtain sufficient resources to hire a larger staff, open branch offices, and the like. By definition, however, the ACM remains a small, largely autonomous organization, which may obtain support or resources from religious denominations or governmental entities but which is in no sense under the control of these larger entities. The key test to be applied to the potential ACM, and the primary factor that differentiates the ACM from a church or denominational body with which it might otherwise be identified, is the "single issue" nature of the ACM's mission. The ACM expends its full energies on combating the particular group(s) or movement(s) that it deems threatening. An individual church body, a religious denomination, or for that matter an agency of the state may fully share the ACM's concerns but will have a considerably wider scope of interests and activities.

It should be noted that while the term may be of recent vintage, the perception that it is imperative to form an organized resistance to new religious movements is of considerable antiquity. Melton points out that the first of the modern anti-cult books appeared in 1917,[3] and it was not long after this date that individual polemical works gave way to the formation of organized groups, the earliest of which were aimed primarily at the Jehovah's Witnesses and the Church of Jesus Christ of Latter Day Saints. The 1970s saw a tremendous explosion of creative expressions of religiosity, paralleled by a fantastic proliferation of religious ACMs directed against a bewildering variety of targets.[4] In addition, complementing the work of the religious component of the anti-cult movement are a number of purely secular political organizations that have attached themselves to particular movements.

The Anti-Cult Constellation

To more fully illustrate the rich variety of active ACMs, a preliminary taxonomy is offered below. In this framework, the primary categories of ACMs include: family centered and apostate groups; political, denominational, or philanthropic subgroups; ACM clearinghouses; and mirror image ACMs.

Family Centered and Apostate Groups

This is the level on which the popular conception of anti-cult groups—and virtually the whole of the sociological literature dealing with the subject—concentrates. The sociologists David Bromley and Anson Shupe offer a three-stage model of ACM groups of this type,[5] positing first a formative stage in which relatives and a circle of other concerned individuals come together in response to the decision of a loved one to join one of the many New Religious Movements that emerged in the late 1960s. An important component of these nascent groups are former cult members who, having either left the new religious movement of their own volition or who were "rescued" by a professional deprogrammer, become key ACM figures.[6] Indeed, a number of ACM groups were formed by disaffected apostate members of New Religious Movements.

Should the group survive beyond this initial stage, a period of expansion occurs, in which the movement begins to transcend its ad hoc origins and to formulate a long-term strategy that looks beyond the immediate "rescue" of individual "cultists" toward the means that could be taken to combat the cult groups themselves. It is at this point that the ACM begins the process of making effective contacts with governmental agencies and with other like-minded private organizations, regularizing fund raising, and at last taking its case to the broader public through the media. Finally, the ACM may reach an institutional stage in which the organization's personnel become fulltime employees, allowing it to find its niche in the crowded ecology of American interest groups. It is important to note that in the category of family centered groups, it is possible to find secular groups of parents worried both about their children in the immediate sense and about the impact of the target movements on the polity in the broader sense. It is equally common to find specifically religious organizations, including most prominently evangelical and fundamentalist Protestants and Conservative and Orthodox Jews.[7] Additionally, it is not unusual to find in this category "integrated" ACM groups containing both secular and religious members.

Denominational, Philanthropic, or Political Subgroups

These anti-cult groups often began their organizational existence either as ad hoc committees formed within larger organizations or as service organizations whose original mission had been accomplished to such a degree that in order to assure continued relevance—and thus survival—a more generalized watchdog role had to be adopted. Regardless of the precise origins of the group, however, they are now configured entirely within the definition of an anti-cult group offered above: a small, relatively autonomous organization that exists solely to monitor its target movement(s) and that, by virtue of its near monopoly of information on the group, forms a kind of exclusive priesthood that assumes an almost proprietary right to interpret and disseminate information about its "esoteric deity."

Perhaps the least crowded constituent of this category is that of denominational subgroups, representing subcommittees of established religious denominations. They are somewhat unusual in that the majority of religiously oriented family centered groups are peopled by members of independent fundamentalist or evangelical Protestant churches. Thus, not surprisingly, denominational ACMs tend to be comprised of more liberal churchmen and -women, and as a result, the targets of these groups are invariably right-wing, racialist movements.

A good example of a denominational ACM in its earliest stages is provided by an ad hoc subgroup of the Presbyterian Church that was formed as a result of concerns expressed at its 198th General Assembly in 1987 regarding the apparent growth of American right-wing movements. The report of the subgroup, issued by Dr. John R. Fry and his colleagues, reflects alarm at the dangers to society posed by the radical right, with Christian Identity (because of its intense biblicism) singled out for particular attention.[8] The report also outlines a program of study materials including Anti-Defamation League publications, Center for Democratic Renewal tracts, works by Leonard Zeskind and Lyn Wells, the popular Hollywood film *Betrayed* (Deborah Winger's portrayal is noted for special study), and books such as *The Silent Brotherhood*. These materials are to be presented to local groups in three successive meetings, which are to culminate in a cathartic final session in which representatives of minority organizations are invited to share their perceptions of victimization, thus giving the assembled Presbyterians an opportunity for a cleansing joint *mea culpa*. Suggested minority "confessors" include rabbis or other representatives of organized Jewry, the NAACP, the Urban League, La Raza Unida, or the League of United Latin American Citizens (LULAC), and representatives of gay rights groups or family planning clinics. How this exercise should ideally work is suggested by the authors:

> When, for instance, a rabbi or other representative of the synagog directs attention to the majoritarian prejudice involved in the public celebration of Christmas, do group members feel that they are actively part of the prejudiced group? When representatives of racial minorities explain that racial jokes are a particularly virulent form of racial prejudice, do group members identify with the victims of the violence or with the joke tellers? When gay persons describe the violence and abuse they endure, do group members feel that they hold views similar to the perpetrators of the violence or the victim?[9]

Then, having exposed and overcome the latent hostilities that the group might hold towards any or all of these victims, arrangements are to be made to create an ongoing watchdog group from a core constituency of those attending the meeting: "Before the meeting is concluded, the leader should make sure that each member has a grasp on how to track the white supremacist movement [in their area] from now on."[10] This last is perhaps the most telling factor in the context of the institutionalization of the ad hoc group as a fully fledged denominational ACM. The work of the group, it must be noted, although funded by the denomination, is largely free of official interference (or perhaps, of official interest). It forms but one of a number of activities sanctioned by the denomination's General Assembly.

Closely related to denominational subgroups are philanthropic subgroups. The only real difference between these two categories of ACMs is the direct relationship of the denominational ACMs to their church's sanctioning mechanism as compared to the philanthropic ACMs' distance from their own religious hierarchies. Thus, the most important of these groups, the Anti-Defamation League—universally identified with Judaism and with Jewish interests—was born as a subgroup of a philanthropic organization, the B'nai B'rith, rather than as an organizational arm of any particular "denomination" of American Judaism. The independence from outside control that the ADL has come to enjoy has proved advantageous to the group, allowing it to undertake actions that no responsible denomination would condone and that few government agencies would dare to undertake.

How closely tied to American internal security agencies the ADL has become has been a matter of conjecture in right-wing circles for many years. It was, however, not until a series of legal suits were filed against the ADL by the Lyndon H. LaRouche organization, beginning in 1980, that documentary evidence of this relationship began to emerge.[11] As part of this ongoing legal action, LaRouche filed a Freedom of Information Act request for pertinent FBI documents detailing that agency's cooperation with the ADL. One of the documents obtained through this action was a two-page memo with cover sheet dated 4 February 1985, which was transmitted from the office of the director of the FBI to twenty-five field offices across the country, accompanied by copies of the ADL's 1984 status report on the Ku Klux Klan and on neo-Nazi activities. The document presents the ADL as "undertaking" to monitor the activities of "domestic terrorist groups" and to report any information touching on criminal activities to the FBI:

> Each [FBI field] office is requested to review the attached documents. The Anti-Defamation League of the B'Nai B'Rith [sic] (ADL) has undertaken to monitor and report the activities of domestic terrorists groups [sic], particularly the Ku Klux Klan. On 1/18/85 the New York Division initiated contact with [deleted] These individuals were advised of the primary jurisdiction of the FBI in civil rights matters. Further, they were advised that any legitimate civil rights allegation should be immediately brought to the attention of the appropriate FBI offi[deleted] expressed his desire to cooperate and stated he would notify all regional ADL offices of the FBI's responsibility. It was also established that each FBI office contact each regional office to establish a liaison and line of communication to promptly receive any allegations of civil rights violations.
>
> Each receiving office should contact the regional ADL Director(s) listed in your Division and establish this liaison. FBIHQ need not be notified of the results of these contacts with the exception of any sig-

nificant cases or problems. These contacts should be documented in each field office 44-0 file.[12]

Conversely, the ADL has had very real difficulties with branches of the U.S. government over the accuracy and tactics of its investigations.[13] The ADL's tactics of infiltration and disruption of targeted movements came most glaringly to light in 1993 when an ADL operative, Roy Bullock, was found to have illegally obtained sensitive files from the San Francisco Police Department's Organized Crime Intelligence Division through the cooperation of an officer in that division, Tom Gerard. The discovery of this operation led to a brief flood of unwelcome publicity in the California press, covering a broad range of the ADL's covert activities. Eventually, the ADL was able to maneuver out of the embarrassing situation by claiming to be a "news gathering" organization whose files thus were protected by the First Amendment. This effectively stifled legal action by the groups who were the recipients of the ADL's unwelcome attentions. In the end, the government declined to prosecute, the ADL "contributed" $75,000 to a fund to fight hate crimes, and the case was officially closed.[14] Undaunted by the public relations nightmare, the ADL's national director Abraham Foxman revealed much about the role of the ACM high priesthood in America when he noted:

> The press that dealt with us continues to call on us as a source and a resource . . . With law enforcement and government, we continue our relationships . . .
>
> [Despite] attempts to bring into question our existence and our techniques, the end result is that we are with the people we started with [including the National Association for the Advancement of Colored People, the Urban League, and the Southern Poverty Law Center] . . .
>
> We see no change in their attitudes toward us and our relationship with them . . . [It] reaffirms that which we have done and we will continue to do without any hindrance.[15]

Despite such incidents, the ADL stands unchallenged as the most successful model of a philanthropic ACM in the United States. It long ago defeated its primary rival, the American Jewish Committee, for predominance in the priesthood of the radical right.[16] Its latest challenger, the Simon Wiesenthal Center, cognizant of the fact that Nazi war criminals are not a renewable resource and casting about for a new niche in the American organizational universe, seized on the right wing as the most logical complement to its ongoing Holocaust education program.[17]

It has yet to make any impression on the ADL's near-monopoly position, however.

Political ACMs differ from denominational and philanthropic subgroups only in that they see their mission as entirely secular: combating racism, or more broadly, "hate," and (not coincidentally) promoting their own particular political agendas. As these agendas are invariably drawn from the left, it is natural that these groups would aim at right-wing movements, often stripping them of their veneer of religiosity to "reveal" the basic political agendas that (they are convinced) lurk beneath the "insincere" cover of spirituality. If this approach smacks somewhat of Marxism, that too is no coincidence, as many of the leaders of these groups—Leonard Zeskind and Lyn Wells of the Center for Democratic Renewal, or Chip Berlet of the Political Research Associates—are said to hail from leftist backgrounds.[18] Morris Dees, a flamboyant lawyer from the liberal wing of Democratic politics, directs the Southern Poverty Law Center (SPLC). *Klanwatch* is the SPLC's influential publication, and the term is often used to denote the organization. The SPLC is the final member of the group of major political ACMs in the United States.

Dees found his distinctive niche in the ACM constellation through his innovative use of civil suits to effectively put Klan factions out of business (mentioned in Chapter 1). His greatest success, however, stems from the civil suit which he filed against Tom Metzger's White Aryan Resistance in the aftermath of the murder of an Ethiopian immigrant in Portland, Oregon, by a group of skinheads who, according to the complaint, were incited to action by Metzger. The success of the action, temporarily closed down Metzger's operation and garnished 40% of any future moneys he may manage to earn.[19] The real effectiveness of the suit is best illustrated by the nearly hysterical warnings to potential WAR recruits emanating from such movement figures as Harold Covington, who claims that as a result of the suit, Dees has gained control of the organization's post office box. This, according to Covington, not only makes Klanwatch and thus the FBI privy to every communication sent to Metzger but also allows Klanwatch to seize a significant percentage of the funds sent to WAR's burgeoning mail order trade.[20]

In fact, Covington seems to have been prescient in warning of yet another danger to the movement. In November 1995, another set of alarums belatedly reverberated through the movement, from Dr. Edward Fields' virulently racist newspaper *The Truth at Last* to the e-mail service associated with the National Socialist figure Milton Kleim, the Aryan News Service. Fields offers the observation that "(if) they want their letters to reach Metzger faster, they should write directly to Tom Metzger c/o Morris Dees (at the Southern Poverty Law Center's Alabama address). Covington is typically more outspoken. In an open letter to Fields, he writes:

> Dear Dr. Fields,
>
> Regarding your article about Morris Dees of the Poverty Law Center receiving Tom Metzger's mail, it should be emphasized that this has been going on for over three years now. Metzger's treachery has given the radical left the most important "observation post" into the activities of the patriotic movement that they have ever enjoyed . . . I am especially concerned about the number of young people who have written to Metzger and had their correspondence turned over to Dees. At least one young man, Mark Lane of Birmingham, Ala, has been sentenced to prison in part due to "evidence" provided to the federal government by Morris Dees, in the form of Lane's private correspondence sent to Tom Metzger's WAR post office box. The truth is that Morris Dees is now the de facto publisher of the WAR newspaper . . . Dees allowed Metzger to remain in business in return for allowing Dees' legally appointed agent, San Diego attorney James McElroy, the authority to open all the mail going to Metzger's Fallbrook P.O. Box, forwarding copies of all letters to the Southern Poverty Law Center and depositing all the money in a Dees controlled bank account. At the end of each month. McElroy writes Metzger a check for 50% of the "take" so he can keep publishing and keep his increasingly bizarre and hysterical telephone recordings on the air.

Covington goes on to perceptively describe the utility to the watchdog groups' fundraising appeals of the most virulent examples of racist propaganda:

> A year ago, Metzger published a crude cartoon showing beheaded Mexicans lying in a field. Then Dees ran this cartoon in a fund raising letter to show how awful these "evil racists are". Thus Dees is actually financing an operation which spies on the right-wing and also provides ammunition for his money-begging racket at the same time.[21]

Taken together, then, the activities of Klanwatch, the Center for Democratic Renewal, Political Research Associates, and other political ACMs tend to support and magnify the work of the ADL, as they too struggle for the recognition—and thus the funding—accorded the high priesthood of the esoteric gods of the extreme right wing.

ACM Clearinghouses

The ACM clearinghouse stands at the apex of the religious anti-cult movement. Such a group may have started its life as a family centered group, but it has gone beyond Bromley and Shupe's conception of an institutionalized ACM in that it has become a repository of information, files, documents, and teaching materials such as videos and cassette recordings, which the anti-cult movement as a whole is able to access as a primary resource. Further, the mark of a successful ACM clearinghouse is its ability to transcend the world of the ACMs and the wider universe of the religious community and to serve as a resource for the dominant culture, fielding inquiries from the public, the press, academics, and governmental agencies. The primary keys to membership in this category are nearly unfettered autonomy and the ability of the organization to enjoy its status as a reliable resource for the secular society *without having to compromise its original character in any way.* Interestingly, the most successful of these groups—the Cult Awareness Network (CAN) in Chicago, the Christian Apologetics: Research and Information Service (CARIS) of Milwaukee, or the Spiritual Counterfeits Project (SCP) in California—are the smallest ACM groups in terms of professional staff; CARIS is essentially a one-man operation headed by Jack Roper, while CAN has but five paid staff members divided between headquarters in Chicago and Los Angeles.[22] With the sole exception of the Cult Awareness Network, at the level of the ACM clearinghouse, there appear to be only organizations emanating from the conservative Protestant world, with fundamentalist and evangelical adherents predominating.

The most direct impact of the American ACM clearinghouses are on the "grand demons" of U.S. society, the "Satanism scare" standing out as the most visible. Their real importance, however, is less in what actions they may take directly (indeed, they undertake very few actions) than in the influence they exert over other ACMs, the news media, and the American judicial and political system. This influence is magnified by the ability of these clearinghouses to network and to share their resources with other forms of ACM organization.[23]

Mirror Image ACMs

There are remarkably few organizations that fit the description of mirror image ACMs, but they are important in that they illustrate the degree to which the members of the millennial community come to communicate primarily with each other. Over time, they even come to resemble each other, despite anguished protestations to the contrary by all concerned. Thus, a mirror image ACM is a watchdog group formed by a target movement that seeks either to consciously act in the image of the group that has undertaken to monitor it, or to set itself up in the image of a well-known member of the watchdog community whose success the mirror image ACM wishes either to emulate or to parody.

A striking example of a mirror image ACM is Der Freikorps, centered in Victoria, Texas. Der Freikorps, a small group of Hitler cultists, created a publication in conscious imitation of Morris Dees' *Klanwatch,* which they dubbed *Jew Watch. Jew Watch* intermixes translations of Nazi-era anti-Semitic propaganda with current news. The latter is notable for inserting into standard news wire stories adjectival phrases advising the reader of the Jewish ancestry of many of the newsmakers of the day, as well as superimposing Nazi-era yellow stars onto the clothing of Jews depicted in news photos. In August 1992, Der Freikorps began a new publication that purports to be the revival of the Nazi-era German newspaper *Der Stürmer.* The premier issue demonstrates a considerable diminution of the basic literacy of *Jew Watch,* but it does show the same remarkable touch with photographs. Depicted on the cover is Bill Clinton speaking at a Friends of Israel podium while above him a dwarfish Micky Cantor sits on a cloud manipulating strings attached to Clinton's hands, with a six-pointed star floating like a halo over Cantor's head.[24]

The occult world too is developing some facility with mirror image ACMs. One of the more effective of these is from the world of Wiccan witchcraft: the Wiccan Information Network (WIN), run by a Vancouver neopagan policeman, Kerr Cuhulain.[25] WIN developed out of the Witches League for Public Awareness, a group that Cuhulain cofounded with the intention of combating the perceived negative images of witches in popular culture while opposing the work of such ACM figures as Jack Roper and Jack Chick as well as of such "occult cops" as Larry Jones.[26] It is with WIN, however, that the concept of the mirror image ACM is made explicit:

> We've found in our work [at WIN] that some of our greatest support comes from other anti-defamation leagues, like the Anti-Defamation League of the B'nai B'rith, because they're in the same boat. When you find somebody who is anti-Pagan, they are almost invariably anti-Catholic, anti-Semitic, anti-Freemason, anti-everything, you name it, because their way is the only way.[27]

In the world of the mirror-image ACMs, the ADL remains an organizational model for emulation; witness another entry in the field from the neopagan world, the Witches' Anti-Defamation League in New York.[28]

A short-lived entrant into the world of mirror image ACMs was the remarkable grouping of self-styled academic "forensic religionists," the Association of World Academics for Religious Education, which was headed by James R. Lewis of the Center for Academic Publication in Goleta, California. Under the acronym AWARE, this organization was formed as a conscious anti-anti-cult grouping in reaction to the deprogramming controversies that erupted in the late 1970s. The original impetus for the group appears to have been a series of contacts in 1989 spearheaded by Jeffrey Hadden of the University of Virginia, Eileen Barker of the London School of Economics, and David Bromley of Virginia Commonwealth University, who sought to form an effective organization of academics who would be ready and willing to enter into the battle as expert witnesses in civil and criminal court cases, countering the ACM "experts" who appeared to have a monopoly in the forensic field.[29] Although such goals are laudable, the organization has been controversial both because of the risks for academics of active participation in the cult wars and because of its appeals to various new religious movements for funding. These appeals do not seem to have been successful; a letter from Hadden bemoans the fact that NRMs with resources of this magnitude are notoriously loath to fund groups that they don't fully control. Nevertheless, by 1992 AWARE was sufficiently organized to begin announcing its existence with a series of press conferences at which its founding document, a four-page press release (replete with footnotes), was distributed to all and sundry.[30]

One such press conference, in Los Angeles on 9 November, featured a joint appearance by James Lewis and Henry Kriegal, who, according to ACM sources, is associated with the Church Universal and Triumphant (CUT) headed by Elizabeth Clair Prophet. This direct association of AWARE with adherents of NRMs is at the heart of the ACM criticism of the organization, and indeed, this close association ultimately led to AWARE's demise. In a 1995 letter to AWARE members, Lewis announced the dissolution of the organization in response to the complaints of AWARE advisory board members that Lewis's increasingly controversial relationship with such NRMs as CUT had become problematic for all concerned.[31]

Finally, in perhaps the most remarkable case of an attempt—ultimately stillborn—to form a mirror image ACM, a group of senior Identity pastors led by such figures as Earl Jones and Paul Hall attempted to set up a watchdog group to monitor the B'nai Noah! This oddity will be considered more fully below. First, however, we must consider Identity's own experience as the object of such scrutiny.

Christian Identity

From its inception as a religious movement marked by a prophetic sense of mission and a high level of proselytizing activity, Christian Identity's forerunner, British Israelism, found itself under siege from opponents who were connected primarily with the Anglican Church.[32] This controversy did not constitute an ACM activity, however, as the

Church had numerous other interests on its plate; moreover, the controversy remained "in-house" in that British Israelism never took sectarian form, and thus its adherents remained within their home churches. Indeed, the British government was rather friendly towards a movement that lent its idiosyncratic support to Britain's imperial policies. The Anglican attack on British Israel doctrines left behind a legacy of polemic literature that later critics and ACM leaders would effectively mine.[33]

In the United States, Christian apologists tended to concentrate their criticisms of British Israel doctrines on what they believed to be the deviant hermeneutics of British Israelites rather than on the social or political ramifications of the belief system. This line of argumentation arose in response to the influential body of nineteenth-century British Israel literature that was on the whole quite philo-Semitic in tone. This school of British Israelism, more reminiscent of Richard Brothers than of Richard Butler, saw the movement as reuniting the house of Israel by bringing the House of Judah (i.e., modern day Jews) together with the lost tribes, revealed at last as the European nations.[34] The criticism of British Israel hermeneutics took two complimentary tracks. First, it countered the British Israelite contention that irrefutable proof for the identification of the Anglo-Saxon peoples with Israel had been found in certain biblical passages. These texts, their critics insisted, were taken wildly out of context or interpreted through baseless linguistic suppositions. Second, these religious critics derided the many layers of occult beliefs—pyramidism in particular—that had over the years become central strands of British Israel doctrine.

A good sampling of this criticism was offered in the 1920s by Rev. L. E. P. Erith, the Warden of St. Peter's Theological College in Kingston, Jamaica. In blunt terms, he states the case against British Israelism:

> we can easily understand why all theologians and historians ignore [British Israelism]; for all British-Israel "proofs" are based on impossible exegesis and untrue history, and form a lamentable compound of prejudice and credulity. In pursuing a chimera of ignorance the British-Israelites find themselves overwhelmed by the magnitude of the task they have undertaken, and so they are led on from one absurdity to another . . . in their efforts to establish a fallacy.[35]

Rev. Erith goes on to take British Israelites to task for a variety of scholarly sins. Specific linguistic errors are decried, but at the center of the attack is British Israel's melange of historical suppositions, ancient folk tales, and pre-Christian myths. (The results of such syncretism included the claim that the genealogy of King George V could be traced back to King David via the marriage of an Irish king to an Israelite woman, Tea-

Tephi by name.)[36] Later Christian apologists would take up and expand this line of attack considerably, arguably the most influential of these polemics being the work of a Duke University professor of Old Testament studies, Allen H. Godby. Godby did not write specifically against British Israel theory, but in over seven-hundred pages, he managed to destroy virtually every facet of British Israel belief.[37] Apologists taking aim specifically at British Israelism soon appropriated his material.

Following closely upon the anti–British Israel school of Christian apologetics came a body of literature that can be identified as true anti-cult polemic. For the first time, not only was British Israelism decried as a modern day heresy, its organized existence was posited as a threat to the Christian community. The most important early figure in this development was J. K. Van Baalen. In Van Baalen's writings, British Israel hermeneutics were again an object of derision, and the occultist aspects of the belief system were held up to ridicule. Pyramidism in particular is utilized in Van Baalen's skillful prose to evoke contempt for British Israel theology even before the central doctrine was put on the dissecting table.[38] Although Van Baalen to be sure incorporated the work of the earlier apologists, his approach was considerably different than theirs. He saw British Israel as but one of a number of new religious movements that he identified in aggregate as cults, defined expansively as any belief system which deviated from the dogma of Protestant Christianity—especially in its evangelical form. Indeed, he felt constrained to begin his book with a defense of his decision to exclude Roman Catholicism from his list of cults.[39] What was new, however, was that his comparative approach provided insights unavailable to the earlier apologists. In particular, Van Baalen was the first to identify the strong doctrinal affinity between Mormonism and British Israelism.[40] This affinity is reaffirmed today in the person of Dan Gayman's evolution from a Mormon splinter sect to the heart of the Identity world, and does much to explain why a current epicenter of Identity theology is the American mountain west.

A second innovation of Van Baalen's approach was the assertion that British Israelism threatened the peace and prosperity of the state itself. This view involved two related areas, social tranquillity and political stability. Of the former, Van Baalen was one of the first to note the drift of British Israelism from its rather philo-Semitic origins to the anti-Semitic doctrine of Christian Identity in the 1930s:

> British-Israel literature does not bother with speaking of the deity of the savior or the atonement of the unworthy ones in His blood. It speaks of the greatness of men, of some, nay, many men. Their greatness is to be sought in physical descent or adoption, as the Pharisees of

old considered themselves the chosen people, and despised all others except those drawn into their own circle as proselytes.[41]

Politically, Van Baalen warned that British Israelism is in essence an imperialistic doctrine, which risks shifting public attention from the "spiritual to the material and economic" and which would "lull us to sleep in a time of world distress, substituting for the one time Pax Romanica and Hitler's dream of a Pax Germanica a fancied Pax Saxonica."[42] Moreover, he correctly recognized the manichaean implications of British Israel doctrine: "It makes a stench in the nostrils of the communists and other foes of the democratic nations by declaring them to be invincible according to Isaiah 54:17, and stating that their foot shall be on the neck of their enemies."[43]

After Van Baalen a curious event occurred, or more precisely, failed to occur. While other "cults" were becoming the target of structured Christian anti-cult organizations, British Israelism—now almost fully transformed into Christian Identity—simply dropped off the map. Identity drew no organized Christian opposition through the 1950s and 1960s, and even the counter-cult polemicists whose numbers exploded in the 1970s seemed to have forgotten that the movement existed. Although it is impossible to explain this marked lack of ACM interest with certainty, several developments in the critical World War II period suggest a possible explanation. As British Israelism metamorphosed into Christian Identity, mainstream American Christianity simply does not seem to have retained great interest in the movement. The great questions that roiled the churches in the late 1930s and in the aftermath of the war centered on questions considered by most churchmen to be more pressing than the pursuit of a small, heterodox sect. Ecumenism was debated, a primary facet of this debate on the national level concerning the activities of the National Council of Churches. More sharply politicized debates surrounded the so-called Faith and Order Movement, coming to a head in 1948 at the first assembly of the World Council of Churches in Amsterdam. Moreover, the vital religious questions of the day rapidly devolved into a reflection of the cold war.[44] Christian Identity, with its virulent anti-Communism and extraordinary millennial excitement, was in no position to weigh into this debate. Finally, evangelicals—the backbone of the early formally constituted anti-cult movements—were themselves becoming increasingly marginal actors in the American body politic.[45]

This is not to say that the Identity movement was left to its own devices. Instead, a new, far more secular constellation of foes discovered Identity, found it to be the antithesis of all that was good and true, and locked onto the movement in an embrace that has yet to abate. This new enemy arose in the form of the organized American Jewish community, no surprise given the Identity doctrine of Jews being the descendants of the unholy coupling of Eve and Satan in the Garden of Eden! The Jewish groups, concerned entirely with secular politics, had little interest in refuting Identity hermeneutics. Rather, their actions were aimed at isolating Identity from contact with the surrounding culture.

How the Jewish community first became aware of the esoteric world of Christian Identity is a question of some interest. The discovery of Christian Identity by the organized Jewish community—in the form of the American Jewish Committee (AJC) and the Anti-Defamation League of the B'nai B'rith—probably resulted from these organizations' intense interest in the movement found around Gerald L. K. Smith. At the heart of this movement was Wesley Swift, a young Ku Klux Klansman and Christian Identity minister who would have a profound impact on Smith's later years, and even more, upon the radicalization of the Identity movement itself. It is highly likely that the AJC and the ADL first discovered the Identity world through its investigations of Smith, and that Wesley Swift soon came to personify the Identity message.

The American Jewish Committee first took formal notice of the activities of Gerald L. K. Smith in May 1947 when, alarmed at the apparent success of Smith and other right wingers at linking Jews to Soviet communism, the AJC executive committee met to form a plan of attack against the Smith crusade.[46] This and subsequent meetings failed to produce agreement on a coherent strategy, primarily because of the delicate balance of the American body politic in the first flush of the cold war. Jews in fact were simply too deeply involved both in the Soviet state and in the international communist movement to risk touching any particular aspect of the communism controversy. Moreover, the fate of Jews in the Soviet Union was another critical factor in this decision.[47]

The ADL and AJC eventually arrived at a strategy that was termed at the time "dynamic silence." Championed by Rabbi S. A. Fineberg of the AJC, the idea was to close off all access to the public media—and thus to the larger culture—by "rabble rousers" such as Smith. The strategy was born of Rabbi Fineberg's observation that organized opposition to one of Smith's meetings would only swell the crowds eager to see the spectacle. Dynamic silence was from its inception a source of considerable controversy within the Jewish community itself. On the left, civil libertarians worried about the chilling effect of the policy on American public discourse. Fineberg's response to the civil libertarian critique is of relevance to the debate in the 1990s regarding "hate speech":

What we have been trying to do is to confine and quarantine the rabble-rouser's influence to as small a segment of the population as we
possibly can. To deny him freedom of speech would negate a fundamental democratic principle. Such violation would soon be turned
against liberals who would meet with a similar fate from those who
despise and fear liberals as much as a rabble-rouser is feared and hated
by some of his opponents.[48]

More problematic to the success of Fineberg's vision of isolating high
profile anti-Semites was the critique from the Jewish right that the policy was too weak, furthering the image of the Jew as having gone sub-
missively to their deaths in the Holocaust. In response to this criticism,
Fineberg dropped the pacifist tone of the term "dynamic silence" in
favor of the more robust sounding "quarantine treatment."[49] The full
force of the disaffection with the policy among right-wing Jews however, would not be fully felt until the Jewish War Veterans insisted on
physically confronting the emergent American Nazi Party of George
Lincoln Rockwell in the early 1960s.[50]

Fineberg's strategy succeeded. Powered by his considerable dogged-
ness in confronting any dissent to his tactics from within the fractious
Jewish community, the notion of quarantine benefited as well from an
overall change in American society in the postwar era in which open
expressions of anti-Semitism were becoming increasingly unacceptable.[51]
This allowed Rabbi Fineberg to find a sympathetic audience for his
views not only in the Jewish press but in editorial offices of the major
daily papers as well. Once adopted, quarantine did result in a dramatic
lessening of the press coverage accorded Smith and marked a sharp decline in Smith's popularity. So successful was the strategy that in the
summer of 1947 Fineberg was able to claim:

Even Gerald L. K. Smith has found himself unable to get the ear of
more than a twentieth of one per cent of the residents of the cities
where he has spoken in the past eight months. The one-twentieth of a
per cent were of the lunatic fringe, people who read and hear the same
drivel whether they come to hear Smith or don't.[52]

It was not until the attempt by Smith and others to block the appointment of Anna M. Rosenberg as an assistant secretary of defense in
1950[53] that both the American Jewish Committee and the Anti-Defamation League opened a full-fledged attack on Smith, bringing charges of
anti-Semitism before the United States Senate. By then, the tactics employed by the ADL and the AJC were well honed: identifying potential
anti-Semites and seeking to preempt or halt their activities by putting
pressure on elected officials and on local and national newspapers,

by printing the names of suspected anti-Semites, and by distributing "educational" materials intended to neutralize criticism of the Jewish community.[54]

To be sure, Smith's biographer notes that a component of this rapid decline in Smith's popularity may have been due to such other factors as "the growing popularity of television, the irrelevance of bombastic oratory, the passing of arch-enemies in the press and government to attack, and his stubborn refusal to change his style or issues."[55] In a word, Smith's time had simply passed. With these changes, the millenarian right would gradually fade from direct access to the popular media and thus from the public consciousness, leaving the watchdog organizations such as the ADL and AJC in a position to assume stewardship over the public exposure of the movement.

Given this intensive scrutiny of Gerald Smith, it is inconceivable that so visible a figure as Wesley Swift could have escaped the attention of either the ADL or the AJC. The dynamics of the Smith/Swift relationship appears to be a matter of some controversy among historians of the period, including the question of whether or not Swift converted Smith to a belief in the Christian Identity message. In any case, Smith in his later years had at least a strong familiarity with the Identity gospel, and Identity hermeneutics were a theme to which he would allude often: "True enough, the real Israel which came out of the seed of Abraham . . . were chosen of God for a special holy purpose (the salvation of mankind). But the people who say they are Jews and are not, and who are of the synagogue of Satan . . . have no relationship to the true Israel."[56] It seems probable that Swift indeed opened the door to the Identity kingdom to Smith, and the two came to be closely identified. Smith wrote often and admiringly of Swift in his magazine, *The Cross and the Flag*. Based on a 1949 issue of *The Cross and the Flag*, Ralph Lord Roy writes:

> Perhaps Gerald L. K. Smith's most influential supporter is Anglo-Israelite Wesley Swift, who operates a hate enterprise costing over $40,000 annually in the Los Angeles area. Swift has directed the activities of the Great Pyramid Club, the Anglo-Saxon Christian Congregation, and the Anglo-Saxon Bible Study Group; collectively they are said to constitute the strongest racist element on the West Coast.
>
> At one time Swift was Smith's chauffeur, bodyguard, and research assistant. He has remained intensely loyal to his former boss, co-operating with his program and accompanying him on many of his trips . . . Smith considers him "one of the great Bible students of the nation, and one of the three or four most eloquent preachers to whom I have ever listened."[57]

Although considerable doubts have been raised as to the accuracy and fairness of Roy's book, there can be no denying the importance of the text. Throughout his work, Roy credits the ADL for its assistance in finding source material, indicating the ADL's interest in the far right wing throughout the late 1940s and early 1950s. After the book's publication in 1953, it stood for a generation as the sole source on the religious dimension of the American radical right. Moreover, if the ADL was unaware of or simply indifferent to the power of an anti-Semitic religious appeal to attract disaffected individuals to the growing Identity movement, Roy's research must surely have had a considerable impact on the ADL's perception of the movement.

Roy's characterization of Smith's admiration for Wesley Swift—if not for the details of Swift's operations—is in accord with Smith's own writings. In fact, Roy somewhat underestimates Swift's zeal for organizing racialist groups: Swift's connection to the KKK is well known. Another important movement, the still extant Christian Defense League (CDL), brought Col. William Potter Gale in contact with Swift and would involve a number of prominent Christian Identity figures, including Richard Butler and the current holder of the CDL organizational title, James Warner.[58]

Having come to grips with Swift, and through him Christian Identity,[59] the Jewish watchdog groups have never let go of the legacy of Wesley Swift. In recent years, the ADL has supplanted the AJC in its active opposition to Christian Identity, and every ADL publication touching on Identity does not fail to feature Swift prominently as "[t]he best known advocate of the 'Identity' doctrine in the United States."[60] This use of Swift as the personification of Christian Identity is no accident. It is typical of the ACMs that in opposing a movement as complex and decentralized as Christian Identity, the preferred method is to hold up the most extreme manifestations of the group—a Wesley Swift or, if a living "devil" is of greater use, a Richard Butler—and to offer this example as typical of the movement as a whole.

How successful this effort can be may be demonstrated by the popular press's fixation on Christian Identity as an inherently violent, utterly irrational sect of fanatic haters. This perception was brought home graphically to me in 1992 when *Time Magazine* correspondent Mike Riley requested an interview on the subject of Christian Identity. His knowledge of the movement did not extend beyond Richard Butler and the Dualist figure Robert Miles. Finally, in frustration at not eliciting the blanket condemnation of the movement that he had expected, Riley asked, "But isn't it a theology of hate?" The unconscious use of the title of an ADL tract as a description of Christian Identity theology graphically demonstrates the success of the ADL in assuming the role of the high priest of an esoteric god in relation to the public perception of Christian Identity.

This ACM effort to simplify, caricature, and ultimately demonize the Identity movement is made possible by the virtual isolation of the group from the mainstream culture, the result of a process that began with the quarantine method perfected in the late 1940s and early 1950s. The news that does reach the public concerning Christian Identity is invariably colored by the ACM's "priestly hermeneutics," dispensed preeminently by the ADL but also by latecomers such as Leonard Zeskind, formerly of the Center for Democratic Renewal (which has billed itself as "the principle national clearinghouse for community-based efforts to counter hate group activity").[61] In addition, the Simon Wiesenthal Center in Los Angeles began gathering material for a project dealing with Christian Identity in the early 1990s, while the Wiesenthal Center in Chicago extended its facilities to Elwood McQuad, head of the intensely philo-Semitic Friends of Israel of Bellmar, New Jersey, during McQuad's visit to the Moody Bible Institute.[62]

For its part, however, the ADL is a priesthood jealous of its deities. James Aho discovered this to his dismay when the ADL, learning of his research on Christian Identity in Idaho, formally requested that he present himself to explain his activities.[63] Moreover, the ADL, once fastened on a target, is tenacious in its endeavors to isolate that movement from the mainstream culture. No better example could be given of an attempt to physically isolate a perceived enemy than the 1969 effort by the ADL to prevent the building of a road (at public expense) linking an aging Gerald L. K. Smith's biblical theme park and annual passion play in Eureka Springs, Arkansas, with the main highway.[64] In this effort, the ADL acted along two tracks: a somewhat covert press campaign that attempted to influence local and national newspapers to write in opposition to the road building effort, and a high profile campaign headed by ADL national chairman Don Schary that appealed to high government officials to intervene. Included in this latter campaign were President Richard Nixon, Secretary of Commerce Maurice Stans, and Secretary of Transportation John Volpe. Smith's theme park did in the end get its road, but not before the ADL set out to punish any individual or company having any connection with the project.[65]

Nor are the attentions of the ADL lavished solely on high profile figures such as Smith. Pastor Dave Barley, the heir to Pastor Sheldon Emry's Heirs of the Promise Ministry, is notable for his efforts to oppose the appeal to violence made by Identity supporters of Richard Kelly Hoskins' *Vigilantes of Christendom* fantasy.[66] In a press campaign aimed at stopping Barley from expanding into a satellite television broadcast ministry, however, local newspapers quote the ADL as a source for their condemnation of Barley's church as violent white supremacists similar to Richard Butler's Aryan Nations. From Pastor Barley's point of view, the sudden surge of negative press is a carbon copy of the local media coverage that arose when he moved the Heirs of the Promise ministry from Arizona to Idaho in 1991.[67] As in the case of Smith's road, the ADL effort failed to derail the broadcasts.

ADL campaigns have not been as uniformly unsuccessful as these two examples would indicate. The ADL has proved somewhat ineffectual on the local level—especially when the organization and its allies call on an economically strapped local community to sacrifice jobs for principle (as defined by the ADL), as in Eureka Springs, or seek to arouse local citizens to oppose the actions of Identity congregations that do not seem threatening, as in the satellite television controversy in Idaho. However, the ADL and similar anti-cult groups opposing the right wing can point to successes on two levels.

The first success is primarily psychological, and like success in almost any endeavor, it carries as a price some fascinating implications. What the ADL has managed to do most successfully is to convince Identity adherents of the proposition that the ADL—and the Jewish power behind it—is a ubiquitous fact of their lives. This perception can be seen in the oft-told jokes that conferences such as the annual Aryan Nations jamboree and hootenanny at Hayden Lake, Idaho, are peopled in equal parts by those controlled by the FBI, by operatives of the ADL, and by Richard Butler's followers. Of the three, the latter group should apply for endangered species protection, given the pressure under which they find themselves to act as agents for either watchdog group. It was just such an attempt to force Randy Weaver, then an anonymous visitor to the Aryan Nations' annual gathering, to act as an FBI informer that led to the tragedies at Ruby Ridge, Idaho. Echoes of this perception can be heard also in the elevation of the ADL to the point where they stand for an all-powerful and utterly malignant deity who in reality is the master of this earth. Such perceptions form the bedrock of the image of ZOG (Zionist Occupation Government) that has become universally accepted throughout the international radical right wing.[68]

The specific examples which could be offered here are legion, so ubiquitous is this perception in the Identity literature and in conversation with Identity adherents. Thus, two brief examples will suffice.

The tragedy of the Randy Weaver family was detailed in chapter 1. As the drama unfolded, the Pete Peters' Scriptures for America Bible Camp in Colorado was under way. In an anguished and outraged message, Peters defiantly stated his belief that the audience of his men-only meeting convened to discuss the situation was heavily infiltrated by the ADL, and he challenged them to report back to their masters his angry and violent, words.[69]

A second, far less dramatic example occurred in the early 1990s. Pastor Dan Gayman, upset about the wording of a passage in a draft of an article written for the *Journal of Terrorism and Political Violence,*[70] condemned my entire project as proving that the ADL had succeeded in poisoning the minds of the American public against the Identity message. His letter is worth quoting here, as a clear illustration of the corrosive effect of ACM activities on open discourse:

> Jeffrey, from my perspective here is where I find your presuppositions to be faulty. If I have perceived something that is not true I would surely stand corrected. In all sincerity here is where I perceive you to be in your paper.
>
> You have already established a "mindset" that the Church of Israel was an alien, foreign, un-American blot that did not belong in the democratic process called America. Your manuscript only confirms what all the literature from the various sources such as the Anti-Defamation League of the B'nai B'rith, et al, have been saying. If I read the implications of your position paper correctly the Church of Israel, though presently pursuing a peaceful coexistence with the government and mainstream America, is fully capable of exploding into a millenarian revolution at any time. Given such a possibility might it not be proper to arrest the Pastor and perhaps other Church members, and hold them for crimes that it is thought that one day they might commit? While the above may seem to over accent the issue, I must be honest when I say that the impression that I get from your paper, is that the Church of Israel if not today, may at any given time, represent a very definite threat to the peace and security of other Americans?[71]

To assert that the article actually implied no such thing is not to criticize Gayman's reading of the text. Rather, as with the intrepid *Time* reporter noted above, the ACMs have contributed a great deal to building a wall of fear and suspicion between the millenarian adherents of Christian Identity and the larger public. Further, as a function of their priesthood they provide both Identity and the dominant culture with the "correct" images of one another, and in this respect, the ADL and their imitators have enjoyed considerable influence on a psychological level.

The second success of the ADL and other ACMs has been in the legislative arena. Many examples could be offered, so suffice it to say here that the ADL model statute forbidding paramilitary activity at the Identity and survivalist camps has made these affairs a great deal less attractive to participants, while the ADL-sponsored model hate crime legislation has become law in many states.[72]

These successes, however, point up the single fundamental difference which separates the ADL from the evangelical Christian ACMs: despite enjoying considerably greater resources and political support than are commanded by the evangelical ACMs, the Jewish organizations appear to have little real appetite for doing away with the target movements entirely. By contrast, the evangelicals could have no dearer wish than for the cults to disappear from the face of the earth. This striking difference may be attributed to the evangelical perception that their battle is unambiguously directed at the devil as the ultimate inspiration behind the proliferation of cults, against whom (given the teleological nature of history) the believers' best efforts are in the short run doomed to failure but in the long run will ultimately be crowned with success. The Jewish ACMs are primarily secular and thus tend to see the situation in less manichaean terms. Of greater import, the Jewish ACMs appeal for support to the wider Jewish community and work as part of a matrix of Jewish organizations (service groups, charities, pro-Israel groups, civil rights groups, etc.), many of whom are on the left of the political spectrum and who insist that "even Nazis have first amendment rights." Thus, while opposition to the activities of Identity adherents is desirable, to silence them completely would drive a wedge between the Jewish groups and their liberal supporters that would outweigh the potential benefits of an all-out offensive against the target groups.

The ADL and other Jewish ACMs appear to have as their primary tactical objective the harassment and disruption of the movement, and as a strategic objective the realization of Rabbi Fineberg's strategy of isolating and thus marginalizing the groups and their adherents from the mainstream of American culture. This they have done with considerable success, and in the process have positioned the ACMs as the high priests of a dangerous god for whose relative quiescence the priesthood may take a large measure of public credit. In the process, of course, the status of the priesthood has been raised considerably—indeed, to a point roughly commensurate to the perceived threat which the Identity and other groups are popularly believed to present. Objectively speaking, however, how great is that threat? In terms of numbers, the movement is rather negligible. Although no reliable statistics exist for Christian Identity, for example, there is no question that the movement is minuscule,[73] and those committed to violence are a small minority of an already insignificant remnant. Other right wing groups show the same trend of declining membership; even the Ku Klux Klan, the long-time barometer of racist right wing activity in the United States, is at an all time low, according to the ADL's own figures.[74] Although hate crimes (including those directed at Jews) are on the increase, these seem to be attributable more to "lone wolves" than to organized anti-Semitic movements. Even the skinhead attacks on Jews have been on the decline.[75]

Despite the trends, it remains in the interest of the ADL and similar organizations to maintain the public impression that the target groups do represent a threat, just as is it in the interest of the target groups to maintain the image of the ADL as an all-powerful foe, ruthlessly dedicated to the persecution and destruction of the last righteous remnant of God's chosen people. For Christian Identity, there is no more natural perception of the contemporary United States than the highly manichaean view of a cabal of conspiratorial Jews spearheaded by the ADL and their governmental allies manipulating American political life, siphoning American wealth to Israel, corrupting the churches from the path of true Christianity to the dreaded syncretism of Judeo-Christianity, and of course, relentlessly persecuting the faithful remnant. Is such a scenario not an authentically biblical description of the Last Days? And is there not sufficient evidence to be found in the mass media to justify such a conclusion?

Identity adherents utilize a method of selective retrieval from Jewish texts to form a matrix of beliefs about Jewish perfidy. The mass media serves to provide further evidence to support this matrix of beliefs. No better media evidence of the truth of such assertions could be found than the highly publicized affair involving the American-Israeli Public Affairs Committee, whose president, David Steiner, was taped making assertions of having planted agents in the presidential campaign of Bill Clinton and having cut secret deals with James Baker of the Bush administration. It is a scenario of the anti-Semitic texts from the *Protocols of the Elders of Zion* right down to Elizabeth Dilling come to life.[76]

Thus, to an audience already convinced of the truth of Jewish control, the public successes of the ACMs tend to reinforce the views of the faithful and make it all the more difficult for wavering Identity adherents to question the received wisdom of the far right wing. Indeed, it is arguably the success of the ADL and its allies in isolating the target movement and publicizing only its most extreme tendencies that may be responsible for attracting the most extreme elements in American society to the movements in the first place! Clearly, the case of Christian Identity and the anti-cult movement that has become attached to it demonstrates in graphic terms the extent to which cult and counter-cult can together form a complex symbiosis in which each protagonist appears to fulfill the most dire constructions the one has formed of the other.

B'nai Noah

Despite criticism suggesting that the B'nai Noah in some way constitute a cult movement,[77] no organized ACM group has yet appeared to oppose B'nai Noah activities. The ADL has never contacted the group's leader, J. David Davis, and only one Christian cult awareness group has done so.[78] Indeed, only the Christian Identity movement has shown any interest in forming such an opposition, and for several reasons, the possibility of Identity adherents founding a true anti-cult organization is almost nil. A good deal of the current immunity from ACM opposition enjoyed by the B'nai Noah may be their sudden appearance in 1991: there has simply been insufficient time for them to make many enemies. Moreover, it is probable that the ideology and the organizational structure of the B'nai Noah will insure that this freedom from ACM attention will continue.

On an ideological level, the core message of the B'nai Noah is unquestionably incendiary: the denial of the divinity of Jesus, a Christianity-equals-idolatry polemic, and the embrace of the Jews as teachers and guides under the theory of covenant plurality (i.e., the theory that God may have multiple simultaneous covenantal relationships). However, the B'nai Noah have emerged at a time of unprecedented Jewish-Christian accord in America, a time that gives a dimension of real meaning to the oft-quoted but seldom defined description of American culture as Judeo-Christian.[79] More important, no sector of the American Christian community has been more militantly philo-Semitic and pro-Israel in recent years than have the evangelical and fundamentalist churches (perhaps for reasons dwelling more on eschatology than on ethics). As an attack on the B'nai Noah would surely risk being interpreted as an attack on the movement's Jewish sponsors and supporters, it is unlikely that any such opposition may be anticipated from this sector of Christianity. Given that the evangelical and fundamentalist churches are the backbone of the religious anti-cult movement, without their involvement, the B'nai Noah appear to have little to fear from the Christian ACMs.

The organizational structure of the B'nai Noah further mitigates against a serious risk of the movement being anathematized as a cult. Save for its southern epicenter, the movement is geographically diffuse and very loosely organized. There quite literally exists no machinery of central control by which David Davis or the core group of rabbinical teachers around him could exert effective control, even if they were so inclined. The rabbis at the center of the movement—Manachem Burstin, Yehoshua Friedman, Yoel Schwartz, Israel Chait, and Michael Katz to name a few—are scattered between Israel, New York, and Atlanta.

Moreover, these rabbinical figures are often sharply divided on their religious and organizational views. Satellite groups of B'nai Noah are spread throughout the country (indeed, throughout the world), and they tend to stay in touch with the Athens, Tennessee, center only fitfully, through occasional letters, phone calls, and the annual conference held in Athens which links the B'nai Noah with their Jewish mentors from throughout the world.

Adding to the factor of geographic diffusion is the rudimentary state of B'nai Noah theology. Beyond belief in the seven Noahide commandments, there is as yet little in the way of dogma to unite the movement. This lack of spiritual guidance from the center further accentuates the influence of local rabbinical teachers engaged in instructing the Noahide groups. Lacking a manual of instruction or even a shared conception of what a Noahide should know or do, these local teachers are free to emphasize whatever aspect of Judaism beyond the seven laws that they deem appropriate to their gentile flock. Ironically, it may be the very visible presence of these local rabbis that best serves to insulate the B'nai Noah from accusations of cultism, for these rabbis are invested with an institutional charisma which the dominant culture recognizes as legitimate. The central role played by local Orthodox rabbis virtually insures that no single charismatic leader will come to be seen as dominating the lives of a particular Noahide group, making the epithet "cultist" unlikely to stick to the movement.

Although the B'nai Noah movement is still too young to have drawn the attention of the more secular ACMs, the longer-term outlook here is not as clear as it appears to be with reference to the religious ACMs. Since conversion to Noahidism does not, for most adherents, entail any dramatic break from their preconversion routine (no one quits their job, changes their style of dress, leaves their family, etc.), it is unlikely that a group composed of the relatives of new converts (often the first stage of ACM formation) will arise to challenge the B'nai Noah. In a striking irony, if a secular ACM is to take up the case of the B'nai Noah, it is likely to emerge from Jewish rather than Christian sources. Although such a development seems unlikely, it could result from the B'nai Noah's alignment with several of the most extreme constituents of the Israeli radical right, the Temple Mount movement and (if Rabbi Michael Katz's council prevails) with the settlement movement. Should the B'nai Noah become too closely identified in the Jewish world with the Third Temple Movement or with Gush Emunim, they may well find themselves enmeshed in the intense inter-Jewish polemic surrounding these groups. Indeed, in this respect, the B'nai Noah may have dodged a bullet when cofounder Vendyl Jones's connection with Rabbi Meir Kahane was severed by the rabbi's assassination on 5 November 1990. Even the ADL felt constrained to bring its influence to bear against the late rabbi.[80]

This leaves as a potential anti–B'nai Noah ACM only that most unlikely of candidates, Christian Identity, itself hounded tirelessly by the ADL! In the initial Identity response to the publicity surrounding the B'nai Noah and the 1991 Education Day controversy, a single figure— Pastor Paul Hall of Midpines, California, the publisher of the influential Identity newspaper *Jubilee*—appeared to have the interest and wherewithal to carry through in forming a center of opposition to the B'nai Noah. Hall was the sole Identity figure to continue to follow the progress of the U. S. Congress's genuflection to the Lubavitcher Rebbe Manachem Schneerson through the vehicle of the second Education Day Resolution, Public Law 102-268 (13 April 1992), a resolution that differed from its 1991 predecessor solely in its correction of the Rebbe's birthdate from 22 March to 14 April.[81] Hall even bought *The Path of the Righteous Gentile* to guide his study of the Noahide Laws.[82]

However, despite promises to follow up on the B'nai Noah movement and the wider Noahide controversy, Pastor Hall through the mid-1990s had yet to make good on this vow. Why this should be speaks to the heart of the unsuitability of Identity leaders and indeed of the far right wing as a whole to create an ACM. Quite simply, they are equipped neither temperamentally nor in terms of resources to focus exclusively on any one set of issues or groups. By the next issue of *The Jubilee*, Hall's attention had been drawn to the Earth Summit in Brazil, a gathering of world leaders that struck him as apocalyptic, summoning images of the anti-Christ;[83] the following issues concentrated almost exclusively on the Randy Weaver drama in Idaho. ACMs are simply not built on the rock of so fleeting an attention span. Nor, in the last analysis, should it be any other way! After all, Christian Identity is an apocalyptic millenarian belief system; given the incessant state of eschatological excitement prevalent in the movement, what could possibly motivate an Identity believer to undertake any long-term commitment? Particularly if that commitment is to oppose a sign of the imminence of the End, the chiliastic event that is the primary longing of every Identity Christian!

Ásatrú/Odinism

The capture of the Order and the discovery that its leader, Robert Mathews, was an Odinist made it virtually inevitable that the same Jewish watchdog organizations that have become the most implacable opponents of Christian Identity would set their sights on the Ásatrú/ Odinist community. Indeed, when in the late 1980s the process of monitoring both Christian Identity and National Socialist literature turned up increasing references to Odinism as a natural religion for Aryan youth who could not accept the biblicism of Identity, the Jewish ACMs could not help but take notice. If past practice is any guide, it is only a matter of time before monitoring turns into action and the attempt is made to sever the Odinist/Ásatrú community from any viable contact with the dominant culture.

Before its widespread identification with the racialist right, the Ásatrú/Odinist community was treated by the fundamentalist and evangelical ACMs as a mere appendage of the Wiccan and neopagan community. So undifferentiated is the interpretation of neopaganism by the ACMs that it is no easy task to find a Christian anti-cult group that evinces any specific interest in Norse paganism. What interest there is comes largely from the ACM clearinghouses, and it is clear from a survey of several of the more prominent of these groups that the racialist aspects of Ásatrú/Odinism are decidedly less important to them than is the dogmatic belief that the real issue is Satanism rather than anything specific to the Norse tradition itself.

To give but two examples, the Cult Awareness Network, never having received a complaint from a distraught parent, has little in the files of its Chicago headquarters regarding either Ásatrú or Odinism. CAN, however, is highly decentralized, and its Texas president Sondra Chesky and vice president Jan Keith are well aware of the Ásatrú movement. The source of this knowledge is rather remarkable, and speaks volumes of the symbiosis of cult and countercult in the world of ACMs.

Samuel David Heron claims to be a former teen-aged Satanist from a conservative Baptist family in the Houston area, who had been rescued from the world of the occult by concerned local Christian ministries. Satanism being a subject of great interest to the Houston chapter of CAN, he eventually came to the attention of the Cheskys, who sponsored several speaking engagements in local high schools.[84] Never able to completely eschew the world of the occult mysteries—nor to fully accept the ACM proposition that the occult is wholly the domain of the devil—Heron met Ymir Thunarsson, a former member of the High Rede of the Ásatrú Ring of Troth and the high *ghodi* ("priest" in the loosest sense of the term) of the idiosyncratic Eagles' Reaches kindred. Heron eventually joined both organizations, while retaining his ties with CAN![85] These ties were only broken by the Cheskys when evidence of Heron's increasing mental instability began to cast doubt on his story of Satanist involvement.

Of greater interest than Heron's misadventures is the sympathy of CAN's Jan Kieth for Ásatrú and indeed for the Wiccan/neopagan movement in general.[86] Keith might appear to be "metagenetically" disposed to Ásatrú on the basis of her family history. She claims that she is able trace her German ancestry to Hessia in 1610 and that her grandfather was a ceremonial magician, whose house in Pflugerville, Texas, was adorned with runes for warding and prosperity; through him, she was taught the mythological heritage of the Germanic peoples, and thus considers herself closer to polytheism than to Christianity. This has led to some internal tension in the Houston affiliate, but as CAN is a highly decentralized organization, this is considered an entirely local affair so long as nothing untoward—or public—results from local activities.[87]

This decentralization—fundamentally the result of a dearth of funding—is in fact CAN's primary weakness. Information obtained by an affiliate often does not find its way to Chicago, on occasion leaving the center in a position of not knowing what the affiliates are doing. Of greater concern, however, is the weakness of an ACM clearinghouse that is unable to create a central archives. For its part, CAN is acutely aware of this, but lacks both funds and staff to address the problem.

Jack Roper of the Christian Apologetics: Research and Information Service has been more aware of Odinism (although not Ásatrú) than has CAN. His files at first glance appear voluminous, but on closer examination, consist entirely of issues of Else Christensen's publication *The Odinist* from 1980 to 1983.[88] The focus of both the ACM clearinghouses and the Jewish watchdog groups on Christensen and the Odinist Fellowship may be attributed to her brand of unabashedly racialist Odinism. Christensen has certainly not been without detractors from within the movement as well; numerous figures in the Ásatrú community consider her and the Odinist Fellowship racist, as do other figures in the Wiccan/neopagan community.[89] Christensen, for her part, strongly denies the accusations of racism and counters with a complaint that has taken on considerable resonance among both Ásatrúers and Odinists, religious persecution and outright discrimination.[90] The blame for this atmosphere of alleged religious intolerance is laid at the door of the Christian community and the ACMs. Such complaints have come from throughout the country, and a brief examination of these incidents demonstrates the manichaean analytical model through which Christian ACMs have assessed the origins, activities, and relative level of threat presented by the Ásatrú community.

Else Christensen's complaints of religious persecution have less to do with any negative experiences of her own than with the experiences of the two primary constituencies of the Odinist Fellowship. The Fellowship functions as a mail order ministry, enjoying very little personal contact with its adherents; thus, the members of the Fellowship tend to be either independents who do not have primary ties to a local kindred or prisoners from around the United States. That either group would be by definition the victims of persecution is a dogma of the Odinist community, given the strongly negative view of Christianity held by Odinists and Ásatrúers alike. This anti-Christian polemic has been raised to a manichaean crescendo in the pages of *The Odinist*. In the face of the many forms that persecution is seen as taking, Christensen asserts that her constant council is for patience:

> When letters come in full of anger about obvious discrimination (and there is a lot!) (funny enough, the Blacks say the same!), I act as a conductor. I do not deny the problems, that would be stupid, but in some prisons I have suggested that our men get together with the Muslims to keep order on the compound and/or to negotiate with the administration; a few times it has worked.
>
> I try to get them to use logic and understand that working together is a lot more productive than fighting.[91]

It is important to note that for Christensen, Odinism is a warrior religion, and she thus holds the Christian concept of turning the other cheek in contempt. Nonetheless, extreme anti-Semitism or derogatory language "alienates those who might otherwise work with us, and . . . will put even more people into the jails and prisons."

Where Else Christensen counsels patience and preparation in the face of Christian persecution, Stephen McNallen, founder of the Ásatrú Free Assembly, professes some bemusement at the irony of Christian fundamentalists attacking Ásatrúers who in fact share certain social and political, if not religious, attitudes with American fundamentalism:

> After a period of religious tolerance that has lulled us for several decades—a tolerance that has protected both the best and the worst in American behavior—it is apparent that we are entering a time when we of Ásatrú are going to meet greater and greater resistance from the powers that rule this country . . . [yet] Many of the values championed by those who oppress us are values with which we can readily identify, such as strengthened family, less bureaucratic intervention in the life of the individual.[92]

In interviews with Ásatrúers and Odinists from across the United States, the precise nature of this alleged persecution by Christian groups is difficult to pin down, but clear patterns do emerge. Anecdotes of personal misfortunes blamed directly or indirectly on Christian ACM activity are not uncommon. One of the better known of these involved the current Steersman of the Ring of Troth, William Bainbridge, an Arizona attorney who was forced to resign from his firm when his involvement in the pagan community became known. The problem illustrates the effectiveness of the ACM paganism-equals-Satanism scenario, in that Bainbridge's travails began with a police raid on the home of a local member of the pagan community in a futile search for human remains believed to have been used in a Satanic ceremony. As a member of the Pagan Arizona Network, Bainbridge—promised anonymity—carried a protest to a local detective. The promise was not kept, and Bainbridge's employers offered him the option of resignation or a long and possibly public investigation, which would have effectively ended his professional career in Phoenix.[93]

One of the more picturesque incidents of the persecution of Ásatrúers involved a woman in a town in the Southwest who, in the course of recovering from a recent divorce, joined the local Kiwanas Club. Through this association, she volunteered to coach a local Girl Scouts softball team. When the local newspaper learned of her Ásatrú involvement, it printed a story falsely accusing her of demanding that a cross be removed from the public park. As a result, she not only was removed as a coach but was all but driven from the town.[94]

Upon closer examination, the factor linking these and many more anecdotes of localized persecution invariably turns out not to be local fears of Ásatrú—indeed, few of the family centered ACMs active on the local level have even heard of Ásatrú, and the ACM clearinghouses are not much more enlightened. Rather, the core of the problem is the fear of Satanism, for which neopagan traditions are believed to be but a mask. This identification was brought home in particularly graphic form in an incident at a local public high school when a professional occult investigator projected pictures of Satanic materials on a screen, and the children of an Ásatrú family noted that some of what was referred to as a "Satanic alphabet" consisted of Norse runes. The source for this story, a prominent Ásatrúer, recalls other incidents in the Southwest, including one in which the local sheriff arrived at his door with news of the "ritual killing" of a dog that was found buried in a shallow grave by the roadside. The "indisputable evidence" that the killing was connected to a Satanic rite was the fact that when the dog was found, all the blood had been drained from the body. Local excitement abated, however, when it was learned that the dog had been dead for some time and that the animal's blood had been lost as a result of natural processes.[95]

It is interesting to note that, despite the dogmatic quality of the belief in the formula Ásatrú/Odinism = Wicca/neopaganism = Satanism, no Christian ACM appears to have looked closely enough at the Ásatrú movement to notice that one of the most divisive internal controversies to beset the community centered on the acknowledged presence of Satanists within Ásatrú ranks. Nor were these debates a matter of abstract theory. Rather, Edred Thorsson, then the head of the Ring of Troth and the Rune Guild, revealed himself in 1989 to be a Fifth Degree Magus and the Grand Master of the Order of the Trapezoid in the Temple of Set![96] Moreover, Thorsson was—even before his connection to Michael Aquino and the Temple of Set—active in Anton LaVey's Church of Satan.[97] Thorsson's subsequent departure from the Troth, however, did not end the connection between Satanism and the Northern Way. A significant number of Ásatrúers have passed through the world of Satanism and some maintain their involvement with the left hand path. In Europe, the commingling of Satanism with National Socialist beliefs and racialist Odinism is quite advanced, including a new Paris-based journal, *Filosofem,* which unites such high profile adherents as Norway's Varg Vigerness, New Zealand's Kerry Bolton, and America's Michael Moynihan, among others. Vigerness, more popularly known as "The Count," is currently serving sentences for murder and for his involvement in burning medieval Norwegian churches; he was a leading figure in the Satanist underground before his conversion to a National Socialist form of racialist Odinism.[98] Thus, the fact that so widely known and highly divisive an issue has escaped the notice of the Christian ACMs speaks volumes for the quality of research—and the degree of attention—that the Ásatrú/Odinist community has drawn in these circles.

The Jewish components of the ACM community, especially the Anti-Defamation League, command considerably greater resources than do the Christian ACMs and thus presumably would have been aware of the doings of the Ásatrú/Odinist community. In particular, they could not have failed to note the references to Odinism that have become ever more frequent in the literature of the Ku Klux Klan, National Socialism, and racially oriented skinheads. In addition, the competition for the allegiance of white prisoners waged by Christian Identity, Odinism, the Church of the Creator, and (until his recent death) Robert Miles' Mountain Church has been no secret. In fact, by the time the Order's high profile activities were brought to an end, the Ásatrú/Odinist community had appeared squarely on the radar of the ADL's intrepid Research Department. The situation closely resembles the early demonization of Christian Identity. There is the same almost accidental (or fortuitous, depending on the perspective of the observer) discovery of the movement and the same gathering of preliminary material from the publications of movements already targeted as enemies of the American Jewish community. Perhaps most important, the Jewish ACMs have taken the same undifferentiated approach to the movement, isolating its most extreme elements and presenting them as "typical" members of a dangerous and potentially violent group of right-wing extremists.

The ADL represents a purely secular set of political interests, despite its sectarian base in the Jewish community. Thus, whether or not a particular leader is a Satanist, or whether the movement is an authentic reconstruction of pre-Christian Germanic paganism or a purely modern construct of adherents seeking alternative forms of communal identification, are questions that would evoke little interest in ADL circles. Rather, their concerns appear to be more elemental: are Odinists racist and anti-Semitic, and if so, do they represent an immediate threat to the Jewish community and a long range challenge to the state? By the early 1990s, the ADL had answered this question in the affirmative, at least in so far as Odinism's identification with National Socialism is concerned, as demonstrated by a letter from Alan M. Schwartz, Director of the Research and Evaluation Department of the Anti-Defamation League. He writes:

> While there may be Odinists who are not part of a neo-Nazi or other hate movement . . . Odinism has been a pseudo-religious strain of American neo-Nazi activity and propaganda. These neo-Nazis apparently consider the worship of Odin and other ancient Norse gods as part of their vision of "Aryan" supremacy. I enclose a piece of neo-Nazi propaganda illustrating this link.[99]

The neo-Nazi material to which Schwartz refers is the premier issue of the *Aryan Action Line,* a publication that touts right-wing causes (especially of the National Socialist variety) and tries to find jobs and housing for "comrades" in unfortunate situations. The key passage of this document is worth quoting in full:

> *The Study of our Past Helps to Guarantee our Future*
> The Odinist Fellowship publishes an excellent newsletter called The Odinist. This informative newsletter has many historical and religious facts. Our Aryan roots go further back than the birth of Jesus Christ and every member of our Movement should learn every aspect of our past. Whether you are an Identity Christian or an avowed atheist you should know how our people lived in the ancient past as well as the more recent past.[100]

Despite Schwartz's concern, the ADL has not gone further than identifying Odinism as a neo-Nazi front group. No literature has yet been issued warning of the dangers of Odinism, and no apparent efforts have been made to get the mainstream press to focus on the movement (which it clearly has not done of its own accord). Thus, if it is true that the ADL/Christian Identity relationship could serve as a paradigm for the evolution of the dealings of the ADL and other secular ACMs with the Ásatrú and Odinist communities, there may yet be time to prevent a similar sort of vilification—and ultimate demonization—

of what is in reality a numerically small but highly diverse religious movement.

That time may be running short however. Some local watchdog groups have begun to look more closely at the Ásatrú and Odinist movement and, based on the undeniable presence of racist adherents within its ranks, have begun to research the movement and to publish exposés based on this research. One group that is still very much in the investigative stage is the British watchdog publication *Open Eye,* whose primary interests seem to center in Britain. Further advanced is the work of the Coalition for Human Dignity, based in Portland, Oregon. In a recent publication, the Coalition published an account of a 1993 weekend gathering of Ásatrúers to celebrate "Viking Days" in Vancouver, Washington. The article concentrates on the racist connections of some members of the local kindred as well as "the editor of *Vor Tru* who was present at the event." The article supplies quotations from that journal as well as other Ásatrú publications to bolster the assertion that the Alliance, and indeed the religion itself, is racist.[101]

There are indeed a number of adherents of National Socialism and other far–right wing racialist ideologies in this community, but there also are a number of adherents who abhor this racialist trend and who exert every effort possible to purge the movement of its racialist element.

One of these antiracialist adherents has in fact taken it upon himself to report on the doings of racist Ásatrúers/Odinists to the Klanwatch group in Alabama. (His first inclination was to perform this function for the ADL, but after reading an article of mine in *Syzygy,* he elected to contact Klanwatch instead.) The primary motivation for this mission appears to be a desire to purge the movement of racialist elements so as to avoid the kind of treatment that has been accorded to such racialist religious groups as Christian Identity. Secondarily, it is hoped that an Ásatrú purged of racists and National Socialists will appeal to adherents with stable families and strong ties to the dominant culture; he believes that only in this way will the movement grow into a stable minority religious community within the pluralistic ethos of mainstream America.[102]

In the middle there appears to be a considerable group—perhaps a majority—who could not be described as racialist in any meaningful sense of the term and who simply wish the issue would go away.[103] Indeed, for the last several years there has been a virtual civil war within Ásatrú/Odinist circles for the soul of the movement. Whether in the end the racialist or the nonracialist faction will ultimately inherit control of the tradition is as yet impossible to know. Based on a reading of recent history, however, this much can be said with some certainty: should the racialist adherents of the community achieve predominance—

and given their superior organization and often greater motivation this remains a distinct possibility—the movement can, like Christian Identity, look forward to a future of angry isolation. Stephen McNallen, the founder of the American Ásatrú movement, notes this danger and suggests that such ACM activity may very well constitute a self-fulfilling prophesy:

> If watchdog organizations try to stigmatize all Asafolk or Odinists as haters or paramilitary types, they will hurt the very people within the movement who are a force for moderation. Reasonable individuals will be repelled, and the extremists will be attracted to what they perceive as like-minded folks. These groups—the watchdogs—will have created the very enemy they feared.[104]

6

A Confederacy of Seekers?

Against stupidity, even the gods battle in vain.

Friedrich von Schiller

If the Bible is true, then I'm Christ . . . But so what? Look at 2,000 years ago. What's so great about being Christ? A man nailed to the cross. A man of sorrow acquainted with grief. You know, being Christ ain't nothing.

David Koresh, 1993[1]

It is traditional for a book centering on such esoterica as millenarianism, heterodox religious groups, and eccentric views of modern political culture to conclude with a sort of grand intellectual *apologia* that seeks to make the case that this too is important. Implicit in this formulation is the presumption that, in normal times, the work will be of interest to only a small cadre of like minded scholars. In times of crisis, however, the intrepid scholar may be thrust in front of a camera and asked to explain the inexplicable. It is in the nature of the scholar that he will invariably attempt to do so. Such is the grand conceit of the academy, and such too is the petty conceit of this volume.

On 19 April 1995, just such a crisis occurred. On the second anniversary of the deaths of the Branch Davidians at Waco, Texas, a powerful explosion demolished the Federal Building in Oklahoma City, Oklahoma. Casualties were in the hundreds, and when it became clear that the accused bombers were associated with the radical right wing, the demands for answers and assurances were directed at scholars from a variety of academic backgrounds. With the news that Waco and Oklahoma City were connected—and that the violent denouement of the siege of Randy Weaver's cabin as well was part of the professed motivation for the bombing—even the scholarly community began to profess puzzlement.

As this book documents, there has in recent years been a marked increase in violence directed by federal authorities at oppositional religious and political groups throughout the American cultic milieu. This increase in violence, and the concomitant rejection of mainstream society and all its works on the part of the oppositional religious and political movements, set the stage for Oklahoma City. In this atmosphere, the attack on the Branch Davidians was seen by a wide variety of movements as an attack on all oppositional groups; the battle at Randy Weaver's cabin on Ruby Ridge, Idaho, was interpreted as yet another event in the federal government's continuing war against all who would oppose its dictates.

Paranoia writ large? Perhaps. But not isolated paranoia, for out of the ashes of Waco grew the militia movement. The core members of the various state militias would have no sympathy whatever for the esoteric teachings of David Koresh and would have even less tolerance for his alleged sexual improprieties. Each of them, however, could identify well with Koresh's fate, and each see the federal government as bent on the destruction of all potential centers of opposition. Here lies the glue that binds together the fantastically diverse American cultic milieu: fear of a government seen as beyond the reach of its citizens and a deep longing for individual freedoms held to be the birthright of all Americans, now all but lost. Moreover, it is clear that neither the conspiratorial suspicions of the millenarian adherents nor the government authority's equally strong suspicions of these oppositional religiopolitical appeals is in any way a new or unique phenomenon. In many times, and in many places, we have seen all this before.

It is an accepted truth that in every age and in every corner of the globe, small groups of people have become unalterably convinced that the processes of history are coming to an end. Although such groups of seekers invariably adopt an oppositional stance to the perceived pattern of changes in their respective societies, seldom are these movements catalyzed from the typical response of selective withdrawal from the dominant culture to a violent determination to act on the belief that the final drama has begun. This book, however, has set for itself a more ambitious task than restating the axioms of the field in the context of a selection of little known contemporary movements. Rather, two primary interpretive questions are at the heart of this study. First, when and under what circumstances will an essentially quietist movement evolve from a stance of "warning and rebuke" to one of violent action? Second, can the existence of a "community of seekers" among such disparate and often bitterly confrontational belief systems be documented?

The Question of Millenarian Revolutionary Violence

> How then, shall we begin to think about Jonestown as students of
> religion, as members of the academy? How might we use the resources
> available for thinking about human religious activity within the con-
> text of the corporate endeavor of the human sciences? A basic strategy
> . . . is to remove from Jonestown the aspect of the unique, of its being
> utterly exotic. We must be able to declare that Jonestown on 18 No-
> vember 1978 was an instance of something known, something we have
> seen before . . . We must reduce Jonestown to the category of the
> known and the knowable.[2]

In the case study of Christian Identity, revolution was defined as
either a violent resort to arms to overthrow the established state (and
not coincidentally, to bring about a denouement to history) or a nonviolent but no less transformative, assault on the accepted precepts of a
religious tradition. My initial model for such an understanding was that
of the early-fifteenth-century Hussite/Taborite/Adamite constellation of
religious rebels in Bohemia.[3] A radical offshoot of the nonviolent, reformist Hussite movement within the Church, faced with the frustration of
its immediate goals and with the Church's blatant betrayal of the movement's leader, resorted to a brief spasm of violence, the so-called Prague
Defenstration of 30 July 1419.[4] Soon after these events, a substantial
number of the rebels withdrew into the fortified cities of Tabor and
anxiously awaited the parousia. When attacked, however, they fought
back with unparalleled skill and, it was noted at the time, suicidal sav-
agery. Eventually, with relative success and breathing space, a sect of
radical purists arose from within the rebel ranks. The so-called Adamites challenged the sect to live as if Christ had indeed returned, as if
amidst the splendor of a "new heaven and a new earth" the original
purity of Eden, uncontaminated by original sin, had been reconstituted.
These purists were annihilated by the forces of Tabor.

With this case as a paradigm, and conditioned by years of the unquestioned expertise of the Anti-Defamation League of the B'nai B'rith
on the subject of the far right wing, I began this study fully expecting
that Christian Identity would represent a community of millenarian adherents fulfilling the definition of the term "revolution" in both its violent activist and its nonviolent polemical senses. Further, just as Pius
Aeneas (the future Pope Pius II) learned of the Taborites—a group as
feared and demonized in his day as are the adherents of Identity
today—by going to their cities and finding, much to his surprise, a community of believers whose qualities were at least as deserving of com-
mendation as of condemnation,[5] I chose to eschew the received wisdom
of the established "high priesthood" of these most esoteric of deities

and to attempt to learn from the movement firsthand. My goal was to present the movement in much the same spirit as Max Weber presented his consideration of the pariah people of his day, the Jews, in *Ancient Judaism*.[6]

Thus, readers of this work may be as disappointed I was surprised to find that although the adherents of Christian Identity—apocalyptic millenarians all, and the products of a vastly different sociopolitical context than that of the Taborites—fit the definition of revolution perfectly in its polemical dimension, only once did an Identity group go beyond words and seek to actualize a revolution in its violent sense. American Identity Christians, faced with a state of vastly greater power than that which confronted Jan Hus and his followers, and constituting as they do a pariah sect where the Hussites enjoyed significant popular support in their native Bohemia, encounter far greater obstacles to a resort to violence than did the Hussites after the frustration of their reformist hopes.

It is all the more remarkable, therefore, that one "Identity" movement did turn to organized revolutionary violence. That group, the Order, was, when it finally came to the attention of federal authorities, easily crushed. Making the matter more confusing from an analytical perspective, the Order was led by an Odinist, not an Identity Christian, and almost half of its core membership was comprised of Odinists. Clearly, Identity presents a case of something more complex than a "theology of violence," as the ADL would have it.

In fact, in recent years Identity adherents have been more the target of violence than its initiator. This was as true for Randy Weaver at Ruby Ridge as it was for James Ellison, who found federal agents surrounding his Covenant, Sword and Arm of the Lord compound in Missouri in 1985.[7] Granted, Richard Butler talks a violent game, as did Wesley Swift and William Potter Gale and as on occasion does Pete Peters. With the sole, ambiguous exception of the Order, however, Identity rhetoric has never catalyzed into actual organized violence—even despite the social upheavals of the late 1960s and early 1970s and the tumultuous changes in the world scene since then. Theoretically, these were the very conditions that had created revolutionary movements in the past; social dislocation of this kind has been posited as constituting the origins of millenarian revolutionary groups by scholars from Norman Cohn to Michael Barkun. But until Oklahoma City, still they slept.

Why then have the adherents of Christian Identity eschewed revolutionary violence, and what, if anything, would catalyze the movement into a confrontational mode? The answer to the former question seems much clearer than that to the latter. Quite simply, as with other historical cases of millenarianism, Identity Christians resist the call to violence for the simple reason that, given the imminent coming of Jesus, what could a premature confrontation with secular authorities accomplish? Hopelessly outgunned and relegated to the distant fringes of society, they know all too well that they will never be more than a numerically insignificant righteous remnant.

In the corpus of non-Western millenarian movements, such balance-of-forces considerations meant little to indigenous groups whose time-honored customs and way of life appeared on the verge of extinction.[8] Western millenarians, however, have historically been more prudent, expecting the imminent return of Christ but planting crops for the spring. When confrontation was on the horizon, these believers took considerable care to cement alliances and timed their actions according to the best available "rational calculus."[9] Compare the situation of Christian Identity in America with the widespread popularity and comparative affluence of the Hussite reformers or the numerical strength and military power of the Taborite cities! Acutely aware of their numbers, despairing of ever being able either to mobilize support in the dominant culture or to right the course of a nation "in the hands of an angry God" (to use Dan Gayman's words), what choice do Identity Christians have but to wait and to watch?

Indeed, watching is what millenarians do best. They watch for the signs of the End of Days. So sensitive are their antennae that the very process of enacting the timeless role of "watchmen on the wall" mitigates against deducing with certainty the onset of the End: as the technology of mass communication improves, adherents are so bombarded with signs and portents that they are unable to focus on any one subject that could be presented as proof of the End. Thus, although Randy Weaver's travails were held as apocalyptic for a season, this incident followed the Noahide Laws controversy and the Los Angeles riots and preceded in short order the Earth Summit in Brazil, the American incursion into Somalia, and then the horrific end to the federal siege of the Branch Davidian compound in Waco.

With such an abundance of Signs of the End, what, if anything, would catalyze Christian Identity into a violent confrontation with the powers that be? For the movement as a whole, it would be hard to envision many circumstances that would bring about such a change short of the return of Jesus or a CNN broadcast from Jerusalem in which the anti-Christ chooses to reveal himself to a breathless populace. Although direct attack on a particular Identity compound or community would be likely to spark a violent response, the movement remains too dispersed, too few, and too internally divided for any particular event to be apprehended and interpreted as a sure sign of the End by the community as a whole.

If Christian Identity is loath to become involved in physical violence, how much less the likelihood of other millenarians or messianists
doing so? Certainly, the B'nai Noah show no signs of preparing an ar-
mory for Armageddon. Ásatrúers will on occasion threaten violence—
to each other—but even with the catalysts of strong drink and a surfeit
of weapons, not one of these occasional threats has been carried out.
Revolutionary violence is a thought that would not be likely to arise in
even the most expansive adherent; Vikings may be a favorite Golden
Age model, but in the real world, rape, pillage, and plunder are all
activities best left to Hollywood Vikings.

Odinists, however, present a more interesting case. At the fringes of
the movement, there is an identifiable subculture that, given leadership,
arms, and a ray of hope, does offer some potential for genuine revolutionary violence. This fringe appears to be comprised primarily of white
prisoners, skinheads, and adherents of the radical right for whom Identity Christians are too old and too conservative and for whom other
racialist ideologies are too secular. It was out of this milieu that the
Order recruited key adherents, and it is thus of some interest to better
understand how such a belief system is formed and catalyzed from mere
discontent into a religious quest and ultimately into a revolutionary
zeal. Consider, then, a letter from a prisoner in Oklahoma to an Odinist
leader. This prisoner, possessed of an extraordinary talent for drawing
(employed in the creation of idealized Viking warriors), writes:

> I know about berserkers, I'm kind of a modern day version, a *skin-*
> *head*. I therefore like the image of the warrior-type Vikings. I also
> know about the gentle, peaceful side of their culture . . . As you may
> have guessed, I am a "Nazi," a "Radical," a "Racist," and most of all,
> a *Revolutionary*. After all, isn't Asatru a "revolution" of values and
> thought? I have heard of Odinists being rabidly anti-Nazi—"Oooh,
> those Nazis gave us a bad name." Well, admittedly Hitler made a lot
> of mistakes, but all "*National Socialism*" really was, was a revival of
> tribal and nationalistic instincts . . . The Third Reich produced some of
> the hardest "berserkers" modern times has seen.[10]

The letter is typical of the genre and suggests some potential for
alliance making and the transformation of a diffuse movement into a
revolutionary force aimed both at a radical reformation of the religious
tradition and at the destruction of the political system. However, the
very real limits of this potential are revealed in a subsequent letter from
the same prisoner:

> [skinhead actions are] to show that we are not a part of the main-
> stream sheepish society running around kissing up to the Jews. We are

proud of our Race and unafraid to fight to defend it . . . But that does scare some Racists off. Most of the Klan hates us. They say we are too violent and act like pagan Vandals. That's ok though they are not what they used to be.[11]

In other words, the right wing talks a better revolution than it is prepared to fight. The movement remains bitterly divided, and nowhere is that division more glaring than in the isolation of the violent fringe of the Odinist movement from other centers of the right-wing constellation or for that matter from the Ásatrúers. Moreover, should a leader arise who appears to have the potential to give shape and substance to this movement, it is a safe assumption that he will be neutralized by federal authorities at the first opportunity.[12]

For its part, the anti-cult movement in its various guises utilizes violence only sporadically—most notably in the kidnapping of "brainwashed cultists"—and its members are hardly exponents of revolution of any sort, be it within the tradition or against the authorities.

Given this marked disinclination toward violence, how are we to explain the bombing in Oklahoma City? Was it an isolated incident carried out by an individual or a small group of radicals, which has no relation to the movement's quietist majority? Will the radical right wing turn increasingly to acts of anti-state violence? Although it is impossible to know for certain, the evolution of views within the prolife "rescue" movement may provide a useful analogy. As the rescue message went unheeded by both the churches and the larger society and as punitive legislation increasingly forced all but the most committed of the rescue community to the sidelines, rescuers began to debate the utility of violence.[13] Then, a peripheral member of the rescue community, Michael Griffin, acted upon this rhetoric and shot Dr. David Gunn to death. This act definitively breached the barriers: within two years Shelley Shannon and Paul Hill had taken up the gun, and a minority of the movement were applauding their acts. Given the demonization which currently typifies the dominant society's perception of the radical right—and vice versa—it is not unlikely that the accused Oklahoma City bomber, Tim McVeigh, will be remembered as the Michael Griffin of the radical right wing. It is only necessary for others to follow his example.

This unhappy scenario is not inevitable, however. The invitation to a group of high profile militia leaders to testify before Congress in June 1995 suggests the possibility of a different outcome. Few would agree with the testimony of James Johnson, a black militia spokesman from Ohio, that the militias are the civil rights movement of the 1990s. Nonetheless, the opening of a dialogue with government authorities offers an avenue through which the cycle of right-wing suspicions and government repression might be broken. Another healthy development was the convening of congressional hearings into the tragedies at Waco and Ruby Ridge. The demotion of a prominent FBI official for his actions in the latter case is notable as well, as are changes that are being instituted by the FBI regarding its handling of such situations in the future.[14] In the final analysis, it is a process of dialogue—rather than punitive legislation or efforts to limit the protections afforded to all by the First and Second Amendments—that will best avoid another Oklahoma City.

The seeming incongruity between the public image of right wing millenarian adherents and the more pedestrian reality of their lives is a fitting place to end this meditation. At root, what advantage did the fifteenth-century Taborites possess that is unavailable to the contemporary millenarian/messianic movements? It would appear that two elements stand out: relative isolation—i.e., sacred space—and the manichaeism that is so rooted in the millenarian *weltanschauung*.

The Taborites could withdraw from the cities, from Prague, from Brno, and leave behind—along with the comforts of home and the familiarity of community—the machinery of state power. What the Taborites discovered was that, having renounced their ties to the world, the world found it difficult to enforce its writ upon them. Moreover, with isolation comes not only consolidation but radicalization. Millenarian expectations, it seems, if they are to catalyze into revolutionary movements, require isolation in which charismatic leaders may subtly reshape the adherents' perceptions of the world, of the times, and even of reality. In the process of creating this new reality, millenarian leaders have all too often succumbed to the temptations of antinomianism; the leader may begin to see himself—and be seen by his flock—as omnipotent, as Christ's Endtime vicar on earth. The leader's ambitions are often accepted by the group because in accepting these claims, the group too is assured of immortality and of final victory. Thus is the finely honed survival instinct of the millenarian dulled.

Manichaeism is, in this model, very much imbedded in the worldview of the millenarian. A manichaean framework requires the adherent to see the world as the devil's domain, in which the tiny, helpless "righteous remnant" perseveres through the protection of God in the hope that, soon, God will see fit to intervene once and for all in the life of this world. This self-perception as a tiny and powerless band of the faithful acts as a powerful check on the catalyzation of violence. Millenarians are no fools. They are canny judges of the prevailing balance of forces. That judgment can be dulled, or with time atrophy altogether, in conditions of angry isolation from the mainstream society.

It is this space, this enclave, that is so sorely lacking among the modern movements.[15] Identity Christians can withdraw to their cabins or compounds, but as Randy Weaver and James Ellison will attest, they live there on sufferance. The American government is fully capable of projecting its power into the most distant Identity redoubt. Indeed, just as Jim Jones fantasized over official suppression and so transmuted the fantasy into reality, and David Koresh saw the realization of Jones's worst paranoid fears in the apocalypse at Waco, it appears that in the modern world, full-scale millenarian revolutionary movements have become relics of a simpler time and a less regulated place.

Is, then, violent millenarian revolutionary activism a thing of the past? No, not yet. As Oklahoma City graphically demonstrates, the instruments of state control are not yet so developed as to preclude an individual or a small group from taking action. This truth was not lost on William Pierce or Richard Kelly Hoskins, authors of *Hunter* and *Vigilantes of Christendom* respectively, although neither would deign to involve himself personally in anything as perilous as revolution. Nor has this truth been lost on the American millennial community. Consider the following observations from a member of the most radical sector of the rescue movement:

> About myself: I'm in prison for burning an abortion clinic in Norfolk, Virginia in May 1993 . . . I'm a student of Bible Prophesy . . . I'm also a Vietnam veteran who has fought Communism. Partly because of that I was determined from the start to fit Communism into Bible Prophesy, if at all possible. I looked for evidence that the Antichrist, the Beast, the Man of Sin, Gog (all names for the same man) was a Soviet leader. I found it.
>
> I looked for evidence that the Endtime dictatorship in Western Europe would be due to Soviet conquest of Europe. I found it. I looked for evidence there would be a nuclear war (Soviet attack upon America). I found it, I'm sad to say.[16]

Or these, expressing a similar perspective:

> millenarianism . . . influenced my compulsion to defend the cause of the unborn . . . it led me to exert the use of actual force in defense the little ones' lives. You may or may not be aware that unlike Operation Rescue's participants, whose approach is one of passive resistance, I chose to apply active force.
>
> On 12/30/85 I left my house in Hebron, Kentucky, and drove across the Ohio River to Cincinnati where, using gasoline, I set fire to Planned Parenthood's abortion chamber and a late-term facility about a quarter mile away. Planned parenthood was destroyed, but the late term target was only damaged extensively enough to be shut down

for 6 months. Therefore, I decided to use explosives in any future operations.[17]

Like the model of the lone-wolf assassin in Pierce's novel, and like many of Hoskins's fanciful Christian vigilantes—and unlike the skinheads who hunt in packs and strike only when they know the victim to be helpless and harmless—these letters from millenarians active on the fringes of the prolife rescue movement indicate that there remains, in selected instances and among a small group of activists, an obligation to strike back, to take up arms and act on the knowledge that this is the End of Days. Thus, although the instruments of state power may destroy a millennial movement with impunity, even the powers of this world as yet struggle in vain against a single committed individual.

Toward an Interactive Model of a Millenarian Community

The "reborn" earth is overflowing with the anguished and frantic cries of those who mourn their dead and the screams of those mutilated and dying in religious battle zones from Waco, Texas to New York City's World Trade Center; from northern Ireland to Bosnia-Herzogovina; from the Arab-Israeli conflict in the Middle East to the killing fields and mosques of India.[18]

What do I do now? [Robert Redford in the film *The Candidate,* after being apprised of his electoral success]

If the question of millenarian revolutionary violence has proven on close examination to be something of a chimera, the same cannot be said for the existence of a "millennial community," that is, a community of adherents of widely differing religious belief systems who, lacking significant access to the dominant culture, talk largely to—and about— each other. This study has examined in exhaustive detail the process by which such exclusion comes about, the rise of a mediating "priesthood" whose self-appointed task it is to propitiate the distant and exotic "deities" of the millennial community, and the web of communication that binds together the disparate sectors of this remarkably large and wondrously diverse confederacy of seekers. Thus, again, Colin Campbell's theory of the cultic milieu as accurately portrays the movements considered here—as well as the international millenarian subculture of the eighteenth century[19]—as it does the equally colorful world of the New Religious Movements of the 1970s that were Campbell's primary focus. It will be enough, then, to once again borrow the conceptual apparatus of the religious map in order to locate each of the communities considered here in relation to each other and, perhaps of greater import, in relation to the dominant culture.

Before venturing out into the terra incognita that has come to be the abode of many of the subjects of this book, it would be well to consider for a moment the safe ground of terra firma upon which these words are being written. Here, safely ensconced in the comfortably secularized heart of the American civil religion, it is easy to rest in the assurance that, if there indeed be monsters out there,[20] we need know nothing of them. This peace of mind is the primary reason for the existence of the anti-cult movement, and if the ministrations of this high priesthood should prove ineffectual, well, there is always the police. Or the FBI. Or the Bureau of Alcohol, Tobacco, and Firearms. The monsters, however, have a disconcerting habit of reappearing. In Jonestown. In Waco. In the great cities and in the suburbs. In the countryside. In recent years they are seemingly everywhere, and yet—given the state of our knowledge of them—they would seem to have materialized from the very ether itself. Before offering a map by which these exotic forms of belief can be located, however, it is important to reiterate that, just as these communities can be viewed from the comfort of the homogenized American civil religion, they too can peer in from the fringes and they too have a name for the dominant religious terrain. For the racialist belief systems, that name is Judeo-Christianity, and this "syncretic pseudo-religion" represents for them the veritable incarnation of all evil—a last redoubt of the Babylonian darkness that their particular approach to hermeneutics has taught them to fear and despise.[21]

With this relativizing proviso, then, the first millenarian community considered above, Christian Identity, is also in many ways the most distant, spatially and spiritually. This was not always so. In its original form, as British Israelism, this small community could once count among its adherents the elite of nineteenth-century British society. It was in those days a rather genteel and generally philo-Semitic affair, offering an idiosyncratic biblicism in support of Great Britain's colonial enterprise. Upon crossing the Atlantic, however, the belief system was adopted in the twentieth century in various forms by such disparate leaders as Herbert W. Armstrong and his Worldwide Church of God, the *Dearborn Independent*'s W. J. Cameron, Howard Rand, Wesley Swift, and perhaps Gerald L. K. Smith himself. Genteel British Israelism was by World War II transformed into Christian Identity, a virulently racialist and anti-Semitic doctrine, and with the decision of the organized Jewish community to strike back, coupled with American security concerns in its conflict with the Axis powers, the process of banishing Identity to the fringes of American culture had begun. By the 1990s, Identity can no longer be found on the map of American religious communities. Instead, it resides among the monsters great and small in the wilderness of terra incognita, in an exile that gives every appearance of permanence. Thus, although the Identity message is on occasion relayed directly into the American cultural center through suitably packaged radio or satellite television broadcasts, Identity's principle point of contact with the mainstream culture is through the movement's most vociferous foes—the Anti-Defamation League, the Center for Democratic Renewal, and ultimately, the security organs of the state.

Identity, however, does not exist in lonely isolation. Rather, terra incognita is peopled with numerous small and bitterly divided theologies and ideologies, who together comprise what Michael Barkun has termed the white supremacist constellation. The interactions of these movements with each other and with the wider culture have been considered in some detail above. As far as the dominant culture is concerned, however, all of these racialist groups remain very much apart, every bit the "other" with whom respectable folk will have no truck and in righteous opposition to whom the high priests of the anti-cult movement and the security services justify their budgets—and their existence.

Again, Identity Christians are apocalyptic millenarians by definition, and as such, are ever on the alert for signs and portents of the expected divine judgment to be visited upon the mainstream culture. Thus, when a dissident sect—however aberrant it may be to Identity sensibilities—appears anywhere on terra incognita, it is a certainty that its existence will be quickly detected by and interpreted for the movement's adherents. It is thus not surprising that the early stirrings of the fledgling B'nai Noah community first came to my attention through the pages of Identity journals, which distinctly heard the hoofbeats of the apocalypse on the heels of the Children of Noah.

Remarkably, many of the B'nai Noah themselves heard echoes of the same horsemen, albeit with the interpretation that these dread riders were but a vanguard for the long tarrying Jewish Messiah. The connection between the two communities, bitterly oppositional as they are, is in the context of the American religious landscape not as odd a pairing as it would appear on the surface. Core members of both movements trace their origins to a border outpost, Protestant fundamentalism, whose bids for mainstream respectability (most recently under the guise of the New Christian Right) alienated certain seekers sufficiently to drive them "back to the Book" in a hermeneutic quest that led to the severing of their fundamentalist affiliations. Those who adopted Identity soon all but disappeared from the map. The B'nai Noah, however, cling tenaciously to the borderland by maintaining their connection to the "Judeo-Christian" mainstream through submission to the Orthodox rabbinate (or at least those members of the rabbinate who accept them as students). Moreover, these Orthodox connections serve to link the B'nai Noah to the constellation of Israeli messianists centered around the Temple Mount movement—the Jerusalem Temple Foundation first and foremost—and the Chief Rabbinate in the person of the Sephardi Chief Rabbi. Thus, the B'nai Noah reside on a double border between the American and the Israeli religious heartlands. Further, by virtue of Christian Identity's hostility toward them, the Noahide movement maintains a connection with the white supremacist constellation as well—a remarkable if perilous location.

Where the B'nai Noah can be found in a distinctive border zone, the Ásatrú and Odinist communities reside in a remarkable geographic niche of their own. Odinism is, of course, very much a denizen of the terra incognita of the white supremacist constellation. At the same time, it retains a connection to Ásatrú, and through Ásatrú to the wider oc- cult and magical community. Ásatrú itself is painfully aware of its con- nection to the "dragons which dwell beyond the pale"—Odinists and neo-Nazis and Klansmen and Identity Christians. Ásatrúers as individ- uals, however, reside (albeit often covertly) in the mainstream culture as lawyers, as military officers, and as college professors, to name but a few of the diverse pursuits of members of this community. At heart, however, Ásatrú is a magical religion, and it is to the community of Wiccans and neopagans that they most often turn for solace—and mar- riage partners. Indeed, Ásatrú inhabits the most perilous of border re- gions, at once warding the gateway to the terra incognita of the racialist right and providing a well-traveled bridge between the white suprema- cist constellation and the magical/occult community.

Finally, although each movement covered in this book has found its own unique location in the universe of American religiosity, and each has its own web of interactions both with like-minded and oppositional religious communities, the most intimate relationship that each move- ment "enjoys" is arguably that which binds the movement to its anti- cult "priesthood." In the final analysis, it is the anti-cult movement that forms the key connection between each movement and the dominant culture. The ACM watchdogs are truly the "watchmen on the wall," keeping their vigil over the borders of terra firma, monitoring the do- ings of the distant "monsters" beyond the horizon, and through their access to the mass media, creating the public's image of the target group.

The "anti-cult" image of the millennial community brings my work on this book full circle, for it was with the ADL's manichaean construc- tion of Christian Identity that my research started. When upon closer examination this most terrifying of the denizens of the unmapped re-gions proved to be considerably less threatening than their public image suggested, the need to throw light on the darkest corners of the community of seekers became clear. It is hoped that in this respect at least, this book has achieved some measure of success.

Notes
Bibliography
Index

Notes

Introduction

1. A good introduction to the various millennial positions may be found in Robert G. Clouse, ed., *The Meaning of the Millennium: Four Views* (Downers Grove, Ill.: Inter-Varsity, 1977) and Paul Boyer, *When Time Shall Be No More* (Cambridge, Mass.: Harvard Univ. Press, 1992). Cf. Michael J. St. Clair, *Millenarian Movements in Historical Context* (New York: Garland, 1992). For a lively history of American millenarian belief, see Timothy Weber, *Living in the Shadow of the Second Coming* (Chicago: Univ. of Chicago Press, 1987). Apocalyptic millenarianism is best presented by Bernard McGinn in his *Visions of the End: Apocalyptic Traditions in the Middle Ages* (New York: Columbia Univ. Press, 1979).

2. Bryan R. Wilson, "Millenarianism in Comparative Perspective," *Comparative Studies in Society and History* 6 (1963–64): 93.

3. Michael Barkun, "Millenarian Aspects of 'White Supremacist' Movements," *Terrorism and Political Violence* 1, no. 4 (Oct. 1989). For a further elaboration on the theme, see Jeffrey Kaplan, "Context of American Millenarian Revolutionary Theology: The Case of the 'Identity Christian' Church of Israel," *Terrorism and Political Violence* 5, no. 1 (Spring 1993).

4. Martin E. Marty, *A Nation Of Behavers* (Chicago: Univ. of Chicago Press, 1976); Colin Campbell, "The Cult, the Cultic Milieu and Secularization," *Sociological Yearbook of Religion in Britain* 5 (1972): 119–36.

5. Campbell, 121–22.

6. A good example of the search for rejected and suppressed knowledge is James Webb, *The Occult Establishment* (La Salle, Ill.: Open Court, 1991).

7. See, for example, Mark Koernke's videos "America In Peril Parts I & II" (n.d.) and "Mark Koernke at Meadville, PA 1995." The former video opens with a telephone number for a BBS line that features "100 Other Suppressed Files." Cf. also a video by Linda Thompson, "America Under Siege" (u.d). A good source for Patriot Videos is the Underground Hotline, P.O. Box 339, Adrian, Mich. 49221. For the costs paid by an earlier generation of seekers, see Lawrence Dennis and Maximillian St. George, *A Trial on Trial: The Great Sedition Trial of 1944* (Torrance, Calif.: Institute for Historical Review, 1984). The contemporary echo of the great sedition trial of 1944, the Fort Smith, Arkansas, sedition trial of 1989, will be considered at some length. Beyond these easily documented legal difficulties, every conspiracy theorist worth his salt will offer dark suspicions of persecution and harrowing tales of near escapes. The truth of any of this is, by its very nature, impossible to verify. However—not for the last time in these pages—it should be noted that even paranoids have real enemies.

8. Robert N. Bellah, *The Broken Covenant: American Civil Religion in Time of Trial* (New York: Seabury, 1975).

181

1. The American Millenial Community

1. Stated by an anonymous follower of William Potter Gale's California Identity ministry in Cheri Seymour, *Committee of the States: Inside the Radical Right* (Mariposa, Calif.: Camden Place Communications, 1991), 265.

2. The only comprehensive history of the evolution of the Identity movement is Michael Barkun, *Religion and the Racist Right: The Origins of the Christian Identity Movement* (Chapel Hill: Univ. of North Carolina Press, 1994), which serves as the basis for much of this section. Cf. Jeffrey Kaplan, "The Far Side of the Far Right," *Christian Century*, 2 Sept. 1994.

3. Richard Brothers, *A Revealed Knowledge of the Prophesies and Times . . . Containing with Other Great and Remarkable Things, Not Revealed to Any Other Person on Earth, The Restoration of the Hebrews to Jerusalem, by the Year 1798, Under Their Revealed Prophet.* Two parts in one volume (London, 1794); J. F. C. Harrison, *The Second Coming: Popular Millenarianism 1780–1850* (New Brunswick, N.J.: Rutgers Univ. Press, 1979), ch. 4.

4. Howard Rand, *The Servant People: A Brochure on Anglo-Saxon Identity and Responsibility*, pamphlet distributed by Destiny Publishers (n.d.), 13.

5. Glen Jeansonne, *Gerald L. K. Smith: Minister of Hate* (New Haven, Conn.: Yale Univ. Press, 1988), 103; Barkun, *Religion and the Racist Right*, 56.

6. Gerald L. K. Smith, *Besieged Patriot*, ed. Elma M. Smith and Charles F. Robinson (Eureka Springs, Ark.: Elma M. Smith Foundation, 1978), 238–39.

7. Gerald L. K. Smith, *Who Are The Chosen People? Certainly Not The Jews! (As We Now Know Jews)* (n.p., n.d.). Cf. idem, *Satan's New Testament* (Los Angeles: Christian Nationalist Crusade, 1975), 25.

8. "'Identity Churches': A Theology of Hate," *ADL Facts* 28 (Spring 1983); Leonard Zeskind, *The "Christian Identity" Movement: Analyzing Its Theological Rationalization for Racist and Anti-Semitic Violence* (Atlanta: Center for Democratic Renewal, 1986).

9. "Extremism Targets the Prisons," *ADL Special Report* (June 1986): 5–8.

10. For details on Order related activities, see Thomas Martinez (with John Guinther), *Brotherhood of Murder* (New York: Pocket Books, 1990), and Kevin Flynn and Gary Gerhardt, *The Silent Brotherhood* (New York: Signet, 1990).

11. Martinez, 270–71.

12. Pete Peters, *Death Penalty for Homosexuals* (Laporte, Colo.: Scriptures for America, 1993). The timing of the tract's appearance indicates that it was intended as a riposte to Bo Gritze's reluctance to endorse capital punishment for homosexuality before a gathering of Identity ministers during the 1992 American presidential campaign. Peters in this period was embroiled in a legal battle with the state of Colorado regarding a technical violation of the election law in regard to his activities in support of Amendment 2, a controversial measure that sought to remove homosexuals from legally protected status as members of a minority group.

13. Pete Peters, "Special Message and Alert from Pastor Peters," Scriptures for America cassette #552 (n.d.). The similarity of the tactics employed at Waco with those utilized against the far right wing did not go unnoticed. See Michael Barkun, "Reflections after Waco: Millennialists and the State," and Jeffrey Kaplan, "The Millennial Dream," both in *From the Ashes: Making Sense of Waco*, ed. James R. Lewis (Lanham, Md.: Rowman & Littlefield, 1994), 41–53. The plans themselves were published under the ungainly title *Special Report on the Meeting of Christian Men Held in Estes Park, Colorado October 23, 24, 25, 1992 Concerning the Killing of Vickie and Samuel Weaver by the United States Government* (Laporte, Colo.: Scriptures for America, n.d.).

14. On Peters' legal dilemma, see "Identity Minister's Church and Property Seized,"

Klanwatch Intelligence Report (Apr. 1993): 4. On the authoritarian personality, see Seymour Martin Lipset and Earl Raab, *The Politics of Unreason: Right Wing Extremism in America, 1790–1977* (Chicago: Univ. of Chicago Press, 1978), 477–82. Cf. the criticism of Lipset's findings in James Aho, *The Politics of Righteousness: Idaho Christian Patriotism* (Seattle: Univ. of Washington Press, 1990), ch. 7.

15. Dan Gayman's biography has been pieced together from the following sources: Dan Gayman, "For Readers of Zion's Watchman," *Zion's Watchman* 1 (Jan. 1977): 6; idem, telephone conversation with author, 17 Aug. 1991; idem, interview with author, 9–11 Dec. 1991; idem, "Kitchen Table Talk," *Watchman* 4 (Fall 1991): 36–37; J. Gordon Melton, *Encyclopedic Handbook of Cults in America* (New York: Garland, 1986), 57; and Anti-Defamation League, *Extremism on the Right: A Handbook* (New York: Anti-Defamation League, 1988), 98.

16. Gayman today seeks to downplay his Mormon roots. The historical record, however, is clear. The Church of Christ (Temple Lot), a schismatic Mormon sect, suffered a doctrinal schism in 1936. The leaders of the breakaway faction, including Dan's father Leo Gayman and his maternal grandfather Jesse Cruz, moved the sect to Halley's Bluff and Schell City, both in Missouri, in 1945. On this history, see Melton, *Encyclopedic Handbook of Cults*, 57; Steven L. Shields, *Divergent Paths of the Restoration: A History of the Latter Day Saint Movement* (Los Angeles: Restoration Research, 1990), 138–39, 194; and Dwain A. Jenista, "The Church of Christ at Halley's Bluff" (unpublished term paper, Univ. of Kansas at Lawrence, 1977).

17. Aho, *Politics of Righteousness,* 127–32, 167. Aho's research indicates that 32.3% of his subjects professing Christian Patriot beliefs came from Mormon backgrounds, a significant finding even in the Mormon heartland of Idaho.

18. Jenista, 6–10.

19. Kenneth Goff, an influential Identity pastor in the late 1940s and 1950s, is an interesting figure. The 1944 national chairman of Gerald L. K. Smith's Christian Youth for America group (of which Dan Gayman later became a member) and a self-proclaimed reformed communist, Goff emerges from the literature and the reminiscences of those who knew him as a decidedly equivocal man, described alternately as a brilliant preacher, a mentally unstable individual, a great patriot, and a shady character, often all in the same breath. He died several years ago, reportedly in a Chicago telephone booth while racing between speaking engagements, according to one of his students and admirers. For a printed accolade, see Jack Mohr's dedication to *The Satanic Counterfeit* (Muskogee, Okla.: Hoffman Printing, 1982):

> To the memory of a good friend, a kinsman by blood and through the blood of Jesus Christ, Kenneth Goff. As a dedicated soldier of the Cross, he was without excellence [i.e., a prophet without honor] in the roll call of modern day American heroes. Few men faced tremendous odds and danger, with the spirit of Christ, as he did. I predict that one day soon, when the battle for righteousness has been won, he will be recognized as the great American hero he was.

Cf. such secondary sources as Ralph Lord Roy, *Apostles of Discord* (Boston: Beacon, 1953), and Jeansonne, *Gerald L. K. Smith,* 119. Goff's writings, however, have little flavor of Identity doctrine.

20. Dan Gayman, *Articles of Faith and Doctrine for the Church of Israel* [pamphlet from the Church of Israel, Shell City, Mo.; 1982], 8. The document further indicates that Pastor Gayman had not yet altogether quit his Mormon beliefs, pledging allegiance to the truth of Holy Scripture and the Nephite Record.

21. The South African branch of the movement owes its existence to a pilgrimage to that then bastion of apartheid by a young Swedish racialist, Tommy Rydén. In a letter

dated 29 Feb. 1988, Gayman wrote: "Tommy, please share these tapes with other Isra-elites [in South Africa] if you will." He did, and Gayman's South African flock is the result (letter from Tommy Rydén to author, 23 Sept. 1995). In a fax to the author dated 14 Nov. 1995, Tommy Rydén notes that most South African Identity believers now follow Pete Peters' ministry rather than that of Dan Gayman.

22. The term "subscriber" may be misleading. The COI asks no money either for the *Watchman* or for the tape ministry. It does accept tithes and irregular offerings, but the literature of the church is at pains not to appear to stress finances. The exact number of persons on the mailing list, tithing, or sending irregular offerings is unavailable to the author; these numbers might be inferred, however, from the outreach of those centers of Identity or other religious ministries who do discuss their mailing lists. For example, the moderate *Identity News* from Minnesota, a newer and far less well established Identity center than the COI, began with a bulk mailing of 1,000 copies and within a year had expanded to 2,000 copies. However, these numbers are misleading, as "only about 2% of those who received the paper actually requested it. The rest went to people whose names I pulled from phone books" ("Letters," *Identity News* [Feb. 1992]: 8. Lest this sound too idiosyncratic to serve as a model, consider the experience of Gary North of Christian Reconstruction fame. After 15 years of tireless outreach, and a veritable mountain of published work, the Institute for Christian Economics can boast a mailing list of only 2,000 names! See Gary North, "Fifteen Years of Invested Time," letter to all ICE sub-scribers, Apr., 1992.

23. Dan Gayman, *Handbook for Establishing a Home Church* (pamphlet from the Church of Israel, 1990); idem, "Drawing Battle Lines," *Watchman* 3 (Summer 1991): 19–22; Leni Walker, "Building Your Home Altar" *Watchman* 3 (Spring 1991): 8–9.

24. Expressed by Louis Beam in John C. Calhoun and Louis Beam, "The Perfected Order of the Klan," *Inter-Klan Newsletter and Survival Alert* 5 (1984): 3.

25. Klanwatch, *The Ku Klux Klan: A History of Racism and Violence,* 4th ed. (Montgomery, Ala.: Klanwatch, 1991), 30–31. The Donald case is recounted in Bill Stan-ton, *Klanwatch: Bringing the Ku Klux Klan to Justice* (New York: Grove Weidenfeld, 1991). Cf. "Invisible Empire Turns Over Assets to the NAACP," *Klanwatch Intelligence Report* 69 (Oct. 1993): 1, detailing the demise of Imperial Wizard James W. Ferrands' North Carolina based Klan group.

26. The split by 1992 had come to the attention of the watchdog groups as well. See "Hate Groups in Bitter Struggle Over Public Image: Militants Call for Violence; Old Style Groups Claim to Condemn It," *Klanwatch Intelligence Report* 59 (1992): 3–4. Perhaps the best introduction to Beam's vision for the Klan and the country is Louis Beam, "On Revolutionary Majorities," *Inter-Klan Newsletter and Survival Alert* 4 (1984): 1. For Beam at his most vociferous, promising to one day "round up those guilty of heinous crimes like the mad dogs they are and execute the ones guilty, hang 'um,' deport them or otherwise rid our Nation of their miserable presence," see idem, "We Are At War," *The Seditionist* 10 (Summer 1991): 1.

27. Beam, "On Revolutionary Majorities," 7.

28. Dennis Mahon, "It's Now War!," *Oklahoma Excalibur* 1 (Mar./May 1992): 1.

29. See for example the remarkably sympathetic portrait of Robb by Michael Riley, "White & Wrong: New Klan, Old Hatred," *Time,* 6 June 1992, 25–27. For another view of Robb, see "Robb's Knights of the KKK Stage Small Comeback," *The Monitor* 25 (May 1992): 11. Cf. the media success of Robb acolyte and former skinhead Shawn Slater ("Colo-rado Klansman Refines Message for the '90s," *New York Times,* 22 Feb. 1992, 10).

30. Anti-Defamation League, *Hate Groups in America: A Record of Bigotry and Violence* (New York: Anti-Defamation League, 1988), 3–4; "The Hate Movement Today: A Chronicle of Violence and Disarray," *ADL Special Report* (1987): 4; and *Klanwatch, Special Report,* 47.

31. "The KKK Today: A 1991 Status Report," *ADL Special Report* (1991): 21.

32. Odin's description of Ragnarök from *The Prose Edda,* 12th c., in Snorri Sturluson, *The Prose Edda,* trans. Jean I. Young (Berkeley: Univ. of California Press, 1966), 86. The marked similarity of this description of Ragnarök, the Twilight of the Gods, to Jewish and Christian apocalyptic texts demonstrates the compatibility of the reconstruction of the Norse tradition with the monotheistic apocalypticists who people the radical right wing. With Ragnarök, the gods and a great deal of the potential for human happiness disappeared from the earth, leaving the Odinist/Ásatrú literature to refer to the contemporary world as the Wolf Age, based on this and similar texts.

33. To date, the only published account of the history of Ásatrú is Stephen E. Flowers, "Revival of Germanic Religion in Contemporary Anglo-American Culture," *Mankind Quarterly* 21, no. 3 (Spring 1981). Stephen Flowers is the birth name of Edred Thorsson, currently a primary Ásatrú theorist and a leader of a wing of the Satanist Temple of Set. A complete documentary history of the Ásatrú/Odinist community will appear as: Jeffrey Kaplan, "The Reconstruction of the Ásatrú and Odinist Traditions," in both *Magical Religions and Modern Witchcraft,* ed. James R. Lewis (Albany: State Univ. of New York Press, 1996) and *April 19 and Terror From the Right,* ed. David C. Rapoport (London: Cass & Co., forthcoming). The research for this article was conducted in the early 1990s, making it rather badly dated by the time it will appear in print. Parts of this work have been serialized and made available to the Ásatrú community through the journal *Thèod,* edited by Garman Lord.

34. "Wicca" is the name for the multifaceted reconstruction of a much romanticized version of the medieval witch cult. On the romantic roots of the reconstruction, see Jules Michelet, *Satanism and Witchcraft,* trans. A. R. Allison (New York: Walden, 1939). The modern reconstruction is based on the work of Gerald Gardner in England in the 1940s; see Gerald Brosseau Gardner, *Meaning of Witchcraft* (London: Aquarian, 1959). For evidence that Gardner's fanciful "discovery" of a surviving descendent of the ancient cult owes more to his own fertile imagination than it does to the Middle Ages, see Aidan A. Kelly, *Crafting the Art of Magic, Book 1: A History of Modern Witchcraft 1939–1964* (St. Paul, Minn.: Llewellyn, 1991). "Neopaganism" refers to reconstructions of a wide variety of pre-Christian religious traditions. For an introduction to the variety of these traditions in contemporary America, see Margot Adler, *Drawing Down the Moon,* 2nd ed. (Boston: Beacon, 1986).

35. Jung, C. G., "Wotan," in *C. G. Jung: The Collected Works,* vol. 10 (New York: Pantheon, 1964), 180. "Wotan" first appeared in *Neue Schweizer Rundschau* (Zurich) in 1936. The intellectual roots of the Odinist revival may be found in the nineteenth century of such German and Austrian occultists as Guido von List. See Nicholas Goodrick-Clark, *The Occult Roots of Nazism* (New York: New York Univ. Press, 1985).

36. See for example, Dusty Sklar, *Gods and Beasts: The Nazis and the Occult* (New York: Thomas Y. Crowell, 1977); Trevor Ravenscroft, *The Spear of Destiny* (York Beach, Maine: Samuel Weiser, 1982); and Jean-Michel Angel, *The Occult and the Third Reich: The Mystical Origins of Nazism and the Search for the Holy Grail* (New York: Macmillan, 1974).

37. A. Rud Mills, *The Odinist Religion: Overcoming Jewish Christianity* (Melbourne, Australia: A. Rud Mills, 1930).

38. Else Christensen, interview with author, 27 Nov. 1992. Mills is presented to the readers of *The Odinist* in "The Wisdom of A. Rud Mills," *The Odinist* 65 (1982): 1. Yockey would deservedly be accorded greater attention than Mills, however. See "Our View of History," *The Odinist* 10 (Dec. 1973): 1; "The Structure of History," *The Odinist* 11 (Mar. 1974): 1; and "More Yockey," *The Odinist* 12 (June 1974): 1. The octogenarian Christensen's long time association with the denizens of the American prison system caught up with her in 1993 when she was arrested and sent to prison after being caught in a car filled with marijuana.

39. Ásatrúers were belatedly treated to a discussion of Mills in the Ásatrú Alliance organ, *Vor Trú* 45 (Summer 1992).

40. Ron Hand, telephone conversation with author, 12 Sept. 1992. Hand is the source of much of what follows on Dietz and on the Odinist Study Group.

41. Stephen McNallen, interview with author, 4 Jan. 1993.

42. Flowers, "Revival of Germanic Religion," 282. Beinteinsson died in 1993, but during his life he was something of an icon for American Odinists. *The Odinist* carries the remarkable story of one young American who made the journey to see Beinteinsson, only to find the language barrier impassable. One is reminded of religious seekers of an earlier day who would make pilgrimages to distant holy men only to discover that they were equipped linguistically and culturally to do little more than stare at the radiant countenance of the learned one and to write moving accounts to the effect that the seeker's life was changed by the worthy's beatific smile. For just such a touching account, see P.F.B., "Visiting Iceland," *The Odinist* 49 (1980): 9.

43. Odinism made an early appearance in George Lincoln Rockwell's American Nazi Party barracks, possibly through the eccentric Jewish Nazi Daniel Burros in the early 1960s. A. M. Rosenthal and Arthur Gelb, *One More Victim: The Life and Death of a Jewish Nazi* (New York: New American Library, 1967). Burros rose to the position of political education officer in Rockwell's ANP. His legacy is the ANP's official manual which was distributed to all recruits: Lt. Dan Burros, *Official Stormtrooper's Manual* ([New York]: Dan Burros, 1961). It is dedicated to Horst Wessel.

44. The quote is taken from a typescript of McNallen's summer 1978 statement. The statement is accompanied by an internal NSWUP letter dated 24 June 1978 advising members to eschew their Nazi uniforms and paraphernalia for the "Odinist" event.

45. Peter Berger, *The Sacred Canopy* (New York: Doubleday, 1967).

46. Steven McNallen interview with author, 1 May 1996. Robert Stine interview with author 22–24 Dec. 1992. McNallen in 1996 feels that, in retrospect, it was simply "not the time" for an organization like the AFA and has taken from this experience the lesson that Ásatrú should not be made into a mass movement today. For greater detail of the AFA breakup, see chap. 3.

47. Mike Murray, interview with author, 29 Apr. 1996.

48. Mike Murray, letter dated 11 Aug. 1988, published in *Vor Trú* 30 (Haust/Fall 2238 R.E./1988): 12. *The New Dawn* was another of the several interchangeable publications issued by New Dawn.

49. Edred Thorsson interview with author, 20 Sept. 1992; idem, *A Book of Troth* (St. Paul, Minn.: Llewellyn, 1992), xii.

50. A letter from McNallen to Thorsson, dated 20 Jan. 1987, contains the last line: "Thanks also for the Temple of Set information!" This acknowledgment does prove that McNallen was aware of the TOS connection in 1986, but it falls well short of approval. In retrospect, he does not share Thorsson's sanguine recollections of the subject:

> Edred seems to have had much more diverse [interests] than most of us in the movement thought! As I recall, all this burst on Ásatrú after the demise of the AFA. I took no position on it though I feel that Ásatrú and Satanism are incompatible belief systems for one person to hold, just as Ásatrú and Christianity would also be incompatible. I suspect that the vast majority of Asafolk would agree. (McNallen, interview)

51. James Chisholm, interview with author, 17 Nov. 1992.

52. Edred Thorsson, interview with author, 15 Apr. 1993. Thorsson in fact felt that with a renewal of hostilities between the Vanes and the Æsir, all was right with the universe.

53. Thorsson has kindly made his letter, addressed to the Arizona Kindred, available

to this research. It is in fact a rather moderate attempt to explain his position, wrapped in salutations to the Althing and attacks on reactionary Christian forces bent on sullying the reputation of the good Dr. Michael Aquino: "the source of the problem—the dying force of the decrepit White-Krist . . . Michael A. Aquino is in full support of the Ásatrú movement and its aims in the world. This is also true of MANY others (some of your close acquaintance) who follow the Left-Hand Path. Don't reject your friends and kinsmen for the sake of your enemies." Thorsson then attempts once again to explain his quest for the shamanic experience of the light and dark paths of Odin ("An Open Letter to Members of the Arizona Kindred From Edred Thorsson, Odhinsgodhi and Yrmin-Drighten," 30 May 1989). Interviewed on 20 Sept. 1992, Thorsson denied that Aquino had any "interest in or knowledge of, the Ring of Troth."

54. KveldúlfR Gundarsson, interview with author, Jan. 1993.

55. The "rehabilitation of Nazi occultism" charge, carrying with it the implication that Thorsson subscribed in some way to subtly packaged National Socialist doctrine, is clearly a sore point with Thorsson. In an article which decries racialism as a "nineteenth century dualist construct," Thorsson fails to address the issue of how the Order of the Trapezoid (which goes unmentioned) can claim to have been reconstituted through Michael Aquino's magical working at Himmler's castle without having raised the shade of "Nazi occultism"; see Edred Thorsson, "Who Will Build the Hearths of the Troth: Are Racial Considerations Appropriate?" *Idunna* 1, no. 2 (July 1989): 16–24. Even today, Thorsson remains incredulous that Mike Murray of all people would criticize anyone on the basis of neo-Nazi ideology (Thorsson, interview, 15 Apr. 1993).

56. Cassette recording of Althing 9, June 1989. The statement went on to condemn Chisholm but otherwise declined to become entangled in the chaotic situation that was then unfolding in Texas, or to take sides in the Rob Meek–Edred Thorsson feud.

57. Letter from Dianne Luark Ross to all *Idunna* subscribers, 29 July 1989.

58. Thorsson interview, 15 Apr. 1993. Cf. Pauline Réage, *Story of O* (New York: Ballentine, 1965).

59. Edred Thorsson, *Northern Magic* (St. Paul, Minn.: Llewellyn, 1992), 161.

60. Thorsson, interview, 15 Apr. 1993. Cf. Edred Thorsson, "Order of the Triskelion," unpublished, privately circulated form letters which outline the general tenets of the Order (n.d.).

61. Meek was at the time a member of the Society for Creative Anachronism, and this group had been invited by McNallen to put on a demonstration of medieval costumes and jousting for the Heritage Center's Grand Opening. Meek stayed on to learn more of the Nothern Way. Robert Stine, interview with author, 1 Apr. 1993.

62. Meek's biography was printed in *Idunna* before his fall from grace; he was held up as a model for all to emulate. See "Announcements," *Idunna* 1, no. 4 (Feb. 1989): 34–35.

63. See, for example, letters to the editor, *Vor Trú* 41 (Summer 2241/1991): 30.

64. Indeed, some still believe that Meek's fall was engineered magically by Thorsson in his role as a Satanist. Thorsson denies this, saying that the Temple of Set—unlike the Church of Satan—does not use magical means to deal with mundane attacks. He was confident from the beginning that Meek would ultimately be destroyed—but by the gods, not by a magical working (Thorsson, interview, 15 Apr. 1993).

65. William Bainbridge, interview with author, 24 Jan. 1993.

66. Letter from Phil Nearing to the Ásatrú Alliance, 6 Jan. 1991. In an undated accompanying letter, Nearing tendered his formal resignation as Thingspeaker as well.

67. "Satanism, murder and S&M just ain't going to make it for a religion that wants to grow . . ." (Phil Nearing, interview with author, 9 Apr. 1993).

68. Thorsson, interview, 15 Apr. 1993.

69. Independent Ásatrúer (name withheld), interview with author, 14 Oct. 1992.

Thorsson adds that Priest, with whom he had once considered coauthoring a book, was a Bainbridge choice; however, Thorsson prefers to reserve further comment, noting only that of the potential candidates, "she doesn't have anything that is terribly bad, and people like her" (Thorsson, interview, 15 Apr. 1993).

70. J. Gordon Melton, "Introduction: When Prophets Die: The Succession Crisis in New Religions," in *When Prophets Die: The Postcharismatic Fate of New Religious Movements,* ed. Timothy Miller (Albany: State Univ. of New York Press, 1991); Bryan R. Wilson, "Factors in the Failure of the New Religious Movements," in *The Future of New Religious Movements,* ed. David G. Bromley and Phillip E. Hammond (Macon, Ga.: Mercer Press, 1987), 33.

71. "Robert N. Taylor, Part II," *Nexus* no. 1 (Aug. 1995), 16.

72. Tobias Brook, "Can the Troth Recover: Shakedown in Troth Leadership Leave Many Doubtful," *Heathen Times* 1, no. 1 (midsummer 1995), 1.

73. Mike Murray, interview with author 29 Apr. 1996. Steve McNallen interview with author 1 May 1996.

74. Mike Murray, interview with author 29 Apr. 1996; Robert Taylor, e-mail message to author, 27 Apr. 1996.

75. Steve McNallen, interview with author 1 May 1996. McNallen offers the analogy of Native American spirituality as his operant model. In this community, he notes, most Native Americans have adopted Christianity and, therefore, do not retain their traditional religious orientation, but the cultural value of the traditions remain unquestioned.

76. Ibid.

77. Stephen McNallen, "The Asatru Folk Assembly: Asatru Faq," e-text from computer BBS (1995).

78. Harold Covington, *What Have We Learned?,* undated pamphlet published by the National Socialist Party of America. The quotes are taken from pages 17–18 and 11–13 respectively. These sentiments are ubiquitous in the writings of American National Socialists. In George Lincoln Rockwell's view: "I learned from bitter experience that the human material of the right wing consists 90 percent of cowards, dopes, nuts, one-track minds, blabbermouths, boobs, incurable tight-wads and—worst of all—hobbyists." (George Lincoln Rockwell, *This Time the World* [Arlington, Va.: Parliament House, 1963], 193).

79. Fredrick J. Simonelli, "American Fuehrer: George Lincoln Rockwell and the American Nazi Party" (Ph.D. diss., Univ. of Nevada, Reno, 1995).

80. For an early example, see James Warner's open letter to "Fellow National Socialists" dated January 1968, which denounces Forbes and explains that his decision to lead a breakaway faction from the NSWPP to form a new American Nazi Party was taken after Matt Koehl failed to resolve a dispute among Los Angeles–based Nazis to his satisfaction. A much stronger denunciation of Koehl and the NSWPP is offered in a report marked "confidential" (on every page!) from the grandiosly styled National Socialist Defense Force Stormtroops Central Command Organization of the National Socialist Party of America. The work of Harold Covington in the early 1980s, the report, titled "NSPA Security Division Report on the Current Status of the National Socialist White People's Party (NSWPP)," systematically holds up to ridicule virtually every facet of Koehl's leadership. On the internecine rivalry that pervaded ANP ranks during the Commander's lifetime, see the acerbic record of life in Rockwell's barracks in Rosenthal and Gelb, or Simonelli.

81. For Mason's account of the mass action vs. revolutionary violence split in National Socialist ranks, and for over 400 pages of the NSLF's newsletter, see James Mason, *Siege* (Denver: Colo.: Storm, 1992).

82. Anti-Defamation League, *Extremism on the Right,* 111; Rick Cooper, "No Man Knows the Date," *NSV Report* 11, no. 3 (July/Sept. 1993): 1. For a strong argument

favoring the millennial interpretation of German National Socialism, see Norman Cohn, *The Pursuit of the Millennium* (New York: Oxford Univ. Press, 1970). Cf. Michael Barkun, *Disaster and the Millennium* (New Haven, Conn.: Yale Univ. Press, 1974), 186–94; and in particular James M. Rhodes, *The Hitler Movement: A Modern Millenarian Revolution* (Stanford, Calif.: Hoover Institution Press, 1980), 18.

83. Martinez, 35–47, 93–100; Anti-Defamation League, *Extremism on the Right,* 39–40, 144–45; Laird Wilcox and John George, *Nazis, Communists, Klansmen and Others on the Fringe* (Buffalo, N.Y.: Prometheus, 1992), 364–65.

84. "Church of the Creator Founder Ben Klassen Commits Suicide," *Klanwatch Intelligence Report* 68 (Aug. 1993): 7. The article states that Pierce immediately put the property back on the market with an asking price of $300,000. For a remarkable record of the blossoming of the Pierce-Klassen relationship, see the correspondence of Ben Klassen, *The Klassen Letters Volume One 1969–1976* (Otto, N.C.: Church of the Creator, 1988), 212, 220–22, 286–88; and Ben Klassen, *The Klassen Letters Volume Two 1976–1981* (Otto, N.C.: Church of the Creator, 1988), 8–9, 29–33.

85. Andrew Macdonald [William Pierce], *The Turner Diaries* (Arlington, Va.: National Vanguard, 1978); idem, *Hunter* (Arlington, Va.: National Vanguard, 1989). For a discussion of the impact of these two volumes, see Kaplan, "The Context of American Millenarian Revolutionary Theology," 59–60, 65n. 28. An early introduction to this tactical change is Louis Beam, "Leaderless Resistance," in Peters, *Special Report on the Meeting of Christian Men,* 20–23.

86. Wilcox and George, 366–67, and on the Covington/Collin imbroglio, 360–61. Cf. Anti-Defamation League, *Extremism on the Right,* 118–19. For a first person account of Lauck's meetings with German comrades in third countries, see "Gerhard Lauck in Europe," *New Order* 96 (Jan./Feb. 1992): 3. On Lauck's success in importing National Socialist materials into Germany, see Tamara Jones, " 'Farm-Belt Fuehrer' Feeds German Market for Hatred," *Anchorage Daily News,* 9 Sept. 1993.

87. The saga of the NSV is best found in its breezy newsletter, the *NSV Report.* See in particular *NSV Report* 1, no. 1 (Jan./Mar. 1983) and 2, no. 3 (July/Sept. 1984) for the Wolf Stadt dream and biographies of the leaders.

88. Rick Cooper, "Brief History of the White Nationalist Movement," e-text from the *NSV Report* (n.d.).

89. Church of Israel, *Articles of Faith and Doctrine,* booklet published by Church of Israel, Schell City, Missouri, 10 Jan. 1982, 31; Jenista, 18. The 6 June 1976 edition of the *Nevada Herald* described Gayman as "dressed in a white uniform, with knee length storm trooper boots, and an empty pistol holder and belt slung over one shoulder."

90. J. Gordon Melton, ed., *The Encyclopedia of American Religions,* Vol. 2 (Tarrytown, N.Y.: Triumph, 1991), 178.

91. The primary texts for the COTC are Ben Klassen's *Nature's Eternal Religion, The White Man's Bible, Expanding Creativity, Building a Whiter and Brighter World,* and *Rahowa! The Planet is Ours.* The latter volume, published in 1989, is an acronym of RAcial HOly WAr, and spells out Klassen's dreams for bringing about, in COTC parlance, "a whiter, brighter world." This output is impressive, but also somewhat less than meets the eye: after *The White Man's Bible,* most of these volumes merely reprint material from *Racial Loyalty.* Most recently, several volumes of Klassen's letters have appeared as well. All of the volumes above were originally published by the Church of the Creator, Otto, N.C. After Klassen's suicide, various successor organizations claim to have reprinted this material under their own imprimatur.

92. Ben Klassen, *The White Man's Bible* (Otto, N.C.: Church of the Creator, 1981), 313, 325. Klassen is more succinct in *Nature's Eternal Religion:* "Christianity was invented by the jews [sic] as a tool with which to destroy the White Race" (Ben Klassen, *Nature's Eternal Religion* [Otto, N.C.: Church of the Creator, 1973], 258).

93. Klassen provides his own exegesis in his *Nature's Eternal Religion*, 256–76.

94. "Church of the Creator in Turmoil Over Leadership Change," *Klanwatch Intelligence Report* 66 (Apr. 1993), 1; "Church of the Creator Founder Ben Klassen Commits Suicide," *Klanwatch Intelligence Report* 68 (August 1993), 7.

95. Letter to all Creators from Dr. Rick McCarty, 12 Aug. 1993.

96. Winston Smith [Harold Covington], "Sayonara to a Sodomite," e-text file obtained from Minuteman BBS, n.d.

97. For the purposes of this book, Christian millenarianism and Jewish messianism—the belief in the coming of a messianic figure whose advent will be accompanied by such phenomena as the full realization of the Law (halacha), the reconstitution of worship in the Third Temple in Jerusalem, God's granting to man of a new Torah, and much more—will be considered together. On the multiple strands of Jewish messianic beliefs, see Raphael Patai, *The Messiah Texts* (Detroit: Wayne State Univ. Press, 1979).

98. J. David Davis, telephone conversation with author, 13 Nov. 1995. Davis states that there are about 70 Noahides living in the Athens area, with several thousand more worldwide on the group's mailing list. It is impossible to determine how many of these would describe themselves as Noahide believers.

99. Aaron Lichtenstein, *The Seven Laws of Noah*, 2nd ed. (New York: Rabbi Jacob Joseph School Press, 1986).

100. Harvey Falk, *Jesus the Pharisee: A New Look at the Jewishness of Jesus* (New York: Paulist, 1985), 17–23. What follows is based on J. David Davis, interview with author, 12 Mar. 1992.

101. B'nai Noah, *What is the B'nai Noah?* (Athens, Tenn.: Echoes of Immanuel, 1991), 4.

102. Rabbi Dov Ber Haskelevich, interview with author, 23 Mar. 1992. Rabbi Schneerson suffered an incapacitating stroke in 1993 and died on 12 June 1994.

103. *The Root and Branch Noahide Guide, 1991/5752* (New York: Root and Branch Association, 1991), 21; cf. the photograph of David Davis with Sephardi Chief Rabbi Mordechai Eliahu in "B'nai Noah: Bible believers neither Christian nor Jewish," *Jerusalem Post International Edition*, 22 February 1992, 17.

104. The Jerusalem Temple Foundation links American evangelical and fundamentalist Protestants (and their money) with Israeli activists. The Israeli front man for this activity is Stanley Goldfoot; American adherents include Terry Reisenhoover, Doug Krieger, and (sometimes) Lambert Dolphin. For varying views on the JTF and related groups, see Louis Rapoport, "Slouching Towards Armageddon: Links with Evangelicals," *Jerusalem Post International Edition*, 17 June 1984; Barbara Ledeen and Michael Ledeen, "The Temple Mount Plot," *New Republic* 3 (18 June 1984): 21–22; Grace Halsell, *Prophesy and Politics* (Westport, Conn.: Lawrence Hill, 1986); and "The Temple Institute Update," *The Gap* (Jan./Feb. 1992): 8.

105. "Tennessee Baptists Turn to Judaism for New Inspiration," *Wall Street Journal*, 20 Mar. 1991.

106. The text of the resolution has been reprinted verbatim in a number of sources. The B'nai Noah offer the text in *Root and Branch Noahide Guide*, 56. Cf. Earl F. Jones, "Public Law 102–14," *Christian Crusade for Truth Intelligence Newsletter* (July/Aug. 1991): 2–5. Pastor Jones's material on this subject has been widely reprinted throughout the Identity movement.

107. I. B. Pranaitis, *The Talmud Unmasked* (St. Petersburg: n.p., 1892); *The Protocols of the Elders of Zion*, trans. Victor Marsden (no publication data); Elizabeth Dilling, *The Jewish Religion: Its Influence Today* (Torrance, Calif.: Noontide, 1983).

108. For a good early presentation of this view see Gerald B. Winrod, *Adam Weishaupt A Human Devil* (no publication data, c. 1935); Kenneth Goff, *Traitors in the*

Pulpit (Englewood, Colo.: Kenneth Goff, 1946); or Jack Mohr, *Woe unto Ye Fundamentalists,* self-published booklet (n.p.: n.d.).

2. Christian Identity

1. "Robert N. Taylor, Part II," *Nexus,* no. 1 (Aug. 1995), 15. Taylor was at one time interim head of the Minutemen during the incarceration of its founder Robert dePugh in 1967. He has since largely abandoned the overtly political path in favor of an approach emphasizing spirituality and artistic expression; a quest which led him from the satanic orientation of the Process Church to his current primary identification with Ásatrú, where he and his wife Karen were primary actors in the formation of the Ásatrú Alliance. Taylor's biography is supplied by the *Nexus* interview noted above, by an interview to be forthcoming in the French journal *Omega,* and in an ongoing e-mail correspondence with the author which began in 1996.

2. Barkun, *Religion and the Racist Right.* Cf. Isaac La Peyrére, *Men Before Adam* (London, 1656); Richard H. Popkin, *Isaac La Peyrére (1596–1676): His Life, Work and Influence* (Leiden: E. J. Brill, 1987).

3. Identity's primary source for the Khazar theory is Arthur Koestler, *The Thirteenth Tribe* (New York: Random House, 1976). Earlier references to the Khazars as part of a broader anti-Semitic tirade is offered in Benjamin H. Friedman's long, rambling letter dated 10 Oct. 1954 to Dr. David Goldstein on the occasion of Goldstein's conversion to Catholicism, reprinted as "The Truth About Khazars," e-text distributed by Scriptures for America (n.d.). For various interpretations, see Gerald Winrod in *The Winrod Letter* 158 (Mar. 1978) and any of many expositions by Jack Mohr. For a good, brief formulation of this doctrine, see Jack Mohr, *Exploding the "Chosen People" Myth,* self-published pamphlet (Bay St. Louis, Miss.: n.d.), or for a more complete formulation, idem, *Satanic Counterfeit.*

4. Francis Parker Yockey, *Imperium* (Costa Mesa, Calif.: Noontide, 1962). The most accessible source of this anti-Semitic amalgamation is Dilling, *Jewish Religion.*

5. Mohr, *Exploding the "Chosen People" Myth,* 10–11.

6. The adherent has a number of these eschatological scenarios from which to choose. Typical examples include Dan Gayman, "Then Cometh the Condemnation," *Message of Old Monthly* 4, nos. 2–3 (May 1971), and idem, "America in the Hands Pof an Angry God," *Zion's Watchman* 4, no. 1 (Jan. 1977).

7. Dan Gayman, "The Bible Case Against Miscegenation," *Watchman* 3 (Spring 1991): 22.

8. See, for example, St. Clair.

9. McGinn, *Visions of the End,* 61.

10. Dan Gayman, "Warning From the Watchman Standing in the American Watchtower," *Zions Watchman* 8 (July 1977): 16, and 12 (Nov. 1977): 11.

11. Dan Gayman, "Personally . . . From the Editor," *Watchman* 3 (Summer 1991): 14–15. These themes are reinforced in his cassette tape ministry; hear, for example, "The Divine Call to be a Separated People," 19 Aug. 1989; "Apocalyptic Millenarianism," 17 Aug. 1991; or "Remnant Response to the Gulf War," 30 Jan. 1991. Cf. for other examples, the step-by-step apocalyptic analysis of the news in 1979–80 offered by the Servants of Messiah in their newsletter, *Age-Ending* 1, no. 1 (1980) or "All Fall Down: AIDS and the End of Civilization," *America's Promise Newsletter* (Oct. 1987).

12. See for example, John R. Harrell, *WANTED: Places to Gather Patriots in Times of Crisis,* and idem, *Mid-America Survival Area,* both undated CDPL publications. The latter includes a "Mid-America Survival Map" which draws a rectangular box from Colorado in the west to Pennsylvania in the east as the most survivable locations in America when

the nuclear attack comes. Pastor Harrell's Flora, Illinois, home constitutes the northern-most edge of the safe area.

13. Contemporary sources recounting this vision are numerous throughout Christian Identity. See for example such diverse contexts as "George Washington's Vision" *Aryan Nations Newsletter* 7 (c. 1978): 1,7; John Harrell, "George Washington's Vision and Prophesy for the United States of America," flier lacking date or publication data currently distributed by both John Harrell and Jack Mohr's Christian Patriots Defense League; and "The Washington Vision," *Newsviews,* undated flier distributed by the Joppa Gospel Tabernacle & Kinship Ministries of Baltimore, Maryland.

14. For a document of this importance, it is probably safe to assume that Rand himself wrote this introduction and did much of the research on the pedigree of the document. For a moving eulogy of Rand, who died on 17 Oct. 1991 at the age of 102, see Michael A. Clark, "Howard B. Rand—The Greatest Identity Pastor Of Our Time Has Passed To His Rest," *Wake Up!* 9 (Jan./Feb. 1992). *Wake Up!* is the organ of the Christian Israel Foundation of Ayrshire, Scotland.

15. "George Washington's Vision," mimeographed reprint from *Destiny Magazine* (Sept. 1958). This introduction traces the earliest known source of the vision to Charles A. L. Totten's Sept. 1898 *Our Race Leaflet;* on Totten, see Barkun, *Religion and the Racist Right,* 18–21. Cf. idem, "From British Israelism to Christian Identity: The Evolution of White Supremacist Religious Doctrine," *Syzygy* 1, no. 1 (Winter 1992): 56.

16. Harrell, "George Washington's Vision and Prophesy."

17. Undated fund raising letter from C. A. "Eddie" Seckinger. An accompanying letter expounds further on Washington's vision, stating explicitly: "George Washington was not just the first president of the United States, but he was a prophet also." See C. A. "Eddie" Seckinger, "What Is to Happen to the United States and Why," undated paper from the Christian Anti-communist Party.

18. Benjamin Franklin's prophesy may be found in Smith, *Satan's New Testament,* 24. It is frequently reprinted in various right-wing sources and is currently being circulated by Family Farm Preservation (in reality remnants of the Posse Comitatus) in Tigerton, Wisconsin; see "Benjamin Franklin Warned Against Jews," undated mimeographed sheet containing as a bonus a special report on Jewish ritual murder today.

19. Gayman, Interview with Dan 9–11 Dec. 1991.

20. See "'Identity Churches': A Theology of Hate," and Zeskind, *"Christian Identity" Movement.* Michael Barkun dedicates the final three chapters of his book to a consideration of the violent implications of Identity rhetoric, but concludes that "there is no evidence that more than a minority have taken Identity beliefs to their logical political conclusions" (*Religion and the Racist Right,* 199).

21. For an insider's view of the process of radicalization, alienation, and ultimately, the decision to opt for millenarian violence, see Jeffrey Kaplan, "Absolute Rescue: Absolutism, Defensive Action and the Resort to Force," *Terrorism and Political Violence* 7, no. 3 (Autumn 1995).

22. See "Extremism Targets the Prisons," 5–8.

23. "Race Traitors," undated flier from the Aryan Nation.

24. "The White Supremacist Movement: 1992 at a Glance," *Klanwatch Intelligence Report* (Feb. 1993): 10–11; "White Supremacist Movement Reels from Severe Setbacks in 1993," *Klanwatch Intelligence Report* (Feb. 1994): 12–13.

25. "White Supremacist Movement: 1992 at a Glance," 11; "White Supremacist Movement Reels," 12–13; "From Aryan Nations to Anti-Hate: Floyd Cochrane Talks About the White Supremacist Movement and the Reasons He Left It," *Klanwatch Intelligence Report* (Oct. 1993): 4–6.

26. On Gayman's career, see Kaplan, "Context of American Millenarian Revolutionary Theology," especially 81n. 190 for his denial of any knowledge of Order activities

or of conversations he was alleged to have had with Order member Richard Scutari. For the allegations themselves, see Flynn and Gerhardt, 305n. 6.

27. Church of Israel, *Articles of Faith and Doctrine*, 31.

28. On submission to state authority, see Dan Gayman, *Romans 13: A Primer in Government for Patriotic Christians*, pamphlet from the Church of Israel, 1989; idem, *Rebellion or Repentance: Which Way Modern Israel?*, pamphlet from the Church of Israel, 1987; and idem, *Christian Conscience Towards Government*, pamphlet from the Church of Israel, 1988. Cf. his four-hour cassette series, "The Bible and Civil Disobedience," 1 Jan. 1989. On the Phineas Priesthood, see idem, *Can There Be Vigilantes in Christendom?*, pamphlet from the Church of Israel, 1991.

29. Raymond Bray, letter to acquaintance of author, 24 Feb. 1992.

30. The concept of defensive violence is borrowed from Ehud Sprinzak's observations on violence emanating from the Heredim in Israel; Ehud Sprinzak, "Three Models of Religious Violence: The Case of Jewish Fundamentalism in Israel," in *Fundamentalisms and the State*, ed. Martin E. Marty and R. Scott Appleby (Chicago: Univ. of Chicago Press, 1993), 463–69.

31. Flynn and Gerhardt, 256–61. For a humorous running commentary on the mentally unstable Ellison's Fort Smith performance, see Robert Miles's articles in *From the Mountain* (Mar./Apr. 1987–Mar./Apr. 1988).

32. "Why Do We Hate the Jews?" *C.S.A. Journal* 9 (1982): 20. Gen. 3:15 reads:

> And I will put enmity
> between you and the woman,
> and between your offspring and hers;
> he will crush your head,
> and you will strike his heel.

33. Covenant, Sword, and Arm of the Lord, *C.S.A. Survival Manual* (N.p., n.d.).

34. James Ellison, letter to Tommy Rydén, 26 May 1987.

35. James Ellison, letter to Tommy Rydén, 17 Aug. 1987. Rydén broke off this correspondence when he was informed by Richard Butler of Ellison's role at Fort Smith.

36. Flynn and Gerhardt, 260–61.

37. Psychological analysis is at best a risky undertaking. For an object lesson in the pleasures and the perils of this methodology, see Raphael Ezekial, *The Racist Mind* (New York: Viking, 1995).

38. Richard Wayne Snell, "Ed Sez," *The Seekers* (Mar./Apr. 1992). All subsequent quotes are taken from this source. Cf. Snell's own death row meditation: idem, *The Shadow of Death! (Is There Life After Death?)* (self published and privately distributed, c. 1986).

39. "En Hyllning," from the Swedish skinhead band Division S's CD *Attack*. Translated by Helene Lööw.

40. Robert Mathews, open letter, obtained as a text file from Don Black's Stormfront BBS.

41. A chronology of Order actions is available in the Center for Democratic Renewal booklet, *Aryan Nations Far Right Underground Movement* (Atlanta: Center for Democratic Renewal, 1986), 47–50. On Alan Berg, see Stephan Singular, *Talked to Death: The Life and Murder of Alan Berg* (New York: Beech Tree, 1987). The best source for the Order is Flynn and Gerhardt; they detail some of these transactions, including $10,000 given to Dan Gayman, who in turn promised to care for Mathews' mistress, Zillah Craig. In a letter to the author that was received 26 Dec. 1991, Pastor Gayman wrote: "I was very stunned to read the information printed . . . [in] The Silent Brotherhood. I had absolutely no knowledge whatever of any counterfeiting ring in the Pacific

Northwest or anyplace else. And never did such a conversation about such take place between myself and Richard Scutari or anyone else, including Robert Mathews."

42. Rick Cooper, "Warning," *NSV Report* (July/Sept. 1984): 6.

43. Rockwell, 193.

44. Richard Kelly Hoskins, *Vigilantes of Christendom* (Lynchburg, Va.: Virginia Publishing Co., 1990). For a discussion of the importance of this text to the world of the radical right, see my review in *Syzygy* 1, no. 3 (Summer 1992).

45. Ehud Sprinzak, "The Process of Deligitimation: Towards a Linkage Theory of Political Terrorism," *Terrorism and Political Violence* 3, no. 1 (Spring 1991). The theory is updated and enhanced with a discussion of millenarian terrorism emanating from the radical right in idem, "Right-Wing Terrorism in Comparative Perspective: The Case of Deligitimation," *Terrorism and Political Violence* 7, no. 1 (Spring 1995).

46. Flynn and Gerhardt, 422–23.

47. Helene Lööw, "Racist Violence and Criminal Behaviour in Sweden: Myths and Realities," *Terrorism and Political Violence* 7, no. 1 (Spring 1995).

48. Hoskins, 435–42. Hoskins' source is Bruce Pierce, an Order member currently serving a 250-year federal prison sentence. Pierce claims that not only David Lane but Bob Mathews himself was an Odinist. Hoskins sees in the emergence of Odinism evidence of a conspiracy against Christianity by the demonic hybrid, Judeo-Christianity.

49. This text is widely circulated around the radical right and is taken from the Cyberspace Minuteman BBS. All quotes are taken from this document.

3. Odinism and Ásatrú

1. Mark L. Mirabello, *The Odin Brotherhood* (Edmonds, Wash.: Sure Fire, 1993), 57. The words are attributed to Baldur to announce the return of the old gods to the earth following the defeat of Christiantiy.

2. Letter dated 11 Jan. 1992 to the leader of an Odinist organization from a skinhead incarcerated in California for hate crimes. Names of correspondents withheld by request. For an interesting interpretation of Ragnarök from a scholarly perspective, see J. Oosten, "The War of the Gods in Scandinavian Mythology," in *Struggles of the Gods: Papers of the Groningen Work Group for the Study of the History of Religions*, ed. Hans G. Kippenberg (Berlin: Moulton, 1984), 214–21.

3. Adler, 273–82. Cf. J. Gordon Melton, *The Encyclopedia of American Religions*, Supplement to 2nd ed., (Detroit: Gale Research, 1987), 641.

4. Success has been defined by Rodney Stark as the "degree to which a religious movement is able to dominate one or more societies" (Rodney Stark, "How New Religions Succeed: A Theoretical Model," in *The Future of New Religious Movements*, ed. David G. Bromley and Phillip E. Hammond [Macon, Ga.: Mercer Univ. Press, 1987], 12). This standard seems unduly rigorous. J. Gordon Melton's standard, which defines success simply as institutionalizing the tradition on a foundation that will survive the passing of the original founder(s), appears more realistic. See Melton, "Introduction: When Prophets Die," 1–12.

5. For a discussion of the key Ásatrú ritual texts, see my review essay in *Syzygy* 2, nos. 3–4 (Summer/Fall 1993). By contrast, see my review of the Wiccan texts in Chas. S. Clifton, ed., *The Modern Craft Movement: Witchcraft Today, Book I* (St. Paul, Minn.: Llewellyn, 1992), in *Syzygy* 2, nos. 1–2 (Winter/Spring 1993). For a definitive discussion of Wicca's purely modern sources, see Kelly.

6. Georges Dumézil, *Gods of the Ancient Northmen*, ed. Einar Haugen (Berkeley: Univ. of California Press, 1973).

7. KveldúlfR Gundarsson, *Teutonic Religion* (St. Paul, Minn.: Llewellyn, 1994), ch. 3, provides a concise argument for the difficulty of fitting Dumézil's theory to the Norse/

Germanic pantheon. A Ph.D. thesis by Stephen Grundy at Cambridge Univ. in England makes this same point in discussing the intricacies of the Odinnic cult; Stephen Grundy, "The Cult of Odinn, God of Death." For a counter argument by a true believer in the Dumézilian theory, see Thorsson, *Northern Magic*, 27–29. *Northern Magic* is a popular market account by Edred Thorsson, who (under his birth name of Stephen Flowers) is a Ph.D. scholar in Germanic studies. Also arguing for Dumézil's view is Stephen McNallen, "Magic, Asafolk and Spiritual Development," *Mountain Thunder* 4 (1992): 5–6; Gundarsson responds in his "Wisdom, Might and Fruitfulness: Dumézil's Theory in the Germanic Rebirth," *Mountain Thunder* 6 (1992): 5–9.

8. Wilfred von Dauster, "How Can You Believe That Junk?" *Mountain Thunder* 4 (1992): 20–21.

9. Gundarsson, *Teutonic Religion,* App. 4. Iceland, primary source of the surviving Eddas and Sagas, has a particular impact on the reconstructive effort today. See for example, Joe Simpson, "The Catastrophic Eleventh Century," *Vor Trú* 31 (Yule/Winter 2238/1988): 10.

10. KveldúlfR Gundarsson, *Teutonic Magic* (St. Paul, Minn.: Llewellyn, 1990); Thorsson, *Northern Magic.*

11. Gundarsson, *Teutonic Religion,* App. 2. For (far) greater detail, see Gundarsson, *Teutonic Magic;* and for a good, brief, introduction bridging the two texts, see KveldúlfR Gundarsson, "The Runes: A Brief Introduction," *Mountain Thunder* 4 (1992): 7–9.

12. Thorsson remains master of the Rune Gild. This organization is much reduced from its pre–Temple of Set membership, although this may be due as much to the fact that Thorsson has already published much of the material that the Rune Gild sold in small increments. Thorsson's bibliography of purely runic material is impressive. Beginning with the publication of his doctoral dissertation (written as Stephen E. Flowers), this list includes: Stephen E. Flowers, *Runes and Magic: Magic Formulaic Elements in the Older Runic Tradition,* Series I Germanic Languages and Literature, vol. 53, (New York: Peter Lang, 1986); Edred Thorsson, *Futhark: A Handbook of Rune Magic* (York Beach, Maine: Weiser, 1984); idem, *Runelore: A Handbook of Esoteric Runology* (York Beach, Maine: Weiser, 1987); idem, *At the Well of Wyrd: A Handbook of Runic Divination* (York Beach, Maine: Weiser, 1988); and idem, *Rune-Might: Secret Practices of the German Rune Magicians* (St. Paul, Minn.: Llewellyn, 1989). Cf. Freyja Aswynn, *Leaves of Yggdrasil* (St. Paul, Minn.: Llewellyn, 1990). Freyja Aswynn has become an increasingly sought after figure among American Ásatrúers since the Temple of Set controversy placed a shadow over Thorsson's work. In Apr., 1993, an anonymous American adherent bought her an air ticket and financed a brief American tour (author's conversation with that anonymous adherent, 4 Apr. 1993). It should be noted too that she is, in Edred Thorsson's description, "the spiritual leader of the Rune Gild for me in U. K." Edred Thorsson, letter to author, 13 May 1993).

13. E. O. G. Turville-Petre, *Myth and Religion of the North* (London: Weidenfeld and Nicolson, 1964), 42–51. Cf. H. R. Ellis Davidson, *Gods and Myths of Northern Europe* (Middlesex, England: Penguin, 1964), 143–45.

14. Thorsson, *Northern Magic,* 54–55. The enigmatic stanza in question, taken from the *Vafþrúdnismál* (54), reads:

> What did Odin whisper
> before he climbed on the pyre
> into the ear of his son?

(Turville-Petre, 110). The somewhat abbreviated version of this episode is found in the Younger Edda (Prose Edda) in Sturluson, 80–82. Dumézil's interesting interpretation of this—in which the myth itself is broken down into a three stage drama—is found in Dumézil, 58–65.

15. Thorsson, *Northern Magic*, 56.

16. KveldúlfR Gundarsson, "The Magic and Making of the Drinking Horn," *Mountain Thunder* 8 (Spring Equinox 1993): 11–12. Gundarsson offers a number of runic inscriptions with their English translations, which may be used for specific purposes including love, power, health, and inspiration.

17. Gamlinginn, "The Standard International Futhark," *Mountain Thunder* 6 (1992): 4.

18. Ymir Thunarsson, "The Importance of Daily Workings," *On Wings of Eagles* 1, no. 1 (Dec./Jan. 1992): 10. Thunarsson is actually a bit harsh with regard to the intellectual elite of the Troth in this passage. Thorsson's *A Book of Troth* is nothing if not a how-to manual for daily practice, and *Idunna* is not without articles on daily rituals. Gundarsson is perhaps the richest source of ritual practice—including rituals performed at Eagles' Reaches' functions. See KveldúlfR Gundarsson, "Yule at Eagles' Reaches," *Mountain Thunder* 8 (Spring Equinox 1993): 28, in which Gundarsson recounts the sacrifice of a pig in epic terms (albeit considerably sanitized from the messy and chaotic event).

19. James Chisholm, "Working with the Wights and Forces of the Lay of Alvis," *Idunna* 2, no. 2 (Oct. 1989): 2–12. Wights refer to a number of supernatural beings, of whom the dwarves, elves, Vanes, giants, and trolls are but a few.

20. James Chisholm, "The Rites of Ostara: Possibilities for Today," *Idunna* 1, no. 4 (Feb. 1989): 7–10.

21. Charles Armour, "Mortar & Pestle," *Mountain Thunder* 1 (1991): 9–10. Every subsequent issue of *Mountain Thunder* carried a "Mortar & Pestle" feature by Armour.

22. Tony Wolf, "Rammaukin: Esoteric Aspects of the Northern Warrior Tradition," *Mountain Thunder* 2 (1991): 7–11; idem, "Ordeal: The Ritual Trials of Rammaukin," *Mountain Thunder* 4 (1992): 22–24; idem, "The Godlauss: Atheism in the Northern Warrior Tradition," *Mountain Thunder* 5 (1992): 19–20; idem, "The Rite of the Flaming Arrow," *Mountain Thunder* 7 (1992): 5; and idem, "Re-Forging the Blade: Practical Aspects of the Northern Warrior Tradition Riddaraskap," *Mountain Thunder* 8 (Spring Equinox 1993): 17–18.

23. No real documentation is ever offered in support of this proposition, and in truth, it appears to reflect a modern American consciousness, in which race is an important (or obsessive) facet of everyday life, more than a pagan Norse or Germanic view of the world. See George W. Stocking, Jr., *Race, Culture and Evolution* (New York: Free Press, 1968).

24. The term is borrowed from Wilfred von Dauster, "The PC Pagan?" *Mountain Thunder* 5 (1992): 3. Von Dauster, the editor of *Mountain Thunder* and an independent Ásatrúer, is himself a powerful voice against racialism in the religion. In this article, he decries racism and anti-Semitism; in a more recent issue, he goes so far as to voice support for gay rights in Colorado in the context of the Amendment 2 controversy in the early 1990s, in which Colorado voters decided to invalidate local ordinances that, it was felt, offered special rights to the gay community. See idem, "Who's Next?" *Mountain Thunder* 8 (Spring Equinox 1993): 3–4.

25. KveldúlfR Gundarsson, "Race, Inheritance and Ásatrú Today," *Mountain Thunder* 5 (1992): 8.

26. Ibid., 9–10. The fetch is an animal or human spirit or projection, which functions in the supernatural realm in service to a single true man or woman throughout his or her life. In the operation of seith magic, the fetch is a central feature of the magical working. For an interesting account of an Odinist group claiming unbroken succession from the pagan era Norse, see Mirabello.

27. Gamlinginn, "Speech at Althing 12 of the Ásatrú Alliance (22–24 May 1992)," *Mountain Thunder* 5 (1992): 4.

28. Ibid., 5.

29. Gamlinginn, "Race and Religion," *Mountain Thunder* 8 (Spring Equinox 1993): 9–10. Gamlinginn also utilizes an apologetic device that has been heard in pleas for universal brotherhood in Islamic and Christian cultures throughout the world, by asking for textual evidence for the color of the eyes and hair (and by implication, the skin) of the first man and the first woman (Ask and Embla). It was in answer to that question that Christian Identity evolved its doctrine that Adam was white because he could blush, or have "blood in the face." For these hermeneutics, see Dan Gayman, *The Holy Bible: The Book of Adam's Race,* pamphlet published by the Church of Israel (n.d.), 1.

30. Gamlinginn, "Race and Religion," 10.

31. Ibid.

32. This story was gathered from several Ring of Troth and independent Ásatrú sources, all of whom prefer their name not be included.

33. Letter to author from Ásatrú adherent (name withheld), n.d.

34. Gamlinginn, interview with author, 14 Oct. 1992. One well known female Ásatrúer (name withheld) recalls that, as she was breaking up with her boyfriend, she saw Odin standing behind him as they sat together in a pub. She took this as a sign that she must leave him as a sacrifice to Odin. Finally, Gundarsson notes that although he and other Ásatrúers have had experience with the gods in the course of mystical practices—and a number of people in contemporary Iceland believe in and propitiate the wights—the direct waking experience of the gods is quite rare. (KveldúlfR Gundarsson, letter to author, 14 Apr. 1993). For a description of Gundarsson's encounter with the gods, see Matt Zoller Seitz, "The Mythic Journey of Stephen Grundy," *Dallas Observer,* 21–27 July 1994.

35. The article was recently reprinted as [Stephe McNallen], "Metagenetics," in *Selections from Runestone: An Odinist Anthology,* (Grass Valley, Calif.: Ásatrú Free Assembly, 1983), 21–25. The article is unsigned, but does carry the preface: "This is the most important article ever to appear in *The Runestone.*"

36. Robert Stine, interview with author, 23–24 Dec. 1992.; James Chisholm, interview. Conversely, the idea does hold considerable appeal to some within the Ásatrú Alliance. Mike Murray, interview with author, 29 Apr. 1996.

37. McNallen, "Metagenetics," McNallen today recalls that Jung's "Wotan" essay was not central to the concept because of its over emphasis on the National Socialist phenomenon in 1930s Germany. "The key point is the biological, inheritable nature of archetypes" (McNallen interview).

38. Jung, "Wotan," 179–93. For a complete consideration of archetypes, see C. G. Jung, *The Archetypes and the Collective Unconscious,* trans. R. F. C. Hull (New York: Pantheon, 1959).

39. McNallen, "Metagenetics," 21.

40. Ibid., 23–24.

41. Ibid., 25.

42. Ibid.

43. Thorsson, "Who Will Build the Hearths of the Troth"; Thorsson, *A Book of Troth,* 59–62; and Edred Thorsson, "How to be a Heathen: A Methodology for the Awakening of Traditional Systems," talk given to the Pagan Student Alliance at the Univ. of Texas at Austin, 22 Nov. 1991.

44. Thorsson, interview, 20 Sept. 1992.

45. Thorsson, "How to be a Heathen," 1.

46. In fact, the *Idunna* article (Thorsson, "Who Will Build the Hearths of the Troth") is a reworking of an earlier piece, which appeared under the aegis of the Rune Gild as Edred Thorsson, "Rune-Wisdom and Race," *Runa* 1, no. 2 (Yule 1982).

47. Thorsson, "Who Will Build the Hearths of the Troth," 22–23.

48. Coriolanus, "Wotan Speaks to His Children," distributed as e-text by the Nordic Heritage and History Club of Chicago, Ill. (n.d.).

49. David Lane, "ODINISM," distributed as e-text on movement BBS (n.d.). Lane also uses the name Wodensson.

50. See, for example, the numerous writings of Jost, a neighbor of Stephen Mc-Nallen in rural California and head of what he styles the National Socialist Kindred; one piece is entitled "NATIONAL SOCIALISM: Adolf Hitler's Revelations of the Eternal Laws of Nature for Family and Folk" (distributed as e-text by the National Socialist Kindred [n.d.]).

51. Stine, interview, 22–24 Dec. 1992.

52. Ibid. Bob Stine is himself an interesting illustration of the contradictions—and possibilities—inherent in Ásatrú. As a young man, he was loosely involved in Ku Klux Klan and Nazi party activities, but following a stint in the army, he turned away from these groups and became (along with Phil Nearing) one of the strongest opponents of racialism in Ásatrú.

53. Cassette recording of Althing 9, June 1989; Phil Nearing, conversation with author, 4 Apr. 1993.

54. William Bainbridge, telephone conversation with author, 3 Apr. 1993. Mike Murray, interview with author, 29 Apr. 1996.

55. This adherent has since left active participation in Ásatrú and is pursuing Ph.D. studies at a university in the Midwest. For this reason, his name will be withheld.

56. Nearing, conversation. Nearing recalls Thor's Hammer Kindred as one of the most extreme proponents of racialism in the AA. Also known as the Troll Kindred for the remarkable physical ugliness of its members, Thor's Hammer Kindred won a measure of renown when, in the latter days of the AFA, the group demonstrated its disgust with McNallen's failure to adopt an openly racialist position and with his having ended the practice of chartering kindreds by returning its charter document with a .44 caliber bullet hole in it. Some, speaking on condition of anonymity, interpreted this as a death threat, and note that McNallen may have received several of these in this period; others, however, were simply amused—and somewhat critical—of Redbeard's marksmanship.

57. Nearing, conversation. In strictly not-for-attribution conversations with Ás-atrúers, it is apparent that some adherents do have Jewish family members, while the kindred headed by former Ring of Troth Steerswoman Prudence Priest contains one Jewish convert to Ásatrú, memorably named Thor Bernstein (Prudence Priest, conversation with author, 22 Nov. 1992). Cf. *Yggdrasil* 9, no. 3 (Freyfaxi 1992): 1.

58. Nearing, conversation. Murray recalls making the remark but adds that Enslin provoked him into saying it. Mike Murray, interview with author, 29 Apr. 1996.

59. Phil Nearing, conversation with author, 4 Apr. 1993; Bainbridge, telephone conversation, 3 Apr. 1993; and Robert Stine, conversation with author, 4 Apr. 1993. In something of a remarkable *volte face,* this same Filssennu, who in 1989 posited a strong racialist stand as the key to Ásatrú's survival, would only two years later decry the entry of Identity Christians and other far rightists into Odinism, which—purged of its most virulently racialist elements—should be reunited with Ásatrú! See "Ocean Kindred of New York News," *Vor Trú* 35 (Yule 2239/1989): 28, and "Letters," *Vor Trú* 39 (Winter 2241/1991): 26–27.

60. Stine, conversation. It is clear that there were variations of opinion within the Kindred over tactics, if not the moral imperative of removing the banner. Nearing, counting on his election as Thingspeaker, was more conciliatory than he in retrospect feels he should have been, while the head of the Brewers Gild (considered by some in the Arizona Kindred as the guiding light of the affair) was most anxious for battle. Stine, typically, seems to have held his own council, but in the event was perhaps the most effective member of the Kindred in what followed (Nearing, conversation; Bainbridge, conversation).

61. Bainbridge, conversation, Murray, interview. It is important to note that the flag itself was not the same as the Warrior Gild flag.

62. In the event, the Arizona Kindred were by no means the monolith that Old Northwest had expected. It was arguably the wide spectrum of opinion within Arizona Kindred ranks that was a key to diffusing the situation. Indeed, in the end, Bainbridge opened negotiations aimed at a compromise with Old Northwest (Stine, conversation). Bainbridge's legalistic diplomacy, technicalities and all, is captured on the cassette recording of Althing 9, June 1989.

63. Stine, conversation.

64. Cassette recording of Althing 9, June 1989.

65. Nearing, conversation.

66. Stein, conversation; Bainbridge, interview. Another attempt was made to turn the Alliance away from racialism at Althing 12 in 1992 by Gamlinginn; see Gamlinginn, "Speech at Althing 12," 4–5. This seems to have had no visible effect. One significant change that did take place in the AA in the wake of Althing 9 was the adoption of a new addition to the by-laws: "All major additions or changes to the Alliance By-Laws should when possible be submitted in advance to each Kindred, either in writing or by phone." No more surprises, please! "By-Laws of the Ásatrú Alliance As Approved at Althing— July 6, 2241 Runic Era [1991]," *Vor Trú* 41 (Summer 2241/1991): 24.

67. Mike Murray, interview with author, 29 Apr. 1996.

68. "By Laws of the Ásatrú Alliance," paper supplied by World Tree Publications, 30 Apr. 1996. On the ethnic qualification for membership, Mike Murray notes: "Anyone can call themselves Ásatrú, but to be an Ásatrúer you must be of the folk." Mike Murray, interview with author, 29 Apr. 1996.

69. Lane, "ODINISM."

70. Christensen, interview.

71. Kevin Hunt, "An Open Letter to the Ásatrú Community," *Vor Trú* 33 (Midyear/ Summer 2239/1989): 19.

72. Ibid.

73. "Letters to the Editor," *Vor Trú* 37 (Summer 2240/1990): 24–26.

74. "Letter to Ed" *Vor Trú* 38 (Fall 2240/1990): 26.

75. This affinity of view between Odinists and Identity adherents made for the smooth functioning of the Order. For a criticism of this cooperation from the Identity perspective, see Hoskins, 435–42. The language of the letter is also strongly suggestive of the English translations of the pronouncements of Islamist activists, as recorded in the popular press. The terminology is so closely tied to a manichaean strain of the Abrahamic traditions that it is likely to have been borrowed from Islamic rather than pagan sources; this likelihood is strengthened by Dane's incarceration—an environment in which Nation of Islam rhetoric employing terminology such as this is rife.

76. "Letter to Ed" *Vor Trú* 38 (Fall 2240/1990): 26. Compare to Else Christensen, speaking from an Odinist perspective: "We have kept contact with [white prisoners who have] scared AA people stiff, but for example, one of the former hard core has recently written me that he finally realize[d] that he was on the wrong track . . . There has [*sic*] been other individuals like that, and I cut another notch on my rune stave, so to speak" (Christensen, interview).

77. The 14 words are reprinted *ad infinitum* in the texts of racialist Odinism. See, for example, David Lane, "Wotan Is Coming," *WAR* (Apr. 1993).

78. Letter from a prisoner in California to a prominent Odinist leader (n.d.). Names withheld by request. The letter continues with a number of specific questions regarding the tenets of Odinism.

79. "News and Views," *Resistance* 4 (Spring 1995): 42.

80. Lane, "Wotan Is Coming."

81. "I don't endorse the atheistic concept known as the Church of the Creator. I've

expressed admiration for those portions of COTC teachings which seem valuable, but I'm not an Atheist anymore than a Theist or biblical religionist" (Lane, "ODINISM").

82. David Lane, "88 Precepts," e-text provided by the Aryan Women's League (n.d.). All discussion of the "88 Precepts" is based on this text; numbers in parentheses refer to precept numbers, not page numbers.

83. Lane, "ODINISM."

4. The B'nai Noah

1. See Donald S. McAlvany, "Encouragement for the Remnant," *McAlvany Intelligence Advisor* (Dec. 1991): 3. This article touched many who read it, as evidenced by its being picked up in other Identity journals; see, for example, "The Remnant," *Kinship Communication* (Jan. 1992): 1.

2. J. David Davis, *Finding the God of Noah: The Spiritual Journey of a Baptist Minister from Jesus to the Laws of Noah* (Hoboken, N.J.: Ktav, forthcoming).

3. Laura Morgan, interview with author, Hoschton, Ga., 11 Apr. 1992. Morgan points out that as a long time religious seeker, she had drifted from Baptist sects to Charismatic groups before finding the B'nai Noah; in each of these commitments, her entire social world was constructed upon the church community. Thus, in opting out of Christianity, she also was indirectly making a very public renunciation of her former community. Another B'nai Noah adherent in rural Georgia, however, was never closely identified with his Baptist community, remaining "unsaved" until he was over 40 years old. In his case, he is far more circumspect about public professions of his new found faith and has thus suffered far fewer repercussions within the community (interview with B'nai Noah adherent [name withheld on request], 11 Apr. 1992).

4. Martin E. Marty and R. Scott Appleby, "Conclusion: An Interim Report on a Hypothetical Family," in *Fundamentalism Observed,* ed. Martin E. Marty and R. Scott Appleby (Chicago: Univ. of Chicago Press, 1991), 818; Stark, "How New Religions Succeed." For a study applying this theory to a new religious movement, the Holy Order of MANS, see Philip Lucas, "Social Factors in the Failure of New Religious Movements: A Case Study Using Stark's Success Model," *Syzygy* 1 (Winter 1992): 42–43.

5. This is a point made to the author by James Tabor in an interview on 23 Mar. 1992. Cf. "Tennessee Baptists Turn to Judaism for New Inspiration," *Wall Street Journal,* 20 Mar. 1991.

6. Jack E. Saunders, "Ben Ish vs Ben Adam—Emotion vs Intellect," *The Gap* (Mar./ Apr. 1992): 8.

7. "Friends Respond," *The Gap* (Jan./Feb. 1992): 6. Portion of a letter from Joyce Williams.

8. "Tennessee Baptists Turn to Judaism for New Inspiration," *Wall Street Journal,* 20 Mar. 1991; "Dixie Noahides Practice Despite Problems," *The Jewish Week,* 17 Aug. 1990. This has led to some defensiveness in the movement over the charge that in dividing families, the B'nai Noah constitute a religious cult. The reply of the movement to such charges is unequivocal: "This is the faith of Abel, Enoch, Noah, and even Abraham (before his circumcision). You could not find a religious Faith on this planet with older roots than the Noahide one! *You would hardly call the religion of these Patriarchs a 'cult.'* It is the very foundation of Western ethical and moral values" (B'nai Noah, *What is the B'nai Noah?,* 4–5).

9. The Root and Branch Association, publisher of the *Noahide Guide,* exists "to promote knowledge of the Noahide Covenant and observance of the Noahide Laws" (*Root and Branch Noahide Guide,* 54). The same publication lists the names, addresses, and telephone numbers of 22 individuals, 14 organizations, and 5 publications from around the world. The availability of the B'nai Noah to press coverage of the movement

(which is then carried in full in the *Guide*) is obvious. There are, in addition, public and semipublic conferences, "cassette ministries" (an Identity favorite as well), and the like to spread the word.

10. One of the more interesting (and printable) is "vomit eating dog." See "Noah's Followers Ignore Flood of Jibes," *Atlanta Journal Constitution*, 8 June 1991. Cf. Tabor, interview, 23 Mar. 1992.

11. Davis, interview.

12. Tabor, interview, 23 Mar. 1992.

13. James D. Tabor, "Plain Talk About Christianity Paganism and Torah Faith," *The Gap* (Nov./Dec. 1991): 1–2.

14. B'nai Noah, *What is the B'nai Noah?*, 5.

15. Gayman, "Jewish Fables Capture American Pulpits," 2–3. Pastor Gayman includes in this article a virtual codex of relevant scriptural passages.

16. James Tabor observes that the B'nai Noah are only one of a wider group of Christians who in the last century have sought to rediscover the roots of Christian belief in the early, pre-Hellenic period of Christian history, often coming to what Dr. Tabor calls "some form of Second Temple Judaism, as they imagine it." This diverse group of spiritual pilgrims includes Sacred Name believers of various hues as well as groups as diverse as Herbert W. Armstrong's modified Anglo-Israelite Worldwide Church of God, liberal Protestants and Catholics, and mainstream fundamentalist and evangelical Protestants. (James Tabor, letter to author, 11 May 1992).

17. A group of Christian Identity pastors make an annual pilgrimage to Washington to attempt to interest elected representatives in issues of concern to the Identity community. See Earl F. Jones, "Congressional Visit," *Christian Crusade For Truth Intelligence Newsletter* (Jan./Feb. 1989): 8; and idem, "Our Trip to the Congressmen," *Christian Crusade For Truth Intelligence Newsletter* (Mar./Apr. 1989): 2.

18. Rabbi Israel Chait, interview with author, 13 May 1992.

19. Rabbi Michael Katz, telephone conversation with author, 17 May 1992.

20. *Root and Branch Noahide Guide*, 21.

21. Katz, telephone conversation. On Agudat Israel, see Charles S. Leibman and Eliezer Don-Yehiya, *Religion and Politics in Israel* (Bloomington: Indiana Univ. Press, 1984), chs. 6–7. The Mizrachi movement is largely moribund. From its ashes, however, the National Religious Party has arisen, and from the youth wing of the NRP, Gush Emunim, the Israeli settlement movement, was born. Discussion of various aspects of the NRP and of Agudat Israel may be found in Ehud Sprinzak, *The Ascendance of Israel's Radical Right* (New York: Oxford Univ. Press, 1991), and Rael Jean Isaac, *Israel Divided: Ideological Politics in the Jewish State* (Baltimore: Johns Hopkins Univ. Press, 1976).

22. Rabbi Chaim Richman, "Teachings From the Temple," *The Gap* (Mar./Apr. 1992): 4. The red heifer belief seems to have been a puzzle to the classical rabbinic authorities, who found no biblical foundation for the belief and for whom the resemblance of this belief to certain occult practices then current among the gentile nations was something of an embarrassment. For the flavor of this controversy, see Ephraim E. Urbach, *The Sages* (Cambridge, Mass.: Harvard Univ. Press, 1987), 377–78. The quest for the ashes of the red heifer is the prime concern of Vendyl Jones's archaeological endeavors.

23. Tabor, interview, Mar. 23, 1992. Dr. Tabor appears to have some reservations about the direction of the Temple Mount activities, but appears to see himself as a non-Jewish voice for moderation (James Tabor, telephone conversation with author, 25 May 1992).

24. The sources of this dissent are unanimous in asking that their names not be used. The Neusner quote is from James D. Davis, "Faith and the Mountain," *Ft. Lauderdale Sun Sentinel*, 1 Dec. 1991.

25. The technical process by which the Noahide laws may have been constructed is

demonstrated in David Novak, *The Image of the Non-Jew in Judaism* (New York: Edwin Mellen, 1983), 3–6.

26. Moses Maimonides, *The Code of Maimonides: Book Fourteen, The Book of Judges,* trans. Abraham M. Hershman (New Haven, Conn.: Yale Univ. Press, 1949), 230–31.

27. Urbach, 532–33; Robert M. Seltzer, *Jewish People, Jewish Thought* (New York: Macmillan, 1980), 286. An accessible English language translation of the relevant portion of Talmud is *New Edition of the Babylonian Talmud,* trans. Michael L. Rodkinson, vols. 7–8, *Tract Sanhedrin* (Boston: The Talmud Society, 1918), 166–77. That the Noahides retain their value in Jewish/Christian polemic is demonstrated by Steven S. Schwarzschild, "Judaism, Scriptures and Ecumenism," *Judaism* 13 (Summer 1964): 271–73, where the author uses the Noahide laws as a riposte to the ecumenical outreach to the Jews emanating from Vatican II.

28. Novak, 3. Novak dates the Tosefta at late second century c.e., and Lichtenstein, (a primary source for the B'nai Noah), 11, argues for the late second century as well. Seltzer, 265, more conservatively places the date of this text as anywhere between the third and fifth centuries.

29. Novak, 3–4.

30. The rabbinical authorities quoted in the relevant passages of Sanhedrin date from the third to the fifth centuries c.e. The actual redaction of the Babylonian and Palestinian Talmuds did not take place before the sixth century. For a discussion of the various theories of the redaction, see Julius Kaplan, *The Redaction of the Babylonian Talmud* (New York: Bloch, 1933). Cf. Seltzer, 260–67.

31. *New Edition of the Babylonian Talmud,* 168.

32. Lichtenstein, 15.

33. Rabbi Dr. I. Epstein, trans. and ed., *The Babylonian Talmud* (London: Soncino Press, 1935). Tract Sanhedrin, 56b, 385.

34. *New Edition of the Babylonian Talmud,* 172.

35. J. David Bleich, "Jewish Law and the State's Authority to Punish Crime," *Cardozo Law Review* 12 (Feb./Mar. 1991): 831.

36. This suggestion has been offered by the *Universal Jewish Encyclopedia,* vol. 8 (New York: Works Project Administration, 1942), 227. There remains a body of scholarly opinion (albeit a minority one) that takes the position that, even under the conditions of the Exile, the Noahide code could have been applied somewhere by someone. See *Encyclopedia Judaica,* vol. 12 (Jerusalem: Keter, 1971), 1189. The suggestion that the Noahide code was applied by someone somewhere is repeated, more in hope than in conviction, by Suzanne Last Stone, "Sinaitic and Noahide Law: Legal Pluralism in Jewish Law," *Cardozo Law Review* 12 (Feb./Mar. 1991): 1163.

37. Novak, 60–64.

38. Arnold N. Enker, "Aspects of Interaction Between the Torah Law, the King's Law, and the Noahide Law in Jewish Criminal Law," *Cardozo Law Review* 12 (Feb./Mar. 1991): 1153. It is probably significant in this context that Maimonides' discussion of Noahide law immediately precedes his discourse on the coming of the Messiah; see Maimonides, chs. 9–11.

39. Enker, 1139, raises precisely this question. Novak, 53–83, also addresses the problem. Jonathan Z. Smith, in a conversation with the author, makes this point as well. The answers posited vary, but no source—including the most enthusiastic proponent of Noahide law, Nahum Rakover—is able to point to any documented post-Exilic instance of a practical application of the Noahide code. See Nahum Rakover, "Jewish Law and the Noahide Obligation to Preserve Social Order," *Cardozo Law Review* 12 (Feb./Mar. 1992).

40. Rakover, 1120–22.

41. Novak, 277.

42. Rakover, 1120–30; cf. Lichtenstein, 31–43.

43. Novak, 169–75.

44. Sanhedrin 57b, quoted in Rakover, 1086.

45. *Universal Jewish Encyclopedia,* vol. 8, 227; *Encyclopedia Judaica,* vol. 12, 1191; and *Jewish Encyclopedia,* vol. 7 (New York: Funk and Wagnalls, 1912), 649.

46. The relevant texts are conveniently gathered in Lichtenstein, in which the death penalty for transgression of each of the Noahide laws is considered.

47. Novak, 54.

48. Maimonides, chs. 9–10, 230–38.

49. Ibid., ch. 10, 234–35. Deliberate murder is the major exception to this. In practice, all Noahides are ignorant of the Noahide code.

50. Ibid., ch. 10, 235. As governments were (and are) conceived of as instruments of coercion controlled by men of violence, in theory, any Noahide following the laws of the land is excused from adherence to the Noahide code, *even if he is aware of its existence.*

51. Rakover.

52. Rabbi Elijah Benamozegh, *Israel and Humanity,* trans. and ed. Maxwell Luria (New York: Paulist, 1995), 53–54.

53. Ibid., 252–56.

54. Ibid., 239.

55. The Noahide Code is discussed in ibid., 260–80.

56. Rabbi Abraham Isaac Kook, *Lights of Penitence, Lights of Holiness,* trans. Ben Zion Bokser (New York: Paulist, 1978); HaRav Tzvi Yehuda HaCohen Kook, *Torat Eretz Israel,* trans. and ed. Tzvi Fishman, (Jerusalem: Torat Eretz Yisrael Publications, 1991).

57. Indeed, this is a primary basis for Tabor's theory that early Christianity was in fact an apocalyptic Noahide movement (James Tabor, interview with author, 26 Mar. 1992). Cf. James D. Tabor, "B'nai Noach: The Reappearance of the God-fearers in our Time," unpublished, privately circulated article (1990).

58. Rabbi Joseph Dov Soloveitchik, "Transcriptions of My Lectures by Rabbi Abraham Besdin," in *Man of Faith in the Modern World: Reflections by the Rav* (Hoboken, N.J.: Ktav, 1989), 76. Another student of Rabbi Soloveichik, Rabbi Shlomo Riskin of the West Bank settlement of Efrat, notes the importance of this covenant and of Sanhedrin 56a to the Rav's thought: Shlomo Riskin, "Three Biblical Covenants," *Jerusalem Post International Edition,* 27 Oct. 1990.

59. There may in fact once have been a pseudepigraphic "Book of Noah," but this had long since been absorbed into the Enoch literature and survives today as part of the second-century B.C. Book of Jubilees and in the first-century A.D. Pseudo-Philo. On the historical development of these texts, see Neil Forsyth, *The Old Enemy: Satan & The Combat Myth* (Princeton, N.J.: Princeton Univ. Press, 1987), 161–63, 183–85. The passages themselves may be found in *The Old Testament Psuedepigrapha,* ed. James H. Charlesworth, vol. 2 (Garden City, N.Y.: Doubleday, 1985), 66–67, 307, 328.

60. Bernard McGinn, trans. and ed., *Apocalyptic Spirituality* (New York: Paulist, 1979), 134.

61. D. H. Krominga, *The Millennium in the Church* (Grand Rapids, Mich.: William B. Eerdmans, 1945), 204; George Park Fisher, *History of Christian Doctrine* (New York: Charles Scribners Sons, 1923), 348–49.

62. Glenn T. Miller, "Dispensationalism," in *The Perennial Dictionary of World Religions* (San Francisco: Harper & Row, 1989), 224.

63. George M. Marsden, *Fundamentalism and American Culture* (Oxford: Oxford Univ. Press, 1980), 119.

64. This tortuous spiritual journey is recounted in Pellière's autobiography, Aimé

Pallière, *The Unknown Sanctuary: A Pilgrimage From Rome to Israel,* trans. Louise Waterman Wise (New York: Bloch, 1928). The key documents in this text, the letters written by Rabbi Benamozegh, are reproduced in Lichtenstein, 7–11.

65. Pallière, 204.

66. Lichtenstein, 11n. 19.

67. On the Identity hermeneutics, see "Blessing or Curse," *Smyrna* (July/Aug. 1991), or Jones, "Public Law 102–14," 2–4. On the views of the B'nai Noah: Rabbi Michael Katz, interview with author, 26 Mar. 1992; Haskelevich, interview; Chait, interview; and "Rabbis Differ in their Reaction to David Davis' B'nai Noach," *The Jewish Voice and Opinion,* June 1991.

68. Stephen S. Schwarzschild, "De Idolatria," in *Proceedings of the Academy for Jewish Philosophy,* ed. David Novak and Norbert M. Samuelson (Lanham, Md.: Univ. Press of America, 1992), 236n. 51. A good primary source detailing Maimonides' views on the question of idolatry is H. M. Russell and Rabbi J. Weinberg, trans., *The Book of Knowledge From the Mishnah Torah of Maimonides* (Edinburgh: Royal College of Physicians of Edinburgh, 1981), 70–108.

69. Schwarzschild, "De Idolatria," 213.

70. Barry S. Kogan, "Judaism and the Varieties of Idolatrous Experience," in *Proceedings of the Academy for Jewish Philosophy,* ed. David Novak and Norbert M. Samuelson (Lanham, Md: Univ. Press of America, 1992), 169.

71. Novak, 108, 112.

72. Ibid., 113, 152nn. 37 and 39.

73. Novak, 114–15.

74. Earlier discussions in the Mishnah, in the aggadic literature, and in the Palestinian Talmud seem to center more on dietary restrictions than on the question of idolatry per se; Novak, 115–17. This is consistent with the view of Jonathan Z. Smith as well; he points out (in conversation with author) that the biblical source of the Noahic covenant itself centered primarily on dietary restrictions. The specific sourcing of the idolatry legislation in the Noahide code, tractate Sanhedrin 56–60, was considered in the context of the historical development of the Noahide laws, above.

75. Novak, 124.

76. Lichtenstein, 59–64. Lichtenstein is a key source, as this text appears to have considerable influence among the B'nai Noah. The reasons for this may be largely a function of its comparative simplicity, its length (only 103 pages of text compared, say, to Novak's 416 pages of scholarly prose), and its appealing style. Lichtenstein devotes much of his text to consideration of Maimonides, and it was in the latter that the death penalty was most discussed; the impact of this discussion on those conditioned by a lifetime of Protestant fundamentalism to a literal reading of text is a matter of speculation. Lost in Lichtenstein's presentation, however, is the needed emphasis on the fact that the Jews were not in a position to put anyone to death. Indeed, the evidentiary laws in tractate Sanhedrin suggest that with each step the condemned is to take towards the place of execution, he must be allowed to turn back to the court to see if new exculpatory evidence has been produced! The laws concerning witnesses also make an actual execution on any charge a practical impossibility.

77. Urbach, 26.

78. Alfred L. Ivry, "The Inevitability of Idolatry," in *Proceedings of the Academy for Jewish Philosophy,* ed. David Novak and Norbert M. Samuelson (Lanham, Md.: University Press of America, 1992), 195-96.

79. Novak, 138.

80. Schwarzschild, "De Idolatria," 224–25.

81. For this view, see David Flusser, "Christianity," in *Contemporary Jewish Reli-*

gious Thought, ed. Arthur A. Cohen and Paul Mendes-Flohr (New York: Charles Scribner's Sons, 1987), 61–66.

82. Schwarzschild, "De Idolatria," 222–23.

83. Novak, 134. In the folk practice of both Jews and Muslims, the veneration of the tombs of saints was common.

84. San. 38a. For a discussion of the term *shittuf*, see Novak, 133–38. For its application in terms of Maimonides' thought, see Schwarzschild, "De Idolatria," 223.

85. See his letter in Pallière, 152.

86. Ibid., 136–37.

87. This is the precise wording adopted by Rabbi Israel Chait to express the view that Christianity may now be safely proclaimed to be idolatry (Chait, interview).

88. Schwarzschild, "De Idolatria," 223. It should be noted that Schwarzschild does condition his view with the provisos that Christians need not be treated as idolaters (based on Deut. 23:7, that even Edomites should be treated as brothers) and that as long as Christians live morally by abiding by the other six Noahide laws, logically, they can't be in serious violation of the law of idolatry.

89. Pranaitis, 83–84. Elizabeth Dilling's *The Plot Against Christianity* (Torrance, Calif.: Noontide, 1983) reprises at greater length the themes derived from Pranaitis.

90. The Zohar is in fact part of the thirteenth-century Kabbalistic literature, and was probably written by Moses de Leon of Castile. It is written in the form of a psuedepigraphic work, set in the Bar Kochba period (c. 2nd C.E.) in the name of a prominent figure of the Talmudic literature, Rabbi Simon bar Yohi. It is, however, not a part of the Talmud. See Seltzer, 428–29.

91. Pranaitis, 83.

92. Ibid., 83.

93. Ibid., 80. The Amalekites are used to this day in Jewish polemic as a term of ultimate contempt; it occurs in times of particular tension in the literature of the Israeli settlement movement Gush Emunim, for example.

94. Norman Cohn, *Warrant for Genocide* (New York: Harper, 1969); Dilling, *The Plot Against Christianity*.

95. *The Protocols of the Elders of Zion*, protocol 15, 196.

96. Jones, "Public Law 102-14," 4.

97. Ibid., 3.

98. Ibid., 4.

99. "Lost Discernment," *Smyrna* (Sept./Oct. 1991): 3–4.

100. "Blessing or Curse," 1.

101. Ibid., 2.

102. "Schneerson: 'Have no fear, Gulf crisis heralds Messiah,'" *Jerusalem Post International Edition*, 1 Sept. 1990. Cf. "Waiting for Messiah," *Jerusalem Post International Edition*, 9 Mar. 1991; "Footsteps of Messiah?" *Jerusalem Post International Edition*, 4 May 1991; "Announcing the Days of Redemption," *Jerusalem Post International Edition*, 5 Oct. 1991. The Habad position is set out in a full-page ad titled "The Time for Your Redemption has Arrived," *Jerusalem Post International Edition*, 29 June 1991.

103. "Blessing or Curse," 1–4.

104. Jack Mohr, "The Seven Noahide Laws and Their Implications for Christians," *The Christian Patriot Crusader* 7 (Dec. 1991): 3. Mohr not only borrows this phraseology—without attribution—but centers his presentation on contrasting the replacement of crèche scenes with menorahs.

105. "Blessing or Curse," 2–3.

106. Jones, "Public Law 102-14."

107. I have seen this article only in recycled form, as part of a mimeographed bulletin; thus, it is not possible to provide much more in the way of documentation for this source, save that a portion of the article covers pages 18–21 of an issue of the Foundation's journal (date and title unknown). It is included here to further illuminate the "jungle telegraph" by which ideas are disseminated. The journal, published by the National Justice Foundation, found its way into the hands of one Grant "Wings" Barker, an elderly right wing gadfly loosely associated with the Identity movement from his Gospel of the Kingdom Mission at Wilderness Ranch in El Cajon, California. Pastor Barker in turn has photocopied and remailed not only this journal excerpt but also *Smyrna* and seemingly anything else at hand. Pastor Barker's specialty, however, is divining esoteric meaning from scripture in an effort to "count the End," which he confidently asserts will be: "About the fall Equinox of 1997; Bible years start in the fall [*sic*]." Grant "Wings" Barker, "Jesus Christ Returns in 1998 to Rule and Reign Over His Kingdom On Earth"; letter to Ted Kell, Sunset School of Preaching Extension, Church of Christ, La Mesa, Calif., 19 Dec. 1981. The relevant document is from a mimeographed paper appended to the eight-page Kell letter.

108. Ibid., 21.

109. "Seven Noahide Laws," *The Shepherd's Voice* (Mar./Apr. 1992): 5–9.

110. Ibid., 8.

111. Ibid., 7.

112. John Harrell, interview with author, 13 Mar. 1992.

113. H. Graber, "Judaism, The Legislated Religion of the United States of America," *Kingdom Courier* 11 (Nov. 1991): 1–4.

114. Paul Hall, "Noahide Laws—Religion of a NEW WORLD ORDER," *Jubilee* 3 (Nov./Dec. 1991): 5.

115. "The second resolution was HJ410, Education Day USA." Cf. Paul Hall, "Noahide Laws II," *Jubilee* 4 (Mar./Apr. 1992), 1. Pastor Hall devotes two columns to reprinting the names and districts of the resolution's sponsors, under the title "Who Are the Sellouts?"

116. Hall, "Noahide Laws II," 11–12, 17. Cf. Chaim Clorfene and Yakov Rogalski, *The Path of the Righteous Gentile* (Jerusalem: Targum, 1987).

117. *Omega Times* (July–Nov. 1991): 4. No date is given for the *Tribune* article in question. The *Omega Times* is notably playful when it comes to dating and typesetting their newsletter, making reading it a somewhat wearing experience. The *Omega Times*'s credo is offered in the preamble of each issue, with the assertion that the newsletter is offered to the public at no charge as "evidence of the fulfillment of prophesy and signs of the soon coming of our LORD AND SAVIOR, JESUS CHRIST!"

118. Ibid.

119. The *Omega Times* (Jan.–etc.? 1992): 8.

120. "Bush Merges Church and State—With 'Noahide Law' . . . (PL 102-12 [*sic*])!!" *Criminal Politics* 1 (Jan. 1992): 5–8.

121. This is an astronomical sum in this milieu. *Criminal Politics* publisher Lawrence Patterson advertises his services as a financial consultant to readers for $850 per hour, although his staff can provide the same services at the bargain rate of only $300 per hour.

122. "Bush Merges Church and State," 8.

5. The Anti-Cult Movement/Watchdog Groups

1. J. Gordon Melton and Robert L. Moore, *The Cult Experience: Responding to the New Religious Pluralism* (New York: Pilgrim, 1982), 95.

2. For a cross section of the debate, see Melton, *Encyclopedic Handbook of Cults,*

3–20; Melton and Moore; David G. Bromley and Anson D. Shupe, Jr., *Strange Gods* (Boston: Beacon, 1981), 3–6, 23–24. It should be noted, however, that even so staunch an opponent of the cult stereotype as J. Gordon Melton finds himself constrained to use the term in the titles of his many dictionaries and publications dealing with NRMs. For an ACM perspective, see George A. Mather and Larry A. Nichols, *Dictionary of Cults, Sects, Religions and the Occult* (Grand Rapids, Mich.: William B. Eerdmans, 1993).

3. Melton, *Encyclopedic Handbook of Cults,* 221. The volume was William C. Irvine's *Timely Warnings.*

4. Ibid. Laird Wilcox, in a partial listing of religious ACMs, lists no less than 256, with the majority aimed at the Mormons or the Jehovah's Witnesses! Laird Wilcox, *Guide to the American Occult* (Olathe, Kans.: Editorial Research Service, 1990).

5. David G. Bromley and Anson Shupe, Jr., "The Future of the Anticult Movement," in *The Future of New Religious Movements,* ed. David G. Bromley and Phillip E. Hammond (Macon, Ga.: Mercer Univ. Press, 1987), 235–50.

6. David G. Bromley and Anson D. Shupe, Jr., *The New Vigilantes* (Beverly Hills, Calif.: Sage, 1980), 121–44.

7. The anti-cult literature of the Christian community has been noted above. For a good overview of anti-cult texts emanating from the Jewish community, see J. Gordon Melton, ed., *Cults and the Jewish Community: Representative Works of Jewish Anti-Cult Literature* (New York: Garland, 1990). For a secular Jewish view, see A. James Rudin and Marcia R. Rudin, *Prison or Paradise: The New Religious Cults* (Philadelphia: Fortress, 1980).

8. John R. Fry, "Hate Crime in America," *Church and Society* 80 (May/June 1990).

9. Ibid., 78.

10. Ibid., 79.

11. The LaRouche organization was reacting to the attentions of the ADL which were later published as Anti-Defamation League, *The LaRouche Political Cult: Packaging Extremism* (New York: Anti-Defamation League, 1986), 35–38.

12. Director of the FBI to SACs and ADICs, 4 Feb. 1985. Obtained through Lyndon LaRouche FOIA action, date unknown. The document was provided by non-LaRouche sources who wish to remain anonymous.

13. 26 Mar. 1982 letter from John Hope III to Irwin Suall of the ADL, refusing to publish the Anti-Defamation League's *Hate Groups In America* under the aegis of the U.S. Commission on Civil Rights on the grounds of gross inaccuracies.

14. On the ADL's settlement of the case, see "Jewish Group Settles Spying Case," *Atlanta Journal/Atlanta Constitution,* 18 Nov. 1993. For a complete collection of the relevant news clippings, as well as for a transcript of the FBI's interview with Roy Bullock, see Laird Wilcox, *Anti-Defamation League 1993 Spy Scandal Clipping File* (Olathe, Kans.: Editorial Research Service, n.d.).

15. Debra Nussbaum Cohen, "ADL Settles Case Alleging Illegal Information-Gathering," *Kansas City Jewish Chronicle,* 19 Nov. 1993.

16. Naomi W. Cohen, *Not Free to Desist* (Philadelphia: Jewish Publication Society of America, 1972), 557.

17. This tactical shift is presaged in an undated, four-page fund raising appeal signed by Rabbi Marvin Hier, Dean, Simon Wiesenthal Center, Los Angeles, Calif. (c. Nov. 1991). On the Wiesenthal Center's efforts in the area of Holocaust education, see Simon Wiesenthal Center, *The Holocaust, 1933–1945, Educational Resource Kit* (Los Angeles: Simon Wiesenthal Center, c. 1995); or Simon Wiesenthal Center, *Dignity & Defiance: The Confrontation of Life and Death in the Warsaw Ghetto* (Los Angeles: Simon Wiesenthal Center, c. 1995).

18. Laird Wilcox, "Lenny Zeskind, Lyn Wells and the Center for Democratic Renewal Including Chip Berlet and Political Research Associates: The Hidden 'Links' and

'Ties' of an 'Anti-Extremist' Organization," special report from Editorial Research Service of Olathe, Kans. (Mar. 1989).

19. *Klanwatch Intelligence Report* 54 (Feb. 1991): 2; Bill Moyers, *Hate on Trial,* PBS Documentary, broadcast, 5 Feb. 1992.

20. Harold Covington, "Urgent and Important Security Notice," *Resistance* 38 (May 1994). Note that Covington's *Resistance* newsletter is not the same as George Eric Hawthorn's glossy *Resistance* magazine, which is dedicated to coverage of the white power music scene.

21. The Covington letter is signed in the name of *Resistance,* and was posted via the ANA e-mail list on 11 Nov. 1995. The Edward Fields article is credited to *The Truth At Last* #385 (1995). The original Fields article quotes as his source Morris Dees' own *SPLC Report.*

22. Jack Roper, telephone conversation with author, 23 Dec. 1992; Harold Henderson, "CAN of Worms," *Chicago Reader,* 16 Oct. 1992; *SCP Newsletter* 15, no. 2 (1990); and letter to author from Stuart Chevre, Spiritual Counterfeits Project, 28 June 1991. John A. Saliba, "The Christian Response to the New Religions: A Critical Look at the Spiritual Counterfeits Project," *Journal of Ecumenical Studies* 18 (Summer 1981): 451–73. For a representative sampling of the literature emanating from these groups, see Anson S. Shupe, Jr., David G. Bromley, and Donna L. Oliver, *The Anti-Cult Movement in America: A Bibliography and Historical Survey* (New York: Garland, 1984), 60–80.

23. For example, the May 1991 conference sponsored by the Chicago affiliate of the Anti-Defamation League of the B'nai B'rith featured a program on "Extremist Cults— Purveyors of Bigotry." See "Remarks Presented by Cynthia Kisser, Executive Director, Cult Awareness Network," unpublished speech delivered on 6 May 1991 to the Chicago Anti-Defamation League's Forum Series.

24. "Jew String Puller Behind Clinton," *Der Stürmer* 1 (Aug. 1992): 1.

25. Kerr Cuhulain, "Ritualistic, Cult and Occult Crime," *Witchcraft, Satanism and Occult Crime: Who's Who and What's What,* Third Edition, (Jan. 1991), 7.

26. John Dellea, "Kerr Cuhulain Pagan Policeman," *Llewellyn's New Worlds of Mind and Spirit* (Jan./Feb. 1993): 39. On Larry Jones and his newsletter, *File 18,* see Robert D. Hicks, *In Pursuit of Satan: The Police and the Occult* (Buffalo, N.Y.: Prometheus, 1991), 38–55.

27. Dellea, 39.

28. "Resources and References," *Witchcraft, Satanism and Occult Crime: Who's Who and What's What,* 3d ed. (January 1991), 19.

29. See the confidential memorandum from Jeffrey Hadden (on behalf of Eileen Barker and David Bromley) to concerned social scientists, "Social scientists concerned about forensic and related issues dealing with New Religious Movements," 20 Dec. 1989. The ten-page memorandum, supplied by sources who wish to remain anonymous, offers suggestions for a number of proposed activities for the as-yet unnamed group.

30. Association of World Academics for Religious Education, "A Social-Scientific Perspective on Cults, Brainwashing, and Deprogramming" (n.d.).

31. Form letter from James R. Lewis, 15 Dec. 1995. The specific reason cited by Lewis was that "certain unfriendly parties have chosen to interpret my personal activities as constituting AWARE's activities and opinions. As a result, people who have lent their names to AWARE's advisory board have been placed in the awkward position of having to respond to questions about my activities and opinions as if their advisory position required them to defend my actions."

32. The attack on British Israel beliefs emanating from the Church of England is still recalled with considerable bitterness today. See "The Identity Movement in Britain," *Wake Up!* (Sept./Oct. 1991): 178.

33. The relationship between the British government and Anglo-Israelism is a tortuously complex tale. As early as 1795, parliamentary support (in the person of Nathaniel

Brassey Halhead) for the earliest and most idiosyncratic theorist of what would become British Israel beliefs, Richard Brothers, was offered on the Commons floor (Harrison, 76). This British upper-class following is noted with some disdain by the American critics of British Israelism; see Anton Darms, *The Delusion of British-Israelism* (New York: Loizeaux Brothers Bible Truth Depot, c. 1939), 5; and Herbert M. Wyrick, *Seven Religious Isms: An Historical and Scriptural Review* (Grand Rapids, Mich.: Zondervan, 1941), 90. This latter booklet was recently reprinted in J. Gordon Melton, ed., *The Evangelical Christian Anti-Cult Movement* (New York: Garland, 1990).

34. For a good example of these beliefs, see Rev. Thomas Rosling Howlett, *Anglo-Israel and the Jewish Problem* (Philadelphia: Spangler & Davis, 1892).

35. Rev. L. E. Erith, "The Fallacy of British Israelism," *The Review of the Churches* 6 (Apr. 1929): 194–95.

36. Ibid., 198–99.

37. Allen H. Godby, *The Lost Tribes a Myth: Suggestions Towards Rewriting Hebrew History* (Durham, N.C.: Duke Univ. Press, 1930).

38. Rev. J. K. Van Baalen, *The Gist of the Cults: Christianity Versus False Religion* (Grand Rapids, Mich.: William B. Eerdmans, 1944), 56. This booklet was recently reprinted in Melton, ed., *Evangelical Christian Anti-Cult Movement,* 156.

39. Jan Karel Van Baalen, *The Chaos of the Cults,* 4th ed. (Grand Rapids, Mich.: William B. Eerdmans, 1962), 5–17.

40. Ibid., 162–64; Van Baalen, *The Gist of the Cults,* 56.

41. Van Baalen, *The Chaos of the Cults,* 173. In less allusive language, Van Baalen in the same chapter credits Ralph L. Roy with pointing out the racialist aspects of British Israel, emphasizing in particular Howard Rand, James A. Lovell, Wesley Swift (Van Baalen does not fail to note Swift's connection with the movement of Gerald L. K. Smith), and Denver's William Blessing.

42. Van Baalen, *The Gist of the Cults,* 60.

43. Ibid.

44. For a detailed insider's account of these issues, see David Gaines, *The World Council of Churches* (Peterborough, N.H.: Richard R. Smith Noone House, 1966).

45. T. Weber, ch. 8.

46. Cohen, 346.

47. Ibid.

48. Rabbi S. Andhill Fineberg, "Quarantine Treatment," memorandum published by the Community Service Department of the AJC, 15 Aug. 1947.

49. Simonelli, 93.

50. The best available coverage of these events is provided by Simonelli, ch. 6.

51. A good recent history of this evolution is Leonard Dinnerstein, *Antisemitism in America* (New York: Oxford Univ. Press, 1994).

52. Fineberg.

53. This incident may have stemmed from the long-standing animus that Smith held for President Dwight D. Eisenhower, whose military career he believed was advanced by a sexual liaison with Ms. Rosenberg (Jeansonne, *Gerald L. K. Smith,* 163).

54. Cohen, 360–61, 374–77. Cf. Roy, 65, and David H. Bennett, *Demagogues in the Depression* (New Brunswick, N.J.: Rutgers Univ. Press, 1969), 286. For Smith's side of the alleged persecution visited on him and his associates by the Jewish organizations, see House Committee on Un-American Activities, *Investigation of Un-American Propaganda Activities in the United States (Gerald L. K. Smith),* 79th Congress, 2d sess., H. Res. (Washington, D.C.: Government Printing Office, 1946), 5.

55. Jeansonne, *Gerald L. K. Smith,* 208–9. Cf. Glen Jeansonne, "Combating Anti-Semitism: The Case of Gerald L. K. Smith," in *Anti-Semitism in American History,* ed. David A. Gerber (Urbana: Univ. of Illinois Press, 1986), 158–60.

56. Smith, *Satan's New Testament*, 25. The biblical reference is to Gen. 2:9 and 3:9.

57. Roy, 103–4.

58. On the Swift period of CDL activity, see William W. Turner, *Power on the Right* (Berkeley, Calif.: Ramparts, 1971), 101–3. Later CDL history is available from Richard Butler's perspective in "Foundations: Biography of Pastor Richard G. Butler," *Aryan Nations* (n.d.): 3. On Warner's CDL, see Anti-Defamation League, *Extremism on the Right*, 9.

59. Swift was well aware of this interest, particularly on the part of the ADL and the AJC. He is in fact quoted in an edition of his *Christian Defense News* as having formed the Christian Defense League as a counter to these and other "enemy" organizations (Turner, 101).

60. "'Identity Churches': A Theology of Hate," 6. To drive home this point, a one-page "ADL Special Edition" flier again evokes the shade of Swift, who died in 1970, by publishing an unattributed quote that has become ubiquitous in coverage of Swift: "I prophesy that before Nov. 1953 there will not be a Jew in the United States, and by that I mean a Jew that will be able to walk or talk" ("Religion as Bigotry: The Identity Church Movement," *Anti-Defamation League of the B'nai B'rith Special Edition* [Oct. 1991]).

61. Zeskind, 52. For an example of these "priestly hermeneutics" in action, see "A Sinister Search for Identity," *Time,* 20 Oct. 1986, 74, where the most extreme aspects of the movement are reported using Leonard Zeskind as an "expert" commentator.

62. Telephone conversation with members of the research department of the Wiesenthal Center in Los Angeles, 5 May 1992. Elwood McQuad, letter to author, 3 Mar. 1992. Cf. Elwood McQuaid, "Peril of the Christian Identity Movement," unpublished, privately circulated essay.

63. Aho, *Politics of Righteousness,* 29.

64. Smith died on 15 Apr. 1976, but *The Cross and the Flag* went on briefly, as did the dream of a biblical theme park and passion play at Eureka Springs. See *The Cross and the Flag* 36 (Sept. 1977): 13, for an advertisement for the park, and 23, for a discussion of the project. For a scholarly view, see Jeansonne, *Gerald L. K. Smith,* ch. 11.

65. Arnold Forster and Benjamin R. Epstein, *The New Anti-Semitism* (New York: McGraw-Hill, 1974), 29, 44–45. The Humble Oil Company, for example, which publicized the passion play in a list of outdoor dramas printed in its *Happy Motoring News* newsletter, found its correspondence with the ADL leaked to the press and some credit card holders returned their cards.

66. See my review essay on the impact of this text on the millenarian right wing in America in *Syzygy* 1 (Summer 1992): 271–73.

67. Dave Barley, "A Predictable Event Has Occurred!" *America's Promise Newsletter* (Mar. 1992): 21–25. Included are reprints of the articles from local newspapers in and around Sand Point, Idaho. Barley's move to Idaho is recalled by a local journalist, David Keyes, "Questions Surround Church," *Bonner County Daily Bee* (n.d.).

68. For an international perspective on the phenomenon of the ZOG discourse as it applied even to countries who suffer from a dearth of Jews, see the articles in the special issue "Terror From the Extreme Right," *Terrorism and Political Violence* 7, no. 1 (Spring 1995). For an insight into the phenomenon of anti-Semitism without Jews, see Michael Shafir, "Anti-Semitism without Jews in Romania," *Report on Eastern Europe* 2, no. 26 (28 June 1991), 20–32.

69. "Special Message and Alert from Pastor Peters," Scriptures for America cassette #552 (n.d.). In an accompanying document, Pastor Peters demands to know why the ADL was uncharacteristically silent on the Weaver situation; see Pete Peters, "White Crime in America," special newsletter, Laporte, Colo. (n.d.), 1.

70. Kaplan, "The Context of American Millenarian Revolutionary Theology."

71. Dan Gayman, undated letter to author.

72. The ADL model statute is published in Anti-Defamation League, *Hate Groups In America,* 54. On ADL involvement with "hate crimes" legislation, see Anti-Defamation League, *Hate Crimes Statutes: A 1991 Status Report* (New York: ADL, 1991).

73. Estimates of the size of the Identity community vary wildly, with a range of between 2,000 and 50,000, according to Barkun in *Religion and the Racist Right,* viii. Gail Gans, the Associate Director of the ADL's Research Department, correctly states that "a census of these groups is probably not possible because they come and go" (Gail Gans, fax to author, 14 Nov. 1995). Expanding on the theme in a fax dated 21 Nov. 1995, Ms. Gans states that the ADL "believes it is not possible to make an accurate [estimate of the numbers involved in that] American National Socialist groups which are hard core, *avowed advocates of National Socialist doctrine,* number no more than 1,000: Groups which advocate a 'semi-Nazism' include many more: racist skinheads and some Holocaust deniers for example."

74. Anti-Defamation League, "The KKK Today: A 1991 Status Report," 1.

75. Anti-Defamation League, *1991 Audit of Anti-Semitic Incidents* (New York: Anti-Defamation League, 1992), 3, 19. On right-wing violence emanating from individuals rather than from organizations, see, Tore Bjørgo, "Introduction," *Terrorism and Political Violence* 7, no. 1 (Spring 1995).

76. "Pro-Israel Lobbyist Resigns After Boasts Are Made Public," *New York Times,* 5 Nov. 1992; "A Pro-Israel Lobby Gives Itself a Headache," *New York Times Week in Review,* 8 Nov. 1992.

77. See the early B'nai Noah response to the cult charge in *What is the B'nai Noah?,* 4–5. The suspicion that the B'nai Noah do somehow constitute a cult persists and may be a factor in limiting the movement's growth. Anecdotal evidence of this abounds, although hard data is impossible to obtain. As an example, while in Chicago, I received a call from a potential Noahide who, having read the B'nai Noah literature, was immensely excited and wished to join immediately. After some weeks of reconsideration, however, this potential adherent decided against any further contact with the group, suspecting that it was somehow a cult. This impression seems to be a function of both the widespread misunderstanding of what actually constitutes a cult, and the common belief, fostered by many religious ACMs, that any New Religious Movement is in reality a cult.

78. The Watchman Fellowship belatedly took up the case of the B'nai Noah and scheduled a crusade for J. David Davis' hometown of Athens, Tenn., to take place 6–9 Nov. 1994; see J. David Davis, "Cult Busters A Bust—A Matter of Honor & Integrity," *The Gap* 9403 (May/June 1994): 5–7.

79. This phenomenon has spawned a considerable body of literature. For one of the better examples of this genre, see Marvin R. Wilson, *Our Father Abraham: Jewish Roots of the Christian Faith* (Grand Rapids, Mich.: William B. Eerdmans, 1989).

80. On Kahane's connection with the B'nai Noah, see Vendyl Jones, "A Prince Has Fallen in Israel," and Rabbi Stewart Weiss, "A Great Man Among Our People Is Dead," both in *Researcher* (Oct.–Dec. 1990): 6–7. Cf. Anti-Defamation League, *Meir Kahane: In His Own Words* (New York: Anti-Defamation League, 1985).

81. Paul Hall, "Noahide Laws Part Three: A Continued Look at Talmudic Laws Foisted Upon America," *Jubilee* (May/June 1992): 10–11. For the text of the first Education Day Resolution, see *Root and Branch Noahide Guide,* 56.

82. Hall, "Noahide Laws Part Three." Cf. Clorfene and Rogalski.

83. Paul Hall, "Earth Summit Derision," *Jubilee* (July/Aug. 1992).

84. Sandra Chesky, telephone conversation with author, 13 Mar. 1993. On the low level of concern for Satanism in Chicago, Cynthia Kisser, interview with author, 17 Mar. 1993. In fact, CAN's national office in Chicago received on average of 133 calls per month on Satanism between July 1988 and July 1990, moving Kisser to write an article on the subject. The intractable—and highly polarized—nature of the debate on Satanism

in America accounts for the low priority the issue receives in Chicago. So too does the fact that whatever the truth of this construction, other cult groups are a demonstrably greater problem from the ACM perspective. In Texas, however, Satanism is taken more seriously. See Cynthia S. Kisser, "Satanism as a Social Movement," *Free Inquiry* (Winter 1992/93). Cf. the immediate riposte from Robert Hicks, "The Myth of Satanism: A Response to Cynthia Kisser," *Free Inquiry* (Winter 1992/93). On Satanism's potency in Texas, Jan Keith, telephone conversation with author, 21 Jan. 1993.

85. Samuel David Heron, interview with author, 6 Jan. 1993. Heron, in fact, points out that while Ms. Chesky is a fundamentalist, Ms. Keith is a pagan working with CAN to change the image of pagan traditions "from the inside" (David Heron, interview with author, 13 Jan. 1993).

86. Keith, telephone conversation.

87. Keith, telephone conversation; Chesky, telephone conversation; Kisser, interview.

88. Conversation with and documents from Jack Roper, 20 Nov. 1992.

89. For a good insight into the negative view of the Odinist Fellowship held by other pagans, see Adler, 278: "[The Odinist Fellowship] is frankly racist, although they would probably prefer the term 'racialist.'"

90. Christensen, interview.

91. Ibid.

92. Stephen McNallen, "The Jesus Flag," *Runestone* 51 (Spring 1985): 11, quoted in Adler, 280. McNallen feels that it is important to note that the key difference "is on the matter of tolerance. I think that that most Asafolk are more tolerant than most fundamentalists, in general" (Steve McNallen, letter to author, 31 Dec. 1992).

93. Bainbridge, telephone conversation, 17 Jan. 1993.

94. Gamlinginn, conversation with author, 12 Oct. 1992.

95. Ibid. Confirmation of the identification of Norse runes with Satanism can be found in the unpublished notes to a slide presentation on Satanism offered by Jack Roper of CARIS; see Jack Roper, *Signs Primer: Occult Semiology Investigative Slide Training Series: Slide Script Volume One* (Milwaukee: CARIS, 1991).

96. The sole exception to this ignorance is the Texas CAN group whose investigator, Samuel David Heron, joined the Ring of Troth which Thorsson founded. Heron did discuss Thorsson's Satanism with Jan Chesky, but noted that in a recent talk at the Houston neopagan bookstore and gathering place for the local occult community, the Magic Lantern, Thorsson appeared to downplay the Satanism issue and CAN took no further action. (Samuel David Heron, interview with author, 6 Jan. 1993).

97. Thorsson, interview, 20 Sept. 1992. Despite this divisive controversy—a controversy that has yet to fully abate—Thorsson remains unbowed by his current virtual pariah status in many sectors of Ásatrú/Odinist opinion. He proudly notes his initiatory degrees in both Ásatrú and the Temple of Set on his c.v., and in the interview of 20 Sept. 1992, refers to the Temple of Set controversy in unrepentant terms: "For the most part I have treated my detractors for the ants they are (you know those crawling up the elephant's leg intent on rape)."

98. *Filosophem* is published by Blood Axis in Metz, France. Harr Vidharr Von Herske, letter to author, 8 Jan. 1995; Varg Vigernes, interview with author, 4 Aug. 1995, Oslo, Norway. In this interview, Vigerness discussed quite openly his plans for the large quantity of explosives which police recovered from his apartment during his arrest. The plan was, he states, to blow up the Antifa (Anti-fascist) center in Oslo, the Blitz House. The plan as described was certainly feasible, and only his impulsive decision to break into the home of a rival on the Norwegian Satanism scene—a decision which led to the murder of that rival—prevented his carrying out the operation.

99. Alan M. Schwartz, letter to author, 4 Dec. 1992.

100. *Aryan Action Line* 1 (Fall 1991).

101. On *Open Eye*'s interest, Matthew Kalman, coeditor of *Open Eye,* letter to author, 16 Apr. 1996. Jonathan Mozzochi, Robert Crawford, S. L. Gardner, and R. L. Taylor, *Northwest Imperative: Documenting a Decade of Hate* (Portland, Ore.: Coalition for Human Dignity, 1994), 1.13–1.14. The author of the article, Jonathan Mozzochi, notes that he learned of the Ásatrú Alliance through "sister publications," and then read *Vor Trú* itself, in which he found racist material. The Coalition, he notes, did talk to the Viking Days organizers, but through his previous reading, Mozzochi knew of Ásatrú before the event. In his view, Ásatrú is a racist religion. Mozzochi states that the goal of the public exposure of the racist nature of Ásatrú is to broaden awareness of the movement through public education, which may lead to picketing of Ásatrú activities, so long as those measures are within the bounds of the law. Jonathan Mozzochi, conversation with author, 1 May 1996.

102. Discussion with Ásatrú adherent (name withheld by request), June 1995. Cf. Jeffrey Kaplan, "The Anti-Cult Movement in America: An History of Culture Perspective," *Syzygy* 2, nos. 3–4 (1993).

103. This middle choice is being increasingly challenged by the nonracialist adherents. For example, the now defunct Ásatrú journal *Mountain Thunder* 8 (Spring Equinox 1993) contains several articles on the topic. Cf. the premier issue of the Ásatrú Fellowship's journal, *Ask and Embla,* for writings on this theme.

104. McNallen, interview.

A Confederacy of Seekers?

1. "Scores Die as Compound is Set Afire After F.B.I. Move," *New York Times,* 20 Apr. 1993.

2. Jonathan Z. Smith, "The Devil in Mr. Jones," in *Imagining Religion* (Chicago: Univ. of Chicago Press, 1982), 111–112.

3. The Taborites serve as a paradigmatic case for millenarian violence, but they are hardly the only such case that could be posited. The "Peoples of the Book" (Judaism, Christianity and Islam) have all produced numerous millenarian or messianic movements that, for a time, have turned to violence. For an overview of the phenomenon, see David C. Rapoport, "Fear and Trembling: Terrorism in Three Religious Traditions," *American Political Science Review* 78 (Sept. 1984), and idem, "Messianic Sanctions for Terror," *Comparative Politics* 20 (Jan. 1988). From the Jewish tradition, the most important modern example would be that of the false messiah, Sabbatai Zevi. See Gershom G. Scholem, *Shabbatai Zevi: The Mystical Messiah* (Princeton, N.J.: Princeton Univ. Press, 1973), or for a more global view, idem, *Messianic Idea in Judaism* (New York: Schocken, 1971). For an analysis of a contemporary Islamic case in millenarian terms, see for example Fuad Ajami, *Vanished Imam* (Ithaca, N.Y.: Cornell Univ. Press, 1986).

4. Howard Kaminsky, "The Prague Insurrection of 30 July 1419," *Medievalia et Humanistica* 10 (1956). For the complete history, see idem, *A History of the Hussite Revolution* (Berkeley: Univ. of California Press, 1967).

5. Howard Kaminsky, "Pius Aeneas Among the Taborites," *Church History* 28 (1959).

6. Max Weber, *Ancient Judaism* (New York: Macmillan, 1952).

7. Chris Temple, "A Lesson in Federal Tyranny: The Weaver Family Saga," *Jubilee* 5 (Sept./Oct. 1992), 1. Cf. idem, "Weaver, Harris Face the Death Penalty," *Jubilee* 5 (Nov./Dec. 1992), 1. On Ellison, see Flynn and Gerhardt, 256–61. It is important to note that the charges against Weaver, Ellison, and David Koresh all involved weapons. The charges were apparently well-founded.

8. Michael Adas, *Prophets Of Rebellion : Millenarian Protest Movements Against The European Colonial Order* (Chapel Hill: Univ. of North Carolina Press, 1979).

9. See Boyer; St. Clair.

10. Undated letter from Oklahoma prisoner to an Odinist leader. Names withheld.

11. Undated letter from Oklahoma prisoner to an Odinist leader. Names withheld.

12. Such, apparently, is the fate of Bill Riccio. Riccio, a middle-aged skinhead, Klansman, and neo-Nazi from Alabama, managed to gather perhaps a dozen followers before being incarcerated, again on weapons charges. His story is featured in the television documentary, "Skinheads, U.S.A.," HBO Television Productions, 1993.

13. Kaplan, "Absolute Rescue."

14. "FBI Director Says Agency Blundered in Standoff," *New York Times,* 20 Oct. 1995; "FBI Director Faults Tactics at Sect Siege," *New York Times,* 2 Nov. 1995.

15. The vital role of religious space is considered in Emmanuel Sivan, "The Enclave Culture," in *Fundamentalisms Comprehended,* ed. Martin E. Marty and R. Scott Appleby (Chicago: Univ. of Chicago Press, 1995); and Jonathan Z. Smith, *To Take Place* (Chicago: Univ. of Chicago Press, 1987).

16. Joseph Grace, undated letter to author, Burkeville, Va. It is notable that in a 1992 conversation I had with Identity adherent John Harrell, an identical conclusion (based on biblical hermeneutics) that nuclear apocalypse was imminent was posited, and I was gently urged to flee Chicago for safer environs.

17. John Broekhoft, letter to author, Ashland, Ky., 10 Feb. 1993.

18. J. Tim Thompson, writing for the dissident Philadelphia Church faction of the Worldwide Church of God in "Worldwide Epidemic: Killing in the Name of God," *The Philadelphia Trumpet* 4 (May 1993).

19. James H. Billington, *Fire in the Minds of Men: Origins of the Revolutionary Faith* (New York: Basic Books, 1980).

20. The metaphor (and much more) is borrowed from Martin Marty.

21. Eustice Mullins, *The Curse of Canaan: A Demonology of History* (Staunton, Va.: Revelation, 1987).

Bibliography

Books, Articles, and Theses

Adas, Michael. *Prophets of Rebellion: Millenarian Protest Movements Against the European Colonial Order.* Chapel Hill: Univ. of North Carolina Press, 1979.

Adler, Margot. *Drawing Down the Moon.* 2nd ed. Boston: Beacon, 1986.

Aho, James A. "Out of Hate: A Sociology of Defection from Neo-Nazism." *Current Research on Peace and Violence* 11 (1988): 159–68.

———. *The Politics of Righteousness: Idaho Christian Patriotism.* Seattle: Univ. of Washington Press, 1990.

———. "Reification and Sacrifice: The Goldmark Case." *California Sociologist* 10 (Winter 1987): 79–95.

Ajami, Fuad. *Vanished Imam.* Ithaca, N.Y.: Cornell Univ. Press, 1986.

Allen, J. H. *Judah's Sceptre and Joseph's Birthright.* Merrimac, Mass.: Destiny, n.d.

Anderson, R. B. *Norse Mythology; or, The Religion of Our Forefathers, Containing All of the Myths of the Eddas, Systemized and Interpreted.* Chicago: S. C. Griggs, 1876.

Anderson, Scott, and John Lee Anderson. *Inside the League.* New York: Dodd, Mead, 1982.

Angel, Jean-Michel. *The Occult and the Third Reich: The Mystical Origins of Nazism and the Search for the Holy Grail.* New York: Macmillan, 1974.

Anti-Defamation League. *Extremism on the Right: A Handbook.* New York: Anti-Defamation League, 1988.

———. *Hate Crimes Statutes: A 1991 Status Report.* New York: Anti-Defamation League, 1991.

———. *Hate Groups In America: A Record of Bigotry and Violence.* New York: Anti-Defamation League, 1988.

———. *The LaRouche Political Cult: Packaging Extremism.* New York: Anti-Defamation League, 1986.

———. *Meir Kahane: In His Own Words.* New York: Anti-Defamation League, 1985.

———. *1991 Audit of Anti-Semitic Incidents.* New York: Anti-Defamation League, 1992.

——. *Religion as Bigotry: The Identity Church Movement.* New York: Anti-Defamation League, Oct. 1991.

Ariel, Yaakov S. "American Premillennialism and Its Attitudes Towards the Jewish People, Judaism and Zionism, 1875–1925." Ph.D. diss., Univ. of Chicago, 1986.

Aswynn, Freyja. *Leaves of Yggdrasil.* St. Paul, Minn.: Llewellyn, 1990.

Barkun, Michael. *Disaster and the Millennium.* New Haven, Conn.: Yale Univ. Press, 1974.

——. "From British Israelism to Christian Identity: The Evolution of White Supremacist Religious Doctrine." *Syzygy* 1, no. 1 (Winter 1992): 55–61.

——. "Millenarian Aspects of 'White Supremacist' Movements." *Terrorism and Political Violence* 1, no. 4 (1989): 409–34.

——. "Racist Apocalypse: Millennialism on the Far Right." *American Studies* 31 (1990): 121–40.

——. "Reflections after Waco: Millenialists and the State." In *From the Ashes: Making Sense of Waco,* edited by James R. Lewis, 41–49. Lanham, Md.: Rowman & Littlefield, 1994.

——. *Religion and the Racist Right: The Origins of the Christian Identity Movement.* Chapel Hill: Univ. of North Carolina Press, 1994.

Barrett, Stanley R. *Is God a Racist?* Toronto: Univ. of Toronto Press, 1987.

Bellah, Robert N. *The Broken Covenant: American Civil Religion in Time of Trial.* New York: Seabury, 1975.

Bellah, Robert N., and Frederick E. Greenspahn. *Uncivil Religion: Interreligious Hostility in America.* New York: Crossroad, 1987.

Benamozegh, Rabbi Elijah. *Israel and Humanity.* Translated and edited by Maxwell Luria. Classics of Western Spirituality. New York: Paulist, 1995.

Bennett, David H. *Demagogues in the Depression.* New Brunswick, N.J.: Rutgers Univ. Press, 1969.

——. *Party of Fear: From Nativist Movements to the New Right.* Chapel Hill: Univ. of North Carolina Press, 1988.

Berger, Peter. *The Sacred Canopy.* New York: Doubleday, 1967.

Billington, James H. *Fire in the Minds of Men: Origins of the Revolutionary Faith.* New York: Basic Books, 1980.

Bjørgo, Tore. "Introduction." *Terrorism and Political Violence* 7, no. 1 (Spring 1995): 1–16.

Bleich, J. David. "Jewish Law and the State's Authority to Punish Crime." *Cardozo Law Review* 12 (Feb./Mar. 1991): 829–57.

Boyer, Paul. *When Time Shall Be No More.* Cambridge, Mass.: Harvard Univ. Press, 1992.

Bromley, David G., and Anson D. Shupe, Jr. "The Future of the Anticult Movement." In *The Future of New Religious Movements,* edited by David G. Bromley and Phillip E. Hammond. Macon, Ga.: Mercer Univ. Press, 1987.

——. *The New Vigilantes.* Beverly Hills, Calif.: Sage, 1980.

——. *Strange Gods.* Boston: Beacon, 1981.

Brothers, Richard. *A Revealed Knowledge of the Prophesies and Times . . . Containing with Other Great and Remarkable Things, Not Revealed to Any Other Person on Earth, The Restoration of the Hebrews to Jerusalem, by the Year 1798, Under Their Revealed Prophet.* Two parts in one vol. London, 1794.

Burridge, Kenelm. *New Heaven, New Earth: A Study of Millenarian Activities.* Oxford: Blackwell, 1969.

Campbell, Colin. "The Cult, the Cultic Milieu and Secularization." *Sociological Yearbook of Religion in Britain* 5 (1972): 119–36.

Center for Democratic Renewal. *Aryan Nations Far Right Underground Movement.* Atlanta: Center for Democratic Renewal, 1986.

"Church of the Creator Founder Ben Klassen Commits Suicide." *Klanwatch Intelligence Report* 68 (Aug. 1993): 7.

"Church of the Creator in Turmoil Over Leadership Change." *Klanwatch Intelligence Report* 66 (Apr. 1993): 1–4.

Clifton, Chas. S., ed. *The Modern Craft Movement: Witchcraft Today, Book I.* St. Paul, Minn.: Llewellyn, 1992.

Clorfene, Chaim, and Yakov Rogalski. *The Path of the Righteous Gentile.* Jerusalem: Targum, 1987.

Clouse, Robert G., ed. *The Meaning of the Millennium: Four Views.* Downers Grove, Ill.: InterVarsity, 1977.

Coates, James. *Armed and Dangerous: The Rise of the Survivalist Right.* New York: Hill and Wang, 1987.

Cohen, Naomi W. *Not Free to Desist.* Philadelphia: Jewish Publication Society of America, 1972.

Cohn, Norman. *The Pursuit of the Millennium.* New York: Oxford Univ. Press, 1970.

———. *Warrant for Genocide.* New York: Harper, 1969.

Committee on Un-American Activities. *Investigation of Un-American Propaganda Activities in the United States (Gerald L. K. Smith).* Washington, D.C.: Government Printing Office, 1946.

Corcoran, James. *Bitter Harvest.* New York: Penguin, 1990.

Crawford, Alan. *Thunder on the Right: The 'New Right' and the Politics of Resentment.* New York: Pantheon, 1980.

Darms, Anton. *The Delusion of British-Israelism.* New York: Loizeaux Brothers Bible Truth Depot, 1939.

Davis, J. David. *Finding the God of Noah: The Spiritual Journey of a Baptist Minister from Jesus to the Laws of Noah.* Hoboken, N.J.: Ktav, forthcoming.

Dennis, Lawrence, and Maximillian St. George. *A Trial on Trial: The Great Sedition Trial of 1944.* Torrance, Calif.: Institute for Historical Review, 1984.

Dilling, Elizabeth. *The Jewish Religion: Its Influence Today.* Torrance, Calif.: Noontide, 1983.

———. *The Plot Against Christianity.* Lincoln, Nebr.: Elizabeth Dilling Foundation, 1964.

Dinnerstein, Leonard. *Antisemitism in America.* New York: Oxford Univ. Press, 1994.

Dumézil, Georges. *Gods of the Ancient Northmen.* Edited by Einar Haugen. Berkeley: Univ. of California Press, 1973.

Ellis Davidson, H. R. *Gods and Myths of Northern Europe.* Middlesex, England: Penguin, 1964.

Encyclopedia Judaica. Vol. 12. Jerusalem: Keter, 1971.

Enker, Arnold N. "Aspects of Interaction Between the Torah Law, the King's Law, and the Noahide Law in Jewish Criminal Law." *Cardozo Law Review* 12 (Feb./Mar. 1991): 1137–56.

Epstein, Rabbi J. *The Babylonian Talmud.* London: Soncino Press, 1935.

Erith, Rev. L. E. "The Fallacy of British Israelism." *Review of the Churches* 6 (Apr. 1929): 194–203.

"Extremism Targets the Prisons." *ADL Special Report* (June 1986).

Ezekial, Raphael. *The Racist Mind.* New York: Viking, 1995.

Falk, Harvey. *Jesus the Pharisee: A New Look at the Jewishness of Jesus.* New York: Paulist, 1985.

Festinger, Leon, et al. *When Prophecy Fails.* Minneapolis: Univ. of Minnesota Press, 1956.

Finch, Phillip. *God, Guts and Guns: A Close Look at the Radical Right.* Seaview: Putnam, 1983.

Fisher, George Park. *History of Christian Doctrine.* New York: Charles Scribners Sons, 1923.

Flowers, Stephen E. "Revival of Germanic Religion in Contemporary Anglo-American Culture." *Mankind Quarterly* 21, no. 3 (Spring 1981): 279–94.

———. *Runes and Magic: Magic Formulaic Elements in the Older Runic Tradition.* Series I. Germanic Languages and Literature. Vol. 53. New York: Peter Lang, 1986.

Flynn, Kevin, and Gary Gerhardt. *The Silent Brotherhood.* New York: Signet, 1990.

Forster, Arnold, and Benjamin R. Epstein. *The New Anti-Semitism.* New York: McGraw-Hill, 1974.

Forsyth, Neil. *The Old Enemy: Satan & The Combat Myth.* Princeton, N.J.: Princeton Univ. Press, 1987.

"From Aryan Nations to Anti-Hate: Floyd Cochrane Talks About the White Supremacist Movement and the Reasons He Left It." *Klanwatch Intelligence Report* no. 69 (Oct. 1993): 4–6.

Fry, John R. "Hate Crime in America." *Church and Society* 80 (May/June 1990): 3–81.

Gaines, David. *The World Council of Churches.* Peterborough, N.H.: Richard R. Smith Noone House, 1966.

Gardner, Gerald Brosseau. *Meaning of Witchcraft.* London: Aquarian, 1959.

Garrett, Clarke. *Respectable Folly: Millenarians and the French Revolution in France and England.* Baltimore: Johns Hopkins Univ. Press, 1975.

Gerber, David A., ed. *Anti-Semitism in American History.* Urbana: Univ. of Illinois Press, 1986.

Girard, René. *Violence and the Sacred.* Translated by Patrick Gregory. Baltimore: Johns Hopkins Univ. Press, 1972.

Godby, Allen H. *The Lost Tribes a Myth: Suggestions Towards Rewriting Hebrew History.* Durham, N.C.: Duke Univ. Press, 1930.

Goodrick-Clark, Nicholas. *The Occult Roots of Nazism.* New York: New York Univ. Press, 1985.

Grundy, Stephen. "The Cult of Odinn, God of Death." Ph.D. diss., Cambridge Univ.

Gundarsson, KveldúlfR. *Teutonic Magic.* St. Paul, Minn.: Llewellyn, 1990.

———. *Teutonic Religion.* St. Paul, Minn.: Llewellyn, 1994.

Halsell, Grace. *Prophesy and Politics.* Westport, Conn.: Lawrence Hill & Co.

Harrison, J. F. C. *The Second Coming: Popular Millenarianism 1780–1850.* New Brunswick, N.J.: Rutgers Univ. Press, 1979.

"Hate Groups in Bitter Struggle Over Public Image: Militants Call for Violence; Old Style Groups Claim to Condemn It." *Klanwatch Intelligence Report 59* (1992): 3–4.

"The Hate Movement Today: A Chronicle of Violence and Disarray." *ADL Special Report* (1987).

Hicks, Robert D. *In Pursuit of Satan: The Police and the Occult.* Buffalo, N.Y.: Prometheus, 1991.

———. "The Myth of Satanism: A Response to Cynthia Kisser." *Free Inquiry* (Winter 1992/93).

Hoskins, Richard Kelly. *Vigilantes of Christendom.* Lynchburg, Va.: Virginia Publishing Co., 1990.

Howlett, Rev. Thomas Rosling. *Anglo-Israel and the Jewish Problem.* Philadelphia: Spangler & Davis, 1892.

"'Identity Churches': A Theology of Hate." *ADL Facts* 28 (Spring 1983).

"Identity Minister's Church and Property Seized." *Klanwatch Intelligence Report 66* (Apr. 1993): 4.

"Invisible Empire Turns Over Assets to the NAACP." *Klanwatch Intelligence Report 69* (Oct. 1993): 1, 9.

Isaac, Rael Jean. *Israel Divided: Ideological Politics in the Jewish State.* Baltimore: Johns Hopkins Univ. Press, 1976.

Ivry, Alfred L. "The Inevitability of Idolatry." In *Proceedings of the Academy for Jewish Philosophy,* edited by David Novak and Norbert M. Samuelson. Lanham, Md.: University Press of America, 1992.

Jeansonne, Glen. "Combating Anti-Semitism: The Case of Gerald L. K. Smith." In *Anti-Semitism in American History,* edited by David A. Gerber. Urbana: Univ. of Illinois Press, 1986.

———. *Gerald L. K. Smith: Minister of Hate.* New Haven, Conn.: Yale Univ. Press, 1988.

Jenista, Dwain A. "The Church of Christ at Halley's Bluff." Unpublished paper, Univ. of Kansas at Lawrence, 1977.

Jewish Encyclopedia. Vol. 7. New York: Funk and Wagnalls, 1912.

Johnson, George. *Architects of Fear.* Los Angeles: Jeremy P. Tarcher, 1983.

Jung, Carl G. *The Archetypes and the Collective Unconscious.* Translated by R. F. C. Hull. Bollingen Series XX. New York: Pantheon, 1959.

———. "Wotan." In *C. G. Jung, The Collected Works.* Vol. 10. Bollingen Series XX, 179–93. New York: Pantheon, 1964.

Kaminsky, Howard. *A History of the Hussite Revolution.* Berkeley: Univ. of California Press, 1967.

———. "Pius Aeneas Among the Taborites." *Church History* 28 (1959): 281–306.

———. "The Prague Insurrection of 30 July 1419." *Medievalia et Humanistica* 10 (1956): 106–26.

Kaplan, Jeffrey. "Absolute Rescue: Absolutism, Defensive Action and the Resort to Force." *Journal of Terrorism and Political Violence* 7, no. 3 (Autumn 1995): 128–63.

———. "Context of American Millenarian Revolutionary Theology: The Case of the 'Identity Christian' Church of Israel." *Terrorism and Political Violence* 5, no. 1 (Spring 1993): 30–82.

———. "The Far Side of the Far Right." *Christian Century,* 2 Sept. 1994, 1019–22.

———. "The Millennial Dream." In *From the Ashes: Making Sense of Waco,* edited by James R. Lewis, 51–53. Lanham, Md.: Rowman & Littlefield, 1994.

———. "The Reconstruction of the Asatrú and Odinist Traditions." In *Magical Religions and Modern Witchcraft,* edited by James R. Lewis. Albany: State Univ. of New York Press, 1996.

———. "Right Wing Violence in North America." *Journal of Terrorism and Political Violence* 7, no. 1 (Spring 1995): 44–95.

Kaplan, Julius. *The Redaction of the Babylonian Talmud.* New York: Bloch, 1933.

Kelly, Aidan A. *Crafting the Art of Magic, Book 1: A History of Modern Witchcraft 1939–1964.* St. Paul, Minn.: Llewellyn, 1991.

Kippenberg, Hans G., ed. *Struggles of the Gods: Papers of the Groningen Work Group for the Study of the History of Religions.* Berlin: Moulton, 1984.

Kisser, Cynthia S. "Satanism as a Social Movement." *Free Inquiry* (Winter 1992/93).

"The KKK Today: A 1991 Status Report." *ADL Special Report* (1991).

Klanwatch. *The Ku Klux Klan: A History of Racism and Violence.* 4th ed. Montgomery, Ala.: Klanwatch, 1991.

Koestler, Arthur. *The Thirteenth Tribe.* New York: Random House, 1976.

Kogan, Barry S. "Judaism and the Varieties of Idolatrous Experience." In *Proceedings of the Academy for Jewish Philosophy,* edited by David Novak and Norbert M. Samuelson. Lanham, Md.: University Press of America, 1992.

Kook, HaRav Tzvi Yehuda HaCohen. *Torat Eretz Israel.* Translated and edited by Tzvi Fishman. Jerusalem: Torat Eretz Yisrael Publications, 1991.

Kook, Rabbi Abraham Isaac. *Lights of Penitence, Lights of Holiness.* Translated by Ben Zion Bokser. Classics of Western Spirituality. New York: Paulist, 1978.

Krominga, D. H. *The Millennium in the Church.* Grand Rapids, Mich.: William B. Eerdmans, 1945.

La Peyrére, Isaac de. *Men Before Adam.* London, 1656.

Ledeen, Barbara, and Michael Ledeen. "The Temple Mount Plot." *New Republic,* 18 June 1984, 20–23.

Leese, Arnold Spencer. *Jewish Ritual Murder.* London: International Fascist League, 1938.

Leibman, Charles S., and Eliezer Don-Yehiya. *Religion and Politics in Israel.* Bloomington: Indiana Univ. Press, 1984.

Lewis, James R., ed. *From the Ashes: Making Sense of Waco*. Lanham, Md.: Rowman & Littlefield, 1994.

Lichtenstein, Aaron. *The Seven Laws of Noah*. 2nd ed. New York: Rabbi Jacob Joseph School Press, 1986.

Lipset, Seymour Martin, and Earl Raab. *The Politics of Unreason: Right Wing Extremism in America, 1790–1977*. Chicago: Univ. of Chicago, 1978.

Lööw, Helene. "Racist Violence and Criminal Behaviour in Sweden: Myths and Realities." *Terrorism and Political Violence* 7, no. 1 (Spring 1995): 119–61.

Lucas, Philip. "Social Factors in the Failure of New Religious Movements: A Case Study Using Stark's Success Model." *Syzygy* 1 (Winter 1992): 39–53.

Macdonald, Andrew [William Pierce]. *Hunter*. Arlington, Va.: National Vanguard, 1989.

———. *The Turner Diaries*. Arlington, Va.: National Vanguard, 1978.

Maimonides, Moses. *The Code of Maimonides: Book Fourteen, The Book of Judges*. Translated by Abraham M. Hershman. New Haven, Conn.: Yale Univ. Press, 1949.

Marsden, George M. *Fundamentalism and American Culture*. Oxford: Oxford Univ. Press, 1980.

Martin, Stoddard. *Art, Messianism, and Crime*. New York: St. Martin's, 1986.

Martinez, Thomas (with John Guinther). *Brotherhood of Murder*. New York: Pocket Books, 1990.

Marty, Martin E. *The Irony of It All, 1893–1919*. Chicago: Univ. of Chicago Press, 1986.

———. *A Nation of Behavers*. Chicago: Univ. of Chicago Press, 1976.

———. *The Noise and the Conflict, 1919–1941*. Chicago: Univ. of Chicago Press, 1991.

Marty, Martin E., and R. Scott Appleby. "Conclusion: An Interim Report on a Hypothetical Family." In *Fundamentalism Observed*, edited by Martin E. Marty and R. Scott Appleby, 814–42. Chicago: Univ. of Chicago Press, 1991.

Mason, James. *Siege*. Denver: Storm, 1992.

Mather, George A., and Larry A. Nichols. *Dictionary of Cults, Sects, Religions and the Occult*. Grand Rapids, Mich.: William B. Eerdmans, 1993.

McGinn, Bernard, trans. and ed. *Apocalyptic Spirituality*. Classics of Western Spirituality. New York: Paulist, 1979.

———. *Visions of the End: Apocalyptic Traditions in the Middle Ages*. New York: Columbia Univ. Press, 1979.

Melton, J. Gordon. *The Encyclopedia of American Religions*. Supplement to 2nd ed. Detroit: Gale Research, 1987.

———. *Encyclopedic Handbook of Cults in America*. New York: Garland, 1986.

———. "Introduction: When Prophets Die: The Succession Crisis in New Religions." In *When Prophets Die: The Postcharismatic Fate of New Religious Movements*, edited by Timothy Miller. Albany: State Univ. of New York Press, 1991.

———, ed. *Cults and the Jewish Community: Representative Works of Jewish Anti-Cult Literature*. New York: Garland, 1990.

————, ed. *The Encyclopedia of American Religions*. Vol. 2. Tarrytown, N.Y.: Triumph, 1991.

————, ed. *The Evangelical Christian Anti-Cult Movement*. New York: Garland, 1990.

Melton, J. Gordon, and Robert L. Moore. *The Cult Experience: Responding to the New Religious Pluralism*. New York: Pilgrim, 1982.

Michelet, Jules. *Satanism and Witchcraft*. Translated by A. R. Allison. New York: Walden, 1939.

Miller, Glenn T. "Dispensationalism." In *The Perennial Dictionary of World Religions*. San Francisco: Harper & Row, 1989.

Mirabello, Mark L. *The Other Brotherhood*. Edmonds, Wash.: Sure Fire, 1993.

Moore, Deborah Dash. *B'nai B'rith and the Challenge of Ethnic Leadership*. Albany: State Univ. of New York Press, 1981.

New Edition of the Babylonian Talmud. Translated by Michael L. Rodkinson. Vols. 7–8, *Tract Sanhedrin*. Boston: The Talmud Society, 1918.

Novak, David. *The Image of the Non-Jew in Judaism*. Toronto Studies in Theology. Vol. 14. New York: Edwin Mellen, 1983.

The Old Testament Psuedepigrapha. Edited by James H. Charlesworth. 2 Vol. Garden City, N.Y.: Doubleday, 1985.

Pallière, Aimé. *The Unknown Sanctuary: A Pilgrimage From Rome to Israel*. Translated by Louise Waterman Wise. New York: Bloch, 1928.

Patai, Raphael. *The Messiah Texts*. Detroit: Wayne State Univ. Press, 1979.

Popkin, Richard H. *Isaac La Peyrére (1596–1676): His Life, Work and Influence*. Leiden: E. J. Brill, 1987.

Pranaitis, I. B. *The Talmud Unmasked*. St. Petersburg: n.p., 1892.

Protocols of the Elders of Zion, The. Translated by Victor Marsden. No publication data.

Rakover, Nahum. "Jewish Law and the Noahide Obligation to Preserve Social Order." *Cardozo Law Review* 12 (Feb./Mar. 1991): 1073–1136.

Rapoport, David C. "Fear and Trembling: Terrorism in Three Religious Traditions." *American Political Science Review* 78 (Sept. 1984): 658–77.

————. "Messianic Sanctions for Terror." *Comparative Politics* 20 (1988): 195–213.

Ravenscroft, Trevor. *The Spear of Destiny*. York Beach, Maine: Samuel Weiser, 1982.

Réage, Pauline. *Story of O*. New York: Ballentine, 1965.

Rhodes, James M. *The Hitler Movement: A Modern Millenarian Revolution*. Stanford, Calif.: Hoover Institution Press, 1980.

Ribuffo, Leo P. "Henry Ford and the International Jew." *American Jewish History* 69, no. 4 (June 1980): 437–77.

Ridgeway, James. *Blood in the Face*. New York: Thunder's Mouth, 1990.

Riley, Michael. "White & Wrong: New Klan, Old Hatred." *Time*, 6 June 1992, 24–27.

"Robb's Knights of the KKK Stage Small Comeback." *The Monitor* 25 (May 1992): 11–12.

Rockwell, George Lincoln. *This Time the World*. Arlington, Va.: Parliament House, 1963.

Rosenthal, A. M., and Arthur Gelb. *One More Victim: The Life and Death of a Jewish Nazi*. New York: New American Library, 1967.

Roy, Ralph Lord. *Apostles of Discord*. Boston: Beacon, 1953.

Rudin, James A., and Marcia R. Rudin. *Prison or Paradise: The New Religious Cults*. Philadelphia: Fortress, 1980.

Russell, H. M., and Rabbi J. Weinberg, trans. *The Book of Knowledge from the Mishnah Torah of Maimonides*. Edinburgh: Royal College of Physicians of Edinburgh, 1981.

Saliba, John A. "The Christian Response to the New Religions: A Critical Look at the Spiritual Counterfeits Project." *Journal of Ecumenical Studies* 18 (Summer 1981): 451–73.

Scholem, Gershom G. *Messianic Idea in Judaism*. New York: Schocken, 1971.

——. *Shabbatai Zevi: The Mystical Messiah*. Princeton, N.J.: Princeton Univ. Press, 1973.

Schwarzschild, Steven S. "De Idolatria." In *Proceedings of the Academy for Jewish Philosophy*, edited by David Novak and Norbert M. Samuelson, 259–73. Lanham, Md.: Univ. Press of America, 1992.

——. "Judaism, Scriptures and Ecumenism." *Judaism* 13 (Summer 1964).

Seltzer, Robert M. *Jewish People, Jewish Thought*. New York: Macmillan, 1980.

Seymour, Cheri. *Committee of the States: Inside the Radical Right*. Mariposa, Calif.: Camden Place Communications, 1991.

Shields, Steven L. *Divergent Paths of the Restoration: A History of the Latter Day Saint Movement*. Los Angeles: Restoration Research, 1990.

Shupe, Anson S., Jr., David G. Bromley, and Donna L. Oliver. *The Anti-Cult Movement in America: A Bibliography and Historical Survey*. New York: Garland, 1984.

Simonelli, Fredrick J. "American Fuehrer: George Lincoln Rockwell and the American Nazi Party." Ph.D. diss., Univ. of Nevada, Reno, 1995.

Simon Wiesenthal Center. *Dignity & Defiance: The Confrontation of Life and Death in the Warsaw Ghetto*. Los Angeles: Simon Wiesenthal Center, 1995.

——. *The Holocaust, 1933–1945, Educational Resource Kit*. Los Angeles: Simon Wiesenthal Center, 1995.

Sims, Patsy. *The Klan*. New York: Stein and Day, 1978.

Singular, Stephan. *Talked to Death: The Life and Murder of Alan Berg*. New York: Beech Tree, 1987.

Sivan, Emmanual. "The Enclave Culture." In *Fundamentalisms Comprehended*, edited by Martin E. Marty and R. Scott Appleby. Chicago: Univ. of Chicago Press, 1995.

Sklar, Dusty. *Gods and Beasts: The Nazis and the Occult*. New York: Thomas Y. Crowell, 1977.

Smith, Gerald L. K. *Besieged Patriot*. Edited by Elma M. Smith and Charles F. Robinson. Eureka Springs, Alaska: Elma M. Smith Foundation, 1978.

——. *Satan's New Testament*. Los Angeles: Christian Nationalist Crusade, 1975.

Smith, Jonathan Z. "The Devil in Mr. Jones." In *Imagining Religion*. Chicago: Univ. of Chicago Press, 1982.

———. *To Take Place*. Chicago: Univ. of Chicago Press, 1987.

Soloveitchik, Rabbi Joseph Dov. "Transcriptions of My Lectures by Rabbi Abraham Besdin." In *Man of Faith in the Modern World: Reflections by the Rav*. Hoboken, N.J.: Ktav, 1989.

Sprinzak, Ehud. *The Ascendance of Israel's Radical Right*. New York: Oxford Univ. Press, 1991.

———. "The Process of Deligitimation: Towards a Linkage Theory of Political Terrorism." *Terrorism and Political Violence* 3, no. 1 (Spring 1991): 50–68.

———. "Right-Wing Terrorism in Comparative Perspective: The Case of Deligitimation." *Terrorism and Political Violence* 7, no. 1 (Spring 1995): 17–43.

———. "Three Models of Religious Violence: The Case of Jewish Fundamentalism In Israel." In *Fundamentalisms and the State,* edited by Martin E. Marty and R. Scott Appleby, 462–90. Chicago: Univ. of Chicago Press, 1993.

St. Clair, Michael J. *Millenarian Movements in Historical Context*. New York: Garland, 1992.

Stanton, Bill. *Klanwatch: Bringing the Ku Klux Klan to Justice*. New York: Grove Weidenfeld, 1991.

Stark, Rodney. "How New Religions Succeed: A Theoretical Model." In *The Future of New Religious Movements,* edited by David G. Bromley and Phillip E. Hammond. Macon, Ga.: Mercer Univ. Press, 1987.

Stocking, George W., Jr. *Race, Culture and Evolution*. New York: Free Press, 1968.

Stone, Suzanne Last. "Sinaitic and Noahide Law: Legal Pluralism in Jewish Law." *Cardozo Law Review* 12 (Feb./Mar. 1991): 1157–1214.

Sturluson, Snorri. *The Prose Edda*. Translated by Jean I. Young. Berkeley: Univ. of California Press, 1966.

Thompson, Jerry. *My Life in the Klan*. Nashville, Tenn.: Rutledge Hills, 1982.

Thorsson, Edred. *At the Well of Wyrd: A Handbook of Runic Divination*. York Beach, Maine: Weiser, 1988.

———. *A Book of Troth*. St. Paul, Minn.: Llewellyn, 1992.

———. *Futhark: A Handbook of Rune Magic*. York Beach, Maine: Weiser, 1984.

———. *Northern Magic*. St. Paul, Minn.: Llewellyn, 1992.

———. *Runelore: A Handbook of Esoteric Runology*. York Beach, Maine: Weiser, 1987.

———. *Rune-Might: Secret Practices of the German Rune Magicians*. St. Paul, Minn.: Llewellyn, 1989.

Tucker, Richard K. *The Dragon and the Cross: The Rise and Fall of the Ku Klux Klan in Middle America*. Hamden, Conn.: Archon, 1991.

Turner, William W. *Power on the Right*. Berkeley, Calif.: Ramparts, 1971.

Turville-Petre, E. O. G. *Myth and Religion of the North*. London: Weidenfeld and Nicolson, 1964.

Universal Jewish Encyclopedia. Vol. 8. New York: Works Project Administration, 1942.

Urbach, Ephraim E. *The Sages*. Cambridge, Mass.: Harvard Univ. Press, 1987.

Van Baalen, Rev. Jan Karel. *The Chaos of the Cults*. 4th ed. Grand Rapids, Mich.: William B. Eerdmans, 1962.

———. *The Gist of the Cults: Christianity Versus False Religion*. Grand Rapids, Mich.: William B. Eerdmans, 1944.

Wade, Wyn Craig. *The Fiery Cross*. New York: Simon and Schuster, 1987.

Webb, James. *The Occult Establishment*. La Salle, Ill.: Open Court, 1991.

Weber, Max. *Ancient Judaism*. New York: Macmillan, 1952.

Weber, Timothy. *Living in the Shadow of the Second Coming*. Chicago: Univ. of Chicago Press, 1987.

"The White Supremacist Movement: 1992 at a Glance." *Klanwatch Intelligence Report* 65 (Feb. 1993): 10–13.

"White Supremacist Movement Reels from Severe Setbacks in 1993." *Klanwatch Intelligence Report* 71 (Feb. 1994): 12–13.

Wilcox, Laird. *Anti-Defamation League 1993 Spy Scandal Clipping File*. Olathe, Kans.: Editorial Research Service, n.d.

———. *Guide to the American Occult*. Olathe, Kans.: Editorial Research Service, 1990.

———. *Guide to the American Occult: Directory and Bibliography*. Olathe, Kans.: Editorial Research Service, 1990.

———. *Guide to the American Right: Directory and Bibliography*. Olathe, Kans.: Editorial Research Service, 1995.

———. "Lenny Zeskind, Lyn Wells and the Center for Democratic Renewal Including Chip Berlet and Political Research Associates: The Hidden 'Links' and 'Ties' of an 'Anti-Extremist' Organization." Special report from Editorial Research Service of Olathe, Kans. (Mar. 1989).

Wilcox, Laird, and John George. *Nazis, Communists, Klansmen and Others on the Fringe*. Buffalo, N.Y.: Prometheus, 1992.

Wilson, Bryan R. "Factors in the Failure of the New Religious Movements." In *The Future of New Religious Movements*, edited by David G. Bromley and Phillip E. Hammond. Macon, Ga.: Mercer Univ. Press, 1987.

———. *Magic and the Millennium*. New York: Harper & Row, 1973.

———. "Millenarianism in Comparative Perspective." *Comparative Studies in Society and History* 6 (1963/64).

Wilson, John. *Our Israelite Origin*. Philadelphia: Daniels & Smith, 1850.

———. *Title Deeds of the Holy Land*. London: James Nisbet and Co., n.d.

Wilson, Marvin R. *Our Father Abraham: Jewish Roots of the Christian Faith*. Grand Rapids, Mich.: William B. Eerdmans, 1989: 93–114.

Wyrick, Herbert M. *Seven Religious Isms: An Historical and Scriptural Review*. Grand Rapids, Mich.: Zondervan, 1941.

Yockey, Francis Parker. *Imperium*. Costa Mesa, Calif.: Noontide, 1962.

Zeskind, Leonard. *The "Christian Identity" Movement: Analyzing Its Theological Rationalization for Racist and Anti-Semitic Violence*. Atlanta: Center for Democratic Renewal, 1986.

Movement Periodicals, Pamphlets, Fliers, and Other Ephemera

"All Fall Down: AIDS and the End of Civilization." *America's Promise Newsletter* (Oct. 1987).

Armour, Charles. "Mortar & Pestle." *Mountain Thunder* 1 (1991).

Bainbridge, William. "Some Thoughts on a Good Time." *Vor Trú* 35 (Yule 1989).

Barley, Dave. "A Predictable Event Has Occurred!" *America's Promise Newsletter* (Mar. 1992).

Beam, Louis. "Computers and Patriots." *The Seditionist* 10 (Summer 1991).

———. *Essays of a Klansman.* Hayden Lake, Idaho: AKIA, 1983.

———. "Klansman's Guide to the Fifth Era." *Inter-Klan Newsletter and Survival Alert* 4 (1984).

———. "Leaderless Resistance." In Pete Peters, *Special Report on the Meeting of Christian Men Held in Estes Park, Colorado October 23, 24, 25, 1992 Concerning the Killing of Vickie and Samuel Weaver by the United States Government.* Laporte, Colo.: Scriptures for America, n.d.

———. "On Avoiding Conspiracy Charges and Other Related Matters." *The Seditionist* 10 (Summer 1991).

———. "On Revolutionary Majorities." *Inter-Klan Newsletter and Survival Alert* 4 (1984).

———. "Showdown in Waco." *Jubilee* 5, no. 5 (Mar./Apr. 1993).

———. "We Are At War." *The Seditionist* 10 (Summer 1991).

"Blessing or Curse." *Smyrna* (July/Aug. 1991).

B'nai Noah. *What Is the B'nai Noah?* Athens, Tenn.: Echoes of Immanuel, 1991.

Bruggerman, James W. "Sanitized Talmud." *Kingdom Chronicle* (Oct. 1991).

"Bush Merges Church and State—With 'Noahide Law' . . . (PL 102-12)!!" *Criminal Politics* 1 (Jan. 1992).

"By-Laws of the Asatrú Alliance As Approved at Althing—July 6, 2241 Runic Era [1991]." *Vor Trú* 41 (Summer 2241/1991).

Calhoun, John C., and Louis R. Beam. "The Perfected Order of the Klan." *Inter-Klan Newsletter and Survival Alert* 5 (1984).

Chisholm, James. "The Rites of Ostara: Possibilities for Today." *Idunna* 1, no. 4 (Feb. 1989).

———. "Working with the Wights and Forces of the Lay of Alvis." *Idunna* 2, no. 2 (Oct. 1989).

Church of Israel. *Articles of Faith and Doctrine.* Booklet. Church of Israel, 10 Jan. 1982.

Clark, Michael A. "Howard B. Rand—The Greatest Identity Pastor of Our Time Has Passed to His Rest." *Wake Up!* 9 (Jan./Feb. 1992).

Cooper, Rick. "Brief History of the White Nationalist Movement." E-text from the *NSV Report,* n.d.

———. "No Man Knows the Date." *NSV Report* 11, no. 3 (July–Sept. 1993).

———. "Warning." *NSV Report* (July–Sept. 1984).

Coriolanus. "Wotan Speaks to His Children." E-text distributed by the Nordic Heritage and History Club of Chicago, Illinois, n.d.

Covenant, Sword and Arm of the Lord. *C. S. A. Survival Manual.* No publication data.

Covington, Harold. "Urgent and Important Security Notice." *Resistance* 38 (May 1994).

———. *What Have We Learned?* Pamphlet. National Socialist Party of America, n.d.

Cuhulain, Kerr. "Ritualistic, Cult and Occult Crime." In *Witchcraft, Satanism and Occult Crime: Who's Who and What's What.* Third Edition (Jan. 1991).

Davis, J. David. "Cult Busters a Bust—A Matter of Honor & Integrity." *The Gap* (May/June 1994).

"Deguello Report." Unpublished report, 1976.

Dellea, John. "Kerr Cuhulain Pagan Policeman." *Llewellyn's New Worlds of Mind and Spirit* (Jan./Feb. 1993).

Fineberg, Rabbi S. Andhill. "Quarantine Treatment." Memorandum published by the Community Service Department of the American Jewish Committee, 15 Aug. 1947.

Friedman, Benjamin H. "The Truth About Khazars." E-text distributed by Scriptures for America, n.d.

Gamlinginn. *Ordasafn of Gamlinginn.* Albuquerque, N.M.: Hrafnahús, 1991.

———. "Race and Religion." *Mountain Thunder* 8 (Spring Equinox 1993).

———. "Speech at Althing 12 of the Asatrú Alliance (22–24 May 1992)." *Mountain Thunder* 5 (1992).

———. "The Standard International Futhark." *Mountain Thunder* 6 (1992).

Gayman, Dan. "America in the Hands of an Angry God." *Zions Watchman* 4, no. 1 (Jan. 1977).

———. *Articles of Faith and Doctrine for the Church of Israel.* Pamphlet. Church of Israel [Shell City, Mo.], 1982.

———. "The Bible Case Against Miscegenation." *Watchman* 3 (Spring 1991).

———. *Can There Be Vigilantes in Christendom?* Pamphlet. Church of Israel, 1991.

———. *Christian Conscience Towards Government.* Pamphlet. Church of Israel, 1988.

———. "Drawing Battle Lines." *Watchman* 3 (Summer 1991).

———. "The Fable of Eve and the Apple." *Zions Watchman* 8 (July 1977).

———. "For Readers of Zions Watchman." *Zions Watchman* 1 (Jan. 1977).

———. *Handbook for Establishing a Home Church.* Pamphlet. Church of Israel, 1990.

———. *The Holy Bible: The Book of Adam's Race.* Pamphlet. Church of Israel, n.d.

———. "Jesus Christ Was Not A Jew." *Zions Watchman* 4 (Apr. 1977).

———. "Kitchen Table Talk." *Watchman* 4 (1991).

———. "Personally . . . From the Editor." *Watchman* 3 (Summer 1991).

———. *Rebellion or Repentance: Which Way Modern Israel?* Pamphlet. Church of Israel, 1987.

———. *Romans 13: A Primer in Government for Patriotic Christians.* Pamphlet. Church of Israel, 1989.

————. "Then Cometh the Condemnation." *Message of Old Monthly* 4, no. 2–3 (May 1971).

————. "Warning From the Watchman Standing in the American Watchtower." *Zions Watchman* 8 (July 1977) and 12 (Nov. 1977).

"George Washington's Vision." *Aryan Nations Newsletter* 7 (c. 1978).

"Gerhard Lauck in Europe." *New Order* 96 (Jan./Feb. 1992).

Goff, Kenneth. *Traitors in the Pulpit*. Englewood, Colo.: Kenneth Goff, 1946.

Graber, H. "Judaism, The Legislated Religion of the United States of America." *Kingdom Courier* 11 (Nov. 1991).

Gundarsson, KveldúlfR. "The Magic and Making of the Drinking Horn." *Mountain Thunder* 8 (Spring Equinox 1993).

————. "Race, Inheritance and Asatrú Today." *Mountain Thunder* 5 (1992).

————. "The Runes: A Brief Introduction." *Mountain Thunder* 4 (1992).

————. "Wisdom, Might and Fruitfulness: Dumézil's Theory in the Germanic Rebirth." *Mountain Thunder* 6 (1992).

————. "Yule at Eagles' Reaches." *Mountain Thunder* 8 (Spring Equinox 1993).

Hall, Paul. "Earth Summit Derision." *Jubilee* (July/Aug. 1992).

————. "Noahide Laws—Religion of a NEW WORLD ORDER." *Jubilee* 3 (Nov./Dec. 1991).

————. "Noahide Laws Part Three: A Continued Look at Talmudic Laws Foisted Upon America." *Jubilee* (May/June 1992).

————. "Noahide Laws II." *Jubilee* 4 (Mar./Apr. 1992).

Harrell, John R. "George Washington's Vision and Prophesy for the United States of America." Christian Patriot Defense League, n.d.

————. "Mid-America Survival Area." Christian Patriots Defense League, n.d.

————. "WANTED: Places to Gather Patriots in Times of Crisis." Christian Patriots Defense League, n.d.

Hunt, Kevin. "An Open Letter to the Asatrú Community." *Vor Trú* 33 (Mid-year/Summer 1989).

"The Identity Movement in Britain." *Wake Up!* (Sept./Oct. 1991).

"Jew String Puller Behind Clinton." *Der Stürmer* 1 (Aug. 1992).

Jones, Earl F. "Congressional Visit." *Christian Crusade For Truth Intelligence Newsletter* (Jan./Feb. 1989).

————. "Our Trip to the Congressmen." *Christian Crusade for Truth Intelligence Newsletter* (Mar./Apr. 1989).

————. "Public Law 102-14." *Christian Crusade for Truth Intelligence Newsletter* (July/Aug. 1991).

Jost. "NATIONAL SOCIALISM: Adolf Hitler's Revelations of the Eternal Laws of Nature for Family and Folk." E-text distributed by the National Socialist Kindred, n.d.

Klassen, Ben. *The Klassen Letters Volume One 1969–1976*. Otto, N.C.: Church of the Creator, 1988.

————. *The Klassen Letters Volume Two 1976–1981*. Otto, N.C.: Church of the Creator, 1988.

————. *Nature's Eternal Religion*. Otto, N.C.: Church of the Creator, 1973.

————. *Rahowa! The Planet is Ours*. Otto, N.C.: Church of the Creator, 1989.

———. *The White Man's Bible*. Otto, N.C.: Church of the Creator, 1981.

Lane, David. "88 Precepts." E-text distributed by the Aryan Women's League, n.d.

———. "ODINISM." E-text obtained from movement BBS, n.d.

———. "Wotan Is Coming." *WAR* (Apr. 1993).

"Lost Discernment." *Smyrna* (Sept./Oct. 1991).

Mahon, Dennis. "It's Now War!" *Oklahoma Excalibur* 1 (Mar.–May 1992).

Martin, Len. *Why 'They' Wanted to Get Gordon Kahl*. Detroit Lakes, Minn.: Pro-American, 1986.

Mathews, Robert. Open letter. Text file from Don Black's Stormfront BBS.

McAlvany, Donald S. "Encouragement for the Remnant." *McAlvany Intelligence Advisor* (Dec. 1991).

McNallen, Stephen. "The Asatru Folk Assembly: Asatru Faq." E-text obtained from computer BBS, 1955.

———. "The Jesus Flag." *Runestone* 51 (Spring 1985).

———. "Magic, Asafolk and Spiritual Development." *Mountain Thunder* 4 (1992).

———. "Nazi Exploitation Blocked!" *Runestone* 25 (1978).

———. *Selections from Runestone: An Odinist Anthology*. Grass Valley, Calif.: Ásatrú Free Assembly, 1983.

McQuad, Elwood. "Peril of the Christian Identity Movement." Unpublished essay, n.d.

Mills, A. Rud. *Call of Our Ancient Nordic Religion*. Melbourne, Australia: A. Rud Mills, 1957.

———. *The Odinist Religion: Overcoming Jewish Christianity*. Melbourne, Australia: A. Rud Mills, 1930.

Mohr, Jack. *Exploding the 'Chosen People' Myth*. Pamphlet. Bay St. Louis, Miss.: Jack Mohr, n.d.

———. *Satanic Counterfeit*. Muskogee, Okla.: Hoffman Printing, 1982.

———. "The Seven Noahide Laws and Their Implications for Christians." *Christian Patriot Crusader* 7 (Dec. 1991).

———. *Wanted! A Few Good Men! (a call for volunteers in the army of the Lord!)*. Pamphlet, n.d.

———. *Who Are You and Why Are You Here?* Bay St. Louis, Miss.: Christian Patriots Defense League, n.d.

———. *Woe Unto Ye Fundamentalists*. Pamphlet, n.d.

"More Yockey." *The Odinist* 12 (June 1974).

Mullins, Eustice. *The Curse of Canaan: A Demonology of History*. Staunton, Va.: Revelation, 1987.

North, Gary. "Fifteen Years of Invested Time." Letter to all Institute for Christian Economics subscribers, Apr. 1992.

"Ocean Kindred of New York News." *Vor Trú* 35 (Yule 1989).

"Our View of History." *The Odinist* 10 (Dec. 1973).

Peters, Pete. *Death Penalty for Homosexuals*. Laporte, Colo.: Scriptures for America, 1993.

———. *Special Report on the Meeting of Christian Men Held in Estes Park, Colorado October 23, 24, 25, 1992 Concerning the Killing of Vickie and*

Samuel Weaver by the United States Government. Laporte, Colo.: Scriptures for America, n.d.

———. "White Crime in America." Special Newsletter. Laporte, Colo.: n.d.

P. F. B. "Visiting Iceland." The Odinist." *The Odinist* 49 (1980).

Poole, W. H. *Anglo-Israel or the Saxon Race Proved to be the Lost Ten Tribes of Israel.* Toronto: n.d.

Rand, Howard. "George Washington's Vision." *Destiny Magazine* (Sept. 1958).

———. *The Servant People: A Brochure on Anglo-Saxon Identity and Responsibility.* Pamphlet. Destiny Publishers, n.d.

———. "What Does It Matter if We Are Israel?" *Special Alert* 103 (Fall 1988).

"The Remnant." *Kinship Communication* (Jan. 1992).

Remnant Resolves Committee. *Remnant Resolves.* Laporte, Colo.: Scriptures for America, n.d.

Richman, Rabbi Chaim. "Teachings From the Temple." *The Gap* (Mar./Apr. 1992).

The Root and Branch Noahide Guide, 1991/5752. New York: Root and Branch Association, 1991.

Roper, Jack. *Signs Primer: Occult Semiology Investigative Slide Training Series: Slide Script Volume One.* Milwaukee: CARIS, 1991.

Ross, Dianne Luark. Open letter to all *Idunna* subscribers, 29 July 1989.

Saunders, Jack E. "Ben Ish vs Ben Adam—Emotion vs Intellect." *The Gap* (Mar./Apr. 1992).

"Seven Noahide Laws." *Shepherd's Voice* (Mar./Apr. 1992).

Simpson, Joe. "The Catastrophic Eleventh Century." *Vor Trú* 31 (Yule/Winter 1988).

Smith, Gerald L. K. *Who Are The Chosen People? Certainly Not The Jews! (As We Now Know Jews).* Pamphlet. Gerald L. K. Smith, n.d.

Smith, Winston [Harold Covington]. "Sayonara to a Sodomite." E-text file obtained from Minuteman BBS, n.d.

Snell, Richard Wayne. "Ed Sez." *The Seekers* (Mar./Apr. 1992).

———. *The Shadow of Death! (Is There Life After Death?).* Booklet. Richard Wayne Snell, n.d.

"The Structure of History." *The Odinist* 11 (Mar. 1974).

Tabor, James D. "B'nai Noach: The Reappearance of the God-fearers in our Time." Unpublished article, 1990.

———. "Plain Talk About Christianity Paganism and Torah Faith." *The Gap* (Nov./Dec. 1991).

Temple, Chris. "A Lesson in Federal Tyranny: The Weaver Family Saga." *Jubilee* 5 (Sept./Oct. 1992).

———. "Weaver, Harris Face the Death Penalty." *Jubilee* 5 (Nov./Dec. 1992).

"The Temple Institute Update." *The Gap* (Jan./Feb. 1992).

Thompson, J. Tim. "Worldwide Epidemic: Killing in the Name of God." *Philadelphia Trumpet* 4 (May 1993).

Thorsson, Edred. "How to be a Heathen: A Methodology for the Awakening of Traditional Systems." Talk given to the Pagan Student Alliance at the University of Texas at Austin, 22 Nov. 1991.

———. "An Open Letter to Members of the Arizona Kindred From Edred

Thorsson, Odhinsgodhi and Yrmin-Drighten." Unpublished circulated letter, 30 May 1989.

———. "Order of the Triskelion." Unpublished circulated letter, n.d.

———. "Rune-Wisdom and Race." *Runa* 1, no. 2 (Yule 1982).

———. "Who Will Build the Hearths of the Troth: Are Racial Considerations Appropriate?" *Idunna* 1, no. 2 (July 1989).

Thunarsson, Ymir. "The Importance of Daily Workings." *On Wings of Eagles* 1, no. 1 (Dec. 1991/Jan. 1992).

Turner, Capstan, and A. J. Lowery. *There Was a Man: The Saga of Gordon Kahl.* Nashville, Tenn.: Sozo, 1985.

von Dauster, Wilfred. "How Can You Believe That Junk?" *Mountain Thunder* 4 (1992).

———. "The PC Pagan?" *Mountain Thunder* 5 (1992).

———. "Who's Next?" *Mountain Thunder* 8 (Spring Equinox 1993).

Walker, Leni. "Building Your Home Altar." *Watchman* 3 (Spring 1991).

Warner, James. "Open letter to Fellow National Socialists." No publication data, Jan. 1968.

"The Washington Vision." *Newsviews* (Joppa Gospel Tabernacle & Kinship Ministries, Baltimore), n.d.

Weiss, Rabbi Stewart. "A Great Man Among Our People Is Dead." *Researcher* (Oct.–Dec. 1990).

"Why Do We Hate the Jews?" *C. S. A. Journal* 9 (1982).

Winrod, Gerald B. *Adam Weishaupt A Human Devil.* No publication data.

"The Wisdom of A. Rud Mills." *The Odinist* 65 (1982).

Wolf, Tony. "The Godlauss: Atheism in the Northern Warrior Tradition." *Mountain Thunder* 5 (1992).

———. "Ordeal: The Ritual Trials of Rammaukin." *Mountain Thunder* 4 (1992).

———. "Rammaukin: Esoteric Aspects of the Northern Warrior Tradition." *Mountain Thunder* 2 (1991).

———. "Re-Forging the Blade: Practical Aspects of the Northern Warrior Tradition Riddaraskap." *Mountain Thunder* 8 (Spring Equinox 1993).

———. "The Rite of the Flaming Arrow." *Mountain Thunder* 7 (1992).

Yarbrough, Gary. Open letter. E-text obtained from Minuteman BBS, 1993.

Interviews and Personal Communications

All conversations and interviews are with the author.

Bainbridge, William. Interview. 24 Jan. 1993.

———. Telephone Conversation. 3 Apr. 1993.

———. Telephone Conversation. 17 Aug. 1993.

Chait, Rabbi Israel. Interview. 13 May 1992.

Chesky, Sandra. Telephone Conversation. 13 Mar. 1993.

Chisholm, James. Interview. 17 Nov. 1992.

Christensen, Else. Interview. 27 Nov. 1992.

Davis, J. David. Interview. 12 Mar. 1992.

———. Telephone Conversation. 13 Nov. 1995.

Emon, Randy. Telephone Conversation. 20 Sept. 1991.

Gamlinginn. Interview. 14 Oct. 1992.

Gayman, Dan. Telephone Conversation. 17 Aug. 1991.

———. Interview. 9–11 Dec. 1991.

Gundarsson, KveldúlfR. Interview. Jan. 1993.

Hand, Ron. Telephone Conversation. 12 Sept. 1992.

———. Interview. 30 Dec. 1992.

Harrell, John. Interview. 13 Mar. 1992.

Haskelevich, Rabbi Dov Ber. Interview. 23 Mar. 1992.

Heron, David. Interview. 6 Jan. 1993.

———. Interview. 13 Jan. 1993.

Katz, Rabbi Michael. Interview. 26 Mar. 1992.

———. Telephone Conversation. 17 May 1992.

Keith, Jan. Telephone Conversation. 21 Jan. 1993.

Kisser, Cynthia. Interview. 17 Mar. 1993.

McNallen, Stephen. Interview. 4 Jan. 1993.

———. Interview. 1 May 1996.

McQueen, Gert. Interview. 19 Jan. 1993.

Miles, Robert. Telephone Conversation. 30 Oct. 1991.

Morgan, Laura. Interview. 11 Apr. 1992.

Murray, Mike. Interview. 29 Apr. 1996.

Nearing, Phil. Conversation. 4 Apr. 1993.

———. Interview. 9 Apr. 1993.

Priest, Prudence. Conversation. 22 Nov. 1992.

Rindel, Peter. Interview. 7 Aug. 1995.

Robb, Thom. Interview. 24 Aug. 1991.

Roper, Jack. Conversation. 20 Nov. 1992.

———. Telephone Conversation. 23 Dec. 1992.

Rydén, Tommy. Interview. 28 July 1995.

Stine, Robert. Interview. 23–24 Dec. 1992.

———. Interview. 1 Apr. 1993.

———. Conversation. 4 Apr. 1993

Tabor, James. Interview. 23 Mar. 1992.

———. Interview. 26 Mar. 1992.

———. Telephone Conversation. 25 May 1992.

Thorsson, Edred. Interview 20 Sept. 1992.

———. Interview. 15 Apr. 1993.

Vikernes, Varg. Interview. 4 Aug. 1995.

von Dauster, Will. Interview. 31 Mar. 1993.

White, Larry. Interview. 29 Apr. 1996.

Audio Cassettes

Althing 9. June 1989. Cassette recording.

Barley, Dave. "Conquering the Leviathan (A Message to the Phineas Priests)."
     Feb. 1992.

Gayman, Dan. "Apocalyptic Millenarianism." 17 Aug. 1991.
———. "The Bible and Civil Disobedience." 1 Jan. 1989.
———. "The Divine Call to Be a Separated People." 19 Aug. 1989.
———. "Remnant Response to the Gulf War." 30 Jan. 1991.
Martinez, Tom. Radio interview on WBEZ, Chicago, 24 Oct. 1991.
Peters, Pete. "Special Message and Alert from Pastor Peters." Scriptures for America cassette #552, n.d.

Videos

Koernke, Mark. "Mark Koernke at Meadville, PA 1995."
———. "America In Peril Parts I & II." N.d.
McLamb, Jack. "Jack McLamb." N.d.
Militia of Montana. "Invasion and Betrayal." N.d.
Moyers, Bill. "Hate on Trial." PBS Documentary, broadcast 5 Feb. 1992.
"Skinheads, U.S.A." HBO Television Productions, 1993.
Thompson, Linda. "America Under Siege." N.d.

Selected Internet Resources

BBS Sites

AEN (Indianapolis): (317) 780-5211
Cyberspace Minuteman: (312) 275-6362
Digital Freedom: (416) 462-3327/(416) 465-4767
Politically Incorrect BBS: (416) 467-4975
Soapbox BBS: (919) 387-1152
Stormfront: (407) 833-4986

Listserves

Aryan News Agency (ANA): anton88@cris.com
Canadian Patriots Network/Digital Freedom: freedom@pathcom.com
Stormfront-L: stormfront-l@stormfront.org

Web Pages

Ásatrú Sites

Asatru Tradition Homepage: http://www.webcom.com/~lstead/
Lysator neo-pagan and Satanic archive: http://www.lysator.liu.se/religion
New Mexico Asatru Council: http://www.nmia.com/~seaxnet/Nmac.htm
Lyfjaberg Kindred: http://ww.nmia.com/~seaxnet/Lyfja.htm
Ring of Troth Homepage: http://pobox.com/~troth

Christian Identity

Christian Identity Online WWW Page: http://www.cris.com/~Chrident/
Scriptures for America: http://www.nilenet.com/~TMW

Conspiracy Sites

A-albionic Research: http://msen.com/~jhdaugh/
Chick, Jack Mirror Site: http://boris.qub.ac.uk/tony/Chick/newhome.html
Conspiracy Materials: http://www.primenet.com/~lion/index.html
Conspiracy Nation: http://www.europa.com/~johnlf/cn.html
New Dawn: http://www.peg.apc.org/~newdawn

Holocaust Denial

Greg Raven: http://www.kaiwan.com:80/~greg.ihr/
Bradley Smith: http://www.valleynet.com/~brsmith
Ernst Zundel's (Voice of Freedom):
   http://www.webcom.com/~ezundel/english/
   http://www.kaiwan.com/~ihrgreg/zundel
   http://trend1.com/~phoenix

Militia Sites

Michigan Militia: http://www.grfn.org/~heniy/cmrm.html
Milita Archive: http://www.tezcat.com:80/patriot/
Militia of Montana: http://www.shore.net/~adfx/2455.html
Militias in the United States: http://www.acsys.com/~sims/revolution/
   militia.html

Miscellaneous Right Wing

Anglo-Saxon/Christian Nationalism: http://www.cris.com/~Chrident/
   Nationalism.html
Aryan Crusader's Library: http://www.io.com/~rlogsdon/
Be Wise as Serpents: http://www.pixi.com/~bewise/
Canadian Patriots Network:
   http://www.pathcom.com/~freedom/cpn.
   http://www.pathcom.com/~freedom
C-Far: http://www.pathcom.com/~freedom/c-far
Coming Fall Of The American Empire: http://www2.gsu.edu/~gs02jwb
Flashback News: http://www.oden.se/~empire/nyheter.html
Freedom Site: http://www.pathcom.com/~freedom
Friends of Freedom: http://alpha.ftcnet.com:80
Greater White Amerikkka: http://www.io.com/~wlp/aryan-page/cng/other.html
Heritage Front: http://www.pathcom.com/~freedom/hf
Journal for Patriotic Justice in America: http://
   weber.u.washington.edu/~mcdaniel/

LaRouche Homepage: http://www.clark.net/larouche/welcome.html
New Dawn: http://www.peg.apc.org/~newdawn
Patriots Web Page: http://www.tezcat.com/patriot/
Populist Links: http://www.emf.net/~cr
Spirit of Truth: http://www.ucc.uconn.edu/~jpa94001

National Socialist Sites

The Aryan Crusader's Library: http://www.io.com/~rlogsdon/
Milton Kleim's National Socialist Primer is at 4 web sites:
    http://www.gl.umbc.edu/~laude/natlsocial.html
    file://www.clark.net/pub/murple/local/nazi.faq
    http://204.137.145.254/~tintin/ns/nsprimer.html
The National Alliance: http://www.natvan.com
Stormfront: http://stormfront.wat.com/stormfront

Skinhead/music Sites

The A-political Skinhead WWW page: http://www.ksu.edu/~lashout/skns.html
Resistance Records: http://www.resistance.com
White Devil Records: http://www.buzzcut.com/central/manson
White Terror Records http://www.geocities.com/capitolhill/3088

Satanism Sites

http://ctulhu.tfs.necronomi.com
http://www.marshall.edu/~allen12/organ.html
http://www.marshall.edu/~allen12/pub.html#raven
http://www.calweb.com/~veshef/ or ~reshef/
http://www.nauticom.net/users/vondraco
http://challenge.tiac.net/users/ighf/
http://www.necromi.com/p/bbs/home.html

Watchdog/Anti-Cult Sites

Anti-Defamation League: http://www.adl.org/
Anti-Fascist Germany Alert!: http://www.webcom.com/~chantry/ga/
Anti-Fascist Web (Netherlands): http://huizen.dds.nl/~hiworld
Anti-Racist Action: http://www.web.apc.org/~ara/
Anti-Militia Site: http://www.greyware.com/authors/pitman/militia.htm
Arm The Spirit: http://burn.ucsd.edu/~ats
Canadian Anti-Racist Web: http://www.web.apc.org/~ara
Cornerstone magazine: http://www.power.net/users/aia/ CultsAndReligions/
    CultOrgs.html
European Crosspoint: http://www.euronet.nl/users/magz/ecp.html
McVay, Kenneth OBC. Home Page: http://www.almanac.bc.ca/~kmcvay/
Militia Watch: http://paul.spu.edu/~sinnfein/progressive.html

Nizkor Project: http://www.almanac.bc.ca/

Norwegian Anti-Racist Center: http://www.internet.no/ars/

Ontario Center for Religious Tolerance: http://www.kosone.com/people/ocrt/
ocrt__hp.htm

Sassoon, Vidal: http://www.2.huji.ac.il/www-jcd/top.html

Satanic Ritual Abuse Sites:

   http://www.xrcads.com/users/~feorag/ sram/sraindex.html

   http://parc.power.net/users/aia

   http://www.tardis.ed.ac.uk/~feorag/sram/sraindex.html

   http://www.utu.fi/~jounsmed/asc/hyp/memories.html

   http://user.aol.com.doughskept/witchhunt__links.html

Wiesanthal Center: http://wiesanthal.com/watch.wpers.htm

World Zionist Organization: http://www.wzo.org.il/

Index